Political

Kenneth

The valu   s to foreign
policy ar   istory. Yet,
the inter   iods in our
foreign r   series is to
encourag   y. A second-
ary obje   in political
thought   d the small
group of   centers and
universit   1950s and
1960s th   Foreign Policy gave   ot been the
focus of   ersity Press
and the   ffairs at the
Universi   that has remained

JUL 2 6 '88

Presidents and Foreign Policy Making

Presidents and Foreign Policy Making

FROM FDR TO REAGAN

Cecil V. Crabb, Jr.

Kevin V. Mulcahy

LOUISIANA STATE UNIVERSITY PRESS   BATON ROUGE AND LONDON

Designer: Patricia Douglas Crowder
Typeface: Linotron 202 Aster
Typesetter: G & S Typesetters, Inc.
Printer: Thomson-Shore, Inc.
Binder: John H. Dekker & Sons, Inc.

95 94 93 92 91 90 89 88   5 4 3 2

LIBRARY OF CONGRESS CATALOGING-IN-PUBLICATION DATA

Crabb, Cecil Van Meter, 1924–
    Presidents and foreign policy making.

    (Political traditions in foreign policy series)
    Includes bibliographical references and index.
    1. United States—Foreign relations—20th century.
2. Presidents—United States—History—20th century.
I. Mulcahy, Kevin V. II. Title. III. Series.
E744.C82 1986   327.73   86-7508
ISBN 0-8071-1329-8
ISBN 0-8071-1365-4 (pbk.)

For William V. Aldred, Cornelia M. Crabb
and Emily D. Mulcahy

We can only cooperate with one Secretary of State at a time!

—*Senator Arthur H. Vandenberg*

Contents

Acknowledgments

Louisiana State University has generously supported our research activities for this project, as it has for others. The Louisiana State University Press has been quite helpful and solicitous at all of the stages of the book's gestation. Special thanks are owed to Beverly Jarrett, Catherine Barton, Catherine Silvia, and, particularly, to our editor, John Easterly. The Department of Political Science has been extremely cooperative in providing research support services and in arranging teaching schedules conducive to research. Kenneth Thompson, Director of White Burkett Miller Center for Public Affairs at the University of Virginia and editor of the Political Traditions in Foreign Policy Series, has also encouraged our work.

Several graduate students have provided valuable research assistance: Louise Rosenzweig of the Department of History and Lynn Sadduth and Gregory Russell of the Department of Political Science. Two former undergraduate students in political science, Tobin Lassen and Michael Vancherie, also helped with research. A number of student workers typed successive drafts of the manuscript with remarkable alacrity and even more remarkable good cheer: Peggy Head, Kimberly Mizzell, Deann Gibson, Ellen Hollis, Risa Robert, John Grubb, and Amanda Jones. The staff, both professional and student, of the Troy H. Middleton Library at LSU was also invariably helpful and resourceful in meeting our research needs.

Our study is immensely indebted to the efforts and support of others for the information and ideas reflected in it. Particularly helpful have been the memoirs, firsthand accounts by the political and diplomatic decision makers, and commentaries dealing with American foreign policy making over the past five decades. Many of these sources have been cited in the footnotes.

The contribution of others, of course, in no way relieves the authors of ultimate responsibility for errors of fact or interpretation that may be found in the study. These are ours alone, for which we accept full responsibility.

Presidents and Foreign Policy Making

Introduction

Two key developments in post–World War II American diplomatic experience, separated by more than a generation, illustrate what has become perhaps the most significant problem in the process of the making of foreign policy in the executive branch. One of these occurred early in the postwar era when, on September 12, 1946, Secretary of Commerce Henry A. Wallace (who had been Franklin Roosevelt's vice-president before Harry Truman) made a widely publicized speech at Madison Square Garden that was sharply critical of the Truman administration's policies toward the Soviet Union. In Wallace's view the attitude of the Truman White House toward Moscow was overly negative, unduly suspicious, and unsympathetic both to the Soviet Union's enormous wartime losses and to its postwar security needs. Wallace was particularly critical of the attitudes of prominent members of the Republican party, most of whom were endeavoring to collaborate with the Truman White House on behalf of a bipartisan approach to American foreign policy. Wallace was also outspokenly critical of the emerging containment strategy of the president and his advisers.

When the leading GOP foreign policy spokesman in Congress, Senator Arthur H. Vandenberg of Michigan, learned of Wallace's speech, he was incensed. From Paris, where he was engaged in negotiating peace treaties with the minor Axis powers, Vandenberg forcefully reiterated the necessity for bipartisanship in foreign relations and pledged his best efforts to achieve that goal. At the same time, he pointedly reminded President Truman that "the situation requires unity within the Administration itself. We can only cooperate with one Secretary of State at a time!" Even Secretary of State James F. Byrnes, who was not on good terms with the president, cabled Truman from Paris, "The world is today in doubt not only as to American foreign policy, but as to your foreign policy." Wallace, Byrnes lamented, had largely destroyed bipartisan collaboration in foreign affairs. The following day, Henry Wallace was replaced as the head of the Commerce Department. It was ironic—and an eloquent commentary upon the recurring nature of the problem analyzed in this study—that a few months later Secretary of State Byrnes himself was ousted for challenging the president's dominant role in the foreign policy process.

The second development occurred in the early 1980s under the Reagan administration. Ronald Reagan chose former White House aide and NATO commander Alexander Haig as his first secretary of state. As all chief executives routinely have done since World War II, in appointing Haig to direct the State Department, President Reagan expressed great confidence in him and designated him as the president's chief foreign policy adviser. In Secretary Haig's colorful metaphor, Reagan had appointed him to serve as "vicar" of American foreign policy, and in the months ahead he attempted to assert his primacy against rival claimants within the executive branch—and, it sometimes appeared, even against the president himself. Within some eighteen months after taking office and following a series of highly publicized conflicts between the secretary and the White House staff, Haig was replaced as secretary of state by George Shultz. The personnel change, however, did not eliminate the problem of "incoherence" and "dissonance" among executive officials involved in foreign policy decision making. Indeed, it can be argued that by the mid-1980s the problem appeared to have become endemic to the policy-making process and was seemingly impervious to resolution. Under the Reagan administration, ongoing disunity within the executive branch became one of the conspicuous hallmarks of American diplomacy. It had also characterized relations between Secretary of State Cyrus Vance and National Security Adviser Zbigniew Brzezinski in the Carter administration.

At the outset, four observations may be made about this fragmentation in foreign policy making. In the first place, events have amply demonstrated that this is one of the most important phenomena affecting America's international role. At no time since World War II has there been a greater necessity for forceful and effective diplomatic leadership by the United States. Yet a minimal condition for achieving it is quite clearly a high degree of unity and coherence among executive officials themselves regarding the objectives and means of external policy. Conversely, a situation marked by ongoing policy incoherence and "static" within the executive bureaucracy, as even many national legislators have recognized, makes it extremely difficult for Congress to play its constitutional role in foreign affairs constructively. From a different perspective, the ability of the United States government to formulate cohesive and effective foreign policies and programs in the contemporary era can affect nothing less than the future political destiny of the world, not excluding the probability of global war or peace.

Second, experience since World War II leaves little doubt that the problem of there seeming to be more than one secretary of state at a time is a recurrent phenomenon. To some degree, it has afflicted every administration in the postwar era. Despite forceful actions like President Truman's dismissal of Wallace, the problem shows no tendency to "stay solved." In the 1960s, for example, it recurred under the Kennedy and Johnson administrations. It took a novel form under the Nixon administration, and it reached epidemic proportions under Presidents Carter and Reagan. It seems a safe prediction that, for reasons that are identified more fully in the chapters that follow, it will similarly characterize the foreign policy process of future administrations.

The recurrent nature of the problem also seems to be independent of the political orientation of the administration in power. No convincing evidence exists that it is uniquely a Democratic problem or a Republican problem. Nor does the phenomenon have any evident and direct relationship to the question of whether the White House and Congress are controlled by the same or different political parties. For example, President Jimmy Carter had to contend with a high level of dissidence among his principal foreign policy advisers, even though his party controlled both the House and Senate.

Third, the problem of intraexecutive disunity in the foreign policy field has posed a remarkably intractable obstacle to effective diplomacy by the United States. At best, attempted solutions and remedies for the problem have proved only marginally successful. In some instances, and the establishment of the National Security Council (NSC) and Central Intelligence Agency in 1947 are perhaps the leading examples, the "solution" may well have compounded the problem by adding a new source of intraexecutive conflict to those already present in the American system. Certainly, the office of assistant to the president for national security affairs has acquired an influence that was not foreseen when it was originally created. Far from being simply the NSC's executive director, managing its internal operations and coordinating departmental documents, the national security adviser has found it possible to exercise an advocacy role in foreign policy making. Sometimes the NSC staff has effectively become a White House "foreign office" independent of, and increasingly prone to compete with, the State Department.

In the fourth place, recent developments in American foreign relations provide substantial evidence for concluding that the problem of disunity among executive officials involved in diplomatic decision making is becoming progressively more acute with the passage of time. In retrospect the problem seems considerably more difficult and intractable in the 1980s than was the case in the 1950s—so much so as to offer reasonable grounds for believing that dissonance and fragmentation within the executive branch may now have become a permanent feature of the foreign policy process of the United States.

This conclusion is supported, for example, by a number of developments in American foreign relations since the end of the Vietnam War. That traumatic episode left a legacy likely to affect the conduct of American foreign relations for an indefinite period in the future. Among its more lasting consequences, two seem especially pertinent to our inquiry. One of these has been the tendency toward congressional assertiveness and independence in dealing with foreign policy issues. Determined to end the era of the "imperial presidency" in conducting foreign relations, Congress in the post–Vietnam War period has exerted its foreign policy prerogatives to an unprecedented degree. In turn this tendency reinforces dissonance within the executive branch, and in some instances such as when Congress encourages differences of opinion within the Defense Department on the nation's military needs, it may serve as a primary cause of intraexecutive disagreements over foreign policy questions.

The other post–Vietnam development fostering policy incoherence among executive agencies is that American public opinion has exhibited a high level of diversity and even self-contradiction concerning the nation's international role. In no period of American history, with the possible exception of the late 1930s, has public opinion within the United States been as hesitant, confused, and contradictory on foreign policy questions as in the aftermath of the Vietnam War. As a result of the nation's military and diplomatic defeat in Southeast Asia, the public consensus that had sustained American diplomatic efforts for over twenty years after World War II dissolved, and no new consensus has replaced it.

After Vietnam, American public attitudes toward foreign affairs became more than ordinarily ambivalent and anomalous. To cite but a few examples, in the post–Vietnam War era most Americans evidently supported a high level of national defense spending, as recommended by Presidents Carter and Reagan. Yet in most instances they opposed the president's reliance upon the armed forces to achieve diplomatic objectives. Similarly, events had made clear that majority sentiment in the United States favored the creation and maintenance of a complex and costly intelligence establishment within the American government. Yet public and congressional sentiment also opposed covert intelligence operations and were highly dubious about intervention in the political affairs of other nations by American intelligence agencies. Toward the Soviet Union, American attitudes were no less bewildering and contradictory. Rather consistently since World War II, the American people have remained suspicious of Soviet motives and objectives in global affairs. At the same time, substantial numbers of citizens have also favored negotiations between Washington and Moscow, called for a "nuclear freeze" between the two superpowers, and advocated other steps whose successful implementation required a high level of trust between the United States and the Soviet Union. If dissonance has increasingly characterized executive activities related to foreign affairs, a basic reason may be that such dissonance reflects the underlying confusions and uncertainties marking public attitudes within American society on external questions.

What are the major causes of policy incoherence and disunity within the executive branch in dealing with diplomatic issues? What forms does this disunity take? What forces have transformed this phenomenon into an integral and seemingly enduring feature of the American foreign policy process since World War II? What recurring patterns of intraexecutive relationships in foreign policy decision making may be identified? What distinctive patterns of relationships may be identified between the president and his principal foreign policy advisers, and what have been the more significant consequences of each pattern? What proposals and reforms have been applied in efforts to achieve greater cohesion among executive officials involved in diplomatic decision making, and why have most of them thus far failed to solve or appreciably alleviate the problem?

This study seeks to provide a clear understanding of such key issues. It is divided into three sections. The first (Chapters 1 and 2) presents an overall view of the foreign policy process in the United States. Chapter 1 analyzes the crucial role of the president in American foreign relations, and Chapter 2 focuses upon the role of the federal bureaucracy, with special attention devoted to the contribution of the State Department in the conduct of foreign relations.

Against this overall background the second section examines selected case studies on intraexecutive conflict and cooperation in foreign affairs in the post–World War II era. No effort is made in the case studies to present a comprehensive chronological account of American foreign relations since World War II. With case studies, some selectivity is always necessary. We have chosen what appear to be particularly instructive examples illustrating the overall problem of intraexecutive relations in the foreign policy field.

Chapter 3 analyzes a recurrent tendency in American diplomacy— one that, at some stage, nearly every chief executive has exemplified: the determination of a president—Franklin D. Roosevelt in this case— to serve as "his own secretary of state." As the chapter emphasizes, this proclivity by the chief executive gives rise to certain problems and consequences that can have a momentous effect upon the course of American diplomacy. At the same time, this pattern reflects a firmly established precedent in the management of foreign affairs, one that will undoubtedly be emulated by future occupants of the Oval Office.

The theme of Chapter 4, which deals with the foreign policy process of the Truman administration, is the creation and maintenance of an effective "partnership" between President Truman and Secretary of

State Dean G. Acheson. By nearly any standard, the Truman administration's foreign policy achievements constituted one of the most creative and overtly successful records in that field since World War II. The constructive working relationship between the president and secretary of state during that period was unquestionably one major factor accounting for that result. Yet, for reasons set forth in our study, this pattern of partnership between the president and his chief foreign policy adviser has become one that is extremely difficult to reproduce and to preserve today.

By contrast, Chapter 5 describes the prototype of a "maximalist" model of the modern American secretary of state in the person of John Foster Dulles. The outstanding feature of this pattern perhaps was the extraordinarily high degree of confidence exhibited by President Dwight D. Eisenhower in his secretary of state. The Eisenhower-Dulles relationship was intensely personal if also highly formal. Despite Secretary Dulles' enormous influence upon the process of diplomatic decision making, during the Eisenhower administration the morale of the State Department deteriorated significantly, and its image with Congress and the American people was badly tarnished. Secretary Dulles did little to reverse this process.

With the Johnson administration, an extraordinarily high premium was placed upon "consensual" decision making by executive officials involved with foreign policy issues. As Chapter 6 emphasizes, LBJ valued unity among the members of his foreign policy team. Throughout most of the period of the Vietnam War, an ostensibly high level of consensus among President Johnson and his aides was maintained. Many commentators on recent American foreign relations are convinced that this fact had two highly significant consequences. It fostered "groupthink" among the president and his advisers—a predisposition to consider an unduly narrow range of foreign policy options that in effect reinforced a predetermined diplomatic position. This approach also meant that dissenters were driven to use clandestine channels, such as leaks to the press, to express their disagreement with prevailing policies.

Chapter 7 examines a totally different configuration of intraexecutive relations in the formulation and administration of foreign policy. This is the emergence of what came to be called a "rival State Department" within the White House, whose de facto leader was the president's national security adviser. During the Nixon administration, this role was played forcefully, dramatically, and often highly successfully by Henry Kissinger, who completely eclipsed Secretary of State William Rogers in diplomatic decision making. Indeed, sometimes it appeared that Kissinger overshadowed President Nixon himself as the official who was overtly in charge of America's relations with other countries. This pattern also established a highly important precedent that other White House aides have endeavored to emulate since the Nixon-Kissinger era.

The last case study, Chapter 8, deals with the tribulations of the would-be "vicar" of American foreign policy under the Reagan administration, Secretary of State Alexander Haig. More than most recent occupants of his position, Haig took literally the president's assertion that the secretary of state was his chief foreign policy deputy and was responsible for coordinating executive activities in foreign relations. From Haig's perspective, that proved to be a profound miscalculation. Perhaps more than any recent head of the State Department, Haig faced repeated challenges to his authority and jurisdiction from the White House staff and from other executive departments. Confronted with continued disunity among his principal aides on key foreign policy questions, President Reagan resolved the matter by "accepting" Haig's obviously reluctant resignation less than eighteen months after he was appointed to office. Yet Haig's replacement by Shultz, events made incontestably clear, did not really solve the problem of executive disunity in foreign policy. During some periods at least, the pattern of foreign policy decision making existing within the Reagan administration exemplified what can be described as an "anarchical" model. The level of internal policy incoherence and dissonance among executive officials in dealing with diplomatic issues exceeded any witnessed since World War II.

Postwar experience has demonstrated, therefore, that several models for the formulation and administration of foreign affairs are available for use by the president and his advisers. As the case studies indicate, each has certain advantages and disadvantages for America's efforts to respond effectively to challenges and events abroad. In the final analysis, which pattern is chosen—or whether some new pattern will emerge—will be a presidential decision. In reaiity, of course, an incumbent president may rely upon several of these models during his tenure in the Oval Office.

The third section of the study—Chapter 9—presents our basic findings and recommendations about the problem under investigation. For the sake of better understanding and comparability of cases, a graphic and uniform summary of each case study is included in this final chapter. Before reading the case studies themselves (Chapters 3–8), the reader may find it helpful to read these summaries. Doing so will facilitate the drawing of meaningful comparisons and contrasts among them, and it should also impart a clearer conception of significant trends affecting the American foreign policy process since World War II.

The concluding chapter also considers various proposals that have been made to solve the problem of executive disunity in the American system. After evaluating these proposals, the authors offer their own remedies for resolving, or at least attenuating, the problem.

The reader should be aware that the authors share a certain intellectual disposition. They belong to the school of thought which believes that political scientists always explicitly or implicitly deal with questions of value. They are dubious about the idea that any haven of total objectivity exists in discussing most political issues, particularly one as complex and controversial as how the United States arrives at its foreign policy decisions. For example, in our view it is patently desirable that the process of foreign policy decision making within the American government consistently produce intelligent and effective responses to the diplomatic challenges confronting the nation abroad. Achieving this general goal in turn demands the fulfillment of two specific requirements: a process of rational goal selection in which the principal options available to the United States in dealing with particular diplomatic issues are identified and carefully considered; and the formulation of effective means—statements, proposals, programs, and the like—designed to achieve the goals adopted.

In contrast, we see little value in a decision-making process that inevitably produces disunity and fragmentation among executive officials in dealing with major foreign policy questions. We believe, for example, that an essential prerequisite for a durable bipartisan foreign policy is that there be a foreign policy to begin with—a carefully considered and agreed-upon position, ultimately approved by the president, that key executive policy makers are prepared to support as a matter of conviction and to defend in relations with Congress, with American public opinion, and with foreign governments. To our minds, it was no coincidence, for example, that the kind of "anarchical" pattern of intraexecutive relations existing under the Reagan administration was also associated with two other tendencies vitally affecting American foreign relations—a high and continuing level of executive-legislative conflict in the foreign policy field and an unusually high degree of public uncertainty and ambivalence about the proper role of the United States in global and regional affairs.

Although we have made no attempt to conceal our own preferences among possible models of foreign policy decision making, we also believe that the positions taken here are defensible and are supported by a substantial accumulation of evidence since World War II. No effort has been made in these pages to "indict" particular presidents or other officials who have played a crucial role in diplomatic decision making throughout the postwar era. Our purpose is to understand that process more fully and dispassionately, to bring the critical problem of intraexecutive conflict in foreign affairs into sharper relief, and to provide useful guidelines enabling the interested student of American diplomacy to anticipate and comprehend emerging tendencies and future developments. Our intention is to apply the motto inscribed above the National Archives building in Washington, D.C.— WHAT IS PAST IS PROLOGUE—to a limited but important dimension of American foreign relations. If we have done so successfully, it will be a contribution not only to greater public enlightenment, but also to a more constructive approach by the United States to a wide variety of global challenges in the years ahead.

1

The Presidency and the Foreign Policy Process

The *New Yorker*, ever alert to the absurdities of official power, had a cartoon in 1984 showing a group of what are supposed to be primitive natives being introduced to a group of deplaning American dignitaries. The native interpreter is explaining to the chief, "The Ambassador says he does not care what we have heard—he speaks for both Secretary Weinberger *and* Secretary Shultz." That the reputed differences between the secretaries of defense and state could be so widely known as to constitute the punch line of a cartoon speaks volumes about the perceived state of American diplomacy. On the other hand, rivalry among the various participants in foreign policy making—including the differences between Caspar Weinberger and George Shultz—is neither a recent nor an isolated phenomenon in the conduct of the nation's foreign affairs. Indeed, what may be most amusing about the cartoon's punch line is not that untutored natives in the farthest reaches of the world had heard of the Weinberger-Shultz feud, but that the ambassador could presume that American foreign policy should speak with a single voice.

The Constitution is clear, if a bit too terse, about vesting responsibility for the administration of public affairs in the president: "The executive power shall be vested in the President of the United States of America" (Article II, Section 1, Clause 1). The Constitution, however, also gives Congress a voice in executive affairs. For example, the appointment of executive departmental officials requires confirmation by the Senate, and the revenues necessary to run the executive branch come through congressional appropriations. This example of constitutional engineering, which is termed checks and balances, was clearly designed, along with other constitutional mechanisms such as separation of powers, to maintain a system of limited government. As Justice Brandeis observed, the American constitutional process was designed not to maximize efficiency but to promote ordered liberty.

The benign inefficiency of American government is nowhere better seen than in the administration of foreign affairs. What may have been intended as a self-limiting system of institutional restraints can become an "invitation to struggle" between Congress and the presidency for control over the foreign policy process. The president has strong formal claims to constitutional preeminence in this field, but Congress is certainly well within any reading of constitutional intent when it asserts its right to a collaborative or a consultative role. Yet there is a marked difference between these two roles in their scope and influence on the process of foreign policy making and implementation, and over the years the degree to which Congress has asserted its constitutional prerogatives has varied markedly. These are controversial issues worth discussing in some detail, but this chapter's major concern is with presidential direction of foreign policy.

What this emphasis posits is the president's near suzerainty in the field of foreign affairs. The twentieth century has been a presidential century in American politics—even more in the international than in the domestic arena. Whatever the constitutional basis for congressional claims in the foreign policy process, it is undeniable that custom, tradition, and Supreme Court interpretations have formed a broad expansion of presidential preeminence.[1] It is difficult to question the statement that foreign policy making is dominated by the president and the secretary of state (and more recently, the assistant to the president for national security affairs) and not the president and the chairman of the Senate Committee on Foreign Relations. The reader probably knows the name of the secretary of state. But who is the chairman of the Foreign Relations Committee?

1. For a full discussion of these views, see Cecil V. Crabb, Jr., and Pat M. Holt, *Invitation to Struggle: Congress, the President, and Foreign Policy* (2nd ed.; Washington, D.C., 1984).

The Presidency in an Age of Permanent Crisis

Decision making in the nuclear age must inevitably be fixed in the presidency. Whatever claims that Congress may make for its role in the conduct of foreign affairs, there is no disputing the president's need to have unquestioned command over the nation's responses to a sudden attack. What may be termed the "Pearl Harbor mentality" of presidential authority has been broadened during the persistent tension between the United States and the Soviet Union in the post–World War II era. This "cold war" has flashed hot on enough occasions to warrant the period's description as an "age of permanent crisis." With the consequent need for crisis management, the presidency has consolidated an institutional preeminence in foreign policy making.

The presidency was well prepared to rise to these expectations about its leadership requirements. As the elected head of government, the president is also the head of state; this fuses in one office functions that are more typically kept separate. As head of state, the president engages in a number of public duties that are elsewhere performed by the king of Sweden, the president of Italy, the governor-general of Australia—all of whom are exclusively figureheads (hereditary or elected) rather than political executives. Clinton Rossiter provided an amusing, and not inaccurate, description of the ceremonial demands on the president.

As figurehead rather than working head of our government, he greets distinguished visitors from all parts of the world, lays wreaths on the tomb of the Unknown Soldier and before the statue of Lincoln, makes proclamations of thanksgiving and commemoration, bestows medals on flustered pilots, holds state dinners for the diplomatic corps and the Supreme Court, lights the nation's Christmas tree, buys the first poppy from the Veterans of Foreign Wars, gives the first crisp banknote to the Red Cross, throws out the first ball for the Senators (the harmless ones out at Griffith Stadium), rolls the first egg for the Easter Bunny, and in the course of any month greets a fantastic procession of firemen, athletes, veterans, Boy Scouts, Campfire Girls, boosters, hog callers, exchange students, and heroic school children.[2]

At first glance, the events listed seem so trivial as to make one wonder why a president would bother to involve himself in such affairs.

2. Clinton Rossiter, *The American Presidency* (Rev. ed.; New York, 1962), 15.

The answer, on one level, is that acting as head of state can provide tremendous psychic satisfactions through the attendant deference and exemption from partisan criticism that such occasions can provide. More important, these ceremonial occasions are not all that nonpolitical; in fact, they are of great political value simply by not seeming to be so. A president who shows himself to the people in this way is not campaigning; he is making a "presidential progress"—the customary state journey familiar to George Washington before him.

Most significant, serving as head of state equips the president with an important symbolic aura that provides the disparate elements of a fragmented electorate and pluralistic society at least one nationally elected official with whom all can identify. As head of state, the president "becomes the living embodiment of the ideals that underlie the political system . . . the personification of Americanism."[3] That vesting such monarchical elements in a politician can have potentially undesirable outcomes for a republican form of government, for example, an "imperial presidency," has been a recurring fear among students of the American political system.[4]

Nowhere is the importance of the president's role as head of state greater than in foreign affairs. There is an American tradition, which goes back to World War I, that "politics stops at the water's edge," and when a president asserts that he is defending the national interest and representing American vital interests abroad, he can count on strong political support from other policy makers and from the public at large. At times of international crisis, he becomes the nation's one, agreed-upon rallying point. It is the president alone among political actors who can command the feelings of loyalty and patriotism that transcend ideological and partisan restrictions. Thus, both political friends and foes of Franklin Roosevelt turned to him for leadership when the Japanese attacked Pearl Harbor in December, 1941.[5]

Of course, the bombing of Pearl Harbor was without parallel in American history. Regardless of that fact, presidents are accorded a

3. Philippa Strum, "A Symbolic Attack on the Imperial Presidency," in Thomas E. Cronin and Rexford G. Tugwell (eds.), *The Presidency Reappraised* (2nd ed.; New York, 1977), 254–55.

4. See, for example, Arthur M. Schlesinger, Jr., *The Imperial Presidency* (Boston, 1973).

5. Richard A. Watson and Norman C. Thomas, *The Politics of the Presidency* (New York, 1983), 166.

wide latitude as head of state in directing the nation's foreign affairs. Crises heighten popular awareness of the president's role and dependence on his judgment as the embodiment of the national interest. What the British prime minister asks for in the name of Queen and Country, the American president requests in his own name. "The president, in short, is the one-man distillation of the American people just as surely as the queen is of the British people; he is, in President Taft's words, 'the personal embodiment and representative of their dignity and majesty.'" Joseph Kallenbach is certainly correct when he observes that the distinctive character of the American chief executive is the fusion of the functions of head of state to an office in which are already vested "very substantial powers over the formulation of legislation, execution of the laws, command of the military forces, and supervision of the conduct of external relations."[6] What he might have further observed is that there is great potential for abuse inherent in an office that combines the policy-making powers of a political leader with the ceremonial powers of a monarch.[7]

As Rossiter was quick to emphasize, the president does more than just reign; he also rules: "He symbolizes the people, but he also runs their government." Yet, while the president's powers as head of state outstrip his formal responsibilities, his powers as chief executive have not traditionally been equal to his responsibilities. As the head of government, the president determines public policy from global strategy to the appointment of assistant secretaries of state. Moreover, the president is held responsible for the successful operation of the government as a whole. If administrative agencies default, he is politically liable. Despite these executive responsibilities, the president actually has few powers that he can exercise to control the administrative machinery of the national government. Richard Watson and Norman Thomas have described the situation: "There is an apparent paradox in the president's position as head of a vast and complex military and civilian bureaucracy and his considerable formal legal powers on the one hand and his limited ability to direct that bureaucracy toward the achievement of his program goals and policy

6. Rossiter, *American Presidency*, 16; Joseph E. Kallenbach, *The American Chief Executive* (New York, 1966), 273.

7. This has been referred to as "Caesarism." See M. Amoury de Reincourt, *The Coming Caesars* (New York, 1957).

objectives on the other." Presidential scholar Kallenbach made the same point. In his view, the president and his helpers can at best tinker and adjust, but the preponderance of the world of policy and action belongs to the departments.[8]

This accepted, and historically supportable, conception of the president as chief executive emphasizes the importance of a president's personal abilities to project the goals of his administration through persuasion, personality, and patronage. The exercise of these extraofficial powers should enable the president to overcome the inertia, conservatism, and special pleading of the departments. Certainly, there are considerable grounds for debate about whether this is an accurate, or necessarily pejorative, characterization of administrative behavior. However, the belief that this was the case led to the development of two assumptions about the conditions necessary for good presidential performance. One is that a good president is an assertive, even aggressive, president who actively projects his person and program before the public. The other is that the Executive Office of the President is the indispensable staff agency for administering a presidential agenda.[9]

Nowhere has the preponderance of presidential power been greater than in the president's role as chief diplomat. Whatever the constitutional claims of Congress in the conduct of international relations (which are considerable), the president has been generally recognized as the fount of foreign policy making. In John Marshall's words of 1799, the president is "the sole organ of the nation in its external relations, and its sole representative with foreign nations."[10] "The age of permanent crisis," this post–World War II nuclear age, has immeasurably strengthened the president's diplomatic status. This strengthening has followed not only from popular perceptions about the president's primary responsibility for safeguarding the nation's international interests but also from the growth of a powerful apparatus within the White House itself for overseeing foreign relations.

When the president's constitutional and statutory responsibilities

8. Rossiter, *American Presidency*, 17; Watson and Thomas, *Politics of the Presidency*, 281; Kallenbach, *The American Chief Executive*, 375–80
9. Margaret Wyszomirski, "The De-Institutionalization of Presidential Staff Agencies," *Public Administration Review*, XLII (1982), 448–58.
10. Quoted in Rossiter, *American Presidency*, 23.

as commander in chief and guarantor of national security are considered, he can be judged to have a virtual monopoly in the conduct of international politics—albeit one sharply contested by Congress in recent years. As Kallenbach has said, the president's designation as commander in chief "is unique among the clauses outlining the powers and duties of the President in that it confers an office rather than a mere function upon him. . . . The implication is that whatever powers and duties are necessarily associated with the exercise of supreme military command belong to the President by constitutional prescription and cannot be constitutionally diminished or controlled by statute."[11]

Presidents as commanders in chief have, in fact, operated on the very fringes of constitutionality (and arguably beyond that). Wars have allowed presidents to exercise power so broadly as to lead critics to accuse both Abraham Lincoln and Franklin Roosevelt of having established constitutional dictatorships. Constitutional "niceties" can be among the first victims of states of emergency. Lincoln's suspension of habeas corpus in areas outside of the theater of war and Roosevelt's internment of Japanese-Americans on the West Coast during World War II come to mind. Moreover, Congress largely acquiesced or abetted these wartime expansions of presidential powers, especially in the twenty-five years of Soviet-American hostility after World War II. The War Powers Act of 1973 symbolized congressional dissatisfaction with an unlimited conception of presidential power. Permanent crises, such as the Cold War, and the extraordinary nature of a thermonuclear war have served to institutionalize presidential preeminence in military affairs. "Traditional modes of action have had to give way to the demands of national survival itself. Total war and constitutional government as usual are incompatible bedfellows. So far as the presidency is concerned, the commander-in-chief clause, reinforced as it may be by congressional delegation of authority, becomes a vast reservoir of prescriptive power to act as the public needs require in dealing with the emergencies generated by war."[12]

Congress, while allowing considerable discretionary authority to the president in the conduct of foreign relations, has also mandated

11. Kallenbach, *The American Chief Executive*, 526.
12. *Ibid.*, 533.

that he be specifically responsible for defining national security policy and objectives.[13] The National Security Act of 1947 codified and classified presidential responsibilities for the maintenance of "peace through strength." To some degree this may have constituted a certain abdication of congressional prerogatives, but it is perhaps better judged to be an admission of the realities of the "national security presidency." Regardless, it legitimized the paramount position of the president and made possible the creation of a White House administrative machinery to assist him in meeting these responsibilities. The president's role of guarantor of national security, which results from the fusion of the tasks of chief diplomat and commander in chief, is a subject of central importance to our entire discussion.

In effect, the modern president is a world executive—"the President of the West"—and responsibility for the administration of foreign affairs is his peculiar preserve and one for which he is held almost solely responsible. A president who is identified as mismanaging foreign affairs will find it extremely difficult to maintain his public credibility. The fate of Harry Truman testifies to the unfairness—and that of Jimmy Carter to the fairness—of such judgments about presidential performance. Clinton Rossiter recognized over twenty-five years ago that the president had become in effect, the Defender of the Free World: "The President has a much larger constituency than the American electorate: his words and deeds in behalf of our own survival as a free nation have a direct bearing on the freedom and stability of at least several score other countries." In his work on the development of the presidency into a global institution, Sidney Warren stated, "By the twentieth century he [the president] would be elected to global leadership, the single most important individual on earth, literally holding in his hands the fate of all mankind."[14]

It may not be possible to establish the exact moment when the United States accepted, or assumed, the mantle of defending Western civilization. But the rhetoric of Woodrow Wilson's ringing affirmation of internationalism and American involvement in world affairs illustrates its essential ideology: "Our object now . . . is to vindicate the principles of peace and justice in the life of the world as against self-

---

13. Charles Funderburk, *Presidents and Politics* (Monterey, Calif., 1982), 246.
14. Rossiter, *American Presidency*, 36; Sidney Warren, *The President as World Leader* (New York, 1964), 3.

ish and autocratic power and to set up amongst the really free . . . a concert of purpose and of action as will henceforth insure the observance of these principles. . . . The world must be made safe for democracy."[15] With the energies of the United States as a world power, and four decades of permanent crisis, the prestige and power of the president in foreign policy making is without any equal.

The Constitutional Prerogatives

Although the pendulum has swung between periods of congressional and presidential preeminence in domestic policy making during the two hundred years of American constitutional government, the president's primacy in foreign policy has been established beyond serious question in the post–World War II era. The usual plea of Congress is to be allowed to take part in foreign policy making—not that it should dominate the process. In his discussion of the treaty-making power of the executive in Federalist 75, Alexander Hamilton argued against congressional responsibility for handling foreign affairs: "Accurate and comprehensive knowledge of foreign policies; a steady and systematic adherence to the same views; a nice and uniform sensibility to national character; decision, secrecy, and dispatch, are all incompatible with the genius of a body so variable and so numerous." Although Hamilton was only referring to the House of Representatives, his description can sum up what has been the usual judgment about the institutional deficiencies of Congress for conducting international relations. The earlier experience under the Articles of Confederation with the administration of foreign affairs through legislative boards and commissions had proven manifestly unsuccessful. "As much as any other single factor, it was the mismanagement of foreign affairs by Congress under the Articles of Confederation that led to the calling of the Constitutional Convention in 1787."[16]

The Founding Fathers wanted a president who was capable of acting as a strong chief executive in foreign, as well as domestic, affairs.

15. Quoted in James MacGregor Burns, *Presidential Government: The Crucible of Leadership* (Boston, 1973), 266.
16. John Jay, Alexander Hamilton, James Madison, *The Federalist: A Commentary on the Constitution of the United States* (New York, 1937), 488; Crabb and Holt, *Invitation to Struggle,* 34.

Congress itself has often legislated broad presidential responsibilities for the execution of foreign policy even when this would have domestic policy implications. In upholding such legislation, the Supreme Court in 1936 argued for the broadest possible assumptions about presidential authority: "It is quite apparent that if, in the maintenance of our international relations, embarrassment—perhaps serious embarrassment—is to be avoided and success for our aims achieved, congressional legislation which is to be made effective through negotiation and inquiry within the international field must often accord to the President a degree of discretion and freedom from statutory restriction which would not be admissable were domestic affairs alone involved."[17] In sum, the Supreme Court was recognizing the president as the sole representative of the United States government in the conduct of international relations. It was agreeing with Thomas Jefferson, who said when he was secretary of state, "The transaction of business with foreign nations is executive altogether."[18]

Presidential-congressional relations have not been without conflicts, especially since the disintegration of the bipartisan foreign policy consensus during and after the Vietnam War. Yet as Richard Pious observes, the major problem confronting presidents has been their weakness as managers of foreign relations. There is no unity of purpose within the executive branch.[19] The president's position in foreign policy making is based neither on mere assertions nor sheer aggressiveness, but rather on solid constitutional articles. The oath that the president takes upon assuming office requires that, in the faithful execution of his duties, he will "preserve, protect, and defend the Constitution of the United States" to the best of his abilities (Article II, Section 1, Clause 8). When combined with the first sentence of the article—"The executive power shall be vested in the President of the United States of America"—and with the admonition that he "take care that the laws be faithfully executed" (Article II, Section 3), there exists a strong case for presidential responsibility for all administration. The conduct of foreign affairs is an important part of general expectations about what the chief executive is supposed to do in the

17. *United States* v. *Curtiss-Wright Export Corp.*, 299 U.S. 304 (1936). See also *Goldwater et al.* v. *Carter*, 444 U.S. 996 (1979), which reaffirmed these principles.
18. Quoted in Francis O. Wilcox, *Congress, the Executive, and Foreign Policy* (New York, 1971), 146.
19. Richard M. Pious, *The American Presidency* (New York, 1979), 332.

regular performance of his duties. Even without specific grants of constitutional authority, there would already exist a strong presumption for presidential authority in the administration of foreign policy, and policy in general.

The president's general administrative power is immeasurably expanded and concretized with his designation as "Commander-in-Chief of the Army and the Navy of the United States, and of the militia of the several states when called into the actual service of the United States" (Article II, Section 2, Clause 1). More than any other single constitutional responsibility, the president's role as commander in chief has been the cause of his vast influence in determining the nation's foreign policy. Almost without exception (the timorous James Buchanan in the late 1850s may stand excepted), presidents have interpreted this authority broadly and dynamically. As the article can be construed, the president's powers as commander in chief give him the right to move troops from Point A to Point B and to tell them what to do when they get there. The destination may be Fort Benning or the presidio; it may also be Seoul or Saigon.[20]

The latter destinations refer to but two of the approximately 125 situations in which an American president committed troops to hostilities during the nation's two-hundred-year history. These "undeclared wars" have been of various sorts and have had varying degrees of political effect. When President James K. Polk ordered the army to occupy the territory between the Nueces and the Rio Grande rivers, disputed territory that was claimed by both Texas and Mexico, he knew that war would follow. The Mexican-American War of 1847–1848 marked a high point in the movement for the realization of the United States' so-called "manifest destiny" on the North American continent. Since the Mexicans were at a distinct disadvantage, it was also a quick and popular war, albeit one that was unprovoked. The army was used to put down the southern insurrection without a declaration of war between the Union and the Confederacy. This long and bloody Civil War was conducted by Abraham Lincoln on the basis of his presidential authority as commander in chief. The Supreme Court upheld his actions, arguing that he was obliged to respond to such a grave threat to the nation's unity "without waiting for Congress to

20. One of the purposes of the War Powers Act was to restrict the traditional right of presidents to dispose of troops, especially in "zones of hostilities."

baptize it with a name."[21] Congress, of course, provided a posteriori approval for Lincoln's actions by financing the war and approving expansion of the armed forces.

The nineteenth-century incidence of undeclared wars was frequent but limited in scope. The twentieth century, by contrast, has been marked by full-scale wars that were fought by virtue of the president's command of the armed forces. Both the Korean and the Vietnam wars involved substantial commitments of American troops and heavy casualties. Both were highly political, with right-wing denunciations of a "sellout to communism" in the one and left-wing demonstrations against American "imperialism" in the other. In both wars the final outcomes were on terms that could not be considered a victory for the United States: stalemate and the *status quo ante bellum* in Korea, stalemate and an eventual Communist takeover in Vietnam. Both wars derived from the role that the United States has played at different times in the post–World War II era of acting as the "world's policeman." The decisions to commit troops in these wars were associated with "executive agreements" (rather than treaties) entered into by various American presidents, and both wars, of course, were waged without benefit of congressional declaration.[22]

Article II, Section 2 of the Constitution states in Clause 3 that the president has the power "by and with the advice and consent of the Senate, to make treaties, provided two-thirds of the Senators present concur." A treaty is the most formal commitment that can be reached between two nations and as distinct from executive agreements (oral or written "understandings" between heads of governments) have a coequality with constitutional provisions and statutes as the supreme law of the land (Article VI). The treaty-making process involves two steps, negotiation and ratification. The first step is almost exclusively a matter of the president's proposing and the Senate's disposing. Agreements between the United States and a foreign power are worked out by the executive branch, signed, and submitted to the Senate for its advice and consent. Whatever may have been the original intent of the framers, presidents—beginning with Washington—have taken

21. See the Prize cases, 67 U.S. (2 Black) 635 (1863).
22. Technically, it may be argued that the defense of South Korea was pursuant to a treaty obligation—the United Nations Charter. Supporters of the Vietnam War argued that it was fought under the "functional equivalent" of a declaration of war provided by the Gulf of Tonkin Resolution.

the view that the executive branch negotiates treaties and then submits them to the Senate for acceptance, modification, or rejection.

Despite the usual talk about Senate "ratification" of a treaty, that is not technically what occurs. The Senate may refuse to give the necessary two-thirds approval, which defeats a proposed treaty, or it may grant a treaty extraordinary approval, as it has in the overwhelming number of cases, and send it back to the president for his signature. The Senate may also amend the treaty submitted by the president, and it can append reservations and understandings that purport to clarify the treaty's meaning. In either case, a president may choose not to sign the treaty as altered, justifying his refusal by maintaining that it runs contrary to his original intention.[23] This was the fate of the ill-starred Treaty of Versailles, which President Wilson refused to sign after his Senate opponents, led by the Republican chairman of the Foreign Relations Committee, Henry Cabot Lodge of Massachusetts, amended out of the treaty Wilson's cherished dreams for America's role in the League of Nations.[24] Whether amended or unamended by the Senate, a treaty does not become the law of the land until signed by the president.

The humiliation that Wilson suffered at the hands of a minority of senators during the debate over the treaty served, especially in its more romanticized renditions, as one of those "lessons" that presidents are supposed to have learned from history, the lesson being, "Don't make treaties because they have to be 'ratified' by the Senate." Since 1919–1920, presidents have come to rely heavily on the use of executive agreements. Doubtless the cumbersome, highly formalized, and much publicized nature of the ratification process deters some presidents from framing a foreign policy initiative as a treaty. On the other hand, most of the major elements of postwar American foreign policy were framed as treaties: the United Nations Charter, the North Atlantic Treaty Organization, the peace with Japan, the Nuclear Test Ban, SALT, and a new regime for the Panama Canal. It would seem that the press of international affairs has elevated the treaty to a spe-

23. Thus, the Senate does not technically "ratify" treaties. It does play a part in the ratification process by giving or withholding its "advice and consent." The president must sign the ratification instrument—a fact that gives the executive the last word in the treaty-ratification process.

24. See Foster Rhea Dulles, *America's Rise to World Power* (New York, 1963), 108–27, and Thomas A. Bailey, *Woodrow Wilson and the Lost Peace* (New York, 1944).

cial status for extraordinary policies, whereas the executive agreement takes care of more quotidian international undertakings.

The two-thirds provision for treaty ratification is itself an extraordinary vote and may have been meant to signify the importance of treaty obligations. Certainly this rule makes it possible for senators representing distinctly minority sectional or group interests to thwart the president and a Senate majority. During the Constitutional Convention, the southern states were afraid that their more numerous northern counterparts might negotiate an agreement ceding New Orleans and the mouth of the Mississippi to Spain in exchange for commercial privileges. The two-thirds rule does make it difficult to pass a treaty without a "concurrent majority" that would have to accommodate strongly organized minorities. At the same time, a treaty is not just an international compact but a law whose provisions are enforced by the courts like any other law. It should also be noted that treaties, like statutes, must be in conformity with the Constitution: "A treaty or law implementing a treaty that abridged First Amendment freedoms would be just as unconstitutional as a law that did the same thing."[25]

The Senate and the president are put in contact with each other on a regular and more routine basis in the appointment process. Article II, Section 2 provides that the president "shall appoint ambassadors, other public ministers and consuls . . . and all other officers of the United States" with the advice and consent of the Senate. Subject to this requirement of senatorial confirmation, the president chooses the nation's highest diplomatic officials and senior foreign policy makers.[26] The president, however, is not required to have senatorial approval for removing these executive branch officers.[27]

"Peopling the government" is one of the principal means by which

25. Edward Corwin and J. W. Peltason, *Understanding the Constitution* (4th ed., New York, 1979), 124, 97–98.

26. The requirement of senatorial confirmation extends through the level of assistant secretaries of departments. On the other hand, the national security adviser and many other White House staff members need not be confirmed by the Senate—an increasingly sore point with members of Congress. Modern presidents have been inclined to rely upon other emissaries—such as the vice-president, White House aides, the First Lady, and private citizens—for diplomatic missions.

27. *Myers* v. *United States*, 272 U.S. 52 (1926) vindicated President Andrew Johnson in his opposition to the requirement of Senate approval for the removal of cabinet officers. The Tenure of Office Act of 1867, over which Johnson was impeached, was repealed by Congress in 1887.

the president is able to exert an influence over policy. It seems logical for the chief executive to be able to select those responsible for executing his policies, since he is to be held responsible for their success or failure. Although the president is given a wide latitude in the process of selection, he is required to collaborate with the Senate as those who are confirmed must do in committee testimony if that confidence is to be maintained. As Kallenbach puts it, "The chief executive may be the captain of the Ship of State; but he must function with a crew that is not entirely of his own choosing."[28] In other words, the requirement for senatorial advice and consent has sometimes prevented a president from selecting certain individuals for fear that they would fail to be confirmed.[29]

Most Senate confirmations are routine both because the offices below the cabinet level are noncontroversial and because of a willingness to allow the president "to pick his own team." But this is not always the case. For example, the confirmation hearings of Charles Bohlen to be President Eisenhower's ambassador to the Soviet Union were the occasion for violent denunciations of postwar containment policies. It required a concerted presidential effort to secure Bohlen's approval from a Senate controlled by Eisenhower's own party (see Chapter 5). During the early 1980s, Jesse Helms (R-N.C.) kept the nominations of several key State Department personnel, such as Lawrence Eagleburger to be assistant secretary for European affairs, bottled up in committee as a protest against what he judged to be their identification with the policies of former Secretary of State Henry Kissinger. That both President Reagan and Kissinger were his fellow Republicans seemed not to concern the senator.

The remaining constitutional provision specifying the president's foreign policy making role is in Article II, Section 3. It provides that the president "shall receive ambassadors and other public ministers from the nations of the world."[30] The reception of such foreign representatives constitutes "recognition" of the nation whose credentials are presented. Foreign diplomats, to repeat, are accredited to the

28. Kallenbach, *The American Chief Executive*, 387.
29. It has been said that Adam Yarmolinsky, an influential adviser to Robert McNamara, remained as a special assistant to the secretary of defense rather than risk a difficult confirmation hearing.
30. Technically, the president can also receive ambassadors from the United Nations and from the Organization of American States.

president personally as head of state. Therefore, it is the president's decision alone whether or not to accord recognition to governments.

Usually, this presidential recognition is a formality. As a rule, in extending recognition, presidents apply the usual international standard of whether a government is in effective control of its own territory. Presidents have at times, however, chosen to apply a subjective standard, such as when Woodrow Wilson in 1913 refused to recognize the Huerta regime in Mexico, which he described as a "government of butchers." The difference between the Wilsonian principle of recognition and the traditional tenet of international law is that the criterion for judgment in the former is largely implicit. Concerning Mexico, the American position was that the government did not "represent the wishes" of the Mexican people. Wilson imposed a democratic criterion for recognition. In regard to the USSR, the United States denied recognition because of Moscow's sponsorship of revolutions abroad and failure to pay czarist debts. Franklin Roosevelt ended sixteen years of nonrecognition of the Soviet Union in 1933; similarly, President Carter appointed the first ambassador to the People's Republic of China thirty years after the Communists had come to power. This appointment of Leonard Woodcock to represent the United States in Peking was also the subject of a sharp confirmation battle in the Senate.

Extraconstitutional Prerogatives

The line between constitutional and extraconstitutional prerogatives is a thin one. Activist presidents, including some of the greatest chief executives, have interpreted the powers of the office expansively— certainly far beyond a narrow construction of the duties enumerated in Article II. Moreover, the Supreme Court has recognized that powers that can be legitimately derived from an enumerated power, if not otherwise forbidden, are constitutionally correct.[31] When exactly is a presidential action that is not expressly delegated a legitimate activity? Which powers are implied and which invented?

The recognition power provides a notable example of this ambigu-

31. See *McCulloch* v. *Maryland*, 4 Wheaton 316 (1819).

ity. For the most part, the exchange of diplomatic representation between nations is procedurally routine. As we have seen, however, a president may use the recognition power to achieve a political goal, such as when previously "nonexistent" governments, for example, "Bolshevik Russia" or "Red China," are finally recognized. The Supreme Court, for its part, has refused to rule on such matters, because they are "political"; that is, they are matters not resolvable through the legal process.[32] What is true for so relatively specialized a power as recognition is truer for other important areas of foreign policy making.

Executive agreements represent one such important extraconstitutional presidential prerogative, since these understandings commit the nation to important foreign policy obligations. Presidents from George Washington to Ronald Reagan have entered into various forms of understanding with the heads of other governments. But these instruments of diplomacy have generated great congressional concern when presidents have agreed to covenants with other countries without legislative knowledge or concurrence. It has been estimated that 95 percent of the understandings reached between the United States and other nations in the period since World War II have been by executive agreement and that a total of about seven thousand such agreements were entered into during this period.[33] The dramatic rise in the use of executive agreements as compared with treaties in the postwar era is most striking. Table 1 shows the historical contrast.

The exponential rise in the number of executive agreements reflects the growing complexity of foreign affairs. Moreover, some executive agreements, especially those concerning overseas trade, are made as a result of congressional authorization, perhaps even encouragement. Also, most of these agreements are concerned with routine matters, such as customs enforcement and the regulation of international radio. Yet, as Robert DiClerico has pointed out, "some presidents have viewed the executive agreement as a device for the accomplishment of ends which they knew would be rejected if submitted in the form of

32. In *United States* v. *Belmont*, 301 U.S. 324 (1937), the Supreme Court ruled that "who is sovereign of a territory is not a judicial question but one the determination of which by the political departments conclusively binds the courts."
33. Loch Johnson and James M. McCormick, "Foreign Policy by Executive Fiat," *Foreign Policy*, XXVIII (Fall, 1977), 117.

Table 1 Treaties and Executive Agreements, 1789–1980

Years	Treaties	Executive Agreements
1789–1839	60	27
1839–1889	215	238
1889–1939	524	917
1940–1970	310	5,653
1971–1980	172	3,114

Sources: Joseph Kallenbach, *The American Chief Executive* (New York, 1966), 504; Louis Fisher, *President and Congress* (New York, 1972), 45; Robert E. DiClerico, *The American President* (Englewood Cliffs, N.J., 1979), 49.

a treaty."[34] When the treaty to annex Texas failed to receive a two-thirds majority in 1844, President John Tyler achieved annexation by executive agreement with the concurrence of a simple majority of both houses in a joint resolution. Franklin Roosevelt raised executive agreements to a new pinnacle in 1940 in his famous destroyer-base deal with Great Britain, by which fifty overage American ships were swapped for naval bases in the Caribbean. Despite the abridgement of strict neutrality involved with such military assistance (which was also forbidden by statute as well as international law), President Roosevelt chose not to risk having a treaty defeated by Senate isolationists. As with so many executive agreements, the full nature of the promises involved were not publicly disclosed.

Most important, many executive agreements have had a dramatic effect on the course of American foreign policy: 1) the understandings with the Soviet Union at various conferences during World War II about the disposition of Eastern Europe; 2) a variety of agreements between the United States and governments in Saigon that committed American support for South Vietnam; 3) the assumption by the United States of de facto commitment for guaranteeing Israeli security; 4) the establishment of cultural and scientific exchanges with the People's Republic of China during the Carter administration. These are all examples of the reliance by presidents on executive agreements to further foreign policy objectives.[35]

34. Robert E. DiClerico, *The American President* (Englewood Cliffs, N.J., 1983), 49. Even in the post-Vietnam era, when congressional criticism of executive agreements has been sharpest, Congress has mostly demanded merely that it be informed by the White House concerning any global commitments entered into by the United States.
35. Crabb and Holt, *Invitation to Struggle*, 13.

If executive agreements have had less visible (sometimes even secret) effect on the direction of foreign policy, presidential wars have been at the forefront of political and constitutional controversy. Only five of the approximately 125 incidents in which the United States has applied armed force were carried out with benefit of a formal declaration of war. Both of the two lengthy and costly post–World War II military engagements in which the United States has been involved were undeclared wars: "Truman's war" in Korea and "Johnson's (later Nixon's) war" in Vietnam. The personalization of these conflicts strongly suggests that in the eyes of many Americans these wars were the result of deliberate presidential choice rather than situations in which the president's hand was forced by an unambiguous act, such as the bombing of Pearl Harbor. These presidential wars have also been identified as "police actions" rather than wars of national survival; they have sometimes been called "policy wars," which are fought for principles like containment that are more subtle and debatable than the goals of wars fought "to make the world safe for democracy" or even one associated with a manifest destiny.

The Constitution refers to Congress's war-making role in four provisions of Article I, Section 8 (Clauses 11–14). In a long enumeration of national legislative powers are found those that empower Congress to "declare war," "raise and support Armies," "provide and maintain a Navy," and "make rules for the government and regulation of the land and naval forces."[36] Congress has also been able to influence defense policy through the budgetary process, especially in the appropriations subcommittees responsible for military spending, and it has also maintained an influence on foreign policy through the confirmation process. Prior to the 1970s, however, there was no effective congressional check on the exercise of the chief executive's war powers. As Edward Keynes has observed, "The Framers apparently believed that by separating the power of the purse (appropriations) from the power of the sword (military command), they could curb foreign military adventurism and domestic tyranny."[37]

36. Article I, Section 8 is a constitutional oddity in that Congress (which meets for two years) can "raise and support armies," but it cannot appropriate funds for the army for more than one year. No such limitation presumably exists on funding for the navy or air force. The Founding Fathers were very suspicious concerning the abuse of ground forces, but considerably less apprehensive about naval power.

37. Edward Keynes, *Undeclared War: Twilight Zone of Constitutional Power* (Univer-

From the first Barbary Coast Wars of 1801–1805, presidents have not been deterred from committing the nation to states of belligerency or other functional equivalents of war on their own initiative. And in the Prize cases the Supreme Court held that the president was not required to await a congressional declaration of war before responding to an external threat. Indeed, the Supreme Court has carefully avoided entering this political fray. When it has, the Court has affirmed a broad, even inherent, presidential authority in the conduct of foreign affairs. In the majority opinion of the Curtiss-Wright case, Justice George Sutherland suggested that presidential authority to initiate war was an extraconstitutional power necessary for a sovereign state. Sutherland's opinion also suggests that governmental powers exist along a continuum from internal to external. Keynes has described the situation: "At one end of the continuum, in domestic emergencies, congressional delegations of power are subject to judicial review and the application of judicial criteria based on the separation of powers. At the other end of the continuum, in international emergencies, the congressional and presidential exercise of power is subject to few constitutional limitations."[38]

In the post–World War II period, there has been one notable exception to the pattern of Supreme Court decisions that have sustained presidential war making and congressional ratification of these military actions. The Court's refusal to accept President Truman's seizure of the nation's steel mills during the Korean War to resolve a labor-management dispute is justly celebrated as a victory for separation of powers. It was also very limited in scope and really did not expressly deal with the president's war-making powers. A deeply divided Court refused to approve so sweeping a presidential presumption in domestic affairs with an existing statutory remedy at hand (the Taft-Hartley Act, which had been passed over Truman's veto) even if the president claimed his authority as wartime commander in chief. Justice Robert H. Jackson, in his concurring opinion, stated: "We should not use this occasion to circumscribe, much less to contract, the lawful role of the President as Commander in Chief. I should indulge the widest lati-

sity Park, 1982), 41. See also W. Taylor Reveley III, *War Powers of the President and Congress* (Charlottesville, 1981), 29–115.

38. *United States* v. *Curtiss-Wright Export Corp.*, 299 U.S. 304, 318 (1936); Keynes, *Undeclared War*, 85.

tude of interpretation to sustain his exclusive function to command the instruments of national force, at least when turned against the outside world for the security of our society. But when it is turned inward, not because of rebellion but because of lawful economic struggle between industry and labor, it should have no such indulgence."[39]

President Truman needed to be reminded that "when the President takes measures incompatible with the expressed or implicit will of Congress his power is at its lowest ebb." In addition, when the Court needed to resolve a dispute arising between a presidential claim to power and a congressional denial of such power, it must take into account "the equilibrium established by our constitutional system."[40] On the other hand, the federal courts sustained the military actions in Southeast Asia despite the growing executive-legislative conflict over claims that the president had overstepped his constitutional power by waging war without congressional authorization. Several test cases were brought during the Vietnam War, with the same result, which was to uphold the principle of the Curtiss-Wright case.[41]

The War Powers Act of 1973 represented a major effort on the part of Congress to restore the constitutional balance between itself and the executive branch in war making. In this light, the War Powers Act should be linked with the Church-Case Amendment to the Continuing Appropriations Resolution of 1974, which prohibited the use of federal funds for any "military or paramilitary operations . . . in . . . over," or "off the shore of" the whole of Vietnam, Laos, and Cambodia. By so using its power over the military purse, Congress sought to mandate an end to the decade-long American involvement in Indochina. In the words of W. Taylor Reveley, "Never before had Congress used its appropriations power to withdraw the United States from a major conflict."[42]

The War Powers Act was intended to be more general in scope than

39. *Youngstown Sheet and Tube Co.* v. *Sawyer*, 343 U.S. 579 (1952), 645–46.

40. *Ibid.*, 637–38; Keynes, *Undeclared War*, 87–94. See also Pat Holt, *The War Powers Resolution: the Role of Congress in U.S. Armed Intervention* (Washington, D.C., 1978). A recent commentary on the War Powers Resolution in the light of experience is Jacob K. Javits, "War Powers Reconsidered," *Foreign Affairs*, LXIV (Fall, 1985), 130–41.

41. Anthony A. D'Amato and Robert M. O'Neil, *The Judiciary and Vietnam* (New York, 1972).

42. Reveley, *War Powers*, 226. The Church-Case Amendment is named for its authors, Senator Frank Church (D-Ind.) and Senator Clifford Case (R-N.J.). Church was the chairman of the Foreign Relations Committee at that time.

the Church-Case Amendment and was significant in its attempt to provide a precise definition of the only circumstances in which it would be legally permissible for the president to commit the armed forces to hostilities in the absence of a declaration of war. Both pieces of legislation represent an admission—perhaps an overly belated one—that if the presidential wars of the past two generations have been of dubious constitutionality, they could not have been fought without congressional collaboration.[43]

The War Powers Act has several major provisions.[44]

1. Before introducing the armed forces into hostilities or into situations in which hostilities are imminent, the president shall consult with Congress in every possible instance.
2. Within forty-eight hours after the involvement of the armed forces in hostilities, the president must submit a report to Congress.
3. The president must withdraw the armed forces sixty days after his report (ninety days in certain circumstances) unless Congress declares war or allows a sixty-day extension of the hostilities.
4. Congress by a concurrent resolution[45] may order the withdrawal of armed forces engaged in hostilities outside of the United States if there is no declaration of war or specific statutory authorization.

The War Powers Act, like much corrective legislation, came out of specific historical circumstance. Congress was anxious to avoid being dragged into another Vietnam by presidential fiat. The example of such dictation that is most often cited is the use of the Gulf of Tonkin Resolution as the functional equivalent of a declaration of war, even as President Johnson denied that Congress was delegating its authority in approving his actions. His successor, Richard Nixon, asserted that his power as commander in chief gave him virtually unlimited discretion over troop deployment. According to Graham

43. DiClerico, *The American President*, 43.
44. Reveley, *War Powers*, 228–48; Robert Scigliano, "The War Powers Resolution and the War Powers," in Joseph M. Bessette and Jeffrey Tulis (eds.), *The Presidency in the Constitutional Order* (Baton Rouge, 1981), 115–53.
45. A concurrent resolution is a legislative instrument usually used to express congressional opinion; it requires passage by a majority in both houses and does not require the president's signature. It would seem that the final provision listed amounts to a form of legislative veto. Whether any such actions are legal in the light of the 1983 Supreme Court ruling in *Chadha v. Immigration and Naturalization Service*, 103 S. Ct. 2764 (1983), remains to be seen. Yet to insist that Congress must get a two-thirds vote to override a presidential veto of its order to terminate unauthorized hostilities would allow a president to conduct a war with minority backing. See Louis Fisher, *The Politics of Shared Powers* (Washington, D.C., 1981), 104–105.

Allison, "Nixon claimed that the 'legal justification for the invasion of Cambodia,' for example, 'is the right of the President of the United States under the Constitution to protect the lives of American men. . . . As Commander-in-Chief, I had no choice but to act to defend these men.'"[46] The War Powers Act, incidentally, was passed over President Nixon's veto. He felt that it infringed upon his constitutional powers as commander in chief.

In the face of such assertions of unilateral presidential authority to commit the nation to a decade-long war, there is little wonder that Congress would want to reaffirm its own prerogatives in war making. However, the creation of a general piece of legislation to remedy past wrongs and to prevent future ones is always a difficult task. To legislate in the unsettled territory between the war-powers claims of the two branches is particularly difficult. Not surprisingly, the War Powers Act has not been a panacea for restoring interbranch equilibrium, if such a state ever really existed.

For example, the act's language is awkward and vague on two points. Who is to determine when it is "possible" for the president to consult with Congress? What does it mean "to consult" (to seek advice beforehand or to advise after the fact)? A second problem is inherent in the nature of the conflict itself. Who is to provide the information that Congress could use for an objective determination of the situation in which hostilities have occurred? Moreover, is it reasonable to expect Congress to contradict a president acting as commander in chief with American soldiers under fire or to cut off funds for the armed forces engaged in such "illegal" hostilities, as has been sometimes suggested? These questions suggest a third reason for ambivalence about the War Powers Resolution. The onus is almost entirely on Congress to bring the president to heel in a situation in which the political repercussions could be enormous. In the first decade after its passage, two incidents involving presidential use of the armed forces abroad raised issues of the War Powers Resolution: the rescue of the crew of the *Mayaguez* in May, 1975, and the attempted rescue of the American hostages in Iran in April, 1980. Experience in these circumstances points up a major dilemma for Congress. If a president takes swift, limited military action and it succeeds, as in the *Mayaguez* inci-

46. Graham Allison, "Making War: The President and Congress," in Cronin and Tugwell (eds.), *The Presidency Reappraised*, 241, 230.

dent, the public approval that follows will likely discourage any vigorous objection by Congress, regardless of any doubts it may have about the legality of such action. And, even if such action fails, as in the effort to rescue the hostages, and the public supports the attempt nevertheless, Congress is not likely to call the president to account.[47] The only realistic hope for successful imposition of Congress' statutory powers is in a situation (hardly to be desired) in which the presidential policy fails and also lacks popular support.

During the first eight years in which the War Powers Act was in effect, there were eight occasions on which presidents committed troops abroad. In only three of these incidents were reports submitted to Congress by the president. To the extent that the required congressional consultation took place, it involved the *Mayaguez* and Iranian situations, but the Senate majority leader, Mike Mansfield (D-Mont.) summed up the attitude of many of his colleagues: "I was notified after the fact about what the administration had already decided to do."[48] Given this pattern of congressional reluctance to take issue with the president over compliance with these statutory provisions, it looked as if the War Powers Act was to be consigned to the constitutional attic. However, in 1983 the deployment of American marines in Beirut as part of a Lebanese peace-keeping operation led to growing fears that "another Vietnam" could be in the making. Ronald Reagan, like his predecessors, had not given Congress the notice required by law. This led to the first invocation of the War Powers Act as a congressional attempt to constrain the war-making powers of the presidency. A compromise was worked out between Capitol Hill and the White House, whereby Congress, declaring the act to be in effect, authorized the continued presence of marines in Lebanon for an additional eighteen months, and the president signed the agreement without conceding any limitation on his constitutional authority as commander in chief.[49] Nevertheless, President Reagan became the first president to recognize the validity of the war powers legislation, and the compromise established an "important precedent" and kept the War Powers Act from becoming a "dead letter."[50]

47. DiClerico, *The American President*, 46.
48. Quoted in *ibid.*, 45.
49. For the text of the resolution applying the War Powers Act to Lebanon, see New York *Times*, September 21, 1983.
50. New York *Times*, September 29, 1983.

Yet, before much jubilation breaks out among the proponents of a more constrained presidency, they should realize that the significance of the congressional assertion is not great. There was nothing in the Lebanon compromise over the War Powers Act to negate the precedent that it originally codified—that presidents may commit the armed forces to hostilities without a declaration of war by Congress. While long a debatable point, it had never been conceded by Congress until 1973. One might note, however, that there is always going to be a fundamental stumbling block in efforts by Congress to control presidential use of armed force abroad. This is Congress' extreme reluctance to accept the consequences of cutting off funds for American soldiers engaged in hostile action, such as the marines were in Lebanon. Moreoever, as presidents have repeatedly emphasized, if Congress denies funds for supporting military operations in a country, such as El Salvador, then it becomes responsible for the success or failure of United States policy in the region, which clearly gives most legislators pause. Many congressmen remember the 1930s and do not want to be blamed for another Pearl Harbor.

Nor can critics of presidential power cite the help of the Supreme Court in curbing executive branch activism. *U.S.* v. *Nixon* was hailed in 1974 as a great blow against "presidential tyranny" and for the restoration of the "delicate constitutional balance on which rests separation of powers." Although the decision rebuffed President Nixon's claim to an unqualified presidential immunity from judicial process, it also expanded certain presidential prerogatives. The Court recognized the long-contested presidential claim to an executive privilege in much of the conduct of foreign affairs, that is, the right of the president and his immediate advisers to refuse to disclose certain information in situations in which considerations of "national security" are at stake. Some constitutional scholars have argued that a future chief executive may be able to avoid turning over his subpoenaed tapes on the grounds that such a disclosure would endanger the national security.[51] This is certainly too extreme. As the decision now stands, the president may argue for this executive privilege against a judicial inquiry, and the courts would determine any threat to national security that would be involved through an *in camera* examination of the material.

51. See *U.S.* v. *Nixon*, 418 U.S. 683 (1974); Keynes, *Undeclared War*, 80.

For all of Congress' reliance upon statutory redress, the rise of presidential preeminence in foreign policy making is not easily remedied by formal means. The president's power has grown by means of broad interpretations of constitutional powers and the aggrandizement of ancillary powers. Political tradition and public expectations have served to legitimize the constitutional and institutional evolution that the presidency has undergone. Yet, it needs to be stressed that, however buttressed, the presidency is a peculiarly personal office. In Richard Neustadt's classic formulation, presidential power is dependent on the president's powers of persuasion; his leadership abilities and personal reputation are his greatest resources. The modern presidency has been one in which personal presidential diplomacy has been of central importance (see Chapter 3).[52] One speaks of the Carter and Nixon foreign policies, not those of Brzezinski or Kissinger, let alone of any congressional leader, however prominent. (It is the "Truman Doctrine," not the Vandenberg Doctrine.) An important reason for the poor public evaluation of the Carter presidency was a widespread belief that the president had failed to act decisively in diplomatic affairs and had not "taken charge" of the foreign policy making process. The growth of presidential power can certainly be attributed to instincts for personal aggrandizement or to "imperial" tendencies by occupants of the Oval Office. But it needs to be equally appreciated that presidents have become powerful because the public has expected them to act in such a fashion. Presidential predominance in foreign affairs may disturb constitutional scholars and members of Congress, but it has been a development that has largely reflected the wishes and interests of the American people.[53]

This preemption by presidents of other actors in the policy making process, particularly of Congress but also of the departments in the executive branch, has been termed "prerogative government" by Richard M. Pious: "Several features distinguish such governance: presidential decisions are made without Congressional collaboration, often in secrecy, and announced as *fait accompli;* decisions are implemented by subordinate executive officials, and . . . events are

---

52. Richard E. Neustadt, *Presidential Power* (New York, 1980), especially 26–43; Kallenbach, *The American Chief Executive*, 497–501.

53. Bernard C. Cohen, *The Public's Impact on Foreign Policy* (Boston, 1973); Ralph B. Levering, *The Public and American Foreign Policy, 1918–1978* (New York, 1978).

managed by the White House rather than by the departments. The president justifies his decision on constitutional grounds, on powers enumerated, or on those claimed or created by his application of rules of constitutional construction. When his expansive interpretation is challenged, he appeals to the public for support by defining his actions in terms of 'national security' or 'the national interest.'"[54]

It is in foreign policy making that this prerogative governance is the most pronounced, if incompletely realized. There are in effect two presidencies—one for domestic affairs and the other for international responsibilities.[55] Congress and the public grant a wider latitude to presidential diplomacy than would be the case in domestic policies. Presidents are expected to take command of the conduct of foreign affairs and to put their stamp on international politics. Cabinet secretaries may be simply good administrators, and legislative leaders may be skilled solely as bargainers. But presidents should have both these qualities and should be able to provide national and international leadership as well.

Presidential Leadership

The American political system was distinguished at its beginning by having the very embodiment of heroic leadership in its first president. According to Constitutional Convention delegate Pierce Butler of South Carolina, George Washington's personality had a great influence in determining the extent of the executive powers to be vested in the presidency. "I do not believe they would have been so great had not many members cast their eyes toward George Washington as President; and shaped their Ideas of the Powers to be given the President, by their opinion of his virtue."[56] James MacGregor Burns's description of heroic presidential leadership, while general in application, could have been written about Washington, except for the references to modern phenomena: "The President must be more than

54. Pious, *American Presidency*, 47.
55. The phrase, but not the argument, is from Aaron Wildavsky, "The Two Presidencies," in Aaron Wildavsky (ed.), *Perspectives on the Presidency* (Boston, 1975), 448–61. See also C. Herman Pritchett, "The Presidency at Home Versus the Presidency Abroad," in Cronin and Tugwell (eds.), *Presidency Reappraised*, 19–22.
56. Quoted in Louis W. Koenig, *The Chief Executive* (New York, 1964), 27.

administrative chief or party leader. He must exert great leadership in behalf of the whole nation. . . . Heroic Presidents have some of the qualities of the hero in modern setting: they cut an impressive figure on the hustings and before the television camera; they have style; they speak movingly and even passionately; they seem to establish a direct connection with the mass public. And they are invested by the press and the public with even magical qualities."[57] Few if any presidents since Washington could have laid claim to his epitaph: "First in war, first in peace, first in the hearts of his countrymen." Many presidents have sought to surpass Washington as a leader, but only Lincoln may have realized even an equal stature.

American historians have periodically been asked to rate presidents as leaders. Table 2 presents the results of three such surveys. Besides the high degree of correspondence among the rankings over a thirty-year period, there are other striking similarities about the "great" and "near great". There is no question that the relationship between presidential greatness and the management of international crises is a close one. All of the highest-ranking presidents presided over some great epoch of American foreign policy: Washington (the establishment of the United States in the concert of nations), Lincoln (the Civil War), Franklin Roosevelt (World War II), Woodrow Wilson (World War I), Thomas Jefferson (Barbary War, the Louisiana Purchase), and Theodore Roosevelt (America's emergence as a world power). The remaining candidates for the presidential pantheon were also associated with major foreign involvements: Harry Truman (the Korean War), John Adams (the naval war with France), and James K. Polk (the Mexican War). Only Andrew Jackson and Grover Cleveland may be associated with primarily domestic-policy accomplishments (and Old Hickory was the great hero of the Battle of New Orleans at the end of the War of 1812).

Tocqueville said it was a truism that a nation's chief executive power finds the greatest occasion to exert its strength and skills in the area of foreign relations. Clinton Rossiter explained the inevitability of presidential control of foreign policy axiomatically: "We may take it as an axiom of political science that the more deeply a nation becomes involved in the affairs of another nation, the more powerful be-

57. James MacGregor Burns, *Presidental Government* (Boston, 1965), 113; Burns, *Leadership* (New York, 1978), esp. 385–97.

Table 2 Historians' Rankings of Presidents on the Basis of Leadership

Schlesinger Poll, 1948	Schlesinger Poll, 1962	U.S. Historical Society Poll, 1977
Great	*Great*	*Ten Greatest—Votes*
Lincoln	Lincoln	Lincoln 85
Washington	Washington	Washington 84
F. Roosevelt	F. Roosevelt	F. Roosevelt 81
Wilson	Wilson	Jefferson 79
Jefferson	Jefferson	T. Roosevelt 79
Jackson		Wilson 74
		Jackson 74
Near Great	*Near Great*	Truman 64
T. Roosevelt	Jackson	Polk 38
Cleveland	T. Roosevelt	J. Adams 35
J. Adams	Truman	L. Johnson 24
Polk	J. Adams	Cleveland 21
	Cleveland	

Sources: Robert DiClerico, *The American President* (Englewood Cliffs, N.J., 1979), 332. The 1948 poll by Arthur Schlesinger, Sr., is discussed in "The U.S. Presidents," *Life*, November 1, 1948, p. 65; the 1962 poll, also by Schlesinger, is discussed in "Our Presidents: A Rating by 75 Historians," *New York Times Magazine*, July 29, 1962, p. 12; results of the U.S. Historical Society's poll of 1977 were obtained directly from the society.

comes its executive branch. Another axiom of political science would seem to be this: great emergencies in the life of a constitutional state bring an increase in executive power and prestige, always at least temporarily, more often than not permanently." It is worth noting that Rossiter posited these axioms in 1962; unquestionably, developments in foreign affairs and in the institution of the presidency during the past twenty years have provided extensive confirmation of these theories. The need for crisis management in international affairs has brought about a shift in the locus of decision making from the State Department to the presidential office. Located in the West Wing of the White House is the Situation Room, which processes and analyzes information from throughout the world as the command center for presidential decision making. Aided by the assistant for national security affairs and his staff, the president has created a "little State Department" in his basement. A major factor in the fragmentation of the foreign policy making process is not simply departmental competition but the rise of a White House foreign ministry, especially

with the Kennedy administration and since. By the Nixon administration, Henry Kissinger had accumulated such dominance over
foreign affairs that a member of the Senate Foreign Relations Committee exclaimed that the national security assistant had become secretary of state "in everything but name."[58]

The accumulation of these presidential powers and the longest
presidential war in American history, linked with the abuses of power
and constitutional irregularities associated with the Watergate scandal, brought about a reaction from other institutional actors, reactions such as the War Powers Act and the move to impeach President
Nixon, and from the public at large. Without presuming to judge the
appropriate solution to such complex political debates, one must distinguish between an "imperial" presidency on one hand and a "strong"
presidency on the other. As much as the American public is suspicious
of a presidency that is unrestrained, they are also fearful of one that is
impotent. Similarly, the other branches of government have recognized that, particularly in foreign affairs, the exigencies of America's
position in world affairs dictate a vital presidency. The Supreme
Court, for example, limited its decision in the Nixon case to the issue
of the integrity of a criminal proceeding, and it was with care that
Congress invoked the War Powers Act after a hiatus of over a decade.
A strong president may not be immune from being called a dictator,
as Franklin Roosevelt and Abraham Lincoln were sometimes labeled,
but he will generally enjoy respect as a dynamic and forceful chief
executive, capable of an imaginative conception of the nation's international concerns and the effective projection of these goals at home
and abroad.

58. Alexis de Tocqueville, *Democracy in America*, (New York, 1948), 137–38; Rossiter, *American Presidency*, 81–82; Senator Stewart Symington (D-Mo.), quoted in
Koenig, *American Presidency*, 225.

2

Dissonance in the Foreign Policy Process

After he left office in 1947, former Secretary of State James F. Byrnes wrote, "When the administration itself is divided on its own foreign policy, it cannot hope to convince the world that the American people have a foreign policy." Over a generation later, informed students of American diplomacy were deeply concerned about the incoherence and the disarray that marked the foreign policy process in the United States. Following the dismissal of Alexander Haig as secretary of state and his replacement by George Shultz in 1982, one of the nation's most experienced observers referred to a "host of problems" besetting Shultz in his new assignment. For some eighteen months, "policy confusions" had characterized the diplomacy of the Reagan administration. Lamenting that Secretary Shultz had "inherited a wreckage" in the decision-making process, this observer urged him to give highest priority to restoring coherence and unity to the management of foreign relations by the United States.[1]

A few months earlier, another analysis of the problem employed terms like *ineffectual, confused, chaos,* and *disarray* to describe the conduct of foreign relations by the United States. It depicted a confused and struggling policy-making apparatus, torn by internecine rivalries. There was a "proliferation of agencies" within the executive branch intensely competing "for a piece of the foreign-policy action," and recent years had witnessed "a steady disintegration of the na-

1. James F. Byrnes, *Speaking Frankly* (New York, 1947), 241; James Reston, in New York *Times*, July 21, 1982.

tion's diplomatic corps." The situation held a potential "for disaster for the U.S. in the 1980s." One experienced American ambassador was convinced that the "contradictory voices on international affairs" posed a greater danger to global peace and security than a direct Soviet-American military confrontation.[2]

Extreme and unqualified as such assessments might be, they underscore the fact that throughout the post–World War II era the effectiveness of American diplomacy has been jeopardized, and in many instances unquestionably impaired, by ongoing dissonances, confusions, cross-purposes, and contradictions arising out of uncoordinated executive activities. Disunity in the American foreign policy process can be traced to two broad sources. The first is conflict between the president and Congress over foreign policy issues—or the absence of bipartisanship in foreign relations. This problem has manifold origins and is beyond the purview of our study.[3] Our analysis focuses upon the second source of such policy discord: the challenge presented to the State Department's traditionally paramount position in the field of external policy by a growing number of executive departments and agencies—a phenomenon that has become pervasive and progressively acute since World War II. To date, techniques for achieving a unified and coordinated approach to foreign relations within the executive branch have achieved only limited success.

The Creation of Foreign Policy Machinery

On July 27, 1789, President George Washington signed an act of Congress creating a Department of Foreign Affairs. A few weeks later, its name was changed to the Department of State, with Thomas Jefferson serving as its first head. The secretary of state and his subordinates were to perform such duties as the president might assign them arising out of America's relations with other nations. For many years

2. *U.S. News and World Report*, September 29, 1980, pp. 35–38.
3. See Cecil V. Crabb, Jr., and Pat Holt, *Invitation to Struggle: Congress, the President and Foreign Policy* (2nd ed.; Washington, D.C., 1984); John Spanier and Joseph Nogee (eds.), *Congress, the Presidency, and American Foreign Policy* (New York, Pergamon Press, 1981); Thomas F. Franck and Edward Weisband, *Foreign Policy by Congress* (New York, 1979).

the State Department also had a wide assortment of other duties, such as receiving the resolutions and bills of Congress, serving as keeper of the Great Seal of the United States, and acting as the custodian of records and papers.

From the beginning (and reflecting certain unfortunate experiences arising when the Continental Congress had endeavored to administer foreign affairs during and after the Revolutionary War), it was understood that the secretary of state was responsible to the president for the performance of his duties. While the Constitution granted Congress (and sometimes the Senate alone) important powers in the foreign policy field, the Founding Fathers differentiated the State Department from other executive agencies. In contrast to other departments and agencies, the State Department existed to carry out the chief executive's directives: the president would determine both the policies the State Department was charged with administering and how they were to be carried out.[4]

The Department of State was unique in two other respects. It was the first executive department established under the Constitution, making it the oldest department and elevating its head to the position of the senior officer in the president's cabinet. The State Department is also exempted from the requirement (imposed by Congress upon other departments and executive agencies) that it furnish information about its activities or substantive policy concerns to the House or Senate or both. The State Department (and today, other executive agencies involved in the foreign policy process) may refuse such legislative requests when, in the judgment of the president, release of such information would be inimical to the nation's security and diplomatic interests. Despite possible abuse of the doctrine of executive privilege from time to time, such as during the Watergate crisis of 1972–1973, the concept remains an accepted American constitutional principle.[5]

From modest beginnings—in its first year, the State Department's budget provided for the salaries of the secretary of state, an under

4. See J. Rives Childs, *American Foreign Service* (New York, 1948), 2–4.
5. The doctrine of executive privilege was first asserted by President George Washington in refusing demands of the House of Representatives to inspect papers related to the Jay Treaty (1794). Customarily, Congress requests information of the State Department only "if not incompatible with the public interest." See Louis Henkin, *Foreign Affairs and the Constitution* (Mineola, N.Y., 1972), 112.

secretary, two clerks, a French interpreter (small allowances were provided for other interpreters when needed), a doorkeeper, and a messenger—the department gradually grew to an establishment numbering several thousand officers, staff, and other employees on the eve of World War II. By 1791, a regularly organized foreign service had emerged. American ministers served in London, Paris, Madrid, and other capitals; Secretary of State Jefferson appointed sixteen consular officers to serve abroad, who were normally self-supporting, since they were remunerated from the fees they charged for services such as processing visa applications. Small as it was, the American diplomatic corps nonetheless compared favorably with those of the European powers of the day. A small diplomatic establishment was consonant with the American society's aversion to diplomacy, its apprehension about diplomatic entanglements, and its preoccupation with domestic affairs—as signified by its devotion to an isolationist foreign policy until World War II.[6]

Evolution of the Diplomatic Establishment

Until the mid-twentieth century, the American diplomatic establishment grew slowly, in what one study has called a "series of recognizable waves." After 1800 the independence of the Latin American nations—along with the expansion of official contacts with a widening circle of European states—brought a threefold growth in the number of nations with which the United States maintained official relations. The mid-1800s witnessed another wave of American diplomatic concern, this time with Asia. Again at the turn of the century the United States increased its diplomatic representation abroad, following the Spanish-American War. By World War I, Washington maintained official relations with forty-nine countries. After the war, owing in large measure to the impact of President Woodrow Wilson's doctrine of self-determination, America established relations with the newly independent nations of East Central Europe, South Africa,

6. Childs, *American Foreign Service*, 2–4; Felix Gilbert, *To the Farewell Address: Ideas of Early American Foreign Policy* (Princeton, 1961), 82–85; Graham H. Stuart, *The Department of State: A History of Its Organization, Procedure, and Personnel* (New York, 1949), 14–18.

Canada, and several other states. When the Japanese attacked Pearl Harbor late in 1941, the United States was operating diplomatic missions in some sixty countries, and it had only recently terminated relations with a few others, like the Baltic states, which were now in the Soviet orbit.[7]

Changes, not always for the better, were also being made in the diplomatic machinery and personnel system. During the nineteenth and early twentieth centuries, the attention of Americans was devoted for the most part to internal affairs. Indifference—if not outright antipathy—described the attitudes of most Americans toward diplomacy, and this fact posed a serious impediment to the emergence of a genuinely professional diplomatic corps. More often than not, appointments to diplomatic and consular positions were made according to the dictates of the "spoils system" or because of personal and family connections. In the main, efforts to introduce and enforce merit criteria for appointment and promotion encountered only limited success until after World War I, and even these were normally made by executive order rather than by the action of an apathetic Congress. An exception was the leadership provided by President Theodore Roosevelt and his secretary of state, Elihu Root, who persuaded Congress to undertake a comprehensive reorganization of the consular service and to require that appointments to it be on the basis of merit. Yet it was not until 1915 that Congress provided for the merit system in appointments to both the consular and diplomatic corps. Still another decade was required, however, before it could be said that the United States had attained, or even had laid the foundations for, a professional diplomatic establishment.[8]

From the Rogers Act to World War II

The outstanding landmark in the emergence of the diplomatic establishment before World War II was the Rogers Act of May 24,

---

7. Elmer Plischke, *United States Diplomats and Their Missions: A Profile of American Diplomatic Emissaries Since 1778* (Washington, D.C., 1975), 12–14.
8. W. Wendell Blancke, *The Foreign Service of the United States* (New York, 1969), 11; Childs, *American Foreign Service,* 9.

1924. Named for Representative John J. Rogers (R-Mass.), who was keenly interested in improving the quality of the American diplomatic service, this enactment emerged as the result of joint executive-legislative efforts to achieve the goal. Some two years of congressional deliberations were required before it became law. The Rogers Act consolidated the diplomatic and consular corps into a new Foreign Service of the United States; provided that appointments to the Foreign Service would be made on the basis of competitive examination and promotions made as a result of meritorious performance; and established a new retirement system and better salary incentives to attract well-qualified candidates to diplomatic careers. Among its other goals, the Rogers Act endeavored to "democratize" the service by opening its ranks to qualified applicants from all regions and spheres of American life.[9]

More limited reforms of the diplomatic establishment were carried out in 1931 and 1939. Some changes during the 1930s, however, proved to be primary causes of the kind of intraexecutive conflict over foreign policy issues that became recurrent after World War II. In 1927, for example, Congress permitted the Commerce Department to establish its own overseas service, largely as a means for encouraging American exports. Three years later, the Agriculture Department took the same step, and other governmental agencies quickly followed the precedent. One study found that even before World War II a "multiplicity" of governmental agencies and officials claimed to speak for the United States abroad. Although President Franklin Roosevelt attempted a "reconsolidation" of these separate overseas services, the problem was not altogether solved, in part because FDR himself encouraged and exploited conflicting activities and jurisdictions by the growing number of executive agencies active in foreign affairs. By World War II, the State Department—with a total of 971 employees and a total budget of some three million dollars—was in many respects ill prepared for the diplomatic consequences of the war. And as events proved, it was not disposed to assume new responsibilities growing out of that global conflict.[10]

9. 43 Statutes-at-Large 140; Warren F. Ilchman, *Professional Diplomacy in the United States: 1779–1939* (Chicago, 1961), 184–185; Blancke, *The Foreign Service of the United States*, 18.

10. Blancke, *The Foreign Service of the United States*, 21.

Postwar Challenges and New Obligations

In a number of key respects the end of World War II was a watershed in the saga of American diplomacy. The war witnessed the formal abandonment of America's historic policy of isolationism and the emergence of the United States as a superpower. As a result, the postwar era has been characterized by the steady expansion in the responsibilities and size of the State Department, and as in other walks of American life, the principle of specialization has increasingly been reflected in its organizational structure.

By the early 1980s the State Department comprised a highly diverse and far-flung bureaucracy. The United States operated some 133 embassies and 101 consular posts in approximately 150 foreign countries. Some 3,700 Foreign Service officers (FSOs), along with 900 Foreign Service information officers[11] and 3,700 Foreign Service specialists (*e.g.*, secretaries, personnel managers, and nurses), served the United States at home and abroad. In addition, several thousand "foreign nationals" were employed in various capacities by American embassies. For fiscal year 1983, the State Department's total budget was almost $2.5 billion.

Yet it was indicative of the American people's traditional lack of interest in foreign affairs and the low priority they accorded diplomacy that the State Department's budget ranked close to the bottom among all federal agencies. In the same period, for example, the Department of Health and Human Services had a budget of $274 billion, the Defense Department would expend $216 billion, and even the budget allocations of the National Aeronautics and Space Administration ($6.6 billion) and the Environmental Protection Agency ($4.6 billion) substantially exceeded what Americans spent upon the operations of the State Department.

Traditionally, the bureaucratic province of the State Department has been political relations between the United States and other nations. Its historic primacy in the foreign policy process signified the dominance of this aspect of diplomacy over other dimensions of for-

11. Foreign Service Information Officers were officials engaged in informational and propaganda activities for the United States government. The agency in charge of this aspect of foreign policy is the United States Information Agency (USIA).

eign relations. In response to postwar events and the evolving nature of the international system, however, other aspects of international relations have come increasingly to the fore, and the addition of new administrative units to the department has reflected this reality. Within the department, there has been a steady increase in the number and size of the "functional bureaus" concerned with external problems cutting across national frontiers. Foremost among these perhaps—and a dimension of foreign affairs that now impinges upon nearly all other aspects of America's relations with other countries—is international economic problems. This is the specific responsibility of the Bureau of Economic Affairs, headed by an under secretary of state (although most other administrative units within the department also have become increasingly involved with economic issues). Another example of this tendency is the Bureau for Security Assistance (*i.e.*, military aid), Science and Technology. Still other functional bureaus specialize in international human-rights problems, in the State Department's relations with Congress, in public affairs (*i.e.*, public relations), in oceanic and environmental questions, and—one of the department's newest concerns—the challenge posed by the growth of international terrorism.

Change and adaptation have also occurred in the traditional heart of the State Department—its geographical bureaus. Reflecting the escalation in America's ties with some one hundred nations that have gained their independence since World War II, the pattern of geographical organization recognizes five major regions plus a variety of international organizations to which the United States belongs. The five regions are Europe, Africa, East Asia and the Pacific, the Western Hemisphere, and the Near East and South Asia. In addition, a Bureau of International Organization Affairs supervises America's role in the United Nations and some fifty other international organizations, and State Department participation in about eight hundred international conferences annually.

According to immemorial State Department custom, the "country desks" within these regional bureaus have served as the hub of America's relations with other countries. Relations between the United States and Nigeria, for example, are supervised and coordinated by the Nigerian desk within the Bureau of African Affairs; the assistant secretary of state for African affairs is responsible to the deputy secretary of state and through him to the secretary of state. The country desk (and its size naturally varies with the size and importance of the particular country) is normally staffed by Foreign Service officers who have served in the country or otherwise have acquired expert knowledge about it. The American ambassador who directs the embassy in Lagos, Nigeria, communicates with the State Department through the Nigerian desk, and the latter in turn relays communications and directives from the department to the ambassador and his staff. Because of their expertise and continuing responsibilities, officials from the country desk are frequently called upon to submit policy recommendations and evaluations to their administrative superiors in the State Department and perhaps to the White House. Incumbent presidents may—and do—utilize their advisers in any manner they deem appropriate. Some rely heavily upon the advice of State Department experts, whereas others do so infrequently or in some instances, not at all.

Postwar Reorganization and Reform

Writing in the mid-1960s, an experienced American diplomat observed that the nation's foreign relations "would prosper" if that period "could become known as the decade in which the American Foreign Service was *not* reorganized." Another former American diplomat has referred to an idea in the national ethos that has shown "remarkable survival value": the notion that American foreign policy could be dramatically improved by "restructuring our foreign policy machinery." This has involved periodic "reshuffling and renaming the little boxes on the State Department organization chart." Others have maintained that more effective coordination of foreign policy might be achieved by "beefing up" the State Department.[12]

Since World War II, the impulse for the reorganization of the diplomatic establishment has had multiple origins. One source has been the conviction among informed students of American foreign rela-

12. Ellis Briggs, *Farewell to Foggy Bottom: The Recollections of a Career Diplomat* (New York, 1964), 175; George W. Ball, *Diplomacy for a Crowded World: An American Foreign Policy* (Boston, 1976), 194; Lincoln P. Bloomfield, *The Foreign Policy Process: A Modern Primer* (Englewood Cliffs, N.J., 1982), 30.

tions that fundamental changes were needed in the State Department and in its relations with other executive agencies. (Many were in fact overdue.) Congressional dissatisfaction with the performance and procedures of the State Department has been another impulse providing momentum to the movement. Moreover, successive presidents have expressed a lack of confidence in the department—sometimes openly, at other times by largely bypassing it in arriving at key foreign policy decisions. Behind these forces, there has existed a residual public and congressional disappointment with the state of the world and an implicit belief that, with "improved" and more efficient foreign policy machinery, America's diplomatic fortunes ought to be significantly enhanced.

The first major reorganization effort occurred in the late 1940s, as a result of the Hoover commission's comprehensive study of the entire executive branch of the government. Under the chairmanship of former President Herbert Hoover, this distinguished study group produced a long list of sweeping recommendations for governmental reform, including far-reaching changes within the diplomatic establishment. Even at this early date, the Hoover commission recognized a cardinal fact about American foreign relations in the postwar era: that the traditional line between "foreign" and "domestic" affairs was becoming progressively eroded.

The commission also took note of a long-standing complaint about American behavior in foreign affairs. Customarily, in former Secretary of State Dean Acheson's words, the United States intervened "in world affairs with sporadic and violent bursts of energy and with decisive and definitive effect," as illustrated by the participation of the United States in both world wars in the twentieth century. America's historic propensity had been "to appear on the scene in the nick of time like a knight errant, rescue the lady, and ride away!" After World War II, however, the United States had to assume *continuing* responsibilities for international developments. And if it were to do so successfully, it was required to *anticipate* emerging problems and tendencies in the international environment and to plan its response to them.

The Truman administration established a Policy Planning Staff within the State Department; this new office (headed in time by an assistant secretary of state) was under the direction of one of America's ablest diplomatic officials, George F. Kennan. But within some two years he had resigned from the government. Kennan's experience was a parable about the difficulty of successful diplomatic planning by the United States government. In the years ahead criticisms continued to be expressed that American foreign policy was made on an *ad hoc* basis, with little attention devoted to emerging global tendencies and America's response to them. Later presidents and secretaries of state endeavored to strengthen the planning function within the State Department. But in Lincoln P. Bloomfield's words, their efforts in time were "subordinated to the chronic and perverse pressures of short-run crisis management." This tendency was highlighted, for example, by the American government's lack of preparedness in the late 1970s for the Iranian Revolution and the subsequent seizure of American hostages by the Iranian militants. No responsible American official really anticipated these climactic developments; nor was the Carter administration equipped with a ready response to them.[13]

Another significant reform of the State Department was undertaken in the mid-1950s, as a result of the report of the Public Committee on Personnel (the Wriston committee) in 1954. The process of "Wristonization," according to which the ranks of the Foreign Service were now opened to civil servants and other officials (such as those engaged in informational, propaganda, and educational activities), was traumatic for the State Department. According to one interpretation, the Wriston committee's efforts to make the Foreign Service less "elitist" and more accessible to well-qualified public servants created morale problems that impaired the State Department's performance and primacy in the foreign policy process for many years thereafter. Other changes produced by the committee were more frequent rotation of Foreign Service officers between foreign posts and Washington, intensified recruitment efforts for the service, and more frequent in-service training and language instruction for America's diplomats.[14]

13. Louis J. Halle, *Civilization and Foreign Policy: An Inquiry for Americans* (New York, 1955), xi–xxii; Lincoln P. Bloomfield, *The Foreign Policy Process: A Modern Primer* (Englewood Cliffs, N.J., 1982), 165–93; Jimmy Carter, *Keeping Faith: Memoirs of a President* (New York, 1982), 431–572; Hamilton Jordan, *Crisis: The Last Year of the Carter Presidency* (New York, 1982).
14. The Wriston committee was named for its chairman, Dr. Henry M. Wriston of Brown University. See Henry M. Wriston, *Diplomacy in a Democracy* (New York, 1956).

Again in the early 1960s, the "Herter committee" proposed a new set of changes for the diplomatic establishment.[15] The committee underscored the idea that in the contemporary world, the president continued to rely heavily upon the State Department in the formulation and administration of American foreign policy. Yet, in the committee's view the department had not adequately responded to the challenge of postwar events, and Herter and his colleagues proposed a series of changes in the department's structure and personnel policies designed to achieve that goal.

In 1970 the State Department initiated its own study of the diplomatic machinery and personnel system. In a document entitled "Diplomacy for the '70's," the department identified a number of organizational and personnel improvements needed to make its performance responsive to changing conditions abroad. Under the direction of Deputy Under Secretary of State William B. Macomber, the department placed a new emphasis upon better management principles in its operations, and it sought to achieve a more equal balance between the resources available to the State Department and its responsibilities in the foreign policy field. Among other specific reforms promulgated, an effort was made to clarify the diplomatic chain of command and to strengthen the position of the secretary of state and his principal advisers (sometimes referred to as the "Seventh Floor" of the department) in the foreign policy process. These reforms unquestionably reflected a growing realization within the State Department, no less than outside it, that its traditionally premier position in the sphere of external policy was being seriously challenged.[16]

In the same period Congress directed that another study of the American foreign policy process be undertaken. Chaired by one of the nation's most experienced diplomats, Robert D. Murphy, the "Murphy commission" devoted some three years to its task. In the process, it produced a comprehensive multivolume report covering nearly every aspect of the formulation and administration of foreign policy in the United States. A prominent theme of the commission's findings

15. The Herter committee was named for its chairman, former Secretary of State Christian Herter. See Committee on Foreign Affairs Personnel, *Report on Personnel for the New Diplomacy* (Washington, D.C., 1962).

16. John H. Esterline and Robert B. Black, *Inside Foreign Policy: The Department of State Political System and Its Subsystems* (Palo Alto, 1975), 216–35.

was the widespread and continuing intrusion into the foreign policy process by a steadily expanding circle of governmental agencies. A related theme was the inadequacy of existing methods for imparting coordination and cohesion to executive branch activities in the foreign policy field. Despite the Murphy commission's broad mandate, it could not be said that its report (submitted to the president and Congress on June 30, 1975) fundamentally altered the position of the State Department within the executive branch. Nor did it significantly remove or alleviate many of the problems, such as the growing diffusion of responsibilities for foreign policy decisions among a proliferating number of executive agencies, that largely accounted for the decline of the influence and prestige of the State Department within the executive bureaucracy.[17]

On the basis of this survey of efforts made throughout the postwar period to improve the diplomatic machinery and personnel system in the United States, several conclusions seem warranted. First, since World War II the American approach to foreign relations have been markedly reform-minded, and no reason exists for believing that this propensity is likely to disappear in the future. For Americans, "reform" has always been an emotive and positive idea eliciting popular support. The reform impulse in American foreign policy suggests a pervasive belief that the condition of global affairs both can be and should be improved.

Second, this reformist attitude is essentially nonpartisan. It has been manifested and given tangible expression under Democratic and Republican administrations alike. Put differently, presidents of both political parties—and legislators representing both parties on Capitol Hill—have expressed dissatisfaction with the foreign policy process, and they have supported efforts to change it.

Third, despite this evident reformist zeal, the implementation of many proposed reforms (and those made by the Murphy commission are a leading example) has often been extremely limited. A commitment to study the deficiencies of the State Department, for example, has usually exceeded an evident willingness among executive and legislative leaders to correct the problems identified. This fact raises

17. The Murphy commission's findings are contained in *The Organization of the Government for the Conduct of Foreign Policy* (7 vols.; Washington, D.C., 1975).

a question about whether the reform impetus springs as much from genuine concern about the effectiveness of American diplomacy as from certain extraneous considerations, such as efforts to make the State Department the scapegoat for conditions lying outside its effective control, or failure by Congress and the public to contribute constructively to the solution of external problems.

Fourth, it is evident that the major and minor reforms undertaken within the American foreign policy process since World War II have not, with rare exceptions, yielded the desired results. During the 1980s, no less than in the 1950s, complaints were routinely heard inside and outside the United States that disarray characterized the American foreign policy process, that intraexecutive conflicts were impairing the cohesion of American foreign relations, and that the influence of the secretary of state was being undermined by other officials within the government. Indeed, by the years of the Reagan administration a number of these problems had perhaps become more acute than in any previous stage of American diplomatic history.

Finally, these reform efforts have done little or nothing to mute criticisms and discontents directed specifically at the State Department's role in the American foreign policy process. On Capitol Hill, among informed segments of American opinion, and sometimes even within the White House, dissatisfaction with the performance of the State Department has remained at a high level since World War II. Despite efforts throughout the postwar period to improve the foreign policy process in the United States, disenchantment about it, focusing specifically upon the State Department's role in it, has persisted. In an unusually candid evaluation, for example, President John F. Kennedy expressed his dismay and frustration concerning the State Department's performance. According to a White House adviser, Kennedy was "discouraged with the State Department almost as soon as he took office." He became convinced that it suffered from "built-in inertia which deadened initiative," that it tended toward "excessive delay" in responding to White House inquiries and in formulating needed policy proposals, that it "spoke with too many voices" on diplomatic issues, and that the president's own "policy line seemed consistently to be altered or evaded" by State Department officialdom. Although Kennedy had appointed capable officials to manage the department, collectively they exhibited "an abundance of talent ironically unmatched by production." As a result, President Kennedy repeatedly bypassed the State Department and made a number of key foreign policy decisions with minimal State Department participation.[18] With minor variations, Kennedy's assessment was echoed before and after his time by those with firsthand experience in diplomatic decision making and by informed commentators outside the government.

Criticisms of the State Department's performance since World War II have been numerous and exceedingly varied. A recurrent lament is that the State Department is highly resistant to change and to creative ideas, especially those proposed by individuals or agencies outside its own ranks. In this view, State Department deliberations are outstanding for their leisurely pace, their attachment to "traditionalism," and their premise that the political dimension of foreign relations must be kept uppermost at all times. Even Secretary of State Dean Rusk complained about the bureaucratic "layering" within the department that inhibited prompt and decisive responses to external problems. To Rusk's mind, the usual tendency of State Department officials was to avoid making decisions whenever possible, apparently in the hope that eventually the problem would "solve itself" or disappear. Related motifs have been the department's reluctance to take on new responsibilities in the postwar era: by default—if not on some occasions deliberately—the State Department has *encouraged* the intrusion into its once exclusive domain by other executive departments and agencies. Leading examples of this phenomenon were the State Department's lack of interest in playing a significant role in the occupation of Germany and Japan, in engaging in informational and propaganda activities, and in supervising intelligence operations in the early postwar period. In more recent years, deliberately or indeliberately, the department appeared to be minimally interested in playing a decisive role in such new dimensions of foreign relations as arms-control negotiations, the space program, environmental issues, and many aspects of international economic relations.[19]

18. For Kennedy's views, see Theodore Sorensen, *Kennedy* (New York, 1965), 287–88.
19. Donald P. Warwick, *A Theory of Public Bureaucracy: Politics, Personality and Organization in the State Department* (Cambridge, Mass., 1975), 15–16; Cordell Hull, *The Memoirs of Cordell Hull* (2 vols.; New York, 1948), II, 1602–22; Dean Acheson, *Present at the Creation: My Years in the State Department* (New York, 1969), 9–21, 48–64.

Other critics of the State Department have pointed to the alleged lack of technical competence and expertise possessed by its representatives vis-à-vis those in newer and more specialized governmental agencies. The traditional State Department "generalist" frequently lacks the detailed expertise of his counterpart in the Treasury Department, the Federal Energy Agency, or the National Aeronautics and Space Administration. If the State Department has lost ground to its bureaucratic rivals, one reason is that its spokesmen frequently are unable to hold their own in the bureaucratic give-and-take that is an inevitable part of policy formulation. This is perhaps merely another way of saying that the State Department's postwar emphasis upon functionalism as an organizational principle has been at best only partially successful.[20]

Other criticisms of the State Department have been directed at its ideological bias, which is said to distort its perspective and policy recommendations. During the late 1940s and early 1950s, the department was accused of exhibiting a pro-Communist orientation that, according to critics, was responsible for America's loss of China to communism. Paradoxically, a decade or so later, other detractors were convinced that the State Department was an influential part of the foreign policy establishment, which reflected a deeply ingrained anti-Communist mentality and which was in large part responsible for America's participation and prolonged involvement in the Vietnam War.[21]

Still another criticism is that, as a study of American-Iranian relations expressed it, "Foreign Service officers often wear a set of political, bureaucratic, and cultural blinders. They are accustomed to serving existing policy. Promotion is enhanced by the ability to get along with the ambassador and with the conventional wisdom." The American diplomat's principal incentive is "to reassure Washington that all is going well and that American policy is being effectively implemented." In this assessment the natural tendency of the State Department bureaucracy is toward continued support of the status quo.

20. David H. Davis, *How the Bureaucracy Makes Foreign Policy* (Lexington, Mass., 1972), 18, 59–60, 67–68.
21. Richard J. Barnet, *Roots of War: The Men and Institutions Behind U.S. Foreign Policy* (Baltimore, 1972), 13–137.

Other critics have called attention to the characteristics of what is described as the "Foreign Service Culture," which has traditionally put a premium upon "conformity," upon complying with the requirements of the "system," upon respectfully deferring to the viewpoints of administrative superiors, and upon the lack of creative thinking the culture has usually produced.[22]

One study of the American foreign policy process has asserted that "no Cabinet department is as much criticized as the Department of State, and none is more resentful of the limitations placed upon it."[23] The criticisms made of the State Department's performance since World War II cannot be dismissed lightly. With only a handful of exceptions (and most of these directed the department for relatively brief periods), every postwar secretary of state has faced mounting disaffection on Capitol Hill, in the public media, and sometimes in the White House. Many have relinquished office believing that their job was impossible and that the State Department was being held responsible for a multitude of regional and global problems that Americans found frustrating but that did not lie within the power of the department to solve. Writing in the early 1970s, one observer concluded, "The State Department, once the proud and undisputed steward of foreign policy, has finally acknowledged what others have long been saying: that it is no longer in charge of the United States' foreign policy, and that it cannot reasonably be expected to be so again." In the same period, former Secretary of State Dean Acheson referred to the "eclipse of the State Department" in the decision-making process.[24]

That a significant erosion in the formerly preeminent position of the State Department in the policy-making process has occurred since World War II can hardly be doubted. Yet, as the highly diverse nature of the complaints about its performance suggests, the depart-

22. Barry Rubin, *Paved with Good Intentions: The American Experience and Iran* (New York, 1981), 183; James W. Clark, "Foreign Affairs Personnel Management," in *The Organization of the Government for the Conduct of Foreign Policy*, VI, 181–200.

23. Graham Allison and Peter Szanton, *Remaking Foreign Policy* (New York, 1976), 122–23.

24. See the views of Terence Smith, as cited in Esterline and Black, *Inside Foreign Policy*, viii; and Dean Acheson, "The Eclipse of the State Department," *Foreign Affairs*, XLIX (July, 1971), 593–606.

ment makes an easy and convenient target for overall public, congressional, and perhaps presidential uneasiness about the condition of world affairs. As experienced State Department officials are aware, for example, the White House customarily takes credit for diplomatic accomplishments, while the department shoulders the blame for diplomatic failures.[25] Officials who have served in the department have also repeatedly reminded Americans that its province is foreign affairs—which is, by definition, a realm outside the writ of American law and is increasingly impervious to the American political will. In many key respects, the external political environment in recent years has become even more intractable, and less susceptible to the achievement of America's purposes abroad, than in the early post–World War II era.

Long-standing skepticism in the American mind about the nature and value of diplomacy also no doubt influences congressional and popular attitudes toward the State Department. A former American ambassador has said that in the United States "people have long looked on diplomacy as a mysterious activity on another planet." Almost a century ago, Senator Henry Cabot Lodge observed that foreign affairs filled "but a slight place in American politics and excite only languid interest" among the people—a judgment that has lost little of its saliency in recent years. In the same period, Secretary of State John Hay lamented that his position had become "almost intolerable" because of a lack of legislative and public understanding of it.[26] According to the American ethos, as another study expressed it, in "a reformed world based on reason, foreign policy and diplomacy would become unnecessary," and as the American democratic example influenced the behavior of other governments, the new political order "would be a world without diplomats." To the mind of John Adams, diplomatic intrigues had become particularly "alien and repulsive" for citizens of the New World. In the more recent era, Dean

---

25. Ball, *Diplomacy for a Crowded World*, 200–201.

26. See the views of former Ambassador Hugh S. Gibson in Elmer Plischke (ed.), *Modern Diplomacy: The Art and the Artisans* (Washington, D.C., 1979), xiii. See also Warwick, *A Theory of Public Bureaucracy*, 13; Stuart, *The Department of State*, 200; Felix Gilbert, *To the Farewell Address: Ideas of Early American Foreign Policy* (Princeton, 1961), 17, 65–68; and Norman A. Graebner, *Ideas and Diplomacy: Readings in the Intellectual Tradition of American Foreign Policy* (New York, 1964).

Acheson once observed that the secretary of state "is destined to be a pariah with Congress because he represents problems which the Congress wishes to forget." For most legislators, votes "can be lost but not gained through foreign policy." The secretary of state is "the personification of international difficulties and frustrations." According to another study of American attitudes, the Jacksonian conception of democracy was extremely suspicious of diplomacy, since frontiersmen "denigrated the diplomatic process as mere talk, mere fancy-pants stuff"; instead, they wanted "action and plenty of it, with all the lace and frills aside."[27] Historically, the climate of opinion in the American society has been adverse to a sympathetic view of diplomacy and the officials involved in it.

Fragmentation in the Policy Process

In reality, the diffusion and dissonance that have marked the process of foreign policy decision making since World War II is no new phenomenon in American diplomatic experience. As early as President George Washington's first administration, internal disunity and fundamental disagreement among his advisers beset the formulation and administration of foreign affairs—a fact that debilitated and disillusioned Secretary of State Thomas Jefferson, finally leading to his resignation on July 31, 1793. Overt intrusion into the foreign policy field by Secretary of the Treasury Alexander Hamilton, for example, was directed at counteracting Jefferson's known pro-French sympathies and at reassuring the British that in Britain's impending war with France, the United States would remain neutral, refusing to honor its alliance with the French. In the negotiations with England over the Jay Treaty (1794), Hamilton was instrumental in having John Jay chosen for this assignment, in drafting his instructions, and in communicating with him (without Jefferson's knowledge) during the negotiations. Faced with such disunity within the executive branch on foreign policy issues, President Washington at length lamented:

27. Ronald J. Stupak, *The Shaping of Foreign Policy: The Role of the Secretary of State as Seen by Dean Acheson* (Indianapolis, 1969), 10–11, 99; Acheson, *Present at the Creation*, 93–104; Smith Simpson, *Anatomy of the State Department* (Boston, 1967), 3.

"The affairs of this country cannot go amiss. There are so many watchful guardians of them and such infallible guides that one is at no loss for a director [of foreign policy] at every turn."[28]

On the eve of World War II, according to Dean Acheson, Secretary of State Cordell Hull and other officials in the State Department encountered a similar "anguishing period," when schism and fragmentation characterized the foreign policy process. As Acheson recalled the era: "Poor Mr. Hull's life was one long battle with the bureaucracies of other agencies—the military, Lend Lease, Economic Warfare, Treasury, War Shipping, Relief, Agriculture, and so on. [Secretary Hull] won all the linguistics of decisions and lost all the substance. What little order came out of it all was produced by Harry Hopkins [FDR's personal adviser] at the White House, regarded by Mr. Hull as his mortal enemy."[29]

This phenomenon became even more pronounced after World War II, when what is often described as "fractionation" and "incoherence" became a conspicuous element in the American foreign policy process. This result stemmed from several broad developments and forces. One of these was the emergence of the United States as a superpower and its assumption of a host of new global and regional responsibilities. A second influence was the evolving nature of what is sometimes described as "the foreign policy agenda": those specific problems and undertakings that collectively comprise the "foreign policy" of the United States. In the postwar era, diplomacy has become concerned with a multitude of new problems and novel challenges, from the provision of governmental assistance to needy societies in the Third World, to efforts designed to stabilize global trade and price levels, to mounting concern about the worsening world food crisis. Inevitably, such new concerns have led to the establishment of new bureaucracies and their growing involvement in international activities. By the late 1960s, for example, such governmental agencies as the Justice Department, the Interior Department, the Transportation Department, and the National Aeronautics and Space

28. Nathan Schachner, *Thomas Jefferson: A Biography* (2 vols.; New York, 1951), I, 410, 482, 485; Stuart, *The Department of State,* 25–27; James T. Flexner, *George Washington: Anguish and Farewell (1793–1799)* (Boston, 1972), 147–48.
29. Acheson, "The Eclipse of the State Department," 596.

Administration had employees serving abroad. Even the Library of Congress and the Tennessee Valley Authority (TVA) conducted overseas operations. By the 1980s, out of some sixteen thousand American officials serving in foreign countries, less than one-fourth (23 percent) were State Department personnel.[30]

Accelerating this tendency also has been the inclination of societies throughout the world (less in America perhaps than in most other nations) to look to government for the solutions to their urgent problems. This has led to a massive expansion in the federal bureaucracy in the United States since the New Deal. Since many domestic problems have their origins in developments overseas, or are directly affected by events beyond America's borders, this process has perhaps foreordained the steady intrusion by other governmental agencies into the State Department's traditional domain. It has also greatly compounded the problem of arriving at unified foreign policy decisions within the executive branch.

Expressed differently, since World War II there has occurred a wholesale intrusion into the foreign policy process of governmental agencies whose normal and primary orientation is domestic affairs. Although their participation in foreign policy making may be selective and episodic, it can also be decisive in determining the external behavior of the United States. For example, the Treasury Department's view of America's balance-of-payments problems or the Agriculture Department's position toward the UN's Food and Agriculture Organization can sometimes exert decisive influence in determining the behavior of the American government in certain aspects of its foreign relations.[31]

In general terms, the problem of interagency conflict over foreign policy issues was defined by Harlan Cleveland, when he observed that "nearly every American institution of any size or significance is already partly international." Since World War II, he stated, "the en-

30. Warwick, *A Theory of Public Bureaucracy*, 64–65; Raymond F. Hopkins, "Global Food Management: U.S. Policy Making in an Interdependent World," in *The Organization of the Government for the Conduct of Foreign Policy*, I, 134–59; *U.S. News and World Report*, September 29, 1980, pp. 35–36.
31. These and other examples are discussed in Charles W. Yost, "Conduct of Multilateral Diplomacy by the United States Government," in *The Organization of the Government for the Conduct of Foreign Policy*, I, 283–92.

tire government" has become involved in the foreign policy process, and this fact means that "it becomes more difficult to define a distinctive role for the State Department."[32]

The Military Role in Foreign Policy

Speaking to the Senate Armed Services Committee in 1981, Secretary of State Alexander Haig observed: "There can be no easy distinction drawn between foreign and defense policy. They are inextricably linked." Haig noted that historically Americans had often been prone to ignore this linkage. In the past they had often believed "preparations for war began only after diplomacy had failed" and had been oblivious to "the utility of military power in preventing war." As a superpower, the United States could no longer "accept a policy which draws an artificial line between diplomacy and the ability to project military power." In brief, Haig was urging legislators to bear in mind what has been widely referred to as "Clausewitz's rule": "War is the continuation of politics [or diplomacy] by other means."[33]

The kind of thinking exemplified by Secretary of State Haig's statement is a relatively recent phenomenon in American experience. The historic American frame of mind—which viewed military and political issues as totally separate questions—was illustrated by the attitude of the Roosevelt administration during World War II. According to one of America's most experienced diplomats, the United States "fought the war to win the war. We paid less attention than we should have to the possible [political] consequences, to what kinds of problems we would be facing at the end of the war, to what sort of political matters would require our attention."[34]

32. Harlan Cleveland, "The Management of Multilateralism," in *The Organization of the Government for the Conduct of Foreign Policy*, I, Appendix C, 8.

33. Alexander Haig, "Relationship of Foreign and Defense Policies," in Department of State, *Current Policy*, No. 302 (July 30, 1981), 1. The Prussian general Carl Maria von Clausewitz (1780–1831) wrote a highly influential treatise analyzing the relationship between military force and the achievement of political objectives called *On War*. For a summary and evaluation of his thought, see Roger A. Leonard (ed.), *Clausewitz on War* (New York, 1967). See also the analysis of Clausewitz' ideas in Bernard Brodie, *War and Politics* (New York, 1973), 1–29.

34. Charles E. Bohlen, *The Transformation of American Foreign Policy* (New York, 1969), 21.

Relatively few Americans understood or sensed that many of the most serious challenges confronting the United States after World War II—such as Soviet domination of Eastern Europe, the division of Germany, the wars in Vietnam and Korea, and the precipitous decline of British power—stemmed directly from military decisions and developments during that conflict. The emergence of the cold war, even before World War II ended, however, provided another inescapable reminder of the relevance of Clausewitz' rule.

One far-reaching result of World War II was the comprehensive reorganization of the American military establishment effected by the National Security Act (1947).[35] Following a prolonged study of the problem by private groups and congressional committees, a new Department of Defense (DOD) was established to include the three military services, which at that time were still separate: the army, the navy (including the marine corps), and the air force. In 1947 and afterward, Congress was unwilling to accept the idea of a single, totally unified military establishment; nor did it favor any reorganization plan that would produce a general staff on the Prussian model, potentially capable of dominating national policy making. Instead, to coordinate defense planning and activities, a new office, the Joint Chiefs of Staff (JCS), headed by a rotating chairman appointed by the president, was established. The JCS was expected to represent the military viewpoint to the civilian secretary of defense and to the president. In their individual capacities, the members of JCS also function as the operating heads of their respective military arms. Another innovation was the creation of an important administrative unit within DOD—the Office of International Security Affairs (ISA). Sometimes called "the Pentagon's State Department," ISA exists to serve as the primary channel of communication between military and diplomatic officials to assure the desired blending of these two crucial components of national policy.[36]

It is not necessary to enter into a detailed analysis of the problems of defense organization and administration since the end of World

35. Useful studies of the evolution of the American military establishment after World War II are Timothy W. Stanley, *American Defense and National Security* (Washington, D.C., 1956); and William R. Kinter, *Forging a New Sword* (New York, 1958).

36. Keith C. Clark and Laurence J. Legere (eds.), *The President and the Management of National Security* (New York, 1969), 137–38.

War II. Other, less sweeping changes were made in the structure of the defense establishment after 1947. But two ideas need to be emphasized. In the first place, the postwar era has witnessed unprecedented attention to military dimensions of foreign affairs. From East Asia to Latin America, throughout the postwar era the United States has been confronted repeatedly with the inseparable relationship between military and diplomatic components of national policy. During the Vietnam War, for example, Secretary of Defense Robert McNamara emerged as unquestionably the most influential member of President Lyndon B. Johnson's cabinet, and his viewpoints on the war often appeared decisive in shaping the policies of the Johnson administration. Under the Carter and Reagan administrations, a new interservice military entity—the Rapid Deployment Force (RDF)—was created to preserve access by the United States and its allies to the vital oil reserves of the Persian Gulf area. Both strategically, and from the perspective of maintaining the American standard of living, this objective was viewed as essential in Washington. And in order to achieve it, fundamental changes were required in the American defense establishment.[37]

In the second place, the reorganization of the military establishment carried out in 1947 and in the years that followed has not brought an end to such problems as interservice rivalries, the lack of a clear national military strategy for using American power abroad, and the hiatus between civilian and military aspects of national policy. The complaint was widely heard in the 1980s, for example, that the Reagan administration lacked a clear and consistent rationale for its massive budget requests—$1.6 trillion proposed in 1983 to be spent over a five-year period to improve the nation's military arsenal. In many cases, exactly how the acquisition of some new weapons system, such as the MX missile or a greatly expanded navy, would enhance the security and diplomatic interests of the United States puzzled informed citizens and their representatives on Capitol Hill. In other cases, American diplomatic and military moves in regions such as Latin America often seemed uncoordinated and at variance

---

37. The rationale and objectives of the Rapid Deployment Force are discussed more fully in Cecil V. Crabb, Jr., *The Doctrines of American Foreign Policy: Their Meaning, Role, and Future* (Baton Rouge, 1983), 360–71; and *U.S. Defense Policy: Weapons, Strategy, and Commitments* (2nd ed.; Washington, D.C., 1980), 65–69.

with the declared policies of the United States. Criticisms also persisted concerning the JCS system on the ground that its inherent tendency was to evade difficult strategic issues, to produce vague and lowest-common-denominator recommendations for the secretary of defense and the president, and to leave the still intractable problem of rivalry and competition among the branches of the armed forces largely unresolved.[38]

Based upon the Pentagon's experience since World War II, one fundamental cause of disunity and fragmentation within the American foreign policy process is the existence of bureaucratic rivalries and conflicts *within* executive agencies. If it has proved difficult to obtain agreement upon a unified and coherent foreign policy position within the executive branch, a potent contributing factor has been that little agreement exists within the Department of Defense upon the kind of military strategy that ought to guide the United States and upon how the separate service arms contribute to its implementation.

Intelligence Agencies and Operations

One of America's national heroes—Nathan Hale—was executed by the British because he served as a spy during the Revolutionary War. In the post–World War II era, the rapid expansion in the size and activities of the nation's intelligence arm has had profound consequences for the conduct and administration of American foreign policy. Down to that global conflict, American intelligence operations were fragmentary, uncoordinated, and inadequate. Perhaps even today many Americans still feel the kind of revulsion about intelligence activities conveyed by the remark of former Secretary of State Henry L. Stimson who said, "Gentlemen do not read other people's mail." Still less do they engage in such "dirty tricks" as trying to overthrow other governments or intervening overtly in their political affairs. The continuing controversy over the activities of the CIA and other intelligence units indicates that, for countless Americans and

38. Barry M. Blechman and Stephen S. Kaplan, *Force Without War: U.S. Armed Forces as a Political Instrument* (Washington, D.C., 1979); James Fallows, *National Defense* (New York, 1980); Douglas Kinnard, *The Secretary of Defense* (Lexington, Ky, 1980); David C. Jones, "What's Wrong with Our Defense Establishment," *New York Times Magazine*, August 7, 1983, pp. 38–42, 70–85.

members of the media, many intelligence operations are of dubious legitimacy in a democracy.

The military disaster at Pearl Harbor late in 1941 underscored the crucial contribution of intelligence operations to national security. There was not only the problem of collecting information required upon which to base national policy (in reality, naval intelligence had broken the Japanese naval code and had learned of an impending attack against American bases). There were also perhaps the even more difficult tasks of disseminating intelligence gathered to policy makers who needed it and of evaluating intelligence data and reports accurately and objectively.

During World War II, the basis for a more adequate and permanent intelligence system was laid by the Office of Strategic Services (OSS); many of its officers continued to serve in intelligence capacities in the postwar era. Once again, after the war the State Department appeared to be indifferent to the need for a peacetime intelligence service and exhibited little interest in its creation.[39]

An important provision of the National Security Act of 1947 was the establishment of a new intelligence organization—the Central Intelligence Agency (CIA)—which was given a twofold mission. The CIA was expected both to engage in intelligence operations itself and to serve as the central or coordinating mechanism for all governmental intelligence activities. Over the years that followed, as America's international responsibilities multiplied and as intelligence operations became more specialized, other agencies developed extensive intelligence programs. Within the executive branch, the "intelligence community" now consists of a long list of governmental agencies active in the field, and coordinating their activities in behalf of a unified approach to intelligence problems has itself become a difficult and recurrent challenge.

The CIA continues to serve as the focal point of national intelligence activities. Its director is charged with preparing intelligence reports reflecting the viewpoints of all agencies involved in intelligence operations for submission to the National Security Council and the president. In addition, according to the provisions of the National Se-

39. The title of former Secretary of State Dean Acheson's discussion—"The Department Muffs Its Intelligence Role"—is indicative of its lack of interest in many novel postwar challenges. See his *Present at the Creation*, 157.

curity Act, the CIA may undertake "such other functions and duties related to intelligence affecting the national security as the NSC may from time to time direct." This is the legislative authority whereby, under the president's ultimate direction, the CIA engages in "political" acts and covert operations such as intervention against Marxist regimes abroad and efforts to maintain a pro-American regime in power.

After 1947, several other agencies also became influential actors within the intelligence community. The National Security Agency (NSA), whose budget exceeds the CIA's, supervises and monitors foreign communications and endeavors to preserve the security of America's codes and ciphers. Much of what is known about the armed forces of other countries, for example, comes from NSA's listening posts abroad, which try to intercept radar and radio signals by other nations.

Within the Pentagon, the Defense Intelligence Agency, which reports to the Joint Chiefs of Staff and the secretary of defense, prepares reports and analyses involving the armed forces as a whole. Each separate military service also operates its own intelligence arm. Naval intelligence, for example, gathers information related directly to the navy's unique mission. Within the State Department, the Bureau of Intelligence and Research, the smallest component within the intelligence community, collects intelligence from diplomatic posts abroad and contributes data and conclusions, principally on political and economic issues, to national intelligence reports. In addition, the Federal Bureau of Investigation, the Treasury Department, and the Department of Energy also engage in intelligence operations. The FBI is charged with counterintelligence activities, for example, whereas the Treasury Department is concerned with such issues as counterfeiting and "gun running." Altogether, some eleven different federal agencies comprise the intelligence community. Although budgetary details are seldom made public, it is estimated that collectively the community expends some six to ten billion dollars annually on intelligence operations.[40]

40. For more detailed description and discussion of the intelligence community, see Lyman B. Kirkpatrick, Jr., *The U.S. Intelligence Community* (New York, 1973); Andrew Tully, *The Super Spies* (New York, 1970); David Wise and Thomas B. Ross, *The Invisible Government* (New York, 1974) and also their *The Espionage Establishment* (New York,

Three ongoing problems related to intelligence operations seem pertinent to foreign policy making. One is the question of whether intelligence analyses of important international issues are at a professionally high level, providing the president and his advisers with the best assessments of external issues of which the nation is capable. A second recurrent question is whether intelligence estimates and studies are free of ideological bias and preconceptions. Do they reflect evident agency bias or present data and findings mainly designed to confirm the preexisting beliefs of the president and other policy makers? The failure of the intelligence community to predict the rapid and total collapse of the Iranian monarchy in the late 1970s provided disturbing evidence of this defect in American intelligence operations. A third fundamental question is how the president and his advisers use the intelligence data and reports available to them. An incumbent chief executive may rely for advice upon any source inside or outside the government. Accordingly, he may lean heavily— or not at all—upon the contributions made by the CIA and other intelligence agencies. Alternatively, he may (and many presidents do) utilize only those intelligence findings that support his predispositions and policy inclinations. Unquestionably, a number of America's "intelligence failures" since World War II, such as several during the Vietnam conflict, involved instances in which policy makers disregarded intelligence estimates that did not conform with their preexisting viewpoints.[41]

Economic and Financial Agencies

Close relations between groups like merchants and financiers, on one hand, and officials engaged in the formulation and administration of American foreign policy, on the other, are no new phenomenon in

---

1968). William R. Corson, *The Armies of Ignorance* (New York, 1977), is a history of the American intelligence establishment.

41. An outstanding case was provided by the findings of the CIA during the Vietnam War. Almost alone among governmental agencies, the CIA predicted quite early that the United States was not accomplishing its objectives in Southeast Asia and would be unable to do so successfully. Extensive evidence is presented in Neil Sheehan *et al.*, *The Pentagon Papers: The Secret History of the Vietnam War* (New York, 1971).

American experience. As already observed, even as early as President Washington's first administration, officials other than the secretary of the state, especially Secretary of the Treasury Alexander Hamilton, frequently played a decisive role in foreign affairs. On some occasions Hamilton served as a kind of de facto secretary of state. At the end of the nineteenth century, the influence of merchants and traders was crucial in convincing the McKinley administration to declare the Open Door policy toward China and become inextricably involved with the future of the Nationalist government of China under Chiang Kai-shek. Similarly, the expectation of expanded Soviet-American trade was one factor inducing many groups to favor recognition of the Soviet Union in 1933.[42]

Since World War II, nearly every significant aspect of American foreign policy has come to possess an important economic or financial dimension. The world price level for imported oil, the cost of the American foreign aid program, the increasingly serious monetary and financial crises existing among nations throughout the Third World, the cost of modernizing NATO's armed forces and of restoring a military balance on the European continent, the centrality of trade questions in Japanese-American relations—these are merely a few of the leading international issues having major economic and financial connotations. Sometimes referred to as the "domesticization" of American foreign policy, this phenomenon has drawn an almost endless list of executive agencies into the policy making process; and it has made that process extremely diffuse, cumbersome, bureaucratic, and subject to recurrent interagency conflicts. In its simplest terms, the traditional distinction between domestic and foreign policy questions has all but disappeared. As one study has expressed it, the substance of "foreign economic policy" is now largely indistinguishable from what was once called "political policy." As a result, the United States no longer seeks to achieve merely one or two national aims in its foreign relations. Instead, policy makers must strive for a high degree "of optimization among a substantial number of highly desirable goals" that impinge directly upon internal affairs. Consequently,

42. Charles S. Campbell, Jr., *Special Business Interests and the Open Door Policy* (New Haven, 1951); See William A. Williams, *American-Russian Relations, 1781–1947* (New York, 1952), 236–37.

the national interest of the United States has become subject to an almost endless number of highly subjective intepretations.[43]

Among the departments and agencies involved with economic aspects of foreign affairs, specific mention must be made of the unique status of the Agency for International Development (AID), established to administer the economic foreign aid program. Headed by its own director, AID is linked to the Department of State and takes its policy directives from the latter. Theoretically, this assures a high degree of continuity between the basic foreign policy goals of the United States and the administration of the foreign aid program. With occasional exceptions, this organizational pattern appears to have worked satisfactorily to achieve the desired goal.

For a century or more, the Department of Commerce has played an active role in foreign relations. During the 1930s, for example, the department strongly advocated the lowering of barriers of international trade, which resulted in passage of the Reciprocal Trade Program in 1934. In an increasingly interdependent world, its interest in such goals as maximizing global trade, encouraging American manufacturing, and fostering and protecting American shipping remains intense. Traditionally, officials of the Department of Commerce collect information about business conditions at home and abroad, about opportunities for expanded trade, about the production and distribution of commodities, and about a host of related subjects that they routinely relay to the State Department. Such information is invaluable to the president, the State Department, and other agencies involved in making decisions related to foreign economic policy.[44]

In the postwar era, the Treasury Department has also assumed an important role—and on some aspects of foreign policy, sometimes a decisive role—in the foreign policy process. Its emergence as an influential foreign policy actor illustrates the economic principle of division of labor. Increasingly, on international financial questions, the views of the Treasury Department tend to be decisive in the formulation of national policy. As one study found: "The State Department frequently must defer to the Treasury on matters of international

43. Edward K. Hamilton, "Summary Report: Principal Lessons of the Past Decade and Thoughts on the Next," in *The Organization of the Government for the Conduct of Foreign Policy*, III, 7.

44. Childs, *American Foreign Service*, 55–57.

monetary policy. It must defer because it lacks expertise; it lacks expertise because it enters the financial arena too seldom to justify developing its own specialists. . . . To develop expertise [in international finance] a man must usually devote years to working in a narrow area. Within the State Department the demand is too small to allow this specialization." In part because of the rotation in their assignments, Foreign Service officers seldom develop such skills, and they do not have access to the capital equipment needed to acquire them. The influential role often exercised by the Treasury Department provides a graphic illustration of the principle that, in any bureaucratic tug-of-war, specialized knowledge is power. The decline in the State Department's relative position in the policy process can be accounted for in some degree by the fact that today it is less well informed about certain key areas of foreign policy than its bureaucratic competitors.[45]

Since World War II, the Labor Department has also developed significant global and regional interests. For a generation or more, the Labor Department has reflected the militant opposition of many American labor unions to communism. It has sought to promote the growth of free labor unions in other countries and to protect the rights of workers abroad, and it has cooperated with the State Department in operating a program of exchanges between representatives of the American labor movement and its counterpart abroad. Within the Foreign Service, labor attachés are assigned to most embassies abroad; their reports are received by both the State and Labor departments. In general, relations between the two departments have tended to be mutually supportive and beneficial.[46]

Among the agencies concerned with economic and financial aspects of foreign affairs, those involved in the budget process must not be omitted. For some fifty years, the preparation of the president's budget was the responsibility of the Bureau of the Budget; its name was changed to the Office of Management and Budget (OMB) during the Nixon administration. As is evident, major budgetary allocations and deletions by OMB, and by budgetary units within the principal

45. Davis, *How the Bureaucracy Makes Policy*, 59, 67.
46. Informative studies are Ronald Radosch, *American Labor and United States Foreign Policy* (New York, 1969); and Lane Kirkland *et al.*, "Labor's International Role," *Foreign Policy*, XXVI (Spring, 1977), 204–48.

federal departments and agencies, provide persuasive evidence of the priority that foreign policy undertakings enjoy within the executive branch. In the final analysis, the diplomatic priorities of the United States are accurately reflected in a willingness by the president and Congress to allocate funds for their effective implementation.[47]

In recent years the foreign policy process has become even more diffuse and fragmented because of the inclusion of a growing number of specialized, or what might be called "technological," agencies within it. Two prominent examples may be noted briefly. One is the National Aeronautics and Space Administration (NASA), whose space programs often have significant political implications for America's relations with other countries. NASA has an unusually favorable image with the American people and Congress. As a rule, NASA's activities evoke a favorable response because they are "peaceful, scientific, generous, daring and winning." Because of NASA's daring, America has won many contests with the Soviets in the space race, a fact that the State Department and propaganda agencies exploit to America's advantage.[48] Also among the newer federal agencies is the Department of Energy, whose primary mission is the coordination of governmental activities in the energy field to enable the United States to reduce its dependence upon foreign (notably Persian Gulf) oil sources. Energy questions have repercussions for America's relations not only with the Middle East but also with NATO, Japan, Mexico, and many other nations. The department has a separate bureau in charge of international energy problems.[49]

Cultural, Informational, and Propaganda Activities

The post–World War II era has witnessed an unprecedented and continuing emphasis upon cultural, informational, and propagandist aspects of foreign affairs. This development in turn has resulted in the

47. Esterline and Black, *Inside Foreign Policy,* 26–27.
48. Davis, *How the Bureaucracy Makes Foreign Policy,* 39. A detailed discussion of NASA's activities in foreign affairs is available in Eugene B. Skolnikoff, "Policy Process for Space Satellites," in *The Organization of the Government for the Conduct of Foreign Policy,* I, 177–91.
49. Allison and Szanton, *Remaking Foreign Policy,* 9.

creation of new governmental agencies, and new administrative units within existing ones, that are responsible for activities and programs in this dimension of modern diplomacy.

During World War I, on several occasions President Woodrow Wilson appealed to the people of Germany and other belligerent countries to disavow the policies of their governments. Propaganda by both the Allies and the Central Powers played a prominent role during this conflict. After the war, President Wilson again sought to influence public opinion at home and abroad in behalf of his peace objectives and the new world order that he advocated.

Propaganda and informational activities played an even more crucial role in World War II. Directed by the German Reich's propaganda minister, Joseph Goebbels, Nazi propaganda output reached new levels of intensity and distortion.[50] Since 1917 also, propaganda has been an instrument utilized heavily by the Communist government of the Soviet Union to achieve its goals. During the war, the Roosevelt administration established the Office of War Information (OWI) to spearhead American propaganda activities against the Axis Powers.

In the postwar era, particularly as cold war came to characterize Soviet-American relations, both superpowers emphasized propaganda and informational aspects of foreign affairs. The global broadcasts of Radio Moscow, for example, were rivaled by those of the Voice of America, though the latter has never had the financial support that Moscow gives to its propaganda program. The Truman administration launched a "campaign of truth" to disseminate information globally about America's beliefs and way of life. Under President Eisenhower, the United States Information Agency (USIA) was established as the agency directly involved in informational and propaganda activities abroad. The USIA (for several years it was called the United States International Communication Agency, or USICA) is administratively separate from the Department of State, though it takes its broad policy guidelines and directives from the latter so that, at least in theory, the United States will present a united diplomatic front to the outside world. In part because of the American people's traditional aversion to propaganda and recurrent questions about its

50. Wallace Carroll, *Persuade or Perish* (Boston, 1948); Paul M. A. Linebarger, *Psychological Warfare* (Washington, D.C., 1948).

precise mission and how it should be achieved, USIA has had a rather troubled existence within the American foreign policy process.[51]

A number of related activities are embraced by what is sometimes called "cultural diplomacy," which has come into prominence since World War II. Student and faculty exchange programs, people-to-people movements (such as pen-pal programs and exchange programs by rotary clubs and other civic organizations), visits by the Bolshoi Ballet to America and by the Boston Symphony Orchestra to the Soviet Union, the exchange of medical teams and expertise between the United States and the People's Republic of China, athletic competition and events among the nations of the world, attempts to reduce barriers impeding international access to information in countries throughout the world—these are leading examples of cultural diplomacy in the contemporary international system. When utilized as an instrument of foreign policy, the object of cultural diplomacy is to remove barriers to better international understanding, enhance the prospects for peaceful relations among nations, and win goodwill among the people and governments of other countries.[52]

Coordinating Devices and Mechanisms

Among the State Department's traditional duties is the task of serving as the principal coordinating mechanism for unifying executive efforts in the foreign policy field. But as the overall influence of the department has declined significantly, its ability to perform this essential coordinating function has been increasingly curtailed. The problem of synchronizing the activities of executive agencies dealing with diplomatic issues has existed for some two centuries. A number of responses have been made to the challenge. One of the oldest is reliance

51. John W. Henderson, *The United States Information Agency* (New York, 1969); Thomas C. Sorensen, *The Word War: The Story of American Propaganda* (New York, 1968). More recent information on America's propaganda programs and the problems besetting them may be found in Cecil V. Crabb, Jr., *American Foreign Policy in the Nuclear Age* (4th ed.; New York, 1983), 149–59.

52. A recent and more extended analysis of the subject may be found in Kevin V. Mulcahy, "Cultural Diplomacy: Foreign Policy and the Exchange Program," in Kevin Mulcahy and C. Richard Sawim (eds.), *Public Policy and the Arts* (Boulder, 1982), 269–303. See also Robert Blum (ed.), *Cultural Affairs and Foreign Relations* (Englewood Cliffs, N.J., 1963).

upon the president's cabinet as the instrument for arriving at a unified foreign policy. George Washington began the custom of referring foreign policy issues to the cabinet for discussion and advice. On some diplomatic issues, other cabinet members overshadowed Secretary of State Thomas Jefferson.

Throughout the course of American history, the cabinet has steadily lost its appeal for successive presidents as a device for unifying diplomatic activities. By World War II, former Secretary of State Cordell Hull observed, the cabinet "filled, in general, a very minor role in the formulation of foreign policy."[53] Hull's colleague, Secretary of War Henry Stimson, concurred that cabinet meetings were "no earthly good." To the mind of former Secretary of State Dean Acheson, cabinet meetings could "become an unorganized and discursive waste of time." Although it might have value as a mechanism for keeping the heads of executive departments informed about the administration's policies, the cabinet was not "a major instrument of Government" for formulating foreign policy decisions, he said. President John F. Kennedy believed that meetings of the cabinet were usually a waste of time. In company with other recent chief executives, however, Kennedy distinguished between the useful contributions made by the cabinet collectively and the influence of its members individually in dealing with particular foreign policy issues.[54]

An alternative approach to the problem of successfully integrating executive activities in the foreign policy field has been reliance upon interagency committees to achieve policy coordination. Such committees may be variously composed and may exist at many levels of the federal bureaucracy. Throughout the postwar period, untold hundreds of such committees have been established, and most have in time been quietly disbanded, only to be succeeded by other such committees. The basic idea is to constitute a group of officials from agencies directly involved in particular foreign policy issues, with the expectation that they will arrive at agreed-upon policy recommendations ultimately for the president.

Two basic patterns of use of such interagency committees may be identified. One is the creation of *ad hoc* committees to deal with par-

---

53. Hull's views are quoted in Arthur W. MacMahon, *Administration in Foreign Affairs* (University, Ala., 1953), 39.
54. *Ibid.*, 42; Acheson, *Present at the Creation*, 736; Sorensen, *Kennedy*, 283.

ticular (often urgent) foreign policy issues. A noteworthy example was what came to be called the Executive Committee of the National Security Council (ExComm), established by President Kennedy at the outset of the Cuban missile crisis in 1962. This group consisted of some fifteen high-level advisers, including such officials as the secretaries of state and defense, along with several assistant secretaries and Attorney General Robert Kennedy. ExComm was disbanded after the Cuban missile crisis was resolved.[55] Since World War II, innumerable *ad hoc* committees have been created within the executive branch to deal with less urgent external challenges.

An alternative format is illustrated by the Senior Interdepartmental Group (SIG), set up under the Johnson administration. Headed by an undersecretary of state, SIG was intended to serve as a permanent high-level committee to deal with a variety of international problems involving several executive departments and agencies. The fact that SIG was chaired by an undersecretary of state signified LBJ's recognition of the State Department's historic primacy in dealing with foreign policy questions.[56]

In addition, President Johnson relied heavily upon another committee—the "Tuesday lunch group," which concentrated mainly upon operational questions related to the Vietnam War. It consisted of the president, Secretary of State Dean Rusk, Secretary of Defense Robert McNamara, and the president's national security adviser; other officials were invited to join the group when the discussion dealt with particular issues involving their interests. While the Tuesday lunch group permitted informal and flexible decision making, disadvantages were that decisions were often made hastily and on an *ad hoc* basis, and that many officials, such as the Joint Chiefs of Staff, believed that their viewpoints were inadequately considered by the president.[57]

Early in the Reagan administration a senior-level committee, consisting of the president, White House adviser William P. Clark, Secretary of State George Shultz, and Secretary of Defense Caspar Wein-

55. Arthur Schlesinger, Jr., *A Thousand Days* (Boston, 1965), 802–19.
56. Simpson, *Anatomy of the State Department*, 67–69.
57. I. M. Destler, *Presidents, Bureaucrats, and Foreign Policy: The Politics of Organizational Reform* (Princeton, 1972), 109–11. See also the Murphy Commission's "Conclusions and Recommendations," in *The Organization of the Government for the Conduct of Foreign Policy*, III, 286–87.

berger, concentrated upon American foreign policy toward the Middle East, an issue eliciting widespread disagreement within the executive branch. The group sought to arrive at a consensus ultimately to be approved by the president.[58]

Interagency committees have unquestionably become a permanent feature of the foreign policy process in the United States. In one form or another, they have been used—and doubtless will continue to be used—by every modern president to impart unity to the process of policy formulation and administration. As informed students of bureaucracy are aware, this device suffers from two fundamental defects that frequently prevent it from achieving the intended goal. One is that in striving for an agreed-upon position, interagency committees deliberately or indeliberately permit the quest for consensus among participating agencies to become the dominant objective. As a result, the recommendations of such committees are often so general and ambiguous as to be of questionable value to the president and department heads. In the process, innovative and creative ideas in the diplomatic field become casualties of prolonged interagency deliberations, bureaucratic "trade-offs," and compromises.

A second and not unrelated weakness of this device is that proposals dealing with major policy questions agreed upon by interagency committees are frequently renegotiated again at higher levels. Representing the viewpoints and bureaucratic interests of their respective departments, cabinet officers may, and often do, "appeal" such agreements to the president and seek to reopen the issue with him. If the president does not accept their appeal, the principal actors in the foreign policy process may then be tempted to take their case to sympathetic legislators and committees on Capitol Hill. If he does accept their appeal and reopen the case, then agreement at a lower level has accomplished little more than to add another time-consuming stage to the foreign policy process.

A different approach to the problem, one directed specifically at conflict among agencies of the United States government operating abroad, was adopted by President Kennedy and has been continued by successive chief executives. This is the concept of the "country team," according to which the ambassador resident in a particular

58. See the analysis by Richard Halloran in the New York *Times*, February 17, 1983.

country supervises all official American activities within that country. (Exceptions include the duties assigned to the armed forces and to individuals or groups engaged in certain intelligence missions.) This scheme was designed to avert the kind of interagency rivalry, for example, that subsequently became conspicuous during the Vietnam War.

The concept of the country team implicitly acknowledged three key facts about America's foreign policy activities. One was that in some instances a high degree of intraexecutive conflict existed abroad and that it sometimes seriously impeded the nation's foreign policy efforts. Another was that some official (in this case, the American ambassador) should formally be in charge of all official activities overseas and should coordinate them in behalf of a unified foreign policy. The third realization was that, theoretically, the premier position of the State Department within the foreign policy should be preserved. This principle was underscored by designating the American ambassador, who reports to the State Department, as the head of the country team.

In practice, the country-team technique has produced highly variable results. To no inconsiderable degree, the success of this approach has depended upon the personality and ability of the individual ambassadors within particular countries, and these qualities often vary widely. It has also depended upon White House and State Department interest in the country and the support that the ambassador's efforts to impose central direction upon overseas activities received in Washington. Use of country teams has been unquestionably beneficial in some settings. Yet the continued existence of ununified foreign policy efforts among an expanding number of executive agencies within Washington has inevitably encouraged interagency rivalries in the field.[59]

Alternatively, the most systematic and formal effort to impart and preserve unity to executive branch activities in the foreign policy sphere since World War II has been the attempt to assign that task to the White House staff. The National Security Act of 1947 created a new coordinating mechanism—the National Security Council (NSC)—

59. See the American Assembly's report, *The Representation of the United States Abroad* (New York, 1956), 183–208; and Raymond L. Thurston, "The Ambassador and the CIA," *Foreign Service Journal*, LVI (January, 1979), 22–23.

to act as a high-level advisory organ to the president. NSC's specific mission was to integrate civilian and military components of foreign policy, to produce something called "national security policy"—a successful fusion of civilian and military components into a unified national policy abroad to be supported by all federal agencies. The president was designated the head of NSC. Although its membership has varied since 1947, by the early 1980s its members were the president, the vice-president, the secretary of state, and the secretary of defense. Other governmental officials, such as the United States ambassador to the UN or the chairman of the JCS, could be, and often were, invited to attend meetings of the NSC when particular agenda items involved their interests and responsibilities. It needs to be reiterated that the president is free to solicit advice from any source he chooses in arriving at foreign policy decisions.

Several facts about the operation of the National Security Council must be emphasized. Its existence represents a formal and highly institutionalized approach to the problem of resolving interagency conflict over foreign policy issues. Yet the NSC was intended to be and remains an *advisory body* to the president in reaching foreign policy decisions. Nearly every occupant of the Oval Office has utilized the machinery afforded by the NSC differently. Some, like President Eisenhower, relied upon extensive staff assistance before arriving at decisions. Others, like Presidents Kennedy and Reagan, have been less disposed to rely upon the NSC and more inclined to use informal modes of consultation and liaison within the executive branch. By contrast, President Nixon made clear his determination to rely upon the NSC, whose staff was headed by Henry Kissinger, in order to assert his own authority in the foreign policy field. Some chief executives have preferred for the NSC to arrive at agreed-upon policy positions, reflecting a consensus among the group. Other presidents have viewed it as primarily a device for producing clear policy options for submission to, and final decision by, the president.

Some presidents (and John F. Kennedy was a prominent example) utilized the National Security Council mainly for purposes other than those for which it was created. According to one former State Department official, JFK used the mechanism of NSC to inform his subordinates "of what the President had already decided so they would not deviate from the line" and to give them "at least the illusion of participating in the formulation of foreign policy."[60] Under President Reagan, the National Security Council performed a different function. Reagan's national security adviser, William P. Clark, conceived of his role as serving as an "honest broker of ideas" for the chief executive. Inexperienced in the foreign policy field, Clark believed that his main task was to maintain a low profile and see that the president had full opportunity to consider a broad range of policy recommendations from his advisers. As one commentator expressed it, Clark theoretically "ensures proper procedures and the full debate of the issues so that the President, as jury, can render the policy verdicts."[61]

As the case studies to be presented in future chapters will indicate, the experience of each incumbent administration in utilizing the machinery of the National Security Council has varied widely since 1947. Two polar positions may be discerned. One was exemplified by the experience of the Truman administration and, to a lesser degree, by the Eisenhower administration (see Chapters 4 and 5). In this instance the National Security Council played a relatively uninfluential role in policy making. The NSC functioned primarily as a White House staff agency to clarify policy alternatives, to facilitate the process of policy formulation, and to allocate responsibilities for the implementation of policies decided upon by the president. Under Truman and Eisenhower, the president's national security adviser played a relatively inconspicuous and minor role in the overall foreign policy process.

The other polar position was represented by the extremely influential role of the national security adviser during the Nixon and Ford administrations, when Henry Kissinger held the position. During the early 1970s, Kissinger largely dominated the American foreign policy process; in effect he operated a "rival State Department" in the White House (see Chapter 7). Kissinger's unprecedented influence upon diplomatic decision making was possible, of course, only because of the president's concurrence and, in some instances, encouragement.

The existence of the National Security Council has not really solved the problem of recurrent conflicts and schisms within the executive branch on foreign policy decision making. Indeed, in some respects,

60. Ball, *Diplomacy for a Crowded World*, 199.
61. See the analysis of Hedrick Smith in the New York *Times*, July 8, 1982.

particularly when the NSC is headed by a Henry Kissinger, it may have aggravated the problem by adding another layer to an already complex foreign policy hierarchy, by generating confusion about who is really in charge of American foreign policy, and by providing the president insufficient opportunities to hear the views of experienced State Department officials on complex diplomatic questions before he arrives at decisions.[62]

In characteristically American fashion, for a generation or more, incumbent presidents have relied upon a wide assortment of administrative techniques for attempting to assure a unified foreign policy within the executive branch. It may safely be predicted that this pattern will continue into the future. In George Ball's view, there is no "optimum formula for relating the work of the [State Department] to the rest of the government." Or, as the Murphy Commission concluded in its study of America's foreign policy machinery in 1975, it was "impossible to commend one form [for coordinating foreign policy] to all Presidents at all times," and different coordinating devices and mechanisms "carry different advantages and imply different risks."[63]

62. Many descriptions and evaluations of the National Security Council system are available. Useful ones include Charles W. Yost, "Conduct of Multilateral Diplomacy by the United States Government," in *The Organization of the Government for the Conduct of Foreign Policy*, I, 285–86; James L. McCamy, *Conduct of the New Diplomacy* (New York, 1964), 121–41; Destler, *Presidents, Bureaucrats, and Foreign Policy*, 95–154; Keith C. Clark and Laurence J. Legere (eds.), *The President and the Management of National Security* (New York, 1969), 55–115; and I. M. Destler, "National Security Management: What Presidents Have Wrought," *Political Science Quarterly*, XCV (1980), 573–88.

63. Ball, *Diplomacy for a Crowded World*, 195; "Conclusions and Recommendations," in *The Organization of the Government for the Conduct of Foreign Policy*, III, 284.

3

The President as His Own Secretary of State: FDR and Hull

This chapter is the first of a series of case studies focusing upon leading examples from recent American diplomatic experience of the relationship among the president, the secretary of state, and other
influential actors in the foreign policy process. Within the limits of
the unique circumstances of each case, these chapters utilize a similar format to facilitate making meaningful comparisons and contrasts among them. The conclusions derived from these case studies
should illuminate a number of the significant and recurrent problems
confronting efforts by officials of the United States government to
achieve and maintain a unified approach to American foreign policy.

The era of President Franklin D. Roosevelt and Secretary of State
Cordell Hull was one of the most momentous in the saga of American
diplomacy. The dominant theme of their foreign policy, especially
after FDR's second term began in 1937, was an idea that Roosevelt
expressed forcefully to Britain's Prime Minister Winston Churchill
during World War II: "There is in this global war literally no question, either military or political, in which the United States is not interested." As much as any other statement by FDR during his long
tenure in the Oval Office, this one symbolized the fundamental transition in American diplomacy from the traditional "isolationist" to
the new "internationalist" approach that occurred during and after
World War II.[1] In the expressive words of Herbert Feis, down to the

1. Lloyd C. Gardner, *Imperial America: American Foreign Policy Since 1898* (New
York, 1976), 160. Background on America's isolationist tradition before and during the
New Deal is available in Norman A. Graebner, "Isolationism," in *International Encyclo-*

Japanese attack upon Pearl Harbor on December 7, 1941, the United States had attempted to follow a policy "of *existing* as a great power without acting like one" in its foreign relations.[2] Under Franklin D. Roosevelt, the United States made the historic transition from an isolationist to an internationalist or global policy, according to which America assumed commitments and responsibilities abroad commensurate with its vast power. This change has been accurately referred to as a revolution in American diplomacy, and it had profound implications for the American people and other societies as well.

The diplomacy of the Roosevelt administration was epochal in the nation's experience for another reason more directly related to the problem of disunity in American foreign policy. A leading study of the period has said concerning FDR's foreign policy role that "he took crucial diplomatic negotiations more completely into his own hands than any president before or since." Unlike his political mentor, Woodrow Wilson, Roosevelt largely succeeded in formulating, promulgating, and gaining a wide consensus supporting his foreign policy decisions. Perhaps more than any occupant of the Oval Office, during his long tenure as chief executive FDR largely served as "his own secretary of state." He personally made a number of crucial diplomatic decisions before and during World War II; few presidents have had the overall impact upon the course of American diplomacy that he did. As time passed, the kind of relationship that existed between Roosevelt and his secretary of state, Cordell Hull, was indicated by the latter's remarks to a friend on the eve of his retirement late in 1944. Hull confessed that he was "tired of intrigue . . . tired of being bypassed . . . tired of being relied on in public and ignored in private . . . tired of fighting battles which were not appreciated . . . tired of making speeches and holding press interviews—tired of talking and tired of service." Hull acknowledged that he was leaving the State Depart-

pedia of the Social Sciences (New York, 1968), VIII, 218–22; Wayne S. Cole, *Senator Gerald P. Nye and American Foreign Relations* (Minneapolis, 1962); Walter Lippmann, *Isolation and Alliances: An American Speaks to the British* (Boston, 1952); Raymond L. Buell, *Isolated America* (New York, 1940); Selig Adler, *The Isolationist Impulse: Its Twentieth Century Reaction* (New York, 1957); Albert K. Weinberg, "The Historical Meaning of the American Doctrine of Isolation," *American Political Science Review*, XXXIV (April, 1940), 539–47; Robert Maddox, *William E. Borah and American Foreign Policy* (Baton Rouge, 1969).

2. Herbert Feis, *The Road to Pearl Harbor* (New York, 1963), 19.

ment not with a feeling of satisfaction after his long service but with a feeling of bitterness.[3]

As was no less true of the Roosevelt administration's domestic policies, its diplomacy was controversial during FDR's incumbency and has remained so to this day. In terms of their long-range impact upon the future of American diplomacy, it would be difficult to imagine a more profoundly influential series of decisions than those made (or in some instances, those deferred) by President Roosevelt and his principal foreign policy aides immediately before and during World War II. Aside from merits or defects of the major substantive decisions made by the Roosevelt White House, it is clear that the Rooseveltian model of decision making has become an attractive one. To some degree, every postwar chief executive has been influenced by FDR's example. Some, like President Eisenhower during the closing months of his second term and President Nixon during the celebrated "opening" of China in the early 1970s, have been guided by the Rooseveltian model selectively and episodically. Other chief executives, such as John F. Kennedy, Lyndon Johnson, and Jimmy Carter, have injected themselves actively and decisively into the foreign policy process, often for the same reasons that prompted FDR to do so. In more general terms, the vast growth of presidential power witnessed since the New Deal—leading to the emergence of what is sometimes called the "imperial presidency"—owes much to FDR's determination to function as the de facto secretary of state. It may confidently be predicted that future chief executives will also find Roosevelt's example on the diplomatic front an attractive and useful set of precedents for dealing with external problems.

The Policy-Making Environment

When the Roosevelt administration assumed office early in 1933, conditions could hardly have been less propitious for diplomatic success by the president and his foreign policy team. With twelve million Americans unemployed and many hundreds of business enterprises

3. Dean Acheson, *Present at the Creation: My Years in the State Department* (New York, 1969), 87. See also *The Memoirs of Cordell Hull* (2 vols.; New York, 1948), I, 155–63, 191–210.

facing financial ruin, the United States was in the grip of the most serious economic crisis in its entire history, with no sign that recovery was within sight. Overseas, the government of Japan had already embarked upon its campaign to annex Manchuria and dominate China, and the League of Nations appeared to be powerless to prevent it. In retrospect, Japan's Manchuria venture was perhaps the opening phase of World War II. In the months ahead, Nazi Germany was to defy the Treaty of Versailles and extend its hegemony over weaker countries. It was joined in this aggressive course by Mussolini's Italy. The "appeasement" policies of the Western democracies did nothing to dissuade the Axis dictators from relying upon militarism to achieve their goals. Witnessing these distressing developments abroad, Congress and the American people reacted by clinging doggedly to their historic isolationist policies and seeking protection behind neutrality legislation. Roosevelt had campaigned in 1932 on a platform that rejected American cooperation with the League of Nations in responding to Axis expansionism, and as the months passed, sentiment in Congress and throughout the nation remained overwhelmingly against American participation in collective efforts to preserve peace, especially those that might entail the risk of war.[4]

President-elect Roosevelt selected a distinguished legislator, Cordell Hull of Tennessee, as his new secretary of state. By many criteria, the choice was ideal, as evidenced by Hull's unprecedented service in this position until late 1944. High on the list of FDR's priorities in choosing Hull for the position was the compelling need to unify the Democratic party—the prerequisite for congressional passage of the president's measures for dealing with the manifold problems created by the Great Depression. Hull's appointment was especially popular with the southern wing of the party. Before joining the administration, Hull had been elected to the Tennessee legislature, and he had served as both a representative and a senator in Congress from that state. Hull was, therefore, an experienced legislator who enjoyed wide

4. Major international developments, and America's response to them from 1933 until its entry into World War II, are discussed more fully in Mark L. Chadwin, *The Hawks of World War II* (Chapel Hill, 1968); Wayne S. Cole, *America First: The Battle Against Intervention, 1940–1941* (Madison, 1953); C. G. Fenwick, *American Neutrality: Trial and Failure* (New York, 1940); William L. Langer and S. Everett Gleason, *The Challenge to Isolation, 1937–1940* (New York, 1952), and *The Undeclared War, 1940–1941* (Gloucester, Mass., 1968); D. F. Drummond, *The Passing of American Neutrality, 1937–1941* (Ann Arbor, 1955); Feis, *The Road to Pearl Harbor.*

respect on Capitol Hill and among the Democratic party regulars. (It was no coincidence that he would make one of his most significant contributions in maintaining cooperative executive-legislative relations in behalf of Roosevelt's diplomatic undertakings, especially in postwar planning.) Hull had also served as a past chairman of the Democratic National Committee. He was an early supporter of Roosevelt for the presidency and worked energetically to assure his nomination in 1932 and his election and reelection thereafter. From the beginning then, political considerations had been crucial in FDR's choice of Hull to head the State Department, and throughout Roosevelt's tenure in office, the president never lost sight of Hull's political assets.[5]

In addition, Cordell Hull had certain other personal qualities that FDR admired and believed qualified Hull for the position. With Roosevelt, Hull was a dedicated Wilsonian: he sincerely believed in the rule of world law, in the necessity to resolve international disputes peaceably, in the need for equitable and civilized behavior by powerful nations, and in other Wilsonian precepts. According to one commentator, Roosevelt was also attracted by Hull's "dignity and high-mindedness"; Hull looked and demeaned himself "like a secretary of state." Fundamental agreement also existed between the president and Hull on basic policy issues. (As Hull more than once discovered, FDR's policy statements were not always congruent, however, with his private thoughts, communications, and subsequent behavior.) Shortly after Hull took office, the British ambassador to the United States described him as "an elderly gentleman" who was "amiable and courteous," who expressed idealistic and moralistic principles, but who had trouble "coming to the point" in discussing specific issues. With the passage of time—as Axis expansionism propelled the world closer to the brink of a new war—more than any other member of Roosevelt's official family, it was Cordell Hull who symbolized America's sense of outrage and moral indignation at the collapse of international law and order.[6]

Hull possessed another quality that sometimes contrasted sharply

5. Frank Freidel, *The Triumph* (Boston, 1956), 177–82, 230–31, 243. Vol. III of Freidel, *Franklin D. Roosevelt*, 4 vols. to date; James A. Farley, *Behind the Ballots: The Personal History of a Politician* (New York, 1938), 100–102; Harold B. Hinton, *Cordell Hull: A Biography* (Garden City, N.Y., 1942), 207–208.

6. *Memoirs of Cordell Hull*, I, 191–92; Frank Freidel, *Launching the New Deal* (Boston, 1973), 144–45, 364. Vol. IV of Freidel, *Franklin D. Roosevelt*, 4 vols. to date.

with other members of Roosevelt's entourage. He was described by his contemporaries as an individual of a "retiring disposition," who sought to avoid the limelight. Former Under Secretary of State Sumner Welles said that Hull was the "least self-seeking man I have ever known," that he was "content to stay in the background and let others take the credit and glory"—indispensable qualities for any secretary of state who served one of the most diplomatically active and publicity-minded chief executives in American history.[7]

Experience demonstrated that Hull had another personal quality that made possible his extraordinarily long tenure at the head of the State Department. He was devoted, methodical, and conscientious in performance of his duties and unstinting in his devotion to President Roosevelt and his program. He was also remarkably long-suffering in enduring the repeated slights, humiliations, and confusions resulting from Roosevelt's determination to act as his own secretary of state.[8]

What were the expectations of President Roosevelt and Secretary Hull concerning how the foreign policy process would normally operate after 1932? Hull has left little doubt about his conception of the office when he agreed to accept it. To his mind, it was essential that the chief executive and the secretary of state work "in complete cooperation"; that the president ultimately conduct the foreign affairs of the United States "through the State Department"; that the role of the secretary of state would not be limited merely to "carrying on . . . correspondence with foreign governments"; that he would play an active role "in the formulation and conduct of foreign policy"; and that, following full consultation with State Department experts on particular policy questions, the secretary of state would recommend policies to the president for approval. Once President Roosevelt had decided upon a policy, then the secretary of state would "carry it out through the State Department." Hull believed he had Roosevelt's firm commitment that, in FDR's own words, "We shall function in the manner you've stated." On that basis, Hull accepted the position of secretary of state.[9]

In his memoirs Hull paid tribute to his superior in the White House

7. Farley, *Behind the Ballots*, 101; Hinton, *Cordell Hull*, vi.
8. Farley, *Behind the Ballots*, 100–101; Hinton, *Cordell Hull*, vi–viii; Langer and Gleason, *The Challenge to Isolation*, 7–8, 11.
9. *Memoirs of Cordell Hull*, I, 158.

and expressed overall satisfaction with the kind of personal relationship that evolved between them. Thus, he observed that during his tenure, "never an unfriendly word" passed between himself and FDR and that policy disagreements were "threshed out earnestly and bluntly but in a friendly spirit." Nearly always, a "like-mindedness" governed their approach to external questions, Hull recalled, and in most instances Roosevelt adhered to his promise that Hull would participate fully in the formulation and administration of American foreign policy. To Hull's mind, FDR gave him—and he exercised—wide latitude in negotiations, in reaching certain agreements with other governments, in deciding when to bring external issues to the president's personal attention, in administering the State Department, and in other aspects of his official duties. For example, Hull and his subordinates made numerous policy recommendations to the president, supplied drafts of the president's speeches and other public statements, helped to brief FDR before he met with foreign leaders, and took other steps in the foreign policy field of which the general public was often unaware. Secretary Hull also recorded, with evident approval, that during the New Deal, the cabinet almost never dealt with major foreign policy questions. With other incumbents in the office, Secretary Hull viewed the cabinet as a totally unsuitable instrument of foreign policy decision making.[10]

Despite his evident admiration of, and loyalty to, Roosevelt, even Hull acknowledged that after the beginning of FDR's second term in 1937, the president turned his attention increasingly to foreign affairs. After the United States entered World War II, under his authority as the nation's commander in chief, FDR made innumerable military decisions, many of which had far-reaching diplomatic consequences. As a rule, Hull played little or no part in this process. Moreover, as Hull also admitted, Roosevelt tended to rely increasingly upon his personal envoys, or upon State Department officials and ambassadors with whom he had close personal ties, in making diplomatic decisions. Meanwhile, by the war Hull's health and vitality were beginning to decline. As a result, President Roosevelt became the nation's chief diplomat in fact as well as in name. Secretary Hull and his subordinates in the State Department as often as not were

10. *Ibid.*, 191–210.

bypassed in reaching key diplomatic decisions, and his duties became more and more to preside over a department whose waning influence was evident to observers both within the United States and abroad.

Unlike some other occupants of the office, Secretary of State Hull understood a number of realities governing the influence and public image of the department he led. He knew, for example, that nearly every secretary of state in American history had engaged in battles with Congress. To his mind, by their very nature the State Department and the national legislature had different perspectives on external policy. He believed that diplomatic business could not be conducted "with wide-open publicity"—a fact that often alienated Congress and the news media. He defended another practice that often elicited vocal opposition on Capitol Hill—the making of executive agreements between heads of state, as substitutes for treaties.[11]

Hull comprehended another reality whose effect upon the conduct of American diplomacy was especially potent during the New Deal. American public opinion has always been skeptical about diplomacy, and this skepticism perhaps reached its zenith during the 1930s. During that period, dedicated isolationists were certain that the Roosevelt administration was steadily propelling the nation into the vortex of World War II. Conversely, left-wing radicals and certain liberals were no less critical of the State Department, believing that it was unresponsive to crises abroad, unduly influenced by the British Foreign Office, and devoted to the status quo. Among many influential literary figures and public groups (and Ernest Hemingway and John Dos Passos were prominent examples), a "disillusionist" viewpoint toward war and international politics in general was fashionable. This frame of mind was exemplified by the Nye committee of Congress, which during the mid-1930s conducted a prolonged investigation of America's role in World War I. Although the committee found little reliable evidence to support the contention, many of its members and supporters throughout the United States were convinced that war profiteers and munitions makers at home, in league with the British government, had drawn the United States into that conflict. The implication of the committee's approach was that in the future

11. *Ibid.*, 211–21.

America must not be manipulated into entering a new foreign conflict that did not involve its interests.[12]

National policy makers during the New Deal were familiar with another characteristic of American public opinion as it related to foreign affairs. Frequent changes of mood, cycles, and sudden variations between the extremes of isolationism and interventionism have always characterized American opinion on foreign policy questions, and public attitudes in the United States have been crucially influenced by developments abroad. During the New Deal era, American public opinion toward diplomatic questions was more than ordinarily unstable, confused, and marked by inconsistencies and anomalies.[13]

Down to the Japanese attack on Pearl Harbor, Americans desired to avoid war, to have their neutrality respected by belligerents, and to concentrate upon domestic concerns. As one vulnerable nation after another was subject to Axis domination, however, Americans also condemned aggression and international lawbreaking. They became increasingly disillusioned with the results of appeasement as a response to Axis expansionism, and they were progressively more receptive to providing "all aid short of war" to the beleaguered Allies. Yet, relatively few Americans grasped the implications of their attitudes in terms of the nation's ability to escape involvement in foreign conflicts. As occurred many times in the postwar period, Americans in time wanted the administration to "do something" about events overseas that alarmed them. But they were by no means clear about what steps the president should take; nor did they comprehend the full implications of their demands and discontents. In the prewar era, as in the postwar period, inconsistencies and incongruities were a normal part of the public response to accelerating global and regional crises.[14]

12. See *ibid.*, 216–17, 398–405, 510–11. More extended analyses of the "disillusionist" mentality and its effects upon New Deal diplomacy are available in Walter Lippmann, *The Public Philosophy* (Boston, 1955), 16–28; Wayne S. Cole, *Senator Gerald P. Nye and American Foreign Relations* (Minneapolis, 1962); John E. Wiltz, *In Search of Peace: The Senate Munitions Inquiry, 1934–1936* (Baton Rouge, 1963); and the extensive excerpts from the Nye committee's hearings in Arthur M. Schlesinger, Jr. (ed.), *Congress Investigates: A Documented History, 1792–1974* (5 vols.; New York, 1975), IV, 2735–2919.

13. F. L. Klingberg, "The Historical Alternation of Moods in American Foreign Policy," *World Politics*, IV (January, 1952), 239–73.

14. See Ralph B. Levering, *The Public and American Foreign Policy, 1918–1978* (New York, 1978), 66–86. Other evidence of American public attitudes toward New Deal diplomacy is available in Hadley Cantril (ed.), *Public Opinion, 1935–1946* (Westport,

President Roosevelt and his advisers confronted a public opinion that was highly fragmented on foreign policy issues. In time, not only was public sentiment divided between the polarities of isolationism and interventionism, but significant differences of opinion on the proper course America should follow diplomatically existed within both groups. Among interventionists, for example, some advocated that the United States go it alone, *i.e.*, revert to its customary practice of responding to foreign crises unilaterally, while others called for close American cooperation with the League of Nations. Still other groups believed that America's "moral leadership" could avert the drift toward global war; other organizations (always a minority before Pearl Harbor) advocated all-out American aid to Allies and the application of military power against Axis expansionism. For the majority of Americans, however, public appeals and arguments were probably less decisive in shaping their attitudes toward developments abroad than the momentary ebb and flow of events.[15]

Throughout his presidency, Roosevelt faced a public milieu that was, in the words of one study, "undisciplined, ill-informed, bewildered and insufficiently war-conscious." As late as 1943, America's abandonment of isolationism and its belated adoption of a role of international leadership was viewed as "probably a temporary sentiment which public opinion might whimsically abandon at any time." As in the past, popular attitudes toward foreign policy issues were judged to be "mercurial" and strongly influenced by emotional factors. As one well-informed student of American culture concluded, paradoxical as it might appear, the champions of an isolationist and an interventionist approach to foreign relations perhaps had a common objective. A leading goal of interventionists, for example—the establishment of a new international organization (in time called the United Nations) to maintain global peace and security—could be viewed as simply a different means for accomplishing a purpose shared by isolationists: relieving the United States of the direct responsibility for assuming unwanted international commitments.[16]

Conn., 1978); and Michael Leigh, *Mobilizing Consent: Public Opinion and American Foreign Policy, 1937–1947* (Westport, Conn., 1976).

15. Levering, *The Public and American Foreign Policy*, 71.

16. Thomas E. Hachey (ed.), *Confidential Dispatches: Analyses of America by the British Ambassador, 1939–1945* (Evanston, Ill., 1974), xxx–xxxi; Max Lerner, *America as a Civilization* (New York, 1957), 881–907.

The inconsistent and unstable nature of American public opinion on foreign policy issues during the New Deal unquestionably had an impact upon the formulation and administration of foreign relations. If, for example, the Roosevelt administration's approach to external problems often appeared hesitant, erratic, and unpredictable, that fact could be attributed in no small measure to fundamental divisions among the American people themselves concerning the nation's proper foreign policy role. As the leader of the world's oldest democracy, FDR was of course required to take account of public opinion in the United States. Even more than ordinarily, however, the president was often faced with the extremely difficult challenge of determining what the American people really wanted their leaders to do in responding to external crises and problems.

The inconsistent and confused state of American public opinion on diplomatic questions had another important result in accounting for the kind of relationship that developed between President Roosevelt and Secretary of State Hull. As in other periods of American history, the existence of widespread public anxiety, confusion, and uncertainty toward developments abroad provided wide scope for the exercise of vigorous presidential leadership. As events after World War II repeatedly demonstrated, under such conditions the American people have customarily looked to the White House, rather than to Congress, for guidance and effective action in responding to external challenges. FDR was prepared to supply the dynamic diplomatic leadership that the American people expected.[17]

Roosevelt's Foreign Policy Style and Administrative Principles

During the Roosevelt era, the foreign policy process in the United States was a unique and complex—and in some respects a remark-

17. Roosevelt's diplomatic leadership on the eve of and during World War II provides a classic example of what one study calls the "rally round the flag" phenomenon, *i.e.* the fact that foreign crises almost invariably result in a significant increase in the popularity of the incumbent president. Thus, FDR's popularity soared after the Japanese attack on Pearl Harbor. Perhaps the intensity of the ensuing conflict was a major factor accounting for the fact that Roosevelt was rated by the American people as the most popular (not necessarily of course, the greatest or most successful) president of the United States ever. See John E. Mueller, *War, Presidents and Public Opinion* (New York, 1973), 194, 208–209.

able and mystifying—phenomenon. Some degree of distinctiveness is no doubt characteristic of every administration in Washington, but for several reasons the model of foreign policy making identified with the Roosevelt administration was incomparable.

To no inconsiderable degree, these unique features derived from the personality, goals, and administrative style of President Roosevelt. An accomplished political strategist, FDR relied upon his impressive talents and, despite his physical handicap, enormous personal energy and magnetism to dominate the decision-making process from his inauguration in 1933 until his death in 1945. As much as any chief executive in American history, Roosevelt would be classified as a strong president whose influence was decisive in nearly every major aspect of foreign and domestic policy.

A discernible change in Roosevelt's interest in foreign affairs had occurred by the beginning of his second term in 1937. As time passed, he became increasingly involved in the management of foreign relations. Yet his background, experience, and expertise on diplomatic questions were seldom commensurate with his impact upon external developments. One student of New Deal diplomacy has said concerning FDR's understanding of the principle of collective security and the concept of international organization, for example, that he strongly favored these ideas as embodied by the end of World War II in the nascent United Nations organization. Yet, "characteristically, Roosevelt never made any detailed analysis of the principle of collective security," and he had "few deep convictions regarding the details or structure of the machinery of collective security." Not untypically, Roosevelt's dedication to the goal greatly exceeded his understanding of it and the problems associated with its realization.[18]

Another distinctive trait of Roosevelt's approach to foreign policy questions was his essentially eclectic and pragmatic frame of mind. FDR tended to concern himself with immediate and urgent problems, and he left to his advisers the challenge of explaining his actions by providing a theoretical framework for them. Roosevelt, one commentator has said, "liked it that way: the more theories the better"! In his outlook on foreign affairs, the president often exhibited conflicting

18. Willard Range, "FDR—A Reflection of American Idealism," in Warren F. Kimball (ed.), *Franklin D. Roosevelt and the World Crisis, 1937–1945* (Lexington, Mass., 1973), 249–50.

and incongruous attitudes. For example, although he came to epitomize the new internationalism that governed American policy abroad, in reality many aspects of the New Deal program were highly nationalistic, exhibiting little concern about the economic recovery or welfare of other societies. Roosevelt's approach to the problem of Axis expansionism exhibited a similar duality. On one hand, as in his famous "quarantine speech" of October 5, 1937, he condemned international lawlessness and violence and called for collective action to deter Axis hegemony. On the other hand, a few months later he congratulated British Prime Minister Neville Chamberlain for relying upon appeasement as a method of preserving global peace. Similarly, Roosevelt was a tireless champion of democracy and a defender of the rights of small nations. Yet, as the end of World War II approached, his "grand design" for postwar peace and stability envisioned a decisive role in international decision making by the Big Five (the Soviet Union, Great Britain, France, China, and the United States); for certain key postwar issues, decisions would be made by the Soviet Union and the United States alone. Indeed, FDR believed that the leadership required to usher in a new era of global peace and security might have to be supplied mainly by the United States.[19]

In one of his "fireside chats" to the American people in 1934 President Roosevelt had said: "I believe in practical explanations and in practical policies." A commentator has characterized the New Deal by saying that it was "not so much a consistent, carefully planned, comprehensive program" as it was a series of *ad hoc* responses to immediate internal problems. Basically, the same pragmatic orientation governed FDR's approach to foreign policy issues. As one of his leading biographers has said, he "was a practical man who proceeded now boldly, now cautiously, step by step toward immediate ends." He was both a "Soldier of Faith," whose actions were motivated by high moral and ideological principles, and he was no less a "Prince of the State," determined to protect the interests of the United States in a dangerous and chaotic world.[20]

19. Gardner, *Imperial America*, 124–35; Paul Seabury, *The Rise and Decline of the Cold War* (New York, 1967), 44; Range, "FDR—A Reflection of American Idealism," 250–61.
20. Samuel I. Rosenman (comp.), *The Public Papers and Addresses of Franklin D. Roosevelt, 1934* (13 vols.; New York, 1938–50), III, 312–18; Gerald Nash, *The Great Depres-*

The diplomacy of the New Deal, therefore, was a mélange or patchwork of short-term and long-range goals, of traditional and often highly innovative methods, and of improvised solutions to urgent external problems. As a result, Roosevelt's critics—and sometimes even some of his supporters—doubted whether his administration really had a foreign policy at all in the sense of a coherent, logically consistent, and carefully formulated approach to international problems. In effect, as the manager of American foreign relations for more than a decade, Roosevelt in his approach exemplified a concept—the principle of "the free hand"—that had been a hallmark of American isolationism since the late eighteenth century.[21]

In his effort to function as "his own secretary of state," Roosevelt employed a number of devices and administrative techniques designed to retain the power of ultimate decision making in the White House. For one thing, he relied heavily upon his power to make appointments to subordinate positions in the State Department. For the position of under secretary of state in his new administration, for example, FDR personally chose his old friend William Phillips, a "Boston Brahmin" who was also an experienced diplomat. As in the choice of Cordell Hull to head the department, political considerations loomed large in FDR's appointment of Phillips, who was especially popular with the internationalist wing of the Democratic party. As assistant secretary of state, Roosevelt appointed another trusted friend, a member of the "brain trust" that advised FDR early in the New Deal, Raymond Moley. As one student of the New Deal explained, it was expected that Moley would "act as political and economic ad-

---

sion and World War II: Organizing America, 1933–1945 (New York, 1979), 18; James M. Burns, "FDR—'Both Fixer and Preacher,'" in Kimball (ed.), Franklin D. Roosevelt and the World Crisis, 281–82.

21. See the conclusion of the French diplomat and authority on American affairs André de Laboulaye, for example, that in his diplomacy Roosevelt presented a "complex, enigmatic face of an unpredictable human being," that his diplomatic moves were subject to a wide variety of conflicting interests and forces, and that he was prone to "puzzling vacillations" in foreign affairs. But according to another observer, the key to Roosevelt's external policies was the fact that he was "above all an empiricist" who "lacked doctrine or consistent plans." Howard C. Payne, Raymond Callahan, and Edward M. Bennett, As the Storm Clouds Gathered: European Perceptions of American Foreign Policy in the 1930s (Durham, N.C., 1979), 28. Roosevelt's leadership techniques are discussed in Louis W. Koenig, The Presidency and Crisis: Powers of the Office from the Invasion of Poland to Pearl Harbor (New York, 1944).

viser extraordinary to the President." Secretary of State Hull understood that in fact "Moley would have nothing to do with the State Department" but would deal directly (and over Hull's head) with the
White House. As time passed, another State Department subordinate,
Under Secretary of State Sumner Welles, became FDR's main channel of communication with the department.[22]

In other cases the president personally chose delegates to international conferences, wrote their instructions, and communicated his
views directly to them while negotiations were in progress. In one
celebrated instance—the wartime Casablanca Conference (January
14–24, 1943)—FDR purposely excluded Secretary Hull from the
deliberations.[23]

Another Rooseveltian tactic—one of FDR's singular contributions
to American diplomatic practice—was his reliance upon "direct diplomacy," as exemplified by the direct telephone link connecting the
Oval Office with No. 10 Downing Street during World War II. Using
this device, Roosevelt and Churchill made a number of crucial wartime decisions. FDR was also a strong advocate of "summit diplomacy." Although he did not invent the technique (his mentor, Woodrow
Wilson, had employed it dramatically at the end of World War I),
Roosevelt institutionalized summit conferences, making them a normal and customary feature of the American foreign policy process. In
a series of important wartime conferences—at Casablanca, Quebec,
Moscow, Cairo, Tehran, Yalta, and, under the Truman administration,
Potsdam—Allied leaders dealt with military and political issues related to the war. Some of these meetings, such as the Atlantic Conference in 1941 between Roosevelt and Churchill, were held without
Secretary of State Hull's knowledge; in nearly all instances, even for
those conferences Hull attended, his influence upon the deliberations
was usually minimal.

Extensive and continuing correspondence with other Allied leaders
was another device FDR employed for conducting foreign relations.
A highly influential example is the voluminous Churchill-Roosevelt
correspondence. Supplemented by numerous transatlantic telephone

22. Hinton, *Cordell Hull*, 210; Robert Dallek, *Franklin D. Roosevelt and American Foreign Policy, 1932–1945* (New York, 1979), 33–34.
23. Julius W. Pratt, *Cordell Hull, 1933–1944* (New York, 1964). Vol. II of Robert H.
Ferrell (ed.), *The American Secretaries of State and Their Diplomacy*. 570.

calls between the two leaders, the correspondence dealt with a number of the war's important military and diplomatic questions. In several key instances, especially when absolute secrecy was required to preserve the confidentiality of military moves, FDR deliberately refrained from informing his advisers of the contents of these messages and the commitments he had assumed as a result of them.[24]

As the chief executive, FDR communicated directly with American ambassadors and his own personal agents abroad, and as often as not, the State Department was kept in the dark about these messages and directives. For example, as ambassador to Vichy France during World War II, Admiral William Leahy often corresponded directly with the White House, without routing his messages through the State Department. It was a testimony to Hull's loyalty to Roosevelt that the secretary of state repeatedly and publicly defended the administration's policies toward Vichy France, which were unpopular. A number of foreign governments, such as those of Stalin and Chiang Kai-shek, concluded that Secretary of State Hull had relatively little influence upon the foreign policy process in the United States. They preferred to transact their diplomatic business directly with the president, and FDR did little to discourage this practice.[25]

Another technique relied upon by FDR to preserve his dominant position in the foreign policy process was his determination that the State Department should have no role in deciding "military" questions, many of which of course had far-reaching diplomatic implications. Thus, in 1942, Hull was not consulted when FDR created the Combined Chiefs of Staff and other agencies having military or quasi-military responsibilities. As a result, Hull was cut off "from official concern with military matters" for the duration of his term in office.[26] Among the president's military decisions, three may be specifically mentioned. One was FDR's insistence that the resolution of political issues arising among the Allies must await the achievement of victory. The result, as in the case of the Soviet occupation of Eastern Europe and the division of Korea and Indochina, was that military deci-

24. Koenig, *The Presidency and Crisis*, 18–19; see also Frances E. Lowenheim (ed.), *Roosevelt and Churchill: Their Secret Wartime Correspondence* (New York, 1975).

25. William L. Langer, *Our Vichy Gamble* (New York, 1957); Admiral W. D. Leahy, *I Was There* (New York, 1950); De Conde, *The American Secretary of State*, 105; Pratt, *Cordell Hull*, 648–49.

26. Pratt, *Cordell Hull*, 532.

sions often produced political outcomes that were not in the interest of the United States and its allies. Second, President Roosevelt personally decided that the European theater of war should have priority over the Pacific theater. Third, FDR accepted the advice of his military staff, especially its army spokesman, that Soviet entry into the Pacific war was essential for victory over Japan, to avoid massive American casualties in the final assault on the Japanese homeland. As Stalin pledged, the USSR did join in the war against the Japanese enemy, though the development of the atomic bomb made its participation unnecessary. Soviet entry into the Pacific conflict, however, greatly enhanced Moscow's position in China, Korea, and other Asian settings in the postwar era.

Still another device employed by President Roosevelt for managing foreign affairs was the executive agreement, an understanding with other heads of state arrived at by the president or his designated agents. In many cases an executive agreement entails no participation by Congress. During the Roosevelt administration and since, not infrequently the existence of such agreements has been kept secret from Congress and the American people for varying periods of time. FDR did not invent this diplomatic device, but he frequently relied upon executive agreements to influence the course of American diplomacy during the New Deal. As Louis W. Koenig concluded, it became clear from the experience of the Roosevelt administration that "the President can accomplish by Executive Agreement anything that can be done by treaty."[27]

A celebrated example of Roosevelt's use of executive agreements to accomplish his diplomatic purposes was the "destroyer-base deal," announced on September 3, 1940, between Great Britain and the United States. In exchange for some fifty overage American destroyers badly needed in the defense of Britain, the United States obtained naval-base sites in Newfoundland, Bermuda, and the Caribbean. The fact that this understanding took the form of an executive agreement—and that it was unquestionably at variance with the spirit of

27. Koenig, *The Presidency and Crisis,* 26. More extended discussions of reliance upon executive agreements by modern presidents for managing foreign relations are available in Cecil V. Crabb, Jr., and Pat Holt, *Invitation to Struggle: Congress, the President and Foreign Policy* (Washington, D.C., 1980), 13–14; and Loch Johnson and James M. McCormick, "Foreign Policy by Executive Fiat," *Foreign Policy,* XXVIII (Fall, 1977), 117–39.

American neutrality toward the conflict in Europe—elicited sharp outcries from the administration's critics.[28]

An even more controversial and far-reaching instance of FDR's penchant for understandings among heads of state was the comprehensive set of agreements reached at the Yalta Conference (February 4–9, 1945). This meeting of the "Big Three" (Roosevelt, Churchill, and Stalin) was in many respects the most important summit conference during World War II. The agenda covered such diverse issues as the treatment to be accorded defeated Germany, the future of Poland and Eastern Europe, and plans for the nascent United Nations organization. Some provisions of these agreements remained secret for many months, and for several years after 1945, the results of the Yalta Conference elicited heated political controversy within the United States. Yet, the dominant reality about these understandings perhaps was the fact that their terms bound the Roosevelt and later administrations diplomatically and in many respects determined the nature of the post–World War II international system.[29]

Another noteworthy trait of Roosevelt as a diplomatic leader was his penchant for secrecy and his preference for relying upon a small number of trusted advisers (and even some of these were not always privy to the president's diplomatic transactions). Thus, one biographer refers to the "little cabinet" with which FDR consulted about many wartime decisions. But even with this group of advisers, Roosevelt sometimes personally made decisions without adequate consultation and repeatedly played off one subordinate against another, often to the detriment of morale in the State Department and other federal agencies.[30]

Two other influential techniques of Rooseveltian diplomacy method deserve brief analysis. One was his frequent reliance upon personal representatives and handpicked presidential agents to resolve diplomatic questions. The other was his creation of a host of new "alphabetical agencies," many of which had major and minor responsibili-

28. Thomas A. Bailey, *A Diplomatic History of the American People* (8th ed.; New York, 1968), 718–20.

29. J. L. Snell (ed.), *The Meaning of Yalta* (Baton Rouge, 1956); Edward R. Stettinius, Jr., *Roosevelt and the Russians: The Yalta Conference* (Garden City, N.Y., 1949); Lisle A. Rose, *After Yalta* (New York, 1973).

30. James M. Burns, *Roosevelt: The Lion and the Fox* (New York, 1956), 465. FDR's "little cabinet" consisted of James M. Byrnes, Judge Samuel I. Rosenman, Harry Hopkins, and Admiral William D. Leahy.

ties in the foreign policy field. FDR's fondness for reliance upon his own personal agents for diplomatic assignments became legendary. This technique was symbolized by FDR's delegation to his closest White House aide, Harry Hopkins, of a wide variety of diplomatic missions, many of which Hopkins carried out without the knowledge of the State Department. In time, in Robert Sherwood's words, Hopkins became known "as Roosevelt's own personal Foreign Office," and he assumed "much of the day-to-day business of diplomacy" for the administration. One foreign government after another came to view Hopkins as the de facto secretary of state and to transact their business with him. Again early in 1941, when Roosevelt appointed W. Averell Harriman as the "expediter" of the Lend-Lease Program to Great Britain, Harriman dealt directly with the British government, bypassing the American embassy there, and with the White House, often leaving the State Department ignorant of his activities.[31]

Earlier, FDR had designated William C. Bullitt to carry on negotiations with the Soviet Union. Bullitt later served as American ambassador to the USSR. Another presidential envoy was General Patrick J. Hurley, who served as the president's personal representative, with the rank of ambassador, to Iran late in 1942. Despite Hurley's lack of expertise on the Middle East, Roosevelt said that Hurley was one person on whom he could depend, in contrast to "those career diplomats" in the State Department, of whom he said, "Half the time I can't tell whether I believe them or not." As usual, State Department officials were dubious about Hurley's credentials and the results of his diplomatic activities within the country. In Iran and elsewhere, FDR's reliance upon what one experienced American ambassador derisively called "latter-day circumnavigating Magellans" of diplomacy, such as Hurley, seldom elicited State Department enthusiasm. In this not untypical assessment, such presidential envoys (who seldom possessed any noteworthy training for their tasks) "produced bewilderment or havoc abroad, and not infrequently both," and almost

---

31. Robert E. Sherwood, *Roosevelt and Hopkins: An Intimate History* (2 vols.; New York, 1948), I, 268–69, 169. Harriman's experiences as a personal agent of Roosevelt and President Truman are described in detail in W. Averell Harriman and Elie Abel, *Special Envoy to Churchill and Stalin, 1941–1946* (New York, 1975). See also Robert Murphy, *Diplomat Among Warriors* (New York, 1964).

invariably they detracted from the authority and prestige of the State Department in the foreign policy field.[32]

A Rooseveltian device that gave the diplomacy of the time much of its disorderly character was the creation of a host of new governmental agencies having greater or lesser responsibilities in foreign relations. Roosevelt also permitted (and, not infrequently, encouraged) established agencies to extend their jurisdictions into the foreign policy realm. These tendencies, coupled with Roosevelt's reluctance to dismiss incompetent or overly ambitious subordinates, resulted in the creation of a vast complex of executive departments, agencies, and bureaus that collectively formed the American foreign policy establishment—an intricate network theoretically being coordinated by the White House. Yet by the end of World War II, it was doubtful that even Roosevelt himself was aware of all the federal agencies involved in foreign relations and still less likely that he could untangle their often overlapping functions and jurisdictions. The responsibility for diplomatic decision making, said Dean Acheson, was ultimately "scattered all over Washington," with the State Department becoming "a shrinking place" in the foreign policy process.[33] In limited space, it is possible to convey only a sketchy and suggestive idea of this unprecedented bureaucratic proliferation.

To the State Department, for example, FDR added the Office of the Coordinator of Inter-American Affairs, popularly known as the Rockefeller committee, whose purpose was to generate support for the Good Neighbor policy throughout Latin America and to enhance the influence of the United States south of the border. In time, this new bureau found its domain in turn invaded by another new entry, the Office of the Coordinator of Information, which the White House added to the State Department bureaucracy. This latter office later evolved into the Office of Strategic Services (OSS), headed by another favorite of FDR's, General Wild Bill Donovan. The OSS carried out a number of secret intelligence missions during the war and served as the nucleus after the war of the Central Intelligence Agency (CIA), cre-

32. Bruce R. Kuniholm, *The Origins of the Cold War in the Near East: Great Power Conflict and Diplomacy in Iran, Turkey, and Greece* (Princeton, 1980), 164–77; Ellis Briggs, *Farewell to Foggy Bottom* (New York, 1964), 296; *Memoirs of Cordell Hull*, I, 200–201.
33. Acheson, *Present at the Creation*, 39.

ated in 1947. These additions to the foreign policy bureaucracy were predictably resented by old-line specialists on Latin America and other officials identified with the State Department establishment.[34]

By contrast, the elimination and consolidation of other administrative divisions within the State Department clearly reflected President Roosevelt's diplomatic inclinations and affected the foreign relations of the United States for years to come. A notable case involved closing the Division of Eastern European Affairs as a separate administrative unit. (Its staff was merged with the Division of Western European Affairs.) In some measure, this move was dictated by FDR's conviction that State Department experts were overly critical of his efforts to arrive at and maintain friendly relations with the Soviet Union during and after the war. Admittedly, as the end of the war approached, many State Department officials, such as George F. Kennan and Charles E. Bohlen, seriously questioned whether the "strange alliance" would endure in the postwar era and indeed whether any real community of interests existed between the Western allies and the Soviet state. Yet, despite his own lack of background or expertise on the internal and external policies of the Soviet Union, Roosevelt appeared to be minimally influenced by such doubts.[35]

By executive order in 1942, Roosevelt created the Board of Economic Warfare (BEW), whose assignment was to determine the nature and destination of American exports with a view to facilitating the war effort. Once more, State Department officials were convinced that BEW was exercising its historic functions and intruding upon its historic domain. Under Secretary of State Sumner Welles was reported as having felt anguish over this development. Subsequently, Secretary Hull, who had been absent from Washington when BEW was set up, blamed Welles and other State Department officials for permitting this new encroachment on the department's jurisdiction.[36]

Once America entered World War II, numerous new agencies were created in Washington for such purposes as to administer the Lend-

34. Allen Dulles, *The Craft of Intelligence* (New York, 1965); William R. Corson, *The Armies of Ignorance: The Rise of the American Intelligence Empire* (New York, 1977); Robert Bendiner, *The Riddle of the State Department* (New York, 1942), 208–209.
35. William E. Kinsella, Jr., *Leadership in Isolation: FDR and the Origins of the Second World War* (Cambridge, Mass., 1978), 217–18; George F. Kennan, *Memoirs, 1925–1950* (New York, 1969), esp. 87–90, 173–314.
36. Bendiner, *The Riddle of the State Department*, 209–10.

Lease Program, to mount a propaganda campaign, to conduct economic warfare, to carry out secret intelligence and other missions, and, as the war drew to a close, to administer relief and rehabilitation programs. Some of these activities were nominally under State Department supervision. In reality, however, the result of this bureaucratic proliferation was to create what one former American diplomat called a large circle of "semi-secretaries of state" in the White House and elsewhere in Washington. The progressively infirm and frustrated Hull was compelled to stay in Washington "trying to keep track of what his competitors were up to."[37]

Secretary of State Hull and his State Department aides also encountered continuing intrusions into the diplomatic realm by established departments and agencies. Although Hull himself was widely respected, the department that he headed frequently was not. An outspoken critic of it was Secretary of the Interior Harold Ickes, who believed that, in its negotiations with Japan before Pearl Harbor, the State Department was staffed by "appeasers" who totally misunderstood the nature of the Japanese threat to American security. After 1941, Secretary of War Henry Stimson, who had been the secretary of state in the Hoover administration and was one of two leading Republicans in FDR's cabinet, believed that Hull's strong aversion to the leader of the Free French, General Charles de Gaulle, was an impediment to the Allied war effort. Thus, he urged the president to disregard Hull's advice, and in the main FDR accepted Stimson's view.[38]

The most prominent case of intrusion into the State Department's traditional domain, however, came at the end of World War II when Secretary of the Treasury Henry Morgenthau, Jr., convinced President Roosevelt to adopt what became known as the Morgenthau Plan for the treatment of Germany after the Allied victory. Perhaps because of his Jewish background and his wide connections within the Jewish community, Morgenthau was almost fanatically anti-Nazi and determined to "solve" the German problem once and for all. Accordingly, he rejected the idea of a soft or moderate policy toward defeated Germany; his plan would in effect have dismembered Germany and reduced it to a pastoral nation incapable of waging

37. John P. Davies, Jr., *Foreign and Other Affairs* (New York, 1964), 184.
38. Pratt, *Cordell Hull*, 512, 585.

aggressive war. At the second Quebec Conference in September, 1944, which Secretary Hull did not attend, Morgenthau first obtained President Roosevelt's, and then Prime Minister Churchill's, consent to his scheme for occupied Germany.

Calling the Morgenthau Plan a proposal based upon the idea of "blind vengeance," Secretary Hull, joined in time by Harry Hopkins and other presidential advisers, finally prevailed upon FDR to change his position. Critics of the Morgenthau Plan contended that it was infeasible; that, contrary to its intentions, its effect would be enduring German resentment and ill will, perhaps guaranteeing the emergence of a new war in Europe; and that its administration would constitute an intolerable military and economic burden for the United States. Such arguments ultimately persuaded FDR to abandon the Morgenthau Plan in favor of a much less harsh and vindictive approach to the German question. The stability of West German democracy for more than a generation after World War II, along with the country's successful integration into the regional NATO defense complex, suggests that the State Department assessment was a better one than that of the Treasury Department.[39]

Sources of Roosevelt's Diplomatic Activism

What factors motivated President Roosevelt to serve as his own secretary of state? Mention can be made initially of FDR's distrust of the State Department—not in the sense (as occurred widely in the late 1940s and early 1950s) of doubting its loyalty to the United States, but in the sense of having little confidence in its ability to carry out his policies energetically and imaginatively. Much as the president respected Hull, for example, he regarded him as often unduly cautious, as restrained by the State Department bureaucracy, and as incapable of the kind of bold diplomatic initiatives the president believed were required for responding to fast-moving and often novel developments overseas. As one commentator observed, Roosevelt exhibited a "tolerant amusement" with Secretary Hull, regarding him

39. *Memoirs of Cordell Hull*, II, 1610–15; Sherwood, *Roosevelt and Hopkins*, II, 818–19, 832.

as a "dignified figurehead who went to banquets and conversed amiably with ambassadors."[40]

A second factor was that FDR's own personality, operating style, boundless energy, and imagination combined to produce what one experienced observer described as "a witch's brew of maladministration" in foreign affairs. For example, FDR exhibited little interest in the administrative details of diplomatic undertakings. He preferred to enunciate broad and often vague foreign policy principles that his subordinates were left to interpret and to apply to specific cases. As he assumed a growing burden of foreign policy responsibilities (while he also remained deeply involved in domestic aspects of the New Deal program), he had neither the time nor the inclination to coordinate the vast administrative structure he had created or to impose central direction upon it. The need for such coordination would become a principal argument for the establishment, and the increasing influence, of the White House staff in the foreign policy process (see especially Chapter 7).[41]

Third, considerable impetus for the emergence of President Roosevelt as a dynamic leader in foreign affairs was supplied by foreign opinion, particularly official and unofficial British opinion. During Britain's "darkest hour" before the United States entered World War II, it had become apparent that only America could halt Axis expansionism. The president of the United States, said the London *Times*, had become "unquestionably the most powerful individual in the world"; it voiced a hope that President Roosevelt "appreciates his new strength and that he means to use it for the good . . . of the world." To British minds, FDR personified those ideas and qualities— confidence in an eventual Allied victory, devotion to democracy, power coupled with the lack of hegemonial ambitions, and constructive energy and imagination—required to defeat the Axis threat. Vigorous diplomatic leadership by the American chief executive was viewed as essential for the survival of democracy and the realization of peace.[42]

40. Sherwood, *Roosevelt and Hopkins*, II, 754–55; Kuniholm, *The Origins of the Cold War in the Near East*, 174; Donald P. Warwick, *A Theory of Public Bureaucracy: Politics, Personality, and Organization in the State Department* (Cambridge, Mass., 1975), 15–16; Kinsella, *Leadership in Isolation*, 150.

41. Arthur Krock, quoted in Pratt, *Cordell Hull*, 615–16; Burns, *Roosevelt: The Lion and the Fox*, 371–72; Acheson, *Present at the Creation*, 47.

42. John Dizikes, *Britain, Roosevelt and the New Deal, 1932–1938* (New York, 1979), 290–310.

Fourth, after the United States entered World War II, the wartime need for secrecy prompted Roosevelt to bypass the State Department and to limit his advisers to a small circle of trusted confidants. This was especially true of decisions having military application and of extremely sensitive decisions affecting inter-Allied relations before the Axis defeat, such as the date and terms of the Soviet Union's entry into the Japanese war.[43]

Finally, a number of informed students of the Roosevelt era believe that much of its pattern of foreign policy decision making could be attributed to FDR's divide-and-rule approach to administration. According to this interpretation, Roosevelt tolerated—and in many instances actually encouraged—administrative competition and rivalry within the executive branch. FDR believed in and applied the concept of separation of powers among a widening circle of executive agencies primarily as a means of assuring his personal dominance and ultimate decision-making power. By "pitting bureaucrat against bureaucrat," according to James M. Burns, he left himself free to serve as the "umpire" among competing agencies; in the process he greatly enhanced the power of the White House over the State Department and other federal agencies.[44]

Secretary Hull and the State Department

In spite of these factors, it should not be thought that the influence of Secretary of State Hull and the department he headed was negligible or unimportant in determining the course of New Deal diplomacy. President Roosevelt respected Hull immensely, valued his services as the official in charge of the State Department, and called him "a great American and a great statesman." At the end of Hull's career (his resignation was announced on November 27, 1944), FDR nominated him for the Nobel Peace Prize, which he received in 1945. Hull's eleven-year incumbency, the longest of any secretary of state in American history, provided eloquent testimony to his numerous contributions to the diplomatic accomplishments of the Roosevelt administration. As one commentator has expressed it, the working partnership be-

43. Sherwood, *Roosevelt and Hopkins,* II, 662.
44. Burns, *Roosevelt: The Lion and the Fox,* 371; Acheson, *Present at the Creation,* 47.

tween Roosevelt and Hull—"one daring and pliable, the other circumspect and inflexible"—in many respects "made a good team." [45]

Next to FDR himself, Hull was perhaps the most widely respected member of the Roosevelt administration. Within the United States and on Capitol Hill, throughout his tenure at the head of the State Department he retained a wide following. Even while they often preferred to deal directly with the White House, foreign officials normally accorded Secretary Hull great deference and respect. Perhaps the apogee of Hull's prestige was reached at the wartime Moscow foreign ministers' conference (October 19–30, 1943), where he played an active and often decisive role, especially in dispelling the impression that the Roosevelt administration lacked a foreign policy and in forging more cooperative Soviet-American relations. According to one account, Hull emerged as the dominant figure at the meeting and was acclaimed as something of a national hero. Among its other results, the achievements at this conference significantly enhanced FDR's prospects for reelection in 1944. [46]

In several key areas of Rooseveltian diplomacy, notably, international trade policy, relations with Latin America, negotiations with Japan before Pearl Harbor, and planning for the postwar era, Secretary Hull and his State Department subordinates did participate actively in foreign policy decision making, and resulting policies often clearly bore Hull's imprint. Even in these areas, however, sometimes FDR could not resist the temptation to intervene directly in negotiations with foreign governments.

In his supervision of the State Department, Hull was conscientious and methodical; deliberate and cautious in considering complex policy issues; considerate in dealing with his subordinates, who were usually consulted in matters falling within their spheres of competence; and jealous of the department's historic prerogatives and responsibilities. He could be called a departmental traditionalist who adapted to and perpetuated the procedures and customs of the diplomatic corps rather than endeavoring to change them significantly. [47]

Hull possessed another quality that, in the context of international

45. Pratt, *Cordell Hull*, 768; Langer and Gleason, *The Challenge to Isolation*, 8.
46. Hachey, (ed.), *Confidential Dispatches*, 149; *Memoirs of Cordell Hull*, II, 1274–1314.
47. Graham H. Stuart, *The Department of State: A History of Its Organization, Procedure, and Personnel* (New York, 1949), 314.

events during the war, made a valuable contribution to the administration's foreign policy efforts. Hull, Secretary of the Interior Harold Ickes said on the day the Japanese attacked Pearl Harbor, looked "more than ever like a Christian martyr." A man of firm principles and high ideals, Hull exemplified the moral outrage which Americans widely felt when the Axis powers violated international law with impunity and trampled upon the rights of defenseless nations.[48]

Hull will not be remembered for his administrative ability. One commentator has said of his management of the State Department that, while he took administrative problems seriously, he was not a particularly able administrator since he tended to become immersed in the mass of routine data; he "accustomed himself to the [State Department] bureaucracy instead of mastering it." According to another interpretation, Hull was never able to acquire a firm grasp upon the innovations in American foreign policy introduced during the New Deal. His principal subordinate, Sumner Welles, said that the secretary of state normally preferred to postpone controversial decisions as long as possible; he was inclined to adopt "a remedial policy" rather than a "preventive policy."[49]

He was also prone to use conferences with other members of the cabinet to air his own grievances rather than discuss substantive diplomatic issues. President Roosevelt found his secretary of state "prolix" and often appeared bored with Hull's long-winded disquisitions on pending policy questions. A British observer called them "senatorial" speeches. Hull's statements usually had a strong moralistic tone and sometimes appeared to others as ideologically rigid. On some occasions, he seemed incapable of grappling with concrete problems facing the United States abroad. One interpretation holds that, as Secretary Hull's health became progressively worse, the president relegated him more and more to the sidelines, to concentrate on postwar planning, while FDR made the really crucial diplomatic decisions.[50]

48. Pratt, *Cordell Hull*, 520.

49. Robert E. Elder, *The Policy Machine: The Department of State and American Foreign Policy* (Syracuse, 1960), 158; James L. McCamy, *Conduct of the New Diplomacy* (New York, 1964), 231; Sumner Welles, "Political Cooperation During the War—A Lost Opportunity," in Kimball (ed.), *Franklin D. Roosevelt and the World Crisis*, 130.

50. Pratt, *Cordell Hull*, 767; Acheson, *Present at the Creation*, 20; Sherwood, *Roosevelt and Hopkins*, II, 433–34; Langer and Gleason, *The Challenge to Isolation*, 7; Kennan, *Memoirs, 1925–1950*, 227–28; Freidel, *Launching the New Deal*, 364.

As the administrative head of the State Department, Secretary Hull directed a department in which morale was chronically low, and by many criteria, it was lower when the Roosevelt administration ended than when it began. Critics of the department and of FDR's diplomacy, of course, were not unified in their discontent. Some detractors believed, for example, that the Roosevelt-Hull team was "dragging the United States into war." Others were convinced that the president and his foreign policy advisers were unduly timid and cautious in protecting American interests against steady Axis encroachments. Still others were persuaded that during most of the New Deal the United States really had no coherent foreign policy at all. Ostensibly at least, the Japanese attack on Pearl Harbor on December 7, 1941, silenced most of this public disaffection. For over four years, and in marked contrast with the Vietnam War later, there followed one of the most impressive exhibitions of national unity in American history.

At the urging of Secretary Hull and other professional diplomats, President Roosevelt did not depart significantly from the standard of other administrations in the quality of his diplomatic appointments. As noted, some of FDR's appointments were overtly "political." But with a few exceptions, the individuals selected performed their duties at least moderately well, and some 50 percent of FDR's ambassadorial appointments were chosen from the Foreign Service. In some instances, as in the case of William C. Bullitt, the official in time also became a close adviser to Hull. Occasionally, FDR permitted Hull to select his own appointees for high-level State Department positions. Roosevelt also appointed the first woman to head an embassy, naming Ruth Bryan Owen United States minister to Denmark.[51]

Growing American involvement in international affairs naturally required administrative changes within the Department of State. A broad reorganization of the department was carried out under the direction of Assistant Secretary George Messersmith in 1938; another set of organizational reforms was made in 1944. By the latter date, the department had six assistant secretaries of state, a legal adviser, and a special assistant in charge of international organization and security. This last office was a kind of belated recognition that military and diplomatic decision making were often merely opposite sides of

51. Freidel, *Launching the New Deal*, 363; Stuart, *The Department of State*, 311–12, 317.

the same coin. Another theme in these administrative changes was the new emphasis accorded to cultural and informational aspects of American diplomacy, which foreshadowed the emergence after the war of a separately administered and massive informational and propaganda program operated by the United States Information Agency. (Significantly, responsibility for this novel dimension of American diplomacy was ultimately removed from the State Department and assigned to a new administrative agency.) Other changes within the department were directed at improving reporting by officials stationed overseas and at freeing high-level administrators to concentrate upon overall policy planning.[52]

Despite such changes, however, it cannot be said that Roosevelt and Hull really adapted the Department of State to the existence of a radically new global environment or prepared it adequately for meeting America's responsibilities in the postwar era. During the New Deal, morale within the department remained rather low. In the Roosevelt era, as in the years that followed, State Department officials routinely complained that their advice was ignored by the White House and that individuals and agencies inexperienced in foreign affairs exercised an undue influence in policy formulation and administration. Much as he became accustomed to it, Secretary of State Hull unquestionably resented his frequent exclusion from the process of decision making, and he was personally hurt by the widespread impression that his contributions to American diplomacy were largely routine or ornamental. Hull undoubtedly realized that Secretary of War Stimson sometimes had greater influence in determining FDR's foreign policy viewpoints than he did, and according to his closest associates, this realization was one factor impairing Hull's health and morale.[53]

Secretary Hull and other State Department officials also understood that during the New Deal and World War II, as in other periods of American history, the department served as a kind of lightening rod for unpopular policies promulgated by the White House. Presi-

52. Stuart, *The Department of State*, 333–411. For more detailed analysis of informational and propaganda aspects of American diplomacy before and during World War II see John W. Henderson, *The United States Information Agency* (New York, 1969), 3–21; and Thomas C. Sorensen, *The Word War: The Story of American Propaganda* (New York, 1968), 1–31.

53. Freidel, *Launching the New Deal*, 359.

dent Roosevelt's determination to maintain minimally cordial relations with Vichy France during the war—a policy conferring many benefits upon the United States—was one example of this phenomenon. Among the admirers of Free French leader General Charles de Gaulle, this policy was widely condemned.

Internal schisms and personal rivalries also unquestionably impaired the State Department's influence in the foreign policy process during the Roosevelt years. The leading example perhaps was the increasingly acrimonious dispute between Secretary Hull and Under Secretary Sumner Welles, who had been appointed to that position in 1937. Welles was personally selected by Roosevelt for the position, and in time he largely supplanted Hull as the primary liaison channel between the White House and the State Department. Because of his prestigious family background, his social connections, his *savoir-faire* and his personal ties with the president, Welles acquired an entree to the Oval Office that Hull never possessed. For many of his contemporaries, Welles was regarded as the guiding spirit of the State Department; FDR and foreign diplomats alike often preferred to deal with him rather than Hull. Inevitably, the relationship between Roosevelt and Welles created serious morale problems and schisms within the State Department, and Secretary Hull became convinced that Welles was attempting to make diplomatic decisions without consulting him. A number of subordinate State Department officials became identified as "Welles's men," whose loyalty to Hull was questionable. Finally, on September 25, 1943, after repeated urging by Hull, Roosevelt announced Welles's resignation.[54]

Despite the Hull-Welles imbroglio and less well-publicized instances of morale problems within the State Department, Hull managed somehow to accommodate himself to Roosevelt's diplomatic style and activism. Given Hull's significant contributions and his loyalty, it would be a mistake to view FDR's sometimes fulsome tributes to him as insincere or solely designed to achieve some presidential purpose. FDR also knew that Hull had no political ambitions of his own and would never use his position to challenge or damage the

54. Bendiner, *The Riddle of the State Department,* 150–65; Acheson, *Present at the Creation,* 12; John W. Wheeler-Bennett and Anthony Nicholls, *The Semblance of Peace: The Political Settlement After the Second World War* (New York, 1974), 106–107; *Memoirs of Cordell Hull,* II, 1227–31, 1256.

president politically. To the contrary, Hull remained one of Roosevelt's most dedicated supporters and used his personal influence time and again to enhance FDR's political fortunes.

Hull had another talent that some secretaries of state before and after him lacked. (Alexander Haig, President Reagan's first secretary of state, is a notable example.) Much as he might have personally resented being bypassed or ignored, or believed that the president was misguided in disregarding the advice of State Department experts, Hull fully understood that under the American constitutional system, the chief executive is in charge of American foreign policy. Some presidents, such as Harry Truman, might interpret this constitutional mandate symbolically, delegating the management of foreign relations largely to the secretary of state. Other chief executives—and Roosevelt was perhaps the most conspicuous case in American diplomatic experience—interpret their constitutional responsibility literally and dynamically, injecting themselves frequently and decisively into the formulation and administration of foreign policy. As Secretary Hull came to be reminded almost every day, the nature of the relationship existing between the chief executive and his secretary of state is a matter ultimately determined by the president, who is free to use or to ignore diplomatic advisers in any manner he chooses. An incumbent secretary of state must come to terms with that reality, as Hull somehow managed to do for some eleven years, or else he will become increasingly frustrated, alienated, and, most likely, expendable.

In appointing Hull as his secretary of state, according to one account, Roosevelt believed that Hull's "best service to the country and to the party could be performed on the floor [of Congress] and in the cloakrooms of the Senate."[55] This observation underscores what was most probably Hull's outstanding contribution to American diplomacy from 1933 to late 1944: his indispensable service in laying a bipartisan foundation for the administration's diplomatic efforts, especially in the realm of postwar planning. Roosevelt and Hull were determined to avoid the earlier mistakes of President Wilson, who had largely ignored the Republican opposition in negotiating the new international order after World War I. The subsequent rejection of the

55. Hinton, *Cordell Hull*, 207–208.

League of Nations by the United States embittered Wilson, impaired his health, and seriously jeopardized efforts during the 1920s and 1930s to apply the concept of collective security successfully.

With the lessons of the Wilsonian era in mind, the Roosevelt-Hull team began as early as 1939 to plan a new approach to international relations in the post–World War II period. Throughout the months that followed, Hull and his subordinates solicited the cooperation of leading Democrats and Republicans in Congress so that the nascent United Nations organization would win widespread admiration on Capitol Hill. The climax to this effort came on July 28, 1945, when the Senate voted in favor of the UN Charter by a vote of 89 to 2. That an overwhelming majority of senators now supported this second experiment in international organization owed as much to the efforts of Cordell Hull as to any other single influence.[56] Perhaps even more crucially, the pattern of bipartisan collaboration emerging from the Roosevelt administration toward the end of World War II supplied valuable precedents for the Truman and later administrations when they were faced with the challenge of creating and maintaining maximum unity in the foreign policy field.

The Roosevelt-Hull Model: Profit and Loss

The diplomatic record of the Roosevelt administration contains some of the most epochal developments and accomplishments in the annals of American diplomacy. As distinctive and highly personal as President Roosevelt's approach to American foreign policy may have been, according to one paramount criterion it must be given high marks. This standard is the results the Roosevelt-Hull team achieved in responding to a series of recurrent and grave external challenges.

As was no less true in domestic affairs, the Roosevelt administration carried out what amounted to a revolution in America's international role, and it did so in the face of serious obstacles at home and abroad. Overdue as the transition may have been—and some com-

56. *Memoirs of Cordell Hull*, II, 1625–1713. For a different perspective, see Arthur H. Vandenberg, Jr. (ed.), *The Private Papers of Senator Vandenberg* (Boston, 1952), 1–220; and Cecil V. Crabb, Jr., *Bipartisan Foreign Policy: Myth or Reality?* (New York, 1957), 44–54.

mentators believed the change should have taken place after the First World War—America's eventual abandonment of isolationism, and its commitment to a policy of active and continuous involvement in the solution of global and regional problems, must be viewed as one of the most momentous developments in the American diplomatic record. It affected, of course, not only America's own destiny, but it crucially influenced the nature of the entire international system.

By World War II, in a number of key respects the United States had become the most powerful nation on the globe, and by the end of the war, it had emerged as one of the two superpowers on the global scene. While the war was still in progress, FDR and his aides concluded that the United States must thenceforth play a role in international decision making commensurate with its vast power. From a purely rational perspective this decision was unquestionably defensible. Yet, psychologically and emotionally, it was resisted by countless Americans who preferred the comfortable and cherished isolationist stance. The remarkable fact about this transition to an internationalist diplomatic orientation was not that it was controversial, but that the change was made with the majority support of the American people and the leaders of both political parties.

Among the specific achievements of the Roosevelt administration in external policy, several developments deserve brief mention. America's initiative, for example, in espousing and gaining international support for the reciprocal trade program during the 1930s was a noteworthy and far-reaching accomplishment. The steady growth in the level of international trade in the years ahead—and the many benefits this fact conferred upon consumers inside and outside the United States—provided eloquent testimony to the value of this landmark in American diplomacy.[57] Similarly, the Roosevelt administration's determination to inaugurate a new era in United States–Latin American relations, symbolized by the Good Neighbor policy, was a milestone. Two subsequent events—the establishment and evolution of the Organization of American States and Latin America's support (except for Argentina) for the Allied cause during World War II— testified to this new and more constructive stage in inter-American relations.

57. *Memoirs of Cordell Hull*, I, 352–88; Burns, *Roosevelt: The Lion and the Fox*, 189, 252, 310–11, 322, 418.

Once the United States entered World War II, a pair of interrelated diplomatic goals became uppermost, and again FDR's administration had an outstanding record in accomplishing them. One of these was an Allied victory in the war. The military power, economic resources, and other contributions of the United States were crucial to this outcome. The Roosevelt White House directed the mobilization effort required for ultimate victory against the Axis. America not only supplied its own armed forces but also served as the "arsenal of democracy," providing indispensable assistance to Great Britain, the Soviet Union, and a long list of other countries resisting Axis hegemony. A related objective—and one of the administration's most difficult diplomatic challenges—was the preservation of Allied unity during the conflict. It would be no exaggeration to say that as much as any other single influence affecting the outcome, FDR's personal efforts time and again were crucial in resolving actual or potential controversies among the Allies and in enabling the coalition against the Axis to coordinate its efforts sufficiently to achieve victory. Many of FDR's concessions to the Soviet Union during the war, for example, were designed to accomplish this purpose, and if the Allied partnership had disintegrated before the Axis defeat, the history of international relations thereafter would almost certainly have been profoundly different.[58]

Toward the end of the war the Roosevelt-Hull emphasis upon establishing postwar foreign policy upon a firm bipartisan basis was another significant accomplishment. Roosevelt and Hull successfully avoided the mistakes of the Wilson administration; the bipartisan collaboration displayed toward the nascent United Nations was a remarkable exhibition of national unity seldom rivaled in American history.[59]

Another achievement of the Roosevelt administration's diplomatic efforts was its firm opposition to colonialism and its determination to bring about the liquidation of Western colonial systems in the postwar period. On the colonial question Roosevelt exhibited the essentially pragmatic outlook that marked his approach to other global

58. William H. McNeill, America, *Britain and Russia: Their Co-operation and Conflict, 1941–46* (London, 1953); Herbert Feis, *Churchill, Roosevelt, Stalin: The War They Waged and the Peace They Sought* (Princeton, 1957).
59. *The Private Papers of Senator Vandenberg*, 108–421; *Memoirs of Cordell Hull*, II, 1625–1743; Crabb, *Bipartisan Foreign Policy*.

issues. In ideal terms, he and many of his advisers believed that colonialism was oppressive, ethically indefensible, and inequitable. And realistically, colonialism was doomed: Western colonialism simply could no longer resist the opposition of Afro-Asian nationalist groups, whose efforts had been given new impetus by the events of World War II, such as Japan's defeat of several Western nations. Attempts to reimpose colonialism would be violently resisted by subject peoples and would serve as a new source of international and regional conflict. For these reasons, the Roosevelt White House repeatedly used its influence to bring about the dismantling of colonial structures in Africa, the Middle East, and Asia. In doing so, it laid the basis for the emergence of the Third World, ultimately including some one hundred new nations, in the postwar era. As much as any other force in the twentieth century, decolonization profoundly altered the nature of the international system and of America's role in it.[60]

But there were also a number of total or partial foreign policy failures during FDR's unprecedented tenure in the Oval Office. With regard to substantive diplomatic issues, several major and minor setbacks may be identified. Under FDR's personal direction, diplomacy generally suffered from a certain paradoxical and ambivalent quality that created widespread confusion about the administration's intentions abroad. Roosevelt's diplomatic activities illustrated many of the defects associated with a pragmatically based approach to foreign relations. In the words of one of FDR's biographers, one of his most appealing and universally admired qualities was the absence of "mischievous nonsense about a destiny, a mission" that FDR or America under his leadership was called upon to perform. To the contrary, the "most fascinating thing" about Roosevelt was the "day-to-dayness of his life, the adequate improvisation of what he needed from resources that were never pretentious." The British socialist thinker Harold Laski similarly commended Roosevelt's "brilliance in improvisation" and his "political acumen." For the British, FDR symbolized the force and the power of American society, its activity and energy, its "courage, confidence, and hope." The great hope for the world was that

60. *Memoirs of Cordell Hull*, II, 1234–1305, 1477–78, 1638–39; Gaddis Smith, *American Diplomacy During the Second World War* (New York, 1966), 81–99; Range, "FDR—a Reflection of American Idealism," in Kimball (ed.), *Franklin D. Roosevelt and the World Crisis*, 239–43.

under Roosevelt's leadership, "the American nation could be roused to action."[61]

Roosevelt's dynamism and energy, and his personal involvement in nearly every dimension of foreign relations, illustrate many of the limitations inherent in a pragmatically based approach to diplomacy. As a rule, FDR evinced little interest in theoretical or long-range diplomatic questions. His mind was not attuned to emerging tendencies likely to affect international politics a decade or a half century in the future. Nor was he overly troubled about the existence of contradictions, inconsistencies, anomalies, and the like in his overall foreign policy. His professed idealism, for example, was not infrequently contradicted by his own highly personal and secretive control over foreign relations, which meant that even the secretary of state was not always privy to his actions. On a different front, it was a personal decision by President Roosevelt, who launched the top-secret Project Manhattan during World War II, that was responsible for the dawn of the nuclear age. Roosevelt and his advisers knew that German scientists were energetically seeking to perfect the atomic bomb for use by Hitler's forces. Yet Roosevelt seemed strangely unmindful of the diplomatic implications of this momentous decision and the consequences of this new era.

High on the list of the Roosevelt administration's diplomatic blind spots also must be placed the president's failure to comprehend the integral relationship between military and political power. Along with millions of other Americans, Roosevelt appeared to be totally unfamiliar with Clausewitz's celebrated maxim: "War is the continuation of politics by other means." This principle has many corollaries and implications. In the context of World War II, perhaps the main one might be stated in the maxim: "Wartime military developments crucially affect postwar politics." What Americans often view as purely military decisions made by generals on the battlefield can, and frequently do, place severe limits upon what diplomats may subsequently accomplish at the conference table.[62] Hull justified FDR's almost single-minded concentration upon military issues by saying that his emphasis upon achieving victory "meant everything to us in

61. See the views of Emil Ludwig, Winston Churchill, Laski, and others on Roosevelt's leadership qualities in Dizikes, *Britain, Roosevelt, and the New Deal*, 304–10.
62. See Chapter 2, note 33.

the diplomatic field by giving to the force of our diplomacy the indispensable backing of military success."[63]

Other commentators, however, have taken a considerably less charitable view of Roosevelt's neglect of Clausewitz' dictum. The president's insistence that controversial political questions be deferred until the end of the war meant in practice that many such issues were in effect resolved by the distribution of military forces rather than by diplomats in formal negotiations. One of the most difficult and contentious diplomatic issues arising out of the war, for example—continued Soviet control over Eastern Europe—was primarily the result of the liberation of this region from Nazi domination by the Red Army. Once that result had been accomplished, policy makers in the Kremlin, who *were* familiar with Clausewitz's teachings, were in a position to impose political hegemony, a reality that the West was subsequently powerless to change after the war.[64] While it may be conceded that the Roosevelt administration most likely could not have prevented ultimate Soviet control over Eastern Europe after World War II, the president and his closest advisers could have exhibited greater awareness of the integral relationship between military and diplomatic decision making, and they could have done considerably more to prepare the American people to understand that crucial connection in the postwar era.

Other diplomatic inadequacies of the Roosevelt years include FDR's legalism and his almost limitless faith in the efficacy of written agreements and personal understandings among heads of state to produce a more peaceful and stable international system. This was illustrated perhaps most clearly in the sphere of Soviet-American relations. Relying upon his highly developed political talents and personal charisma, Roosevelt sincerely believed that he could charm, cajole, and otherwise persuade the Soviet dictator, Joseph Stalin, to cooperate in constructing the president's "grand design" for a just and democratic order for the postwar world. That concepts like freedom and democracy had different meanings for Western and Soviet political leaders—or that Stalin might have had no intention from the beginning of honoring his commitments to observe democratic political norms in Eastern Europe and elsewhere—seldom, if ever, occurred to Roose-

63. *Memoirs of Cordell Hull,* II, 1721.
64. Hugh Seton-Watson, *The East European Revolution* (New York, 1956), xi.

velt. Similarly, his efforts to forge a durable coalition agreement between highly antagonistic political factions in China appeared to many informed students of Chinese affairs at the time and afterward as a naïve projection of his often successful domestic political strategy into the arena of global politics.[65]

President Roosevelt's decision to operate as the de facto secretary of state exacted a high price in another respect, one that has posed a serious problem in the conduct of foreign relations by the United States since the New Deal. Looking back on the Roosevelt era, former Secretary of State Dean Acheson described it as an "anguishing period" for the State Department. As one who witnessed it firsthand, Acheson described Secretary of State Hull's experience as "one long battle with the bureaucracies of other agencies" in Washington. What order existed in the management of foreign relations (and it often appeared minimal) was imposed by Roosevelt's close advisers in the White House.[66] Thus, private organizations, legislators, other executive officials, and officials in foreign countries, were likely to conclude that the State Department's role in the American foreign policy process was largely ceremonial and peripheral. This fact impaired morale within the department and inevitably invited intrusions into its customary administrative domain by other governmental agencies. Roosevelt not only tolerated such bureaucratic imperialism, but in some cases he overtly encouraged it.

As a result, the State Department emerged from World War II poorly prepared—and in some instances, it seemed strangely unmotivated—to assume a variety of new responsibilities in the new age of American internationalism. Hull's growing frustrations reflected a deeper conviction within the department that its functions were being usurped by the White House and a host of other departments and agencies and that its expertise was being ignored, wasted, and otherwise inadequately utilized in making some of the most crucial foreign policy decisions in the nation's experience.

The diplomatic record of the New Deal also underscores the point that a heavy price may be paid when an incumbent president decides to serve as his own secretary of state. The period was a landmark in

65. George F. Kennan, *American Diplomacy, 1900–1950* (New York, 1951).
66. Dean Acheson, "The Eclipse of the State Department," *Foreign Affairs*, XLIX (July, 1971), 596.

American history for several reasons, not least because of the mounting burden it placed upon the chief executive in supervising a rapidly growing federal bureaucracy. That task is demanding enough, even when the president delegates substantial foreign policy responsibilities to the secretary of state and other advisers; in recent years, the burdens of the presidential office have become heavier than ever. During the Roosevelt era, the "decline" of the State Department was perhaps given irreversible momentum. Whether intentionally or unintentionally, Roosevelt contributed decisively to that result, with deleterious consequences for the American foreign policy process and for the outcome of the nation's diplomatic efforts from Latin America to East Asia. Although no other individual ever directed the State Department as long as Hull, his growing disenchantment presaged the frame of mind of perhaps a majority of incumbents in the office since World War II. With very few exceptions (see Chapter 5 on Secretary of State John Foster Dulles, perhaps the leading postwar example), they have also found their assignment frustrating, psychologically draining, and even impossible. In company with Hull, they have witnessed inroads upon the State Department's assigned jurisdiction by the president himself, other executive agencies, and Congress. And they have repeatedly been required to take the blame for unpopular diplomatic decisions in which their participation was often minimal (see Chapter 6 on Secretary of State Dean Rusk, for example).

Finally, a transcendent lesson derived from the Roosevelt model clearly is that if a chief executive decides to function as the de facto secretary of state, it is imperative that he endeavor to acquire expertise and genuine understanding concerning the complex issues confronting him abroad. Roosevelt's background and knowledge for many of the important international problems he was called upon to resolve was extremely limited, and the qualifications of many of his trusted advisers, like Harry Hopkins, were even less impressive. Moreover, in too many cases FDR was either too busy to avail himself of expertise from the State Department or he deliberately avoided such advice, believing it to be biased or otherwise suspect. As a substitute, he frequently trusted his own political instincts—cultivated mainly in the arena of American domestic politics—and the recommendations of his domestic advisers, whose knowledge of foreign affairs was usually inferior to his own. As one of the most dynamic chief executives in the nation's history, when conditions abroad became critical FDR simply added the conduct of foreign affairs to a long list of his other responsibilities. The result was a kind of diplomatic dilettantism by the leader of the world's most powerful nation. This dilettantism did little to prepare America for the kind of sustained and informed international role the nation was required to play in the years ahead. In the months following Roosevelt's death, neither the new chief executive, Harry S. Truman, nor the Department of State was adequately prepared to fill the existing policy vacuum.

4

A Successful Partnership: Truman and Acheson

One of the most successful partnerships between a chief executive and his secretary of state in the annals of American diplomacy was that between President Truman and his fourth secretary of state, Dean G. Acheson.[1] A more marked contrast with the Roosevelt-Hull model could hardly be imagined.

The presidency of Harry S. Truman began in war and ended in war. When Truman entered the Oval Office following the sudden death of President Roosevelt on April 12, 1945, World War II had not yet been won. Nazi Germany surrendered on May 7; and after two atomic bombs were dropped on Japan on August 6 and 9, Tokyo surrendered on August 14. Characteristically, Truman personally made the decision to use these new and devastating weapons against the Japanese enemy.[2]

Almost five years later, President Truman made another epochal military decision when he committed the United States to the defense of South Korea after North Korean forces crossed the border on June 25, 1950. The ensuing Korean War proved to be a costly, exhausting, and inconclusive contest—next to the Vietnam War, the most contro-

1. Truman's first secretary of state was Edward R. Stettinius, a carry-over from the Roosevelt administration who served until June 27, 1945. His second was James F. Byrnes, who served from July 3, 1945, until his retirement on January 7, 1947. General George C. Marshall took office as secretary of state on January 21, 1947; he retired on January 7, 1949. Acheson became secretary of state on January 21, 1949, and served until President Eisenhower entered the White House on January 20, 1953.
2. Harry S. Truman, *Year of Decisions* (Garden City, N.Y., 1955), 415–26. Vol. I of Truman, *Memoirs*, 2 vols. Leonard Mosley, *Marshall: Hero of Our Times* (New York, 1982), 337–40.

versial and internally divisive military engagement in American history. It was left for the Eisenhower administration to negotiate an armistice, which went into effect on July 27, 1953. Yet, a generation after its termination, no formal peace treaty among the belligerents has yet been signed, and the Demilitarized Zone (DMZ) between North and South Korea remains among the most volatile frontiers on the globe.[3]

Between the end of World War II and the Korean conflict, there occurred some of the most significant developments in the annals of American diplomacy. Under the supervision of the Truman White House, World War II was fought to a victorious conclusion, and occupation regimes for Germany and Japan were established. During the occupation period, both countries embarked upon democratic experiments that, after some four decades of experience, show every sign of remaining stable and benign. Following the use of atomic weapons against Japan, the Truman administration endeavored unsuccessfully to arrive at a nuclear disarmament agreement with the Soviet Union. As set forth in the Baruch Plan of arms control, the Truman administration's position, which in most crucial respects remained unchanged under later American chief executives, was that the Soviet Union must agree to mutual and verifiable arms reduction before the United States was prepared to relinquish its advantage in nuclear weapons.[4]

The diplomacy of the Truman administration was noteworthy for another reason. Although strains had appeared in Soviet-American relations before Roosevelt's death, under his successor the all-pervasive conflict known as the cold war became the dominating reality of the postwar international system and remained so after 1953. Exactly when the cold war began—and what precise issue or issues precipitated it—remain highly controversial questions among diplomatic historians. In any event, by the early months of the Truman administration the "strange alliance" that had produced an Allied victory in World War II was disintegrating. By mid-1945, growing suspicion and ill-will characterized Soviet-American relations, so much so as to

3. John W. Spanier, *The Truman-MacArthur Controversy and the Korean War* (Cambridge, Mass., 1959); Matthew W. Ridgway, *The Korean War* (New York, 1967).

4. Harry S. Truman, *Years of Trial and Hope* (Garden City, N.Y., 1956), 1–16. Vol. II of Truman, *Memoirs*, 2 vols.; Dean Acheson, *Present at the Creation: My Years in the State Department* (New York, 1969), 149–57.

produce fears among some groups that a military conflict between them was inevitable. The failure of Washington and Moscow to agree upon peace treaties for Germany and Japan; repeated American protests about Soviet hegemony in Eastern Europe and intervention in countries such as Greece, Turkey, and Iran; a rising tide of Communist political activity in Western Europe; Moscow's resentment about the sudden American termination of wartime aid (the Lend-Lease program) and Washington's lack of interest in assisting with Russian postwar recovery; the successful communization of China in 1949; repeated efforts by Stalin's government in 1948–1949 to drive the Western powers out of Berlin, requiring them to undertake an expensive airlift to supply the beleagured city; and Soviet efforts to infiltrate and control Afro-Asian nationalist movements—these were major developments in the emergence of the cold war between the superpowers.[5]

As Soviet-American wartime friendship gave way to suspicion and tension, the Truman administration formulated and carried out a number of foreign policy undertakings that must be regarded as landmarks in the nation's diplomatic experience. Leading ones were the Greek-Turkish aid program, which was the occasion for the promulgation of the Truman Doctrine early in 1947; the Marshall Plan for the long-range reconstruction of war-devastated Western Europe, inaugurated the following year; the North Atlantic Treaty, creating a Western defense organization (NATO) in 1949; and Truman's Point Four program of economic and technical assistance for the developing countries, announced in 1950 and continued, in modified form, by his successors in the White House.

Few developments in the annals of American foreign relations were more momentous than the issuance of the Truman Doctrine committing the United States to the strategy of "containment" of expansive communism. Speaking to a joint session of Congress on March 12, 1947, President Truman asked the legislative branch to provide $400 million for Greece and Turkey to strengthen these countries in the face of internal and external communist pressures. By granting Truman's request, Congress formally repudiated isolationism as the guiding principle of America's relations with Western Europe. The new strategy of containment served notice upon the Kremlin that its expan-

5. Richard F. Haynes, *The Awesome Power: Harry S. Truman as Commander in Chief* (Baton Rouge, 1973), 27–28.

sionist policies and adventurism in the Mediterranean and other areas would be resisted by the United States. America's subsequent involvement in the Korean and Vietnam wars were specific applications of the containment policy.[6]

Postwar American assistance for European reconstruction, in the form of the Marshall Plan, was vital for that region's rapid recovery and for its subsequent economic dynamism and growing sense of political independence from both the United States and the Soviet Union. NATO provided—and continues to provide—a shield behind which the United States and its major allies enjoy political freedom, economic prosperity, and security from Soviet hegemony. The Truman administration recognized a reality that has remained at the center of American diplomacy since World War II: the security of the United States is inseparably linked with the freedom and well-being of Western Europe. Truman's appointment of the avowedly Europe-oriented Acheson as his secretary of state underscored that fundamental transition in American foreign policy.

The efforts by the Roosevelt and Truman administrations to create a new international organization, the United Nations, were brought to fruition at the San Francisco Conference on April 25–June 26, 1945. Largely as a result of American leadership, this second experiment in international organization was launched when the UN Charter was signed by fifty nations and approved by the United States Senate on July 28, 1945.

The diplomatic legacy of the Truman administration toward other regions and international issues may be noted briefly. In inter-American relations, efforts were made to extend and strengthen the Organization of American States (OAS) and to promote hemispheric cooperation. The Rio Treaty of regional defense, which theoretically made the security of the Western Hemisphere the joint responsibility of the American republics, was signed on September 2, 1947.

In the Middle East, the most significant development in the early postwar period was the creation of the state of Israel, which came into existence on May 14, 1948, and immediately found itself at war

6. See the article by George F. Kennan (writing as "X"), "The Sources of Soviet Conduct," *Foreign Affairs*, XXV (July, 1947), 556–83; George F. Kennan, *Memoirs, 1925–1950* (New York, 1969), 198–388; Truman, *Years of Trial and Hope*, 93–109; and Joseph M. Jones, *The Fifteen Weeks* (New York, 1955).

with the surrounding Arab states. The United States played an active and decisive role in the founding of Israel and has remained its principal supporter since 1948. To Arab minds, American support of Zionist goals in the Middle East—entailing massive American assistance to Israel after its establishment—was viewed as a major contributing factor to ongoing violence and turbulence in the region.

Elsewhere in the Afro-Asian world, the Truman administration sought to promote independence for dependent societies. In company with Roosevelt before him, Truman was an outspoken critic of colonialism. Under Truman, the United States honored FDR's pledge to grant independence to the Philippines, which was done on July 4, 1946. Washington expected other colonial powers, such as Great Britain, France, and the Netherlands, to follow its example in regions like Africa, the Middle East, and Asia, and American officials repeatedly used their influence to encourage the process of decolonization in these areas.

Overall, the record of the Truman administration in foreign affairs was one of creativity, imagination, restraint, realism, and foresight in responding to a wide variety of postwar challenges. Its diplomatic efforts laid the foundations for American postwar foreign policy, and in most respects, they have proved remarkably durable. Also according to another criterion, the Truman administration's diplomatic legacy was outstanding: most of the specific diplomatic programs and undertakings emerged as the result of successful team efforts by the president and his advisers, efforts in which Truman's fourth secretary of state, Dean Acheson, nearly always played a pivotal role.

In another significant respect also, the Truman-Acheson diplomatic record merits careful analysis by the informed student of American foreign policy. Under the Truman administration, what might be called the "classical" administrative pattern of the relationship between the president and the secretary of state received its clearest expression since World War II. As was his constitutional responsibility, President Truman ultimately made the required foreign policy decisions to meet the challenges confronting the United States abroad. His secretary of state, most conspicuously General George Marshall and later Dean Acheson, served as his chief deputy and designated spokesman in foreign relations. And the State Department was recognized as the agency that was in charge of American foreign policy under White House direction.

A few months after he entered the Oval Office, President Truman was presented with a challenge to this administrative model, when his secretary of commerce, Henry A. Wallace, delivered the speech at Madison Square Garden in which he was overtly critical of the administration's foreign policy, especially its harshness toward the Soviet Union. This attempt by another cabinet official to usurp the State Department's foreign policy leadership brought a sharp rebuke to the Truman administration by Senator Arthur H. Vandenberg (R-Mich.), who became a symbol of bipartisanship in foreign relations in the early postwar era. Republicans, Vandenberg admonished the White House, wanted to cooperate with Democrats to produce a unified foreign policy, but they could "only cooperate with one Secretary of State at a time." Wallace's resignation from the cabinet followed quickly.[7] After the Wallace incident, the secretary of state's primacy in dealing with external issues during the Truman administration was not usually contested by other rivals. The notable exception was General Douglas MacArthur's diplomatic statements and activities during the Korean War.

Acheson's Background and Appointment

In mid-November, 1948, President Truman asked Under Secretary of State Dean Acheson to meet with him at Blair House. The president informed Acheson that he had selected him to succeed the ailing Secretary of State George C. Marshall, who was planning to retire. To Acheson's demurers about his lack of qualifications and suitability for the position, Truman characteristically replied that others might be better qualified for the position (or even for the office of president) but that Truman was president of the United States, and he wanted Acheson to serve as his chief deputy in foreign affairs![8]

7. Arthur H. Vandenberg, Jr. (ed.), *The Private Papers of Senator Vandenberg* (Boston, 1952), 300–302.

8. Acheson, *Present at the Creation*, 249–50; Gaddis Smith, "Dean Acheson," in Robert H. Ferrell (ed.), *The American Secretaries of State and Their Diplomacy* (New York, 1972), 54–55.

What considerations induced the president to select Acheson as his secretary of state? For Truman, Acheson's appointment had several attractions. Truman's earlier, and sometimes frustrating, experiences with others who had held the position unquestionably influenced his choice. For example, he had inherited Secretary of State Edward R. Stettinius from the Roosevelt administration. One student of the period has described Stettinius as "handsome, smiling, banal," and "better suited to preside over a Rotarian's banquet than the complexities of foreign policy." Stettinius' tenure was brief and undistinguished.[9]

His successor, the former Democratic senator from South Carolina and associate justice of the Supreme Court, James F. Byrnes, who served for some eighteen months, retiring in January, 1947, presented a different, and much more difficult, challenge for the Truman White House. In fact, the Truman-Byrnes relationship became increasingly strained, leading ultimately to the latter's forced retirement. Byrnes possessed considerable political influence in his own right. Some observers believe that Byrnes thought he should have been FDR's vice-presidential running mate in 1944 instead of Truman, and to the latter's mind, Byrnes always remained a serious political rival. Moreover, Byrnes was almost totally inexperienced in foreign affairs, a limitation that did not deter him from asserting his position forcefully on a variety of diplomatic issues. But his most serious defect as secretary of state (a deficiency observed by Byrnes's subordinates in the State Department, like Dean Acheson) was his failure to understand clearly that in the American system of government, the president ultimately makes the foreign policy of the United States, not the secretary of state. More than once, Byrnes neglected to keep President Truman adequately informed of his activities and to obtain the necessary White House approval before issuing statements on diplomatic questions in the name of the Truman administration. After several pointed admonitions, Truman finally relieved Byrnes of his position and appointed Marshall as his replacement.[10]

By contrast, the management of the State Department by General Marshall had the opposite impact upon President Truman and upon

9. Smith, "Dean Acheson," 19.
10. See Truman, *Year of Decisions*, 551–52; Mosley, *Marshall: Hero of Our Times*, 388–89. James F. Byrnes's own account of his service in the State Department is available in his memoirs, *Speaking Frankly* (New York, 1947).

Marshall's protégé Acheson. Marshall had served as President Roosevelt's chief of staff during World War II. After retiring from a distinguished military career, he was sent on an ill-fated mediatory mission to China by President Truman in the early postwar era, as part of America's effort to bring stability to that strife-torn country. Then, at Truman's request, he agreed to become secretary of state, beginning in January, 1947, and he held this position for almost exactly two years, until Acheson replaced him.

Acheson once said that General Marshall and President Truman were the two individuals he most respected as a result of his career in government service. For Acheson, Secretary of State Marshall provided an exemplary role model of an effective State Department head and diplomatic adviser to the president. Marshall was a dedicated, conscientious, and capable administrator who chose able subordinates and knew how to utilize their talents effectively. Some of the most talented and well-qualified State Department officers in postwar experience, such as Acheson, George F. Kennan, and Charles E. Bohlen, served as Marshall's advisers. One of General Marshall's qualities as an administrator was his decisiveness and his insistence that, after appropriate study and discussion, his staff make clear policy recommendations rather than "fight the problem" indefinitely. In common with his superior in the White House, Marshall had little fondness for typical bureaucratic delay and "red tape" that impeded the process.[11] In contrast to his predecessor, Secretary Byrnes, Marshall was also scrupulous about keeping President Truman fully informed of his activities, in recognition that the power of ultimate decision making resided in the White House. For a chief executive like Truman, who valued overt evidence of loyalty from his subordinates, Marshall's management of the State Department elicited nothing but praise and respect from his superior.[12] Acheson and his contemporaries in the State Department could contrast Marshall's effective administration of the diplomatic machinery with the earlier incumbency of Hull. Under Hull the position of secretary of state had severely eroded, and the overall position of the State Department within the executive branch declined significantly.

11. Smith, "Dean Acheson," 43; "Apologia" in Acheson, *Present at the Creation;* Truman, *Years of Trial and Hope*, 112.
12. See the tributes to Marshall in Acheson, *Present at the Creation*, 735–36; Mosley, *Marshall: Hero of Our Times*, 509–24; and Kennan, *Memoirs, 1925–1950*, 363–64.

Born in 1893, the son of the Episcopal bishop of Connecticut, Dean Gooderham Acheson obtained a law degree from Harvard Law School in 1918, served as the law clerk to Supreme Court Justice Louis D. Brandeis, and during the New Deal became a successful Washington attorney. He entered public service in 1933 by accepting a position as under secretary of the treasury in the Roosevelt administration, a post he soon resigned as the result of policy differences with his superiors.[13] Before the United States entered World War II, Acheson spoke publicly about the necessity for the nation to support Great Britain and other Western countries against the Axis danger. Throughout his diplomatic career, his European orientation (vis-à-vis his lack of knowledge of Asia and other regions, like Latin America) was pronounced.

Early in 1941, Acheson was appointed assistant secretary of state for economic affairs. Three years later, he was placed in charge of the State Department's congressional relations, an area in which, ironically, as secretary of state he was to encounter his most severe criticism. Under Byrnes, Acheson was elevated to the second-highest position within the department, a post he held for two years until 1947, when he returned to private life because of financial problems. He resumed his diplomatic career when President Truman designated him as secretary of state. After 1952, he undertook diplomatic assignments for, and served as foreign policy adviser to, several presidents.

During his apprenticeship as a public servant, Acheson had gained experience in several key areas of national policy. He had a legal background and had acquired some familiarity with economic policy questions from his Treasury and State department service. At the State Department, he had played a part in postwar planning for the United Nations and had become acquainted with the importance of congressional relations as a significant and relatively new dimension of the department's activity. He had contributed to studies and planning anticipating the evacuation of British power from the Mediterranean area and to the formulation of the Truman Doctrine's strategy of containment. He had also been instrumental in State Department studies that eventually led to the formulation of the Marshall Plan. During Secretary of State Byrnes's frequent absences from Washing-

13. Acheson, *Present at the Creation*, 3–4.

ton, Acheson had overall responsibility for administering the State Department.[14]

Another factor enhanced Truman's attraction to Acheson as a potential secretary of state. As a former State Department official has emphasized, every administration needs a group of "front men" in the diplomatic establishment, to fulfill such functions as advocating policies, representing the president's views to career specialists, and gaining consensus for particular policies within the executive branch. The articulate and intellectually gifted Acheson was an excellent choice for this role.[15] He also served the Truman administration as a front man in another sense: he represented the viewpoints, and commanded the respect of, an important segment of conservative business and professional opinion within the Democratic party. As the Democratic defeat in the congressional elections of 1946 indicated, Truman needed as much unity within the ranks of the always disparate Democratic party as he could muster, and Acheson's appointment helped him maintain rapport with one influential wing of the party.

On the surface, it would be difficult to conceive of a more unpromising and unlikely partnership than the one between President Truman and Secretary of State Acheson. A former Democratic senator from Missouri, Truman had worked as a haberdasher and had entered political life through the notorious Pendergast machine of Kansas City, which he in time repudiated. By an accident of history, the former vice-president found himself in the Oval Office after Roosevelt's death. Except for his contributions to the war effort as chairman of the Truman committee in the Senate during World War II, Truman had been a largely unknown political figure whose career lacked distinction. After FDR's untimely death, Truman admitted to friends that he possessed few qualifications for the presidency.

Although his formal education was limited, Truman possessed several qualities that contributed significantly to his success in the Oval Office. He was widely read and could analyze internal and external

14. Acheson, *Present at the Creation*, 1–249; Graham H. Stuart, *The Department of State: A History of Its Organization, Procedure, and Personnel* (New York, 1949), 328–456.

15. Roger Hilsman, *The Politics of Policy Making in Defense and Foreign Affairs* (New York, 1971), 181–82.

policy issues against an extensive historical background that many of his advisers lacked. Truman was also concerned about his place in history: he was determined to deal resolutely with the problems confronting the United States during his presidency and to provide the kind of national leadership required by them.

As FDR's successor, Truman had entered the White House with little preparation for the presidency and very limited experience and background in the foreign policy field. He was usually compelled, therefore, to lean heavily upon his advisers. In most instances Truman consulted his advisers regularly, listened to their viewpoints, and then made the necessary decision. His approach to decision making was relatively simple and uncomplicated: he wanted the problem to be studied, the alternatives and consequences examined, and the question resolved decisively within a relatively brief period of time. Truman was not like some chief executives who tended to "remain suspended between alternatives," who "seek escape by postponing the issue" or are tormented by self-doubts and second thoughts. In effect, Truman followed Marshall's admonition to his advisers not to fight the problem but to decide it.[16] Truman unhesitatingly made the crucial decisions, such as to defend Berlin, to assist Greece and Turkey, to commit the United States to the peacetime defense of Western Europe, and to meet the Communist challenge in Korea, decisions which determined the diplomatic course not only of his administration but of the nation for a generation or more after he left the White House.

The highly effective working relationship that evolved between Truman and Acheson is perhaps explicable by the theory that "opposites attract." Acheson and his superior complemented each other almost perfectly. In his physical appearance and demeanor, Acheson looked like a member of the British nobility, a fact that was sometimes a serious barrier in his efforts to reach bipartisan understandings with Congress and to communicate effectively with ordinary citizens. (With his prominent moustache and aristocratic bearing, Acheson appeared to be the prototype of a senior British officer in the

16. Ernst B. Haas, *Tangle of Hopes: American Commitments and World Order* (Englewood Cliffs, N.J., 1969), 55–56. See Acheson's discussion of presidential decision making (in which Truman is obviously his model) in his *This Vast External Realm* (New York, 1973), 199.

Coldstream Guards.) A product of the Ivy League, a former law clerk to Justice Brandeis, a successful Washington lawyer, and an associate of leading business and financial figures, he possessed a keen and highly trained intellect that not infrequently intimidated his contemporaries. Members of Congress found his hauteur and rather stiff, sometimes imperious personality irritating. Acheson's impatience with questions by uninformed interrogators was legendary. It was said of him, especially because of his almost contemptuous attitude toward his critics, that he "did not suffer fools gladly." To this assertion, after he left the State Department, Acheson replied characteristically that it was untrue: doubtless recalling his many hours of testimony before skeptical legislators and his answers to unfriendly news reporters, he observed that he had suffered many fools while he was in charge of the State Department.[17]

Yet, throughout his tenure as secretary of state Acheson retained a high level of respect and admiration for his superior in the White House. At all stages, he was careful to inform Truman fully about major foreign policy developments, to provide him with objective and carefully considered policy recommendations (which Truman nearly always approved), to defend the president's policies at home and abroad, to remember the political constraints under which Truman operated, and to demonstrate his loyalty to the chief executive when circumstances required it. At the same time, to a degree unexcelled by perhaps any other secretary of state since World War II, with Truman's almost unwavering support he usually managed to assert and maintain the State Department's primacy vis-à-vis the other agencies that were increasingly active in the foreign policy field. For his part, Truman defended his secretary of state against a barrage of extreme, unfounded, and continuing criticism. More than once he refused to remove Acheson from office when detractors demanded it. In the end Truman described Acheson one of the most accomplished secretaries of state in American history.[18]

Incongruous as it might have appeared, the Truman-Acheson partnership emerged and proved to be remarkably durable in the face of

17. David S. McLellan, *Dean Acheson: The State Department Years* (New York, 1976), 59; Dean Acheson, *Sketches from Life* (New York, 1961), 133–34, 140.
18. Truman, *Years of Trial and Hope*, 428–29. See also Robert J. Donovan, *Tumultuous Years: The Presidency of Harry S. Truman, 1949–1953* (New York, 1982), 136.

adverse developments at home and abroad. Despite the differences in their experiences and backgrounds, the two men were united by a common bond—fundamental agreement upon the main contours of American postwar foreign policy, especially in responding to the Soviet challenge—that survived continuing political attacks within the United States, as well as setbacks, such as the Korean war stalemate, overseas. Acheson was of course a Democrat in the Roosevelt-Truman tradition (though he disagreed with his party by doubting the ability of the United Nations to preserve peace and security after World War II). Both Truman and Acheson were convinced that the United States must play an active role in global affairs consonant with its vast power, especially in containing expansive Soviet moves abroad. Truman fully supported Acheson's view that the State Department ought to be the agency charged with the responsibility for formulating major foreign policy proposals and administering tthe external relations of the United States. Under Acheson's direction the department demonstrated that it was responsive to the challenges of the postwar international environment.[19]

Elements in the Truman-Acheson Partnership

After assuming his duties at the head of the State Department early in 1949, Acheson forged a close working relationship with Truman that remained intact for the next four years. A student of the Truman-Acheson period has emphasized the latter's understanding that "the first order of business of any Secretary of State is to establish close and cordial working associations with the President." It might be added that the second order of business, which many other incumbents in the position have neglected, is for the secretary of state to *maintain* a constructive working relationship with the chief executive.[20]

Several fundamental principles and administrative maxims guided Acheson's relationship with the president. In later years Acheson re-

19. Smith, *Dean Acheson, 54–55, 248–49; Ronald J. Stupak, The Shaping of Foreign Policy: The Role of the Secretary of State as Seen by Dean Acheson* (New York, 1969), viii–x.
20. Stupak, *The Shaping of Foreign Policy,* 79.

flected upon his constant awareness as secretary of state of "who was President," and of the parallel necessity for the chief executive also to bear in mind at all times "who was Secretary of State." Effective enactment of both roles was essential for American diplomatic success, and "mutual restraint" by both officials was required if a collaborative relationship was to be maintained between them. Implicit in his understanding of the secretary of state's role, however, was Acheson's awareness that the Truman-Acheson partnership was not an equal one. His predecessor, Secretary Byrnes, had been made painfully aware of the reality that the head of the State Department is the president's appointee, serves at his pleasure, and must continually operate with the president's approval and support. Acheson clearly understood that if an incumbent president chooses to function as his own secretary of state (which Truman did infrequently, such as when he extended almost instantaneous recognition to the state of Israel upon its establishment on May 14, 1948), his advisers can do little to prevent it. Acheson was cognizant that his own, and his department's, influence upon the foreign policy process would depend in the final analysis upon the degree to which their views and policy recommendations merited consideration by the White House and were viewed by the president as promoting America's diplomatic interests. In fact, Truman almost never acted in the field of foreign affairs without consulting his secretary of state.[21]

On the personal level, in his dealings with the president, Acheson was courteous, considerate, and respectful. If Acheson tended to be condescending and intimidating in his relations with others, these qualities were seldom evident in his relationship with Truman. Different as their personalities and backgrounds were, Acheson genuinely admired him, appreciated the difficult circumstances that had placed him in the Oval Office, and respected his prerogatives as chief executive. Unlike many other secretaries of state before and after, Acheson did not overtly seek publicity for himself or attempt to upstage the president in the news media; nor did he challenge or threaten Truman as a political leader. If Acheson did in time become something of a political liability for President Truman and other

21. Acheson, *Present at the Creation*, 735, 169–82, 258–59; Truman, *Years of Trial and Hope*, 156–69; Stupak, *The Shaping of Foreign Policy*, 80.

members of his party, it was not because Acheson contested Truman's position as head of the Democratic party.[22]

Consideration for Truman's position led the secretary of state to keep his superior fully and frequently informed about major developments affecting American foreign policy; to present timely, clear, and thoughtful policy proposals to him; to consult other high-ranking executive officials, such as the secretary of defense and the nation's military commanders, in the stage of policy formulation; and, even in the rare instances when his advice was not accepted, to carry out conscientiously those policies that had been approved by the White House. For his part, President Truman no less respected Secretary Acheson's position. Unlike Roosevelt, when he relied upon "presidential agents" such as W. Averell Harriman for diplomatic missions, Truman normally instructed these agents to maintain close communication with the secretary of state. And these presidential envoys were not encouraged to make policy recommendations outside of regular State Department channels.[23]

Another principle motivating Acheson's administration of the State Department was his belief in a "strong presidency." He had first entered government service during the New Deal and would naturally look for dynamic presidential leadership in formulating solutions for the nation's domestic and foreign problems. He could recall the contrasting era of congressional dominance of foreign relations during the 1930s, when the security of the United States and the Western allies was placed in extreme jeopardy by the isolationists on Capitol Hill. In Truman, Acheson had found a chief executive who was prepared to use presidential power as needed to meet the internal and external challenges of the postwar period, and who in fact relished doing so. Accordingly, during his career at the head of the State Department, as one commentator has said, Acheson was "a lion in defense of the President."[24]

But Acheson was also convinced that the concept of the strong president should not degenerate into the model (à la Roosevelt) of the chief executive's attempting to serve as his own secretary of state,

22. Alexander DeConde, *The American Secretary of State: An Interpretation* (New York, 1962), 123–24; Smith, *Dean Acheson*, 43–44; Donovan, *Tumultuous Years*, 35–36.
23. Truman, *Years of Trial and Hope*, 253–54; Smith, *Dean Acheson*, 392.
24. See McLellan, *Dean Acheson*, 95; and Acheson's essay "The Responsibility for Decision in Foreign Policy," in *This Vast External Realm*, 193–208.

thereby relegating his chief diplomatic adviser to the position of a figurehead. He had little confidence in the ability of any president to conduct foreign relations single-handedly. He believed that the president needed an able secretary of state, fully as much as the latter required presidential support. To an even greater extent than FDR, Truman had entered the White House with little or no preparation in foreign affairs. Fortunately for Acheson, the president implicitly acknowledged this fact by a willingness to listen to his foreign policy advisers before he made the ultimate decision. Acheson also understood, however, that a chief executive may seek "advice from whatever quarter he wishes." He accepted this reality stoically, and if he was jealous or resentful of the advice given to President Truman by other advisers, he usually managed to conceal the fact. Acheson believed, however, that the secretary of state should have the last word with the president—and should be able to advise him privately—before the latter made his decision.[25]

Another principle to which Acheson was devoted was the belief that unity within the government was essential for diplomatic success. He was aware that two broad sources of discord and dissension can pose serious obstacles for American diplomatic success. One of these is conflict between the executive and legislative branches in the foreign policy field. Acheson was especially concerned that foreign governments would distrust the reliability and constancy of American foreign policy if executive actions were repudiated or undermined on Capitol Hill. Consequently, he devoted as much as one-third of his time to legislative liaison and to cultivating support on Capitol Hill for the administration's diplomatic undertakings. During the tenure of Secretaries of State Marshall and Acheson, a bipartisan approach to American foreign policy reached its culmination in the postwar period.[26]

The second possible source of division within the government on foreign policy questions was conflict within the executive branch. In his earlier State Department service, Acheson had witnessed and ex-

25. Charles Yost, *The Conduct and Misconduct of Foreign Affairs: Reflections on U.S. Foreign Policy Since World War II* (New York, 1972), 137; Dean Acheson, Introduction to Louis J. Halle, *Civilization and Foreign Policy: An Inquiry for Americans* (New York, 1955), xvii.

26. McLellan, *Dean Acheson*, 49; Acheson, *Present at the Creation*, 89–101; Dean Acheson, *A Citizen Looks at Congress* (New York, 1957).

perienced firsthand the department's decline during and after World War II, a phenomenon to which he believed Secretary of State Hull's inadequate leadership had significantly contributed. In the early postwar era this process had been accelerated by the passage of the National Security Act of 1947, creating the CIA, a new Department of Defense, and a new White House advisory organ—the National Security Council (see Chapter 2). Along with the older executive departments like Commerce and Treasury, these agencies were actual or potential rivals of the State Department in the foreign policy process.

Although he was realistic enough to know that he could not totally undo such administrative changes, Acheson continued to believe in the primacy of the State Department as the agency in charge of American foreign policy under the president's direction. He deplored the department's eclipse, and he was determined to restore it as the spokesman for, and agency for administering, the foreign relations of the United States. As a rule, Acheson served as the spokesman for the Truman administration's foreign policy inside and outside the government, and his position was seldom overtly challenged by other executive officials. His ready and frequent access to the Oval Office (he customarily met with President Truman three or four times per week) signified at least a partial, if in hindsight only a temporary, revival in the State Department's fortunes. At the same time, he rejected the idea (advanced periodically by some students of American foreign policy) that the secretary of state should serve as a kind of "first secretary" within the executive branch, at a level higher than any other cabinet officer. Acheson never forgot that, as with all other members of the cabinet, the secretary of state's position and influence ultimately depend upon the degree of support he receives from the president.[27]

Implicit in Acheson's conception of the relationship between president and secretary of state was his skepticism about the value of coordinating agencies and mechanisms, such as the cabinet and the National Security Council, in the foreign policy field. President Truman was dubious about the value of the NSC. Acheson wanted no other executive agencies to come between the president and his chief for-

27. Stupak, *The Shaping of Foreign Policy*, 67–68, 84–85; I. M. Destler, *Presidents, Bureaucrats, and Foreign Policy: The Politics of Organizational Reform* (Princeton, 1972), 89.

eign policy adviser, and Truman did not encourage that practice. In company with many other experienced diplomatic officials, Acheson was no less skeptical about the value of the president's cabinet as a policy making mechanism. (On foreign policy issues, President Truman used his cabinet primarily as a forum for *informing* department heads of important diplomatic developments.) Truman's reliance upon the NSC and the cabinet in diplomatic decision making was nominal and infrequent. Although Acheson acknowledged the necessity to coordinate the activities of executive agencies in foreign affairs, in his view this could most effectively be done by small, usually *ad hoc* groups of high-ranking officials directly involved with particular diplomatic issues. To his mind, such groups could successfully avoid the temptation to produce innocuous agreed-upon proposals having little to recommend them except that they reflected a vague consensus among those officials involved in formulating them. In all attempts to unify executive branch activities in the foreign policy sphere, the primacy of the State Department had to be recognized and preserved, he thought. He also believed that one method the secretary of state could use to achieve this goal was to play a central role in drafting presidential speeches and policy declarations—one of the most crucial stages in the enunciation of foreign policy.[28]

Acheson and the State Department

Charles Dickens' famous description of Europe during the era of the French Revolution as both "the best of times" and "the worst of times" could well describe the history of the State Department during Acheson's tenure as secretary of state. On one hand, by a number of criteria, under Acheson's forceful and capable direction the State Department reached the pinnacle of its institutional influence as an actor in the foreign policy process in the post–World War II period. (In the Eisenhower-Dulles era, which followed, the influence of the secretary of state, though not of the State Department as an institu-

28. Kenneth C. Clark and Laurence J. Legere, *The President and the Management of National Security: A Report by the Institute of Defense Analysis* (New York, 1969), 58–59; Acheson, *Present at the Creation*, 734–36, 755–57; Stupak, *The Shaping of Foreign Policy*, 85–87; George Ball, *Diplomacy for a Crowded World* (Boston, 1976), 199.

tion, may well have been greater than in the Truman administration.) For a time, Acheson substantially succeeded in his determination to halt the decline of the department within the executive branch and to gain recognition of it—from the president and from other executive agencies—as the premier department in the foreign policy field.

On the other hand, during Acheson's incumbency as secretary of state, the department suffered a series of extremely serious blows to its prestige and morale, which impaired its performance and its influence within the foreign policy process for a generation or more thereafter. If the influence of the State Department has perceptibly declined since World War II, a major reason was its poor image on Capitol Hill and in the news media during the Truman-Acheson period. In the late 1940s, by the time of Acheson's confirmation by the Senate as secretary of state, allegations were being made of pro-Communist influence within the State Department, accusations that received national attention when they were made and amplified by the House Un-American Activities Committee and by Senator Joseph McCarthy (R-Wis.). In time these charges were widely publicized and embellished by right-wing political commentators and organizations. Acheson himself became a prime target of right-wing critics, in part because of his association in the State Department with Alger Hiss. Hiss was ultimately convicted of spying for the Soviet Union, and his conviction was upheld by the Supreme Court. Although Hiss had never held a high-level position within the diplomatic establishment, McCarthyites charged that pro-Communist elements were responsible for such diplomatic setbacks as American membership in the United Nations, the "loss of China" to communism, and America's failure to "win" the cold war. President Truman's decision during the Korean War to relieve the popular General Douglas MacArthur of his command for failure to follow presidential directives also incensed Acheson's right-wing detractors and precipitated new calls for his dismissal—demands that Truman consistently refused to accept.[29]

29. For a more comprehensive discussion, see Alan D. Harper, *The Politics of Loyalty: The White House and the Communist Issue, 1946–1952* (Westport, Conn., 1969). The Hiss case is analyzed in Alistair Cooke, *A Generation on Trial: U.S.A. vs. Alger Hiss* (New York, 1950); and William A. J. Jowitt, *The Strange Case of Alger Hiss* (Garden City, N.Y., 1953). The political movement known as McCarthyism is examined in Joseph McCarthy, *McCarthyism: The Fight for America* (New York, 1952); Fred J. Cook, *The Nightmare Decade: The Life and Times of Senator Joe McCarthy* (New York, 1971); Earl Latham, *The Meaning of McCarthyism* (Boston, 1966).

Despite repeated efforts by Truman, Acheson, and other officials to refute McCarthy's usually baseless allegations, the continuing assault by the radical right exacted a heavy toll from the State Department. Some officials were released because of their alleged pro-Communist connections and inclinations; others resigned rather than be subjected to endless investigations and interrogations before hostile congressional committees. For those who remained in the diplomatic service, the main lesson seemed to be that mindless conformity and the expression of safe viewpoints were the prime requisite for survival and advancement. A number of State Department officials (such as the "old China hands," who had questioned America's generous support of Nationalist China and predicted a Communist victory in China's civil war) found themselves publicly vilified, their careers jeopardized, and their personal reputations irreparably damaged by McCarthy and his disciples, who usually made their accusations within Congress, where they were protected by congressional immunity from lawsuits.

During the McCarthy period, for many Americans—probably always a relatively small, if highly vocal and politically active, minority—Acheson's name became a synonym for America's "defeat" in the cold war and for the alleged influence of Marxist ideas in all spheres of American life. For the last two years or so of his incumbency, hardly a day passed that President Truman was not urged to fire Acheson by some spokesman for the radical right. (Ironically, by the years of the Vietnam War, Acheson and many of his State Department associates were being vocally castigated by the New Left and by the revisionist school of postwar American foreign policy. According to this indictment, Acheson was a prominent spokesman for the "military-industrial complex," whose ingrained *anticommunism*, greed for lucrative defense contracts, political conservatism, and other characteristics were responsible for precipitating and intensifying the cold war.)[30] Within Congress, Senator McCarthy and his followers comprised a small minority of the House and Senate. Time and again during this period, congressional majorities supported the Truman-

30. John C. Donovan, *The Cold Warriors: A Policy-Making Elite* (Lexington, Mass., 1974); Richard J. Barnet, *Roots of War: The Men and Institutions Behind U.S. Foreign Policy* (Baltimore, 1973); N. D. Houghton (ed.), *Struggle Against History: United States Foreign Policy in an Age of Revolution* (New York, 1968); Thomas G. Paterson (ed.), *Cold War Critics: Alternatives to American Foreign Policy in the Truman Years* (Chicago, 1971).

Acheson foreign policy proposals. In time, McCarthy was severely reprimanded by his own Senate colleagues.

Acheson was determined to revitalize the State Department and to restore it to the center of the policy making process. He believed that, to achieve this objective, the department had to demonstrate its competence, its creativity, and the relevance of its policy recommendations to postwar conditions. It had to be responsive to the needs of the president and to the challenges confronting the United States abroad. As secretary of state, Acheson set an example of an energetic, disciplined, hard-working administrator who demanded a comparable performance from his subordinates. He kept himself well informed about current diplomatic issues and participated actively in the deliberations of the department. Secretary Acheson insisted that presidential and other inquiries to the State Department be answered promptly. He regularly consulted his own aides and bureau chiefs in the formulation of major policy proposals, and in turn he made an effort to keep the department informed of current and pending developments. He demanded that position papers and policy recommendations by the department be timely, readable, and pertinent, and he continually reminded his State Department colleagues of the necessity for prompt action rather than bureaucratic indecision and lethargy. In the words of one commentator, Acheson was determined to make his department "the best organized and most efficiently run agency" in Washington, capable of providing the president "the most accurate information and soundest advice possible."[31] As judged by the quality and durability of diplomatic programs undertaken during his tenure, for the most part Acheson succeeded in achieving his objective.

Secretary of State Acheson was not a devotee of the idea that frequent and sweeping organizational reform was the key to American diplomatic success. State Department organizational changes during his tenure were limited, confined primarily to implementing the recommendations of the Hoover commission, which had been created by President Truman to reorganize the executive branch.[32] Instead,

31. McLellan, *Dean Acheson*, 97.
32. The Hoover commission, chaired by ex-President Herbert Hoover, was the popular name of U.S. Commission on the Organization of the Executive Branch of the Government. See its report, *Foreign Affairs: A Report to the Congress* (Washington, D.C., 1949).

Acheson relied upon a well-qualified staff in whom he had confidence—individuals such as Charles E. Bohlen, George F. Kennan, Will Clayton, Charles B. Marshall, Loy Henderson, and Dean Rusk—to supply the creative ideas that were ultimately reflected in the department's position papers and policy recommendations. Acheson was accessible to his subordinates, engaged in frank dialogues with them, and encouraged them to think objectively and independently. On innumerable occasions, he took pains to praise the diplomatic corps, especially after some of its members had come under sharp congressional and media attack from right-wing critics. Not infrequently, he deflected criticism of the State Department from his subordinates to himself.[33]

A perennial complaint about the American foreign policy process is the lack of long-range diplomatic planning engaged in by State Department officials. Because of this deficiency, American diplomacy has frequently been criticized for its incremental or piecemeal character and its preoccupation with immediate crises abroad. On the question of more systematic diplomatic planning, Acheson's views were ambivalent. In principle, he endorsed the idea, believing that American foreign policy needed to be undergirded by "an applicable body of theory" and had to overcome the typical American tendency to respond to external problems by a series of disconnected, often inconsistent, day-by-day policy improvisations.[34] In practice, he continued to utilize the department's Policy Planning Staff instituted by his predecessor, Secretary of State Marshall. But in time, its members, such as Kennan, were increasingly assigned to work on immediate and urgent diplomatic issues, leaving them little time and inclination for planning long-term diplomatic strategy. Ultimately, this tendency convinced Kennan and other State Department officials that policy planning was not a function that enjoyed a high priority with Acheson and with most of his successors.[35]

In another of his official duties—negotiating and maintaining con-

33. McLellan, *Dean Acheson*, 59, 97–98; Smith, *Dean Acheson*, 395–96, 412; Hilsman, *The Politics of Policy Making in Defense and Foreign Affairs*, 156–57.

34. Roger Hilsman, *To Move a Nation: The Politics of Foreign Policy in the Administration of John F. Kennedy* (Garden City, N.Y., 1967); David Halberstam, *The Best and the Brightest* (New York, 1983); Acheson, Introduction to Halle, *Civilization and Foreign Policy*, xi–xxii, and the ensuing exposition by Halle, *passim*.

35. See Kennan, *Memoirs, 1925–1950*, pp. 449–50, 493–94.

structive relations with foreign leaders, especially in Western Europe—Acheson excelled. He was highly regarded in European capitals, and his rapport with the leaders of the region contributed significantly to the success of American diplomacy in Europe during the Truman administration. His strong European orientation, and his belief that European-American relations formed the cornerstone of United States foreign policy, were well known. He was considerably less familiar with, or interested in, regions like Asia and Latin America. One student of the period, for example, has said that Acheson's interest in Latin America was perfunctory: he had little time or inclination to become deeply involved in the region's problems. Nor could it be said that Acheson was particularly well informed about Asia and its contemporary political movements.[36]

Several years after he retired from government service, Acheson observed, "Nobody has been able to run the [State] Department in a hundred and fifty years."[37] As secretary of state, he experienced a number of disappointments and frustrations. Owing largely to the incessant attacks by right-wing critics, he himself became a highly controversial figure and a political liability for the Truman administration, and that fact to some degree weakened the basis of legitimacy that any successful foreign policy requires in the American democracy. With Truman himself, other members of his official family, and millions of Americans, Acheson did not fully understand the relationship between diplomatic and military power. This fact, for example, led the administration to change the goals of the Korean War several times, which in turn contributed significantly to the popular confusion and disaffection about the war's outcome. Despite such deficiencies, Acheson probably ran the State Department as well or better than any secretary of state since World War II.

Acheson and Other Executive Agencies

During the Truman-Acheson period, one commentator has observed, "No other department or agency . . . competed seriously with [the

36. Stupak, *The Shaping of Foreign Policy,* 36; McLellan, *Dean Acheson,* 395; Donald S. Zagoria, "Choices in the Postwar World (2): Containment and China," in Charles Gati (ed.), *Caging the Bear: Containment and the Cold War* (Indianapolis, 1974), 120–22.
37. James L. McCamy, *Conduct of the New Diplomacy* (New York, 1964), 7.

State Department] for control of foreign policy." In that respect Acheson's administration of the department marked the end of an era in the American foreign policy process. After 1952, the influence of the White House staff, the Defense Department, and other executive bureaucracies grew steadily. By the period of the Vietnam War (see Chapter 6), it appeared that the State Department was sometimes a relatively minor actor in the decision-making process. In his relations with other executive agencies, Secretary of State Acheson exhibited what a former State Department official has called "the killer instinct" in defending the prerogatives and jurisdiction of his department. He was avowedly protective of his department and determined to preserve its traditional powers and responsibilities from encroachments by other agencies.[38]

Although the Central Intelligence Agency had been created in 1947, during the Truman presidency its role in the foreign policy process remained limited, and its influence was nearly always eclipsed by that of the State Department as expressed by Acheson. With the collaboration of the Defense Department, Secretary Acheson also prevailed in a clash in late 1949 and early 1950 with the Atomic Energy Commission. President Truman sided with the joint viewpoint of the Defense and State departments by committing the United States to the development of the hydrogen bomb.[39]

In his relations with the military arm of the government—the newly created Department of Defense—Acheson's approach was marked by emphasis upon three fundamental principles. First, military and other forms of power were crucial elements in successful diplomacy. Second, the United States had to possess the power requisite for carrying out its international commitments, and it also had to possess the will to use the power at its disposal for diplomatic ends. Failure in either case risked diplomatic disaster. Third, power, particularly military power, must always be viewed as an adjunct or instrument of diplomacy, not as a substitute for it. The successful application of military power merely made possible acceptable diplomatic solutions; it did not guarantee successful diplomatic results. One of the more in-

38. Smith, *Dean Acheson*, 392; Hilsman, *The Politics of Policy Making in Defense and Foreign Affairs*, 168.
39. Smith, *Dean Acheson*, 393; Smith Simpson, *Anatomy of the State Department* (Boston, 1967), 81.

novative aspects of Acheson's thought about power was his realization, though perhaps he did not fully grasp all its implications, that "limited war," as exemplified in the Korean conflict, was the only kind of military confrontation that could be tolerated in the nuclear age.

Acheson approached international politics from what might be called a pragmatic or "neorealist" perspective. To his mind, political relationships among rival nation-states entailed a dynamic pattern of "challenge and response." The global arena was a universe of contending "forces and counterforces." And in Acheson's expressive metaphor, the objective of diplomacy was to achieve and preserve "the dynamic, precarious, shifting equilibrium of two elephants butting against each other." Contrary to the expectations of many Americans, the Soviet and American "elephants" would never achieve a true condition of peace and friendship. But given enlightened statesmanship on both sides, they did not need to engage in mutual annihilation. Power and power struggles, Acheson asserted, were synonyms for life itself. Life expressed itself in power, and "kinetic energy" was organic to it. He thus rejected the view, identified with idealists like Hull and Roosevelt, that occasional and frenzied applications of American power or crusades could ever free the United States from vexatious international problems and unwanted global responsibilities.[40]

Yet, since he was an American, Acheson's thought was also influenced by certain pragmatic and idealistic desiderata shaping his conception of the foreign policy process. Although he continued, for example, to use the Policy Planning Staff in the State Department, Acheson appeared more dubious than his predecessor about the utility of long-range diplomatic planning divorced from immediate policy questions. In opposition to his right-wing critics, Acheson did not believe that the United States could undertake a diplomatic offensive designed to win the cold war decisively without losing the very qualities that made the United States a democratic nation. As the containment strategy implied and as Acheson's critics complained, the United States was required to limit or constrain Soviet moves with its own countermoves, in the hope that sooner or later, the Kremlin would abandon its expansionist ambitions or, as George Kennan antici-

40. Dean Acheson, *Power and Diplomacy* (Cambridge, Mass., 1958); Acheson, Introduction to Halle, *Civilization and Foreign Policy*, xiv–xxii; Acheson, *This Vast External Realm*, 29–41, 115–26, 146–56.

pated, that the Soviet dictatorship would "mellow" or evolve into a more benign political order. Meanwhile, Acheson was convinced that communism exemplified a "new barbarism" that threatened Western values and principles. The Soviet-American conflict was, therefore, something more than another familiar example of clashing national interests or hegemonic impulses.[41]

While Acheson acknowledged the role of power in international politics, he also believed that the civilian and political dimensions of diplomacy must always remain uppermost. As he assessed it, America's armed forces are essentially a means or adjunct of national policy: they were utilized by civilian policy makers to achieve political objectives. It followed that the military voice in the policy making process should be heard and carefully considered, but it should never be dominant in the highest councils of the American government.[42]

As under secretary of state serving under General Marshall, whose career had been spent in the armed forces, Acheson had become accustomed to maintaining close liaison with the defense establishment. He continued this practice as secretary of state. During the Korean War, for example, Acheson and other State Department officials regularly consulted with their counterparts in the Defense Department and with the Joint Chiefs of Staff. In most instances, State and Defense department spokesmen were able to arrive at agreed-upon positions on problems of mutual concern. In 1949, however, a long-standing feud erupted into overt bureaucratic conflict between Acheson and Secretary of Defense Louis Johnson, who had become highly critical of Acheson and was also politically ambitious. In the end, President Truman resolved the dispute by siding with Acheson and relieving Johnson of his position.[43]

But in some respects Acheson was also in awe of military strategists and appeared reluctant to challenge their judgments directly, even when military decisions had significant diplomatic consequences. For example, along with nearly all other high-ranking officials of the Truman administration, he accepted General MacArthur's strategy of pursuing Communist forces northward across the thirty-eighth par-

---

41. Acheson, Introduction to Halle, *Civilization and Foreign Policy*, xxi; Acheson, *This Vast External Realm*, 35–38, 75–88.
42. Smith, *Dean Acheson*, 392–93.
43. Haynes, *The Awesome Power*, 193–94; Donovan, *Tumultuous Years*, 62–63.

allel in Korea to the Yalu River border with Communist China. As this offensive moved toward the Chinese frontier, Communist China's entry into the war converted it into a destructive Sino-American conflict—a major factor in the more than twenty years of estrangement between the two countries that followed. Acheson did, however, finally urge President Truman to relieve MacArthur of his command. Not unexpectedly, this development incensed the State Department's right-wing critics and triggered new demands for Acheson's resignation.[44]

Truman, Acheson, and the Zenith of Bipartisanship

In sum, the Truman-Acheson foreign policy record had a strangely paradoxical quality. On one hand, it was one of the most intensely partisan and internally divisive periods in post–World War II diplomacy. Once he became a continuing target of right-wing critics, Acheson was a heavy political liability for the Truman administration. On the other hand, the concept of bipartisanship in foreign affairs since World War II reached its zenith during the Truman administration. During the period of Secretaries of State Marshall and Acheson, an unprecedented level of collaboration existed between the White House and Congress in behalf of key foreign policy measures. After 1952, successive administrations were never able to recover a comparable degree of bipartisan cooperation in the foreign policy field, though by the early 1980s, the Reagan administration was endeavoring, not altogether successfully, to revive the concept of bipartisanship in foreign affairs.

From the inception, the precise meaning and requirements of a "bipartisan" approach to foreign relations have remained inexact and poorly defined. According to popular slogans expressing the idea, such as the World War I concept that "politics is adjourned" or the later maxim that "politics stops at the water's edge," the basic goal is the formulation and administration of a foreign policy that is supported by both major political parties and by the executive and legislative branches of the government. Many of the post–World War II

44. Destler, *Presidents, Bureaucrats, and Foreign Policy*, 260–61; Haynes, *The Awesome Power*, 193–94; Truman, *Years of Trial and Hope*, 330–450; Acheson, *Present at the Creation*, 402–14, 512–29.

advocates of bipartisanship had firsthand recollections of two eras when there had been a marked absence of bipartisan collaboration in foreign relations.

One was the period following World War I, when the partisan controversy between opponents and supporters of the League of Nations resulted in America's rejection of that organization and in the nation's relapse into its traditional isolationist stance. Then, during the New Deal the deadlock between the Roosevelt White House and the isolationists on Capitol Hill immobilized American foreign policy and left the nation unprepared for World War II. Roosevelt and his advisers were determined that internal disunity would not once again prevent the United States from assuming its proper international obligations in the post–World War II era. His appointment of two Republicans, Frank Knox as secretary of the navy and Henry L. Stimson as secretary of war, along with the participation of prominent Republicans, such as John Foster Dulles, in wartime planning for the United Nations, prepared the way for even more systematic bipartisan collaboration under the Truman administration.[45]

Truman continued this bipartisan tradition, appointing Republicans as members of the American delegation to the San Francisco Conference, which drafted the UN Charter in 1945, and as negotiators for the minor Axis peace treaties in the early postwar period. Senator Warren Austin (R-Vt.) was also asked by the Truman White House to serve as the nation's first ambassador to the United Nations. During the tenure of Secretaries of State Marshall and Acheson the major diplomatic undertakings, such as the Greek-Turkish aid program, the Marshall Plan, the North Atlantic Treaty, and the Point Four program, emerged as a result of bipartisan collaboration between executive and legislative officials. Even Truman's most controversial act in the foreign policy field—his dismissal of MacArthur—was ultimately accepted as legitimate by majorities in the House and Senate and by the American people.

What factors explain the remarkable bipartisan consensus on foreign policy questions that existed during the Truman administration? Even today, it is difficult to account for the phenomenon satisfactorily and to explain why the same level of bipartisan collaboration could

45. *The Private Papers of Senator Vandenberg,* 1–146; Cordell Hull, *The Memoirs of Cordell Hull* (2 vols.; New York, 1948), II, 1109–1743.

not be reproduced after 1952. In retrospect, it seems clear that from the end of World War II until the early 1950s, an almost ideal combination of factors and developments produced this level bipartisanship. Briefly and at the risk of some oversimplification, several conditions that contributed to this result can be identified.

One was the fact that soon after entering the Oval Office, President Truman pledged to continue the foreign policies of the Roosevelt administration, which included maintaining the bipartisan tradition established by FDR and his advisers. With his predecessor, Truman was determined that partisan acrimony would not destroy the unity and continuity of postwar American foreign policy.[46]

Another development enhancing the prospect for bipartisanship after World War II was the impact of the Pearl Harbor disaster upon both congressional and public opinion in the United States. A pervasive consequence of this event was the conversion of most isolationists in the House and Senate to a foreign policy of internationalism. A noteworthy case was the experience of the individual who came to epitomize bipartisanship after World War II, Senator Vandenberg. Formerly an ardent isolationist, during the war Vandenberg became an outspoken and well-informed advocate of an international leadership role by the United States. In time, he emerged as the most influential Republican spokesman on Capitol Hill on foreign policy issues.[47] Working closely with State Department officials, Vandenberg played a key role in formulating, and in mustering legislative support for, the major diplomatic undertakings of the Truman administration.

When the Republican party gained control of the Eightieth Congress (1947–1948), Senator Vandenberg served as chairman of the Senate Foreign Relations Committee. In this period, in contrast to the 1970s and early 1980s, the Senate was clearly a more influential body than the House in dealing with foreign policy issues, and within the Senate, the Foreign Relations Committee was recognized as having primary, if not usually exclusive, jurisdiction over diplomatic questions. For its part, during the Truman-Acheson period the executive branch also maintained a high degree of internal unity on foreign policy issues. Under the president's direction, Secretary of State Acheson served as the administration's designated foreign policy spokesman:

46. Donovan, *Tumultuous Years*, 68.
47. *The Private Papers of Senator Vandenberg*, 1–21.

Vandenberg could rely upon the fact that agreements arrived at with Acheson or his representatives accurately reflected the viewpoints of the Truman White House. After Vandenberg's retirement and death in 1951, no other individual emerged in Congress who was capable of making his unique contribution to the cause of bipartisan cooperation in the foreign policy sphere.[48]

As early as 1943, Acheson had participated in efforts by the Roosevelt administration to build a bipartisan foundation under postwar American foreign policy. For a brief period he had been in charge of the department's office of congressional relations. As under secretary of state, he had delivered an articulate and moving statement of the rationale for the containment policy to a group of legislators early in 1947, before President Truman asked Congress to approve the Greek-Turkish aid program on March 12. At Senator Vandenberg's instigation, Truman and his advisers were urged to "scare hell out of the country" when they described the Communist threat to Greece and Turkey, advice that the White House followed and that was unquestionably decisive in securing congressional and public approval for this epochal undertaking.[49] In the months ahead, the Marshall Plan, the North Atlantic Treaty, and other programs implementing the containment strategy were adopted by solid bipartisan majorities in Congress. In nearly all instances, Vandenberg's support was crucial to the outcome.

During the tenure of Secretary of State Acheson and of his predecessor General Marshall, certain principles, procedures, and (often informal) understandings evolved in the attempt to maintain a bipartisan approach to American foreign policy. One of these was forcefully communicated in the early postwar period by Senator Vandenberg, when, after reading about an important foreign policy development in the newspaper, he bluntly informed the White House that Republicans wanted to be in on the "takeoffs" as well as the "crash landings" in foreign affairs.[50] For Vandenberg, in other words, genuine bipar-

48. *Ibid.*, 172–581.
49. Truman, *Years of Trial and Hope*, 103–104; Acheson, *Present at the Creation*, 218–20. See also Acheson's sketch of Vandenberg in *Sketches from Life*, 123–47.
50. Two studies focusing upon the foreign policy of the Truman administration that call attention to the principles and procedures of bipartisanship are Cecil V. Crabb, Jr., *Bipartisan Foreign Policy: Myth or Reality?* (New York, 1957); and H. Bradford Westerfield, *Foreign Policy and Party Politics* (New Haven, 1955).

tisanship required meaningful advance consultations between executive and legislative officials in the stage of policy formulation (as distinct from the president's presenting legislators with a *fait accompli* that they were expected to support according to the principle of bipartisanship). As an experienced legislator, Vandenberg knew that his colleagues in Congress were sensitive to the criticism that they often served merely as "rubber stamps" for diplomatic decisions made by the president and his advisers. Consequently, he nearly always insisted that measures like the Greek-Turkish aid program and the Marshall Plan bear the congressional imprint and that changes be made in White House proposals to reflect legislative concerns. Acheson was careful to cooperate with and show respect for Vandenberg's desires.[51]

As head of the State Department, Acheson understood these prerequisites of a bipartisan foreign policy. Different as their backgrounds, personalities, and political orientations were, Secretary Acheson and Senator Vandenberg developed a constructive personal relationship based upon candor, respect, and mutual trust. Acheson was not noted for his admiration of Congress as an institution or his patience with poorly informed (and sometimes highly critical) legislators. He was an outspoken advocate of executive leadership in foreign policy and an opponent of legislative encroachments upon the president's domain. Yet, he managed to maintain a harmonious and constructive relationship with Senator Vandenberg that nearly always produced agreement between them. As one commentator has explained it, Acheson comprehended Vandenberg's mind-set and was careful to give him the "illusion of victory" by incorporating his suggestions into major foreign policy programs.[52]

For his part, Vandenberg made a twofold contribution to the Truman administration's diplomatic record that the president and his advisers could not supply. Having participated in the formulation of important diplomatic programs, Vandenberg defended them vigorously against critics on Capitol Hill. And if he could not altogether prevent attacks in the House and Senate upon Acheson and other State Department officials, he could and did refute these allegations;

51. *The Private Papers of Senator Vandenberg,* 337–99; Crabb, *Bipartisan Foreign Policy,* 54–98; Acheson, *Sketches from Life,* 124–27.
52. Smith, *Dean Acheson,* 407–408; Acheson, *Present at the Creation,* 99–100; Stupak, *The Shaping of Foreign Policy,* 31–32; Michael Leigh, *Mobilizing Consent: Public Opinion and American Foreign Policy, 1937–1947* (Westport, Conn., 1976), 151.

his knowledge of foreign affairs and great prestige often went far toward preventing these criticisms from impairing the credibility of the Truman administration's foreign policy at home and abroad.

The Truman-Acheson era marked the high point of bipartisan collaboration in foreign affairs for another reason that was possibly the most decisive. Theoretically, the American Congress serves as the voice of the people and is usually viewed as the most "representative" branch of the national government. On that assumption, the high level of bipartisan collaboration in the early postwar period can be accounted for by the remarkable degree of unity existing among the American people concerning the nation's global role and, more specifically, its response to the Soviet challenge. By the passage of the Greek-Turkish aid program early in 1947, it had become evident that the wartime goodwill that Americans had exhibited toward the Soviet ally had been superseded by a pervasive feeling of anxiety and distrust. Americans became increasingly skeptical about the prospects of constructive relations with the USSR.

Sometimes public opinion forged ahead of the attitudes of President Truman and his advisers in demanding that national leaders resist the Kremlin's demands. The Truman administration's stance of "patience and firmness" toward Moscow—ultimately translated into the containment strategy—was to no inconsiderable extent an outgrowth of American public opinion. The Republican victory in Congress in 1946, for example, was a forceful message to the Truman White House that the people wanted decisive resistance to Communist expansionist moves. In this public-opinion context, the people's legislative representatives had little choice except to support foreign policy measures reflecting popular concern. In contrast, later administrations (and the Carter and Reagan administrations are noteworthy examples) were usually compelled to make major foreign policy decisions in what was often a highly fragmented, disunited environment of public confusion and uncertainty about the nation's proper international role.[53]

An additional factor facilitating the emergence of bipartisan accords between Democrats and Republicans in foreign affairs during

53. Ralph B. Levering, *The Public and American Foreign Policy, 1918–1978* (New York, 1978), 92–120; Cecil V. Crabb, Jr., *Policy-Makers and Critics: Conflicting Theories of American Foreign Policy* (New York, 1976), 81–128.

the Truman-Acheson period was that a reasonably clear division of labor existed within the Senate on domestic and foreign policy issues. On domestic questions Senator Robert A. Taft (R-Ohio) was recognized as the authoritative GOP spokesman; on external issues most legislators, including Senator Taft, deferred to Senator Vandenberg's judgment. When, therefore, Acheson and his subordinates in the State Department arrived at understandings with Vandenberg, they could usually do so in confidence that these agreements would hold up in the ensuing Senate debate and would be translated into majorities supporting the administration's proposals. Throughout the years that followed, Congress itself became so internally disunified and so devoid of accepted leaders like Senators Taft and Vandenberg that bipartisanship became extremely difficult to achieve.[54]

Yet to Dean Acheson, as desirable as bipartisan understandings were, all participants in the process had to recognize that in the final analysis, the president decided, or made, the foreign policy of the United States. Bipartisanship did not in effect transfer the locus of foreign policy decision making from the White House to Congress. In Acheson's view (and it was an interpretation that came to be sharply challenged by advocates of congressional activism in foreign affairs after the Vietnam War), Congress' role in the foreign policy process consisted primarily of two contributions: imparting to major diplomatic undertakings the legitimacy or broad consensus needed to make them acceptable to American public opinion, and providing the funds, armed forces, and other resources needed to implement policies and programs decided upon by the White House. In brief, Congress "made the results possible." Acheson, in other words, did not believe that a bipartisan approach to foreign policy could be a substitute for imaginative and vigorous White House leadership in foreign relations. Indeed, he believed that a constructive contribution by Congress in responding to external challenges depended upon the exercise of forceful executive direction and guidance in the foreign policy field. Otherwise (as occurred, for example, during the 1970s), what Acheson called "Frenchification"—the immobilization of the national government because neither the president nor Congress was

54. Cecil V. Crabb, Jr., and Pat Holt, *Invitation to Struggle: Congress, the President and Foreign Policy* (2nd ed.; Washington, D.C., 1984), esp. 232–47.

capable of managing foreign relations effectively—would almost certainly occur.[55]

As Robert Elder has emphasized, the career of Dean Acheson as secretary of state shows how politically exposed and vulnerable the position can be and how dependent upon others for political support it remains.[56] Some secretaries of state—and perhaps the leading example in recent experience is Alexander Haig—lacked the requisite base of White House and congressional support to survive in the face of growing criticism of their performance. Acheson faced perhaps even more intense condemnation for a longer period of time, but he continued to head the State Department until President Eisenhower took office in 1953. The crucial difference was that Acheson retained President Truman's unswerving support and loyalty and that he had knowledgeable and highly respected defenders on Capitol Hill, such as Senator Vandenberg, who collaborated with him to gain needed support in the House and Senate. As a result, the State Department's critics had a limited impact upon the evolution of American diplomacy.

55. Acheson, *This Vast External Realm*, 195–97; Acheson, *Sketches from Life*, 130–31; Barton Bernstein (ed.), *Politics and Policies of the Truman Administraton* (Chicago, 1970), 207.

56. Robert E. Elder, *The Policy Machine: The Department of State and American Foreign Policy* (Syracuse, 1960), 145.

5

A Maximalist Secretary of State: Eisenhower and Dulles

Toward the end of the Eisenhower administration, an unknown com-
medienne named Carol Burnett scored a popular hit with a song entitled "I Lost My Heart over John Foster Dulles." It was done as high
burlesque, and its satire in viewing a secretary of state as an object of
amorous desire was heightened by Dulles' aloof manner and pu-
ritanical rhetoric. To his credit, the secretary was said to have taken it
all as good fun. Such a spoof of President Dwight Eisenhower would
not have been conceivable, since he was almost universally beloved
by the public, if not uniformly respected by the elite opinion makers.
"I Like Ike" was a widely, sometimes fervently, expressed feeling on
the part of the American electorate. Indeed, he was one of those rare
presidents who left office with a popular approval rating from a majority of the public.[1] Dulles, by contrast, was a deeply controversial
public figure capable of arousing bitter animosities that were far
from exclusively partisan in origin. For many, he was the embodiment of a strident anticommunism and moral self-righteousness that,
except at the end of his life, deprived him of any substantial popular
affection.[2]

1. On leaving office, Eisenhower and Kennedy enjoyed the approval of 59 percent of
the population. Only one other president since World War II has left office with a
majority of the public approving his performance—Gerald Ford with 53 percent.
Robert E. DiClerico, *The American President* (Englewood Cliffs, N.J., 1979), 158.
2. Townsend Hoopes, *The Devil and John Foster Dulles* (Boston, 1973), 35; Stephen E.
Ambrose, *The President* (New York, 1984), 442. Vol. II of Ambrose, *Eisenhower,* 2 vols.

Despite such a seemingly unbridgeable chasm between these two men in personality and political sensibility, Eisenhower and Dulles forged a close relationship on the personal and political level. Most important, the onetime supreme military commander in Europe and the longtime elder of the Presbyterian church maintained a close relationship in the formulation and execution of American foreign policy. A similar relationship has not been realized by a president and secretary of state since. Indeed, one would have to look back to Warren Harding and Charles Evans Hughes or Theodore Roosevelt and John Hay to find approximations in this century. (Henry Kissinger made his mark as special assistant to the president for national security affairs; see Chapter 7.) Dean Rusk and Lyndon Johnson conducted foreign policy by "consensus," and Dean Acheson and Harry Truman had a successful partnership (see Chapters 4 and 6). But Dulles' position was unique even when compared with Acheson and Rusk.

Whereas Acheson shared responsibility with Harry Truman, and Rusk endured because he facilitated the execution of LBJ's policies, Dulles enjoyed such a position of preeminence and independence in the conduct of foreign relations that he is best described as a "maximalist" secretary of state. He acted as the president's chief spokesman for foreign affairs. He was able to interpret his authority widely and consolidate his formal command of the foreign policy process because of his close personal relationship with Eisenhower. He and the president cooperated closely in both formal and informal discussions throughout all stages of the policy making process. The president deferred to his secretary on foreign policy matters; Dulles, for his part, carefully cultivated Eisenhower's support and never presumed to be doing more than faithfully executing the president's policies. Most significantly, Dulles neither acknowledged nor allowed an equal within his area—no other cabinet officer and certainly not a White House aide. He was not only Eisenhower's chief spokesman for foreign affairs but also the chief architect of the policy process. Yet, it must be remembered how completely Dulles' preeminence was dependent on his successful representation of Eisenhower's policies and his cultivation of the president's confidence.

Communism, Containment, and Cold War

The Eisenhower administration came to power early in 1953 with a strongly voiced opposition to the nation's existing foreign policy. The Republican campaign rhetoric was particularly hard-hitting in its denunciation of the containment policy of the Truman administration. Moreover, the preeminence that was accorded to foreign affairs in the 1952 campaign was unusual. For all of their global significance, foreign policy issues have not been of paramount importance in domestic politics. John Kennedy talked about a "missile gap" in 1960, and Ronald Reagan warned about a "window of vulnerability" in 1980. But most candidates have sought votes with personal appeals, appeals to traditional partisan loyalties, or promises of economic betterment. The 1952 campaign, however, was characterized by harsh partisan indictments and calls for policy revisions that contradicted the principles of continuity and bipartisanship in foreign policy. The Republican platform promised particularly to end "the negative, futile, and immoral policy of 'containment' which abandons countless human beings to a despotism and godless terrorism which in turn enables the rulers to forge the captives into a weapon for our destruction." [3]

Most of the anticontainment rhetoric, however, was only symbolic. As a consummate compromiser, Eisenhower was carefully balancing the two foreign policy wings of the Republican party. The recitation of the litany excoriating the "sellout at Yalta" and the Truman-Acheson "recipe for defeat" was designed largely to appease Senator Robert Taft and his isolationist colleagues. Eisenhower, to the contrary, was the very embodiment of the modern Republican internationalist. As the supreme Allied commander in Europe during and after World War II, Eisenhower could find little agreement with Taft's opposition to NATO and to the Marshall Plan for European reconstruction. Dulles, as a believer in collective security and global interdependence, could find little in common with a Fortress America approach to international relations that advocated "no foreign entanglements." [4]

3. Warren E. Miller and Donald E. Stokes, "Constituency Influence in Congress," *American Political Science Review*, LVII (March, 1963), 45–56; Hoopes, *The Devil and John Foster Dulles*, 130.
4. The Fortress America concept was popular in some conservative political circles in the 1950s. As formulated by ex-President Herbert Hoover, it meant that America's security was best built on a foundation of hemispheric self-sufficiency and nondepen-

But as was so typical of Eisenhower's style of leadership, he and Dulles avoided direct confrontations and sought to appease their opponents with symbolic gestures. Having "romanced" the Republican right wing with denunciations of the immorality of the Truman-Acheson line, they went about applying containment as the basis of the new administration's approach to foreign affairs.[5] This can be seen in the areas of weapons-systems development, alliance formation, and direct intervention in the affairs of other nations. Nothing about the Eisenhower-Dulles execution of foreign policy showed a marked departure from that of their Democratic predecessors. Although containment was criticized, it was also codified as the basic premise of American foreign policy for the next two decades.[6]

A Republican campaign slogan summed up for many Americans the problems that faced the nation: COMMUNISM, CORRUPTION, AND KOREA. Others wanted an answer to the question "Who lost China?" This so-called "China lobby" of Chiang Kai-shek's supporters was made up of such leaders as Henry Luce of Time, Incorporated, Senator William Knowland (R-Calif.), and Representative Walter Judd (R-Minn.). Senator Richard Nixon (R-Calif.) had recently been making serious charges about Communist influence in the administration of American foreign policy during the Roosevelt and Truman years. Veteran Foreign Service officers were examined before State Department and congressional loyalty boards, in the process creating a sense of uneasiness among career diplomats and contributing to popular mistrust of the whole foreign policy making process. This atmosphere would become paranoid during the later investigations by Senator Joseph McCarthy. The international situation as perceived domestically during the early 1950s was grave: "On top of the Soviet atomic debut, Chiang Kai-shek's forces had finally abandoned the mainland and had decided to make the island of Taiwan Chinese. An airlift lasting nearly one year, directed by General Lucius Clay, had been needed

---

dence on allies. While constituting a neoisolationism, it was also predicated on strong naval and sea forces and, ultimately, a strong nuclear arsenal. See Cecil V. Crabb, Jr., *Policymakers and Critics: Conflicting Theories of American Foreign Policy* (New York, 1976), 227–30.

5. Herbert S. Parmet, *Eisenhower and the American Crusades* (New York, 1972), 269.

6. For a discussion of Eisenhower's views on foreign affairs, see Richard M. Saunders, "Military Force in the Foreign Policy of the Eisenhower Presidency," *Political Science Quarterly*, C (Spring, 1985), 99–106.

to defy the Soviet blockade of West Berlin. The Korean War was still being fought. General MacArthur had miscalculated Chinese Communist reactions toward American troops driving to the Yalu River, and a whole 'new war' had developed. Less than a year later, the President fired the determined general."[7]

What Eisenhower promised to do was resolve these problems, "to clean up the mess in Washington." When he said, "I will go to Korea," many Americans breathed a sigh of relief. Eisenhower promised stability, order and a foreign policy that would resist Communist advances while preserving the peace and balancing the budget. Harry A. Bullis, chairman of the board of the General Mills Corporation, wrote to Eisenhower: "The people want another George Washington. They really think of you as a modern George Washington."[8]

The Republicans also pledged new policy directions with special attention to lowering federal spending, especially defense spending. Reduced spending would be accompanied by a greater decisiveness in dealing with international communism that would reject "the negative, futile, and immoral policy of containment." This "New Look" in national security policy involved a greater reliance on the possible retaliatory use of nuclear weapons. Thus, the large amounts of manpower that would be required for a protracted conventional war would not be necessary. The defense budget made up 70 percent of total federal spending in 1953. Substantial reductions in it would do what Eisenhower considered essential for the nation's economic well-being. The New Look's reliance on massive retaliation was admittedly risky, but Eisenhower believed that the deterrence strategy would discourage the Soviet Union from actions that might threaten an all-out war. Given the domestic policy considerations, "the New Look's admitted operational shortcomings seemed an acceptable risk."[9]

The Republicans linked frugality in military spending with a "policy of boldness" in foreign affairs, and the New Look came to be asso-

7. Parmet, *Eisenhower and the American Crusades*, 32.
8. *Ibid.*, 42.
9. Douglas Kinnard, *President Eisenhower and Strategy Management: A Study in Defense Politics* (Lexington, Ky., 1977), esp. 1–36; Dwight D. Eisenhower, *Mandate for Change, 1953–1956* (Garden City, N.Y., 1963), 445–58. Vol. I of Eisenhower, *The White House Years*, 2 vols. Samuel F. Wells, Jr., "The Origins of Massive Retaliation," *Political Science Quarterly*, XCVI (Spring, 1981), 39.

ciated with the doctrine of "massive retaliation" that Dulles is famous for. As early as 1951, he argued for a strategy that, in dealing
with any possible Soviet aggressive move, would rely on "the capacity of counterattack against the aggressor"; the success of such a
counterattack would come from the West's strategic air force and
weapons stockpile. Dulles also linked the threat of nuclear retaliation
against any Soviet aggression with the promise of "liberation" for the
"captive peoples" of Eastern Europe by which the United States
would seek to "roll back" the Soviet domination that had come with
the end of World War II. This expanded notion of massive retaliation
to include the more provocative rollback principle was never implemented. As the result of a White House review of foreign policy in
October, 1953, nicknamed Operation Solarium, the Eisenhower administration decided against renouncing the containment policy of
the Truman years. However, it was suggested that *resistance* might be
a better word than *containment*, presumably because of its less defensive connotations. Samuel F. Wells sums up President Eisenhower's
thinking: "Ultimately the participants in this top-level reassessment
decided not to undertake the policy of 'rollback' promised in the 1952
campaign. Instead they committed the administration to continue
Truman's policy of containment, backed by a more explicit reliance
on the retaliatory deterrent."[10]

Despite the clear official renunciation of any measures of retaliatory rollback, there was a persistent perception to the contrary. Many
people believed that the Eisenhower administration was willing to
use nuclear weapons as a response not just to a first-strike attack but
also to an attack on a nation vital to American security, such as Germany or Japan, or in the event of a resumption of the Korean conflict.
Dulles certainly continued to articulate a "liberationist theology"
that condemned communism in strident and uncompromising terms.
Eisenhower, for his part, espoused a more moderate position while
never contradicting his secretary of state. This "studied ambiguity"
in public pronouncements seemed clearly calculated to allow the
president a greater degree of flexibility in maneuvering among the
various institutions and interests that inhabit the foreign policy

10. John Foster Dulles, "Where Are We? A Five Year Record of America's Response to
the Challenge of Communism," *Department of State Bulletin,* XXIV (January 15, 1951),
85–89; Ambrose, *The President,* 171–72; Wells, "Origins of Massive Retaliation," 44.

sphere. In sum, "the combination of massive retaliation with the hope of an eventual triumph over communism satisfied all the requirements for a new Republican international policy. It exploited America's technological superiority and provided the basis for reduced federal spending; it had broad popular appeal; and it flowed from the strong belief of the president and his top advisers in the utility of nuclear weapons for both deterrent and actual military missions."[11]

Whatever value this strategy may have had domestically, the effect on the external scene was decidedly less than a complete success. The doctrine of massive retaliation may have been valid as a strategic response to a Soviet first strike and, more arguably, for protection of an essential element of our national security from destruction by Soviet conventional forces. However, when massive retaliation is combined with talk of rollback and liberation, it ceases to be a defensive doctrine and becomes offensive, if not provocative, in content. This dichotomized voice inevitably led to confusion and misperceptions about the actual intentions of American foreign policy. Ultimately, the Eisenhower-Dulles legacy in foreign affairs must be judged a mixed one largely because of the strategic ambiguity that made for its domestic successes.

Eisenhower's professional and partisan credentials, on the other hand, allowed him to do what no Democratic president would have dared. First, the Korean War came to an end in 1953 on roughly the *status quo ante bellum*. A general in the White House made the first stalemate in American warfare palatable. Second, military spending was brought under control for perhaps the only time in the postwar period. A general as president could say no to the service chiefs, especially when he had been a service chief himself. Third, American foreign policy was placed firmly on an internationalist footing. The remaining isolationists in the Republican party would have had a strong voice in policy making if Robert Taft had become president rather than Eisenhower (assuming Senator Taft could have beaten the Democratic candidate). Unlike Taft, Eisenhower had internationalist political beliefs rooted in his faith in the European alliance and a Free

11. Wells, "Origins of Massive Retaliation," 35; Kinnard, *Eisenhower and Strategy Management*, 126–27. Emmett John Hughes, *The Ordeal of Power, A Political Memoir of the Eisenhower Years* (New York, 1963), 340; Kinnard, *Eisenhower and Strategy Management*, 123–36.

World led by the United States. Fourth, the Eisenhower presidency stabilized American foreign policy by accepting the containment assumptions of Truman and Acheson. For all the talk of "agonizing reappraisals," the postwar stalemate was accepted. Fifth, the principle of collective security was affirmed with an unswerving commitment to NATO and the creation of other regional defense arrangements. Dulles' obsessive applications of this principle with regional pacts, such as the Central Treaty Organization (CENTO) and the Southeast Asia Treaty Organization (SEATO), were decidedly less important. Sixth, the principle of resistance to aggression that is the supposed lesson of Munich was made applicable to the Soviet Union and also applied in some very controversial cases—Lebanon, Guatemala, and Iran.

The Eisenhower administration's most striking diplomatic achievement was a negative one: the country remained at peace during his two terms, in contrast to the eight years following and preceding. Yet, this period of peace was hardly an era of good feeling. It would be difficult to imagine a more bellicose or intransigent secretary of state than Dulles, even though his policies proved moderate and realistic. So though there was talk of rolling back the Communists in Eastern Europe and unleashing Chiang Kai-shek, neither the Soviet invasion of Hungary nor the military incidents with the People's Republic of China at Quemoy and Matsu became the occasion for war. What alarmed so many was the destabilizing effect of the rhetoric used by the administration, particularly when the words were those of its chief spokesman for foreign affairs. Nothing raised more of a furor than some ruminations by Secretary Dulles in 1956 about how he approached various decisions while in office: "You have to take chances for peace, just as you have to take chances in war. Some say we were brought to the verge of war. Of course we were brought to the verge of war. The ability to get to the verge without getting into war is the necessary art. If you cannot master it, you inevitably get into war. If you try to run away from it, if you are scared to go to the brink, you are lost. We walked to the brink and we looked it in the face. We took strong action." [12]

Brinksmanship entered the lexicon of diplomacy as a synonym for

12. Sherman Adams, *Firsthand Report* (New York, 1961), 118.

recklessness and became as closely associated with the Dulles name as "massive retaliation." As the public furor over these remarks grew, President Eisenhower was obliged to deplore some of their connotations even while affirming that Dulles was the best secretary of state he had ever known. And former White House chief of staff Sherman Adams contends that Eisenhower was never as close to the brink as Dulles asserted. For example, "Eisenhower did not draw a definite line across the Strait of Formosa and warn the Communists that if they crossed it there would be war." Worse is the interpretation offered by Townsend Hoopes of Dulles' thinking: "The interview seemed to reflect the man's strange quintessential inwardness, in its revelation of both his insensitivity to public mood and his tendency to let vanity outrun proportion and truth."[13] Whatever judgment is accepted, the important point is the distorted view of American intentions that attached to this rhetoric. It was an uneasy peace that prevailed in a world in which Dulles was poised at the brink of retaliation.

It is important to remember, however, that the Eisenhower-Dulles era was a peaceful one uninterrupted by a Korea-style "police action" engaged in by the previous administration or the interminable war in Vietnam that was to plague the three administrations that followed. When subsequent generations look back on the 1950s, it is remembered, if selectively, as a time of international tranquillity. The events that might have involved the United States in armed conflicts have been largely forgotten: CIA involvement in the Guatemalan coup of 1954; the intervention of the marines in Lebanon in 1958; the U-2 incident of 1959, in which an American spy plane was shot down over Soviet air space; the military maneuvers involving the islands of Quemoy and Matsu, which were claimed by the People's Republic of China but occupied by Taiwan. Most strikingly, the strident rhetoric that characterized so many of Dulles' public pronouncements was not paralleled by military action. For all the talk of a rollback in Eastern Europe, the Soviet invasion of Hungary in 1956 went unanswered by the United States. Even before the "spirit of Camp David" was proclaimed in 1960, "peaceful coexistence" had characterized Soviet-American relations and the New Look defense budget assumed a limited role for the American military. When the United States was faced with a war in the Middle East started by Britain, France, and Israel,

13. *Ibid.*, 119; Hoopes, *The Devil and John Foster Dulles*, 311.

Dulles and Eisenhower forced a cessation of hostilities by these American allies. Massive retaliation may have been a weak reed on which to base world peace; nevertheless, no politically palatable alternative has been formulated in the intervening decades.

Eisenhower and the Whig Presidency

The Eisenhower portrayed so far is substantially at odds with the Eisenhower of conventional political wisdom. This traditional view of Eisenhower "as a good-natured bumbler, who lacked the leadership qualities to be an effective president," is quite different from the calculating, shrewd chief executive who, with Dulles, formulated this complex and largely successful foreign policy.[14] There have been only a few other presidential candidates with popular credentials and a background in foreign affairs that matched those of Eisenhower in 1952. From the perspective of the 1960s, it was possible to deplore the electorate's lack of wisdom in preferring a "simple soldier" over a "statesman" like Adlai Stevenson, the Democratic presidential candidate in 1952 and 1956. Without meaning to denigrate Stevenson's potential as a leader in foreign affairs, it should be noted that Eisenhower was already a proven international leader who could meet with such redoubtable figures as Winston Churchill and Charles de Gaulle on a level of equality, whereas Stevenson's major political experience was as governor of Illinois. Stephen Ambrose has said of Ike that "in foreign affairs, he was the best-prepared man ever elected to the Presidency."[15] In fact, the "simple soldier" characterization was largely a public-relations device that humanized and domesticated a man who

14. Fred I. Greenstein, *The Hidden-Hand Presidency: Eisenhower as Leader* (New York, 1982), vii. Richard Neustadt thought that Eisenhower neither liked the game he was engaged in nor had gained much understanding of its rules. See Richard Neustadt, *Presidential Power* (New York, 1980), 112–25. For a discussion of the revisionist historiography on Eisenhower, see Greenstein, *Hidden-Hand Presidency*, 251, n. 2; Stephen E. Ambrose, "The Ike Age," *New Republic*, May 9, 1981, pp. 26–34; and Anthony James Jones, "Eisenhower Revisionism: The Tide Comes In," *Presidential Studies Quarterly*, XIV (Fall, 1984), 561–71. In fact, this revisionist view of Eisenhower was held by at least one perceptive contemporary. See Samuel Lubell, *Revolt of the Moderates* (New York, 1956). For an early reevaluation by a political liberal, see Murray Kempton, "The Underestimation of Dwight D. Eisenhower," *Esquire* (September, 1967), 108.
15. Ambrose, *The President*, 18.

had been a general of the army, supreme allied commander in the European Theater, army chief of staff, and NATO supreme commander.

Contemporary perceptions of Eisenhower were often widely off the mark. The "paragon of domesticity" had in fact spent almost all of his adult life either on army bases or overseas—first, in the Philippines as chief of staff to General MacArthur and, then, in Europe during and after World War II. Although he was seemingly overmatched by such larger-than-life colleagues as General Patton and Field Marshal Montgomery, it was the self-effacing Eisenhower who held the alliance together during World War II and kept Patton and Montgomery in line. The description of Eisenhower as a simple soldier also disguised the formidable administrative skills that he wielded as the coordinator of victory. He was a consummate bureaucrat in his ability to marshal and command the resources of large-scale, multinational organizations. This was the Eisenhower who graduated first in his class at the Army General Staff College and who became a masterful bridge player during the tedium of the interwar years. This was also the Eisenhower who, despite his reputation for garbled prose, graduated tenth in English composition in his West Point class.

What was never ambiguous about Eisenhower was the enormous appeal that he had for so many segments of the American public: party stalwart, average voter, independents, Democrats and Republicans alike. Eisenhower enjoyed a "simultaneous appeal to a great array of interests, all of whom were convinced that he was their man." There probably has not been another president in this century who enjoyed such consistently favorable approval from the American public—before, during, and after his term as president. "I like Ike" was a spontaneous and deeply felt chant heard on both sides of the political fence. Indeed, Eisenhower had been approached by the Democrats to run for president, but he decided to identify himself as a Republican, though he demonstrated a continuing distaste for most kinds of partisan politics. He sought from the people a "mandate for change" and he was eagerly taken up on it. This indifference to the more vocal aspects of partisanship again contributed to a perception of Eisenhower as above politics (which would have been news to both Senator Taft and Governor Stevenson). He had the ability to project the image of a man whose behavior contrasted favorably with that of the professional politicians who abounded on the national scene.[16] Eisenhower was that most gifted of all politicians—the kind who can appear to be nonpolitical.

Eisenhower brought to the presidency a somewhat "whiggish" notion of the office. At least compared with the interventionist and highly personal styles of his immediate predecessors, he appeared restrained and uninvolved. In part this image was the result of a philosophical commitment to what he saw as the constitutional principle of separation of powers. But much of this seeming presidential noninvolvement was also just appearance—calculated by Eisenhower to further his political fortunes. Fred I. Greenstein has argued that Eisenhower's was a "hidden-hand" presidency: "He deliberately cultivated the impression that he was not involved even in the most successful of the maneuvers in which he directly participated. . . . He employed his skills to achieve his ends by inconspicuous means and was aware that a reputation as a tough political operator could be inconsistent with acquiring and maintaining another source of presidential influence, namely public prestige."[17] Greenstein concludes that in reality Eisenhower was "politically astute and informed, actively engaged in putting his personal stamp on public policy, and applied a carefully thought-out conception of leadership to the conduct of his presidency."[18]

Eisenhower's approach to the presidency can be characterized by the term *cabinet government*. Although the presidents who followed him entered office pledging to administer the government through their cabinet secretaries, Eisenhower seems to have been the last to have actually done so. The Eisenhower cabinet was derided by some as "nine millionaires and a plumber," the latter being a reference to Secretary of Labor Martin Durkin. But it contained individuals with strong personalities and established reputations: Dulles; Secretary of

16. Parmet, *Eisenhower and the American Crusades*, 7–18, 175.
17. Fred Greenstein, "Eisenhower as an Activist President: A New Look at the Evidence," *Political Science Quarterly*, XCIV (Winter, 1979–80), 597–98. See also Greenstein, *Hidden-Hand Presidency*, 58–63. On Eisenhower's active role in Republican party affairs, see Cornelius P. Cotter, "Eisenhower as a Party Leader," *Political Science Quarterly*, XCVIII (Summer, 1983), 255–83, and Ambrose, *Eisenhower*, 21–22.
18. Greenstein, "Eisenhower as an Activist President," 577; Kinnard, *Eisenhower and Strategy Management*, 128–29; Robert Divine, *Eisenhower and the Cold War* (New York, 1981), 7–11.

the Treasury George Humphrey, a successful businessman; Secretary of Defense Charles Wilson, former president of General Motors; Attorney General Herbert Brownell, a successful Wall Street lawyer; Secretary of Agriculture Ezra Taft Benson, an apostle of the Mormon church. Eisenhower used weekly Friday-morning cabinet meetings as forums for government-wide discussions and consensus-building. Issues were freely discussed, and the agreements reached were considered binding on the entire cabinet. Eisenhower's aide Robert Donovan described his boss's use of the cabinet: "Eisenhower has been very deliberate in attaining final agreement by the Cabinet on questions before it, and this agreement becomes, when the President approves it, the policy of the administration. . . . He has conducted the Cabinet on the principle that since all are free to participate, the ultimate decision is binding upon all. And, under these terms, it would be very bad medicine for one Cabinet member to go off and start feuding with another on a policy that had been settled upon in the Cabinet."[19]

The Eisenhower cabinet, however, rarely debated and decided on significant policy innovations; more often it was involved in modifying departmental compromises. Foreign policy making, moreover, was peculiarly Dulles' preserve, and his presentations at cabinet meetings were rarely questioned. Other cabinet members were aware that Dulles spoke for Eisenhower and that the secretary's policies had been or would be filtered through the National Security Council (NSC) committees. The president's caution against playing politics with foreign affairs also ensured Dulles' supremacy in that sphere.[20]

Eisenhower also greatly strengthened the National Security Council by creating the position of special assistant for national security affairs to coordinate liaison activities among NSC members, to chair the NSC Policy Planning Board, and to brief the president on the international situation. Future special assistants would use this position as a mechanism for providing presidents with independent analy-

19. Robert J. Donovan, *Eisenhower: The Inside Story* (New York, 1963), 67.
20. In a memorandum to Dulles about a press account of some statements by Secretary of Defense Wilson concerning the withdrawal of American troops from Europe, Eisenhower stated that he had pointed out to Wilson "that an NSC decision had been made to refer all statements and investigations on this subject to the Secretary of State." The president also said that he had directed Wilson to answer any further questions on the subject by saying: "Troops stationed outside the United States are always there in support of United States foreign policy. Please take up such questions with the Secretary of State." Ann Whitman File, Dulles-Herter, Box 1, October 22, 1953, Eisenhower Library, Abilene, Kansas.

ses of foreign policy. But those who held the position under Eisenhower (Robert Cutler, Dillon Anderson, and Gordon Gray) had the classic "passion for anonymity" that should supposedly characterize presidential staffers. Moreover, they never overtly challenged the State Department's role in formulating and executing foreign policy. Even the assistant to the president, Sherman Adams, who was anything but anonymous, took no active part in foreign affairs. Although all important political matters and domestic policy issues were first cleared through Adams, foreign policy was thrashed out in the Oval Office.[21]

For all the bad marks that Eisenhower has received from many commentators for his presidential leadership, he initiated some far-reaching administrative procedures. The creation of a cabinet secretariat and chief of staff formalized the decision-making process within the White House. The establishment of the White House office of congressional liaison, set up by retired General Jerry Persons, also provided for better executive-legislative relations. Although ignored and even criticized at the time, these institutional changes have become part of White House organization, as has the National Security Council and its staff. At the time the NSC policy making process was criticized as a cumbersome paper mill, but more recently, it has been pointed out that the system had a number of positive merits, including meticulous staff work, free and open discussion of the various policy perspectives at the subcabinet level, the use of cabinet-level meetings to clarify official policy among those responsible for its execution, and continuous policy planning and frequent cabinet and NSC meetings as means of developing an effective crisis-management team. The process may have been time-consuming, but its very formality imparted clarity to the administration's foreign policy. Later national security assistants like McGeorge Bundy, Walt Rostow, Henry Kissinger, and Zbigniew Brzezinski used the NSC staff for formulating and advocating policy. Under Eisenhower, however, the staff was restricted to compiling, coordinating, and clarifying information, while cabinet secretaries and other line officials were responsible for debating, deciding, and defending the administration's policies.[22]

21. Donovan, *Eisenhower: The Inside Story*, 65–71; Divine, *Eisenhower and the Cold War*, 23–25.
22. Henry M. Jackson (ed.), *The National Security Council: Jackson Subcommittee Papers on Policymaking at the Presidential Level* (New York, 1963); Kinnard, *Eisenhower and Strategy Management*, 14–17, 133–35; Greenstein, "Eisenhower as an Activist

The general observation that was made about Eisenhower's preference for delegation in administration had its variations: at one extreme were Dulles and Secretary of the Treasury Humphrey; at the other were Secretary of Defense Wilson and other Pentagon officials. In effect, Eisenhower was his own secretary of defense. The quip that Eisenhower could not be impressed by the Pentagon brass because he had one more star than their highest-ranking officers was well founded. As Greenstein said, "Eisenhower did not need a military expert to head a department he knew inside out and to determine overall policy; in this sphere, the president's own background and skills scarcely could be equaled." Wilson's responsibilities as secretary were to ensure that what was then the largest executive department was run in an efficient manner while Eisenhower himself largely shaped defense strategy and the military budget. In a memorandum to NSC staff chief Robert Cutler outlining his plans for implementing his New Look military budget, the president flatly stated, "I instructed Mr. Wilson as follows on the budget matters" and went on to the details.[23]

In acting as his own secretary of defense, Eisenhower in 1954, when he submitted his first military budget, imposed on the service chiefs a policy they did not like. The New Look had two components: a cut in overall military spending and a reallocation of resources among existing strategic forces. The budgetary economizing was urged by the president and strongly supported by Secretary of the Treasury Humphrey as a result of a deeply felt conservative principle that too much government spending was bad for the American economy. He and his fiscal advisors identified the Pentagon as the principal offender against the administration's efforts to limit federal spending and balance the budget. As Herbert Parmet has put it, "The civilian businessmen brought to Washington by the Republicans were themselves continually amazed by the tendency of seemingly modest incipient programs to blossom fantastically into major expenditures as they progressed through the Pentagon."[24]

President," 580; Saunders, "Military Force in the Foreign Policy of the Eisenhower Presidency," 111–12; Greenstein, *Hidden-Hand Presidency*, 106–107.

23. Greenstein, *Hidden-Hand Presidency*, 83, 85. See also Saunders, "Military Force in the Foreign Policy of the Eisenhower Presidency," 106.

24. Parmet, *Eisenhower and the American Crusades*, 498.

To accomplish these economies, a reduction in conventional forces (combat forces deployed overseas, forces allocated to keeping the sea-lanes open, and reserve forces) was to be realized with complementary greater emphases on nuclear retaliatory forces and the Continental Air Defense Command. As costly overseas commands were scaled down at the expense of the army and navy, missile-based forces were built up, to the advantage of the air force. In effect, the United States would not attempt to match Soviet manpower and armor in Europe but would rely instead on nuclear weapons to deter any Soviet attack. Fearing instant and massive retaliation, the Soviets would refrain from war. American missile superiority would neutralize the Soviet Union's advantage in conventional forces; in effect, budget reductions were linked to massive retaliation.[25]

The dislocation of traditional service privileges and, in particular, the relatively greater importance attached to the air force under the New Look created a situation ripe for internecine warfare in the Pentagon. The Eisenhower administration, however, was determined not to have a repeat of the bureaucratic conflicts that characterized the Truman years. Eisenhower told Defense Secretary Wilson not to be cowed by the service chiefs' talk of "requirements" that necessitated increased appropriations. Sherman Adams recalled one occasion on which the president spoke sharply to Wilson: "'You people never seem to learn whom you are supposed to be protecting. Not the generals,' he exploded, 'but the American people.' Looking Wilson straight in the eye, he said, 'You have got to be willing to be the most unpopular man in government.'"[26]

Eisenhower also took concrete steps to keep the military chiefs under control. His Reorganization Plan 6, which was submitted to Congress on April 30, 1953, sought to reduce interservice competition for funds by emphasizing the principle of civilian control of the De-

25. For Eisenhower's general thinking about defense spending, see the supplementary notes to the legislative leadership meeting of June 24, 1958, in Legislative Meetings, Box 2, Eisenhower Library: "As for retaliatory forces, the President asked how much is really needed? We have a great force of intercontinental bombers, and four-fifths of our defense money goes into retaliation. The President just didn't know how many times you could kill the same man!" See also Ambrose, *The President*, 224–26, 454–55; and Saunders, "Military Force in the Foreign Policy of the Eisenhower Presidency," 106–107.

26. Eisenhower, *Mandate for Change*, 449–51; Ambrose, *The President*, 171; Adams, *Firsthand Report*, 298–99.

fense Department. He wished to put all budget allocations exclusively in the hands of the secretary of defense, thus preventing special pleading by the services before congressional committees; to confine the authority of the military chiefs and service secretaries to purely administrative matters; to centralize weapons-systems research and development in the office of the secretary of defense; and to create a general staff independent of the services to advise the Joint Chiefs and the secretary on defense policy making.[27] Many of these proposals for strengthening the office of the defense secretary were not realized until Robert McNamara's tenure during the 1960s; some, such as a general staff, have yet to be acted upon.

Throughout all of the reformulation of defense policy that was involved in the New Look, Dulles maintained a hands-off posture. Part of this noninvolvement can be attributed to his preoccupation with foreign policy rather than military affairs. Another source of his basically unrestricted support for the New Look was the importance that it attached to his own well-developed ideas of deterrence and massive retaliation. Perhaps most important, he recognized not only that he was an amateur in these military debates, but that Eisenhower was an expert. As Townsend Hoopes observed, "Thus any effort on his part to debate military issues with Eisenhower could only reveal Eisenhower's greater understanding; this in turn would tend to diminish Eisenhower's respect for Dulles's judgment—a diminution which might extend beyond military affairs into the domain of foreign policy."[28] Dulles was too skilled a bureaucratic actor not to see the wisdom of excluding himself from an area of marginal importance to his interests in exchange for virtual superiority over what was most central to his fortunes.

The Secretary of State as Foreign Secretary

It was said that John Foster Dulles had spent his whole life preparing to be secretary of state. As the grandson of John Foster, Benjamin Harrison's secretary of state, and the nephew (by marriage) of Robert Lansing, Woodrow Wilson's secretary of state, Dulles could affect a

27. Adams, *Firsthand Report*, 404–405.
28. Hoopes, *The Devil and John Foster Dulles*, 197.

proprietary attitude about the office. That his brother, Allen Dulles, was director of the Central Intelligence Agency during the 1950s and his sister, Eleanor Dulles, was head of the State Department's Berlin desk added to the familial sense. As a young man, Dulles had accompanied his uncle to the Paris Peace Conference and had seen Lansing's position as secretary of state progressively undermined by President Wilson's personal emissary, Colonel Edward House. Dulles became convinced that, as the president's "first minister," only the secretary of state should conduct the nation's foreign policy. He also remained a convinced internationalist despite (or perhaps because of) the Versailles treaty's emasculation by the Senate in 1917. For over thirty years, he practiced international law with the New York firm of Sullivan and Cromwell, with time out to serve as part of the American delegation to the San Francisco Conference, which established the United Nations, and to help negotiate the Japanese peace treaty. Dulles was also active as a Presbyterian layman and an advisor to the National Council of Churches on international affairs. He was appointed by Governor Thomas Dewey of New York to fill out the unexpired term of Senator Robert F. Wagner but was defeated in the 1950 general election by the Democratic candidate, Herbert H. Lehman.

Dulles carefully positioned himself to be the Republican party's unchallenged spokesman on foreign affairs. Although an internationalist, his strong anti-Communist convictions made him acceptable to the still-strong Republican isolationists. Dulles, however, was certainly closer in his thinking to Dewey and Senator Vandenberg, chairman of the Foreign Relations Committee in the Eightieth Congress, than to the isolationists, and it was said that he would have been Dewey's choice for secretary of state if Dewey had won the 1948 race against Truman.[29]

Despite this prominence in Republican party affairs, it has been said that Dulles was not Eisenhower's preordained choice for secretary of state. For one thing, he had not been active in the Eisenhower campaign organization. It has also been suggested that Eisenhower wanted his friend and former colleague John J. McCloy for the job. McCloy had been assistant secretary of war and high commissioner for Germany during the Allied occupation after World War II. But ac-

29. Parmet, *Eisenhower and the American Crusades*, 120; Richard Gould-Adams, *John Foster Dulles: A Reappraisal* (New York, 1962), 54.

cording to General Lucius Clay, who along with Herbert Brownell, was one of the principal advisers on cabinet selection, Eisenhower never considered anyone but Dulles.[30]

One scheme that was firmly rejected was an arrangement whereby McCloy would run the State Department "from an administrative point of view" while Dulles planned foreign policy as a White House adviser. The consensus was that the secretary of state should be the president's principal adviser on foreign affairs and that a White House position that was unsupported by tradition would lack the necessary power and prestige.[31] Such a change would have to wait for Henry Kissinger, and there would be rather different consequences than either McCloy or Dulles imagined.

Eisenhower waited three weeks before appointing Dulles, and he named his longtime friend and former chief of staff, General William Bedell Smith, as under secretary of state, possibly to keep an eye on Dulles. But no such vigilance was necessary. Dulles was fully aware of the necessity for open and clear communications with Eisenhower. Indeed, he was a maximalist secretary of state because he realized that the sine qua non of his power was the president's confidence. Dulles assiduously cultivated his relationship with Eisenhower and allowed no encroachment on his role as the president's principal adviser on foreign policy. As Hoopes noted: "Throughout his period as Secretary of State, Dulles never forgot that his relationship to the President was the absolute first priority: the vital lifeline. He nourished it with extreme care. . . . As the relationship developed, the two men would normally talk on the telephone three or four times a day, and when Dulles was out of the country he sent the President each evening a summary cable of his actions and reflections."[32]

Sherman Adams, Eisenhower's chief of staff at the White House, described the Dulles-Eisenhower relationship as close and intimate, with Dulles being given more presidential trust and confidence than any cabinet official in recent history. It should be noted that this effective working relationship was not spontaneous but rather the result of conscious effort on the part of both men. Eisenhower did not socialize with Dulles or relax in his company; he preferred to associ-

30. Hoopes, *The Devil and John Foster Dulles*, 135–36.
31. *Ibid.*, 136–37.
32. *Ibid.*, 138.

ate with old soldiers and successful businessmen in his leisure time. Dulles, for his part, seemed to patronize the president at first, and even as a careful respect grew, their relationship remained formal and reserved. But the professional closeness was clear. Eisenhower respected Dulles' intellectual abilities and paid close attention to his detailed formulations of foreign policy proposals. Eisenhower also admired the secretary of state's stern principles and moral probity, referring to him as an "Old Testament prophet." Dulles, for his part, realized that Eisenhower's confidence was essential to his own continued effectiveness and created a careful lawyer-client relationship with him. He viewed himself as the presidential attorney for foreign affairs and, as in any lawyer-client relationship, felt that "his job was to provide advice and counsel." He also had another quality of a good lawyer, "since he was in no doubt that it was the client who possessed the ultimate authority and power."[33]

While holding the president's brief, Dulles allowed no interference from other administration officials in foreign affairs. Various presidential staffers whose domains overlapped Dulles' territory experienced the skill and ruthlessness with which he would protect his control over the foreign policy turf.[34] This happened with Harold Stassen, cabinet-level assistant for mutual security and disarmament; C. D. Jackson, a specialist on Cold War psychology; Lewis Strauss, an advisor on atomic energy affairs; Robert Cutler and Gordon Gray, special assistants for national security affairs; and even the redoubtable White House chief of staff, Sherman Adams. Dulles alone of the cabinet secretaries would go directly into Eisenhower's office without announcement or a prior appointment. There was little sniping between the State Department and the White House during Dulles' tenure in office. Indeed, Stassen's continued forays into diplomacy led Dulles to demand (and receive) his dismissal by Eisenhower. Nor did the spe-

33. Adams, *Firsthand Report*, 89; Ambrose, *The President*, 438; Richard E. Neustadt, *Alliance Politics* (New York, 1970), 104, 186; Hoopes, *The Devil and John Foster Dulles*, 138. In a letter to Eisenhower accompanying a draft of a proposed speech, Dulles commented, "I always greatly appreciate it if you have the time to look over my speeches, so that I can be sure that I am in harmony with your thinking." Ann Whitman File, Dulles-Herter, Box 5, December 5, 1955, Eisenhower Library.

34. See, for example, the cable of June 4, 1957, from Dulles to Stassen in which the secretary of state sharply reprimands Stassen for unauthorized communication with the Soviet ambassador, in Ann Whitman File, Dulles-Herter, Box 7, Eisenhower Library. See also Ambrose, *The President*, 401, 403, 447–48.

cial assistant for national security affairs seek to challenge the secretary of state's paramount position. Such challenges would be a later
development in the administration of American foreign policy.

Sherman Adams speculated about the causes of Dulles' protective
attitude about his relationship with Eisenhower: "The secretary had
to deal with the President directly on every important development
in world affairs and he wanted no one to come between him and Eisenhower. Dulles had seen his uncle, Robert Lansing, Secretary of State
under Woodrow Wilson, virtually supplanted by Colonel Edward M.
House, Wilson's unofficial adviser. The memory of Cordell Hull's being
ignored while Franklin D. Roosevelt conferred with Sumner Welles,
and Harry Hopkins' shouldering aside Edward Stettinius was vivid
in Dulles' mind. Taking no chances, Dulles saw to it that nobody but
himself talked with Eisenhower about major policy decisions."[35]

Dulles was also careful not to make the same mistake as some of his
predecessors by overly antagonizing congressional leaders. In particular, he assiduously courted the support of the members of the
Senate Foreign Relations Committee. Although hardly a congressional
favorite, he testified forty-eight times during his six years as head of
the State Department. He always made it a point to appear before and
after major international conferences, and he established a reputation
that was characterized as one of "complete frankness and honesty,"
even if many Democratic congressmen thought him self-righteous
and narrow-minded.[36] Dulles was anxious to avoid the fate of his
predecessor, Acheson, who had seen his early rapport with Congress
disintegrate into acrimony and accusations.

For all of Dulles' success with the president, among other department heads, and among members of Congress, his popular reputation
at home and abroad was curiously mixed. In large measure this can
be attributed to his public manner and rhetoric, but it was perhaps
above all due to his temperament. Dulles was not a man of pastels or
neutral colors; rather, he was as close "to being a man of black-and-
white convictions as a rational mind could justify." He described the
world in dichotomous terms: a "godless, atheistic Communism" on
one side and a "god-fearing, righteous capitalism" on the other. He
would brook no intellectual compromise, at least rhetorically, with

35. Adams, *Firsthand Report*, 89–90.
36. Parmet, *Eisenhower and the American Crusades*, 186–87.

what he saw as evil, and for him error had no rights, at least theoretically. A man of peace and an active churchman, he was widely
perceived as bellicose, because of his remarks about "massive retaliation." At times Dulles seemed like a figure from the seventeenth-
century Counter-Reformation, with his view of the world "as an arena
in which the forces of good and evil were continuously at war." Like a
twentieth-century John Calvin or Ignatius Loyola, he had a great respect for his enemy: it was said that his nightstand held the Bible, the
Federalist Papers, and Stalin's *Problems of Leninism*. And Eisenhower
once suggested to associates that they "have Dulles give them a
twenty-minute summary" of Stalin's book, "something the President
once listened to with admiration."[37]

The moral assurance and ideological certainty of Dulles perhaps
gave American foreign policy a firmness and direction that other administrations have lacked. During the Dulles years no one ever suggested that the secretary of state did not run the foreign affairs of the
United States or that he did not articulate a clear set of American
objectives. But even if items like "rollback" could be appraised as
largely rhetorical, other items on the agenda, such as "brinksmanship," were unnerving to American allies and large segments of the
American public. Moreover, there was a strong tendency for the policy
to become inflexible as well as morally self-righteous and ideologically rigid.

Two examples of the limits of Dulles' theological approach to international politics are illustrative. First, his moralistic approach to
international politics led the United States to display strong disap-
proval of any signs of neutrality or of an uncommitted stance by other
nations. For Dulles, you were simply for us or against us: it was a
matter of right against wrong. This attitude not only unnecessarily
estranged the United States from many emerging nations in the 1950s,
but in some cases it led to outright hostilities, such as the conflict with
Egypt over Nasser's acceptance of Soviet financial help in completing
the Aswan Dam project. Second, Dulles' ideological rigidity made him
suspicious of even the most formalized of diplomatic liaisons, such as
international educational and cultural exchanges. That a "free na-

37. Roscoe Drummond and Gaston Coblentz, *Duel at the Brink: John Foster Dulles's
Command of American Power* (Garden City, N.Y., 1960), 14, 15; Donovan, *Eisenhower:
The Inside Story*, 162.

tion" would accept Soviet foreign aid was, to him, unthinkable. The result was not only to distance the United States from the currents of political and social change in the world but to preclude much normal diplomatic intercourse that has since proven strongly beneficial to American interests, such as that with the People's Republic of China.

Emmett John Hughes, a speech writer for the president during the first Eisenhower administration, thought that "the essence of Dulles as Secretary of State—to oversimplify a little—was this: the man was a lawyer. As Secretary, he lived, acted, spoke, reacted, advanced, retreated, threatened, courted, summarized, analyzed, briefed, cross-examined, responded, appealed, objected, thrust, parried—like a lawyer. It is true that he displayed almost two distinct personalities: the public posture, rigid and categorical, righteous and doctrinaire; and the private demeanor, relaxed and communicative, supple and sophisticated. But the two contrasted like that of a lawyer—in and out of the courtroom."[38]

Hughes believed Dulles saw himself not just in an ordinary court, but standing before the bar of history in the role of prosecutor of the Soviet Union "for crimes against freedom and peace."[39] Hughes may have gotten carried away with his analogy, but his basic point has validity. Dulles brought his almost forty years of legal work into the State Department; he also brought with him a comparable period of preparation for the job of secretary of state, as well as a desire to be effective in the job. Given the frequent references to the fate of his uncle, Robert Lansing, Dulles knew that he was arguing a brief for a client who could, if he desired, be his own lawyer. So he sought to maximize his position by effectively representing the interests of his presidential client.

According to Sherman Adams, Dulles told Eisenhower at the beginning of his presidency, "With my understanding of the intricate relationships between the peoples of the world and your sensitiveness to the political considerations involved, we will make the most successful team in history." Adams has caught Dulles in a hyperbole here, but it is nonetheless true that Eisenhower and Dulles were a great success as a partnership. What maximized Dulles' role as secretary was his ability to win the president's unlimited confidence. He

38. Hughes, *Ordeal of Power*, 204–205.
39. *Ibid.*, 205.

did this in three ways: first, by his prodigious mastery of the details of foreign affairs, which could not but impress any chief executive, even one as well-versed in the subject as Eisenhower; second, by using his time with Eisenhower as efficiently as possible—not in "thinking out loud" but in presenting problems and possible solutions; third, by presenting all the possible courses of action involved—including his own preferred solution, though not as a purely parochial State Department viewpoint—while assessing the likely consequences for other policies and departments. These three qualities of Dulles— "detailed knowledge, decisiveness, and objective discussion"—were the basis of a bond between him and Eisenhower that survived policy defeats and public controversy.[40] Dulles was also a strong asset to Eisenhower because he embodied the foreign policy views of many Republicans and conservative Democrats and nicely complemented the president's obvious internationalism. This political attractiveness and Dulles' manifest command of foreign affairs forged a bond between president and secretary of state that ended only with the latter's death from cancer in 1959.

Elements of Maximalism

There are, then, several general observations to be made about the nature of the political and administrative relations between President Eisenhower and Secretary of State Dulles. First, Dulles was able to be a maximalist secretary of state because he maintained a close relationship with the president. He never forgot that Eisenhower was his lifeline, and he carefully cultivated him as confidant, client, and commander. The two men conferred often during the week, conversed several times a day by telephone, and communicated by cable when Dulles was out of the country. (Dulles was the first secretary of state to engage in the now commonplace practice of personally flying to the world's trouble spots.)[41]

Second, as an experienced lawyer, Dulles knew that his counsel

40. Adams, *Firsthand Report*, 89–90; Drummond and Coblentz, *Duel at the Brink*, 32–33, 205.
41. Adams, *Firsthand Report*, 73; Dwight D. Eisenhower, *Waging Peace, 1956–1961* (Garden City, N.Y., 1965), 367. Vol. II of Eisenhower, *The White House Years*, 2 vols.

would only be acceptable if it were consistent with the president's personal values and policy goals. While Eisenhower came increasingly to identify Dulles' ideas as his own, the secretary never forgot that the ultimate authority was a presidential prerogative, and he still scrupulously kept Eisenhower notified about every move. Similarly, Eisenhower's delegation of broad administrative power to a cabinet secretary was predicated upon successful implementation of presidential policies. Eisenhower was fully confident of Dulles' loyalty. He once said of Dulles, "He has never done a thing that I did not approve beforehand."

Third, Dulles was extremely jealous of this delegated authority. The graveyard of the Eisenhower administration is littered with the remains of Republican officials who attempted to poach on what Dulles regarded as his turf. The president himself once said: "Well, it's true that there's no department so jealous of its prerogatives as State. And even Foster's hackles rise when he thinks someone is butting in. Why, when Nelson Rockefeller was on the White House staff here, producing ideas in this area, he got Foster so fuming that I just had to do something about it."[42] Rockefeller was assigned to other duties.

Townsend Hoopes put the matter more bluntly, observing that Dulles was of the mind that there could be only one presidential adviser on foreign policy and that he "was extremely sensitive to the slightest threat of intrusion from any quarter, defending his turf with an aggressive, guileful, absolute single-mindedness that brooked no opposition." Dulles was much more successful in this endeavor than Alexander Haig would prove to be (see Chapter 8). Similarly, when Eisenhower was incapacitated by a heart attack in 1956, Dulles (unlike Haig during the Reagan assassination attempt) was uneasy about seeming to act without the president's active collaboration. Sensing this and knowing that Dulles was off to a foreign ministers' conference, Eisenhower wrote to Vice-President Nixon that Dulles enjoyed his complete confidence: "He must be the one who both at the conference table and before the world speaks for me with authority for our country."[43]

Although Dulles in many ways functioned like a "foreign secretary," it is important not to stretch this analogy to the British political sys-

42. Hughes, *Ordeal of Power,* 280, 281.
43. Hoopes, *The Devil and John Foster Dulles,* 138, 307.

tem too far. The British foreign secretary is a member of Parliament who, as a spokesman for foreign policy, can acquire some political standing independent of the head of the government (but not too much). Some British foreign secretaries in this century have gone on to the premiership; in the post–World War II period Anthony Eden and Alec Douglas-Home are examples. But one would have to go back to John Quincy Adams to find an American secretary of state who became president and to James G. Blaine to find one who even became a presidential candidate. (Charles Evans Hughes was appointed secretary of state in 1920 after having run for president in 1916.)

"Dulles worked for Eisenhower and was dependent on him," Richard Neustadt has said. "Indeed, few Secretaries of State have ever been more conscious of dependence on the President, and none has been more careful of his White House credit." These two observations underestimate Dulles' personal political standing, but they properly emphasize the superior-subordinate relationship involved. There is no constitutional precedent for a dual presidency in the United States, though it has sometimes been proposed that there be one president for domestic affairs and another for foreign affairs. As it stands, the president is both immediately and ultimately responsible for the conduct of American foreign relations, as he is also responsible for national defense and, when necessary, for fighting a war. Despite what seemed to some as passivity, Eisenhower maintained a firm grasp on foreign policy decision making, while offering Dulles a role as his confidant and adviser. For example, Sherman Adams recalled that, during the Suez crisis, Eisenhower stood firmly behind Dulles, "as he always did," and that "every action taken by the Secretary of State in the Middle East negotiations had the personal approval of the President 'from top to bottom.'"[44] Eisenhower believed Dulles to possess a knowledge of and experience in foreign affairs that were without equal. Most important, the president trusted his secretary of state to represent his interests faithfully and jealously and with the firm conviction that Dulles understood that, while he might propose, Eisenhower disposed. "He would not deliver an important speech or statement until after I had read, edited, and approved it," Eisenhower recalled in his memoirs. "He guarded constantly against

44. Neustadt, *Alliance Politics*, 64–65, 103; Adams, *Firsthand Report*, 275.

the possibility that any misunderstanding could arise between us. It was the mutual trust and understanding, thus engendered, that enabled me, with complete confidence, to delegate to him an unusual degree of flexibility as my representative in international conferences, well knowing that he would not in the slightest degree operate outside the limits previously agreed between us."[45]

It is important to stress, however, that the relationship between Eisenhower and Dulles was reciprocal and characterized by mutual respect. If the stereotype of a politically naïve general compliantly following the dictates of his secretary of state is incorrect, so is the converse of a powerless Dulles executing Eisenhower's will. The relationship between the two men demonstrated a working tension, with the hard-line, doctrinaire Dulles juxtaposed with the more accommodating, moderate Eisenhower. Clearly, the general direction of policy was set by the president, but as he himself observed, "I don't like to make a speech on foreign policy that my Secretary of State disagrees with."[46] Indeed, after Dulles died, the Eisenhower administration's foreign policy, with an unaggressive Christian Herter as secretary of state, moderated considerably. Eisenhower perhaps became more his own man and initiated policies such as the "open skies proposal" and inaugurated the early détente associated with the "spirit of Camp David." Yet much of his liberalized image was a verbal softening that, while a significant shift in tone, did not represent a retreat from reliance on massive retaliation or containment.

Whatever the differences in temperaments and emphases between Dulles and Eisenhower, American foreign policy spoke with one voice. In particular, the secretary of state was the unquestioned spokesman for the administration of foreign affairs abroad and in the government.

45. Eisenhower, *Waging Peace*, 365. See also Richard H. Immerman, "Eisenhower and Dulles: Who Made the Decisions?" *Political Psychology*, I (Autumn, 1979), 21–38; Greenstein, *Hidden-Hand Presidency*, 87–88; Bennet C. Rushkoff, "Eisenhower, Dulles, and the Quemoy-Matsu Crisis, 1954–1955," *Political Science Quarterly*, XCVI (Fall, 1981), 465–80; and, also on the Quemoy-Matsu affair, Hoopes, *The Devil and John Foster Dulles*, 280–83. Documents in the Eisenhower Library are replete with examples of Eisenhower's editing, recasting, or substantially amending memoranda, speeches, and policy proposals that Dulles submitted to him for approval. See also Divine, *Eisenhower and the Cold War*, 20–21, which argues that in essence, "Eisenhower used Dulles."

46. Morton H. Halperin, *Bureaucratic Politics and Foreign Policy* (Washington, D.C., 1974), 220.

Dulles was never shunted aside while the president personally conducted foreign policy, unlike Secretary of State Hull (see Chapter 3). Nor was Dulles ever locked in internecine warfare with the White House staff, as Alexander Haig would be (see Chapter 8), let alone superseded by the president's special assistant for national security affairs, as William Rogers would be by Henry Kissinger (see Chapter 7). In the post–World War II period, only Dulles and Dean Rusk did not resign their office (Dulles, of course, died in office), though Rusk often seemed to remain only through the sufferance of the presidents he served. Moreover, Rusk had to contend with a powerful defense secretary, and in the weekly meetings that made decisions on the Vietnam War, he was at best a first among equals in advising the president (see Chapter 6).

Dulles had no competition at the Pentagon, civilian or military; certainly no one on the White House staff contested his authority in foreign policy making. Indeed, it was his very authoritativeness that distinguished him from his successors as secretary of state (except for the special case of Henry Kissinger). For all his subordination to Eisenhower, Dulles acted like, and was widely regarded as, the president's principal foreign policy maker.[47] John Foster Dulles would never have had to learn of a new initiative in American foreign policy by reading the Washington *Post*. Bedell Smith was not a Sumner Welles; nor was Sherman Adams a Harry Hopkins. Eisenhower's style of presidential administration involved a broad delegation of executive responsibility to his principal cabinet officers. Nevertheless, the president extended so much freedom of action to Dulles as to give him a stature among his cabinet colleagues rivaled only by Secretary of the Treasury George Humphrey.

The maximalist secretary of state is a perfectly acceptable model for the conduct of foreign affairs. The president as head of government retains constitutional responsibility for determining the foreign policy of the United States while choosing to delegate to the secretary

47. Responding to a letter from Representative Walter Judd that spoke of an "organized attack" by some in the government against Dulles, the president wrote that he wanted documentation so that he could learn the identities of any such persons. He also said that Dulles had his "total support and confidence" and was "as nearly indispensible as a human being ever becomes." Ann Whitman File, Dulles-Herter, Box 7, January 4, 1958, Eisenhower Library.

of state responsibility for the conduct of foreign relations. In effect, the president acts in the manner of a British prime minister (or perhaps more accurately in Eisenhower's case, a corporate chairman of the board) who grants broad operating authority to his department heads while retaining policy-making, supervisory, and, if necessary, interventionist rights. In addition, under the maximalist model the secretary of state is not simply a *primus inter pares* with other officials who might be involved in foreign policy, such as the secretary of defense, national security assistant, and CIA director. Instead, these officials must defer to him, as well as to the president, on foreign policy matters. But it should be stressed that Eisenhower did not abdicate control of foreign policy making in delegating its execution to Dulles. The relationship between the president and the secretary of state can be summarized in the words of Dulles' assistant Roderic L. O'Connor, who said that Dulles "felt that the Secretary of State really was the President's lawyer of foreign affairs. . . . He thought the relationship was very like a lawyer and a client, and that his job was to advise and counsel, but basically on behalf of his client who ultimately had the authority and the power."[48]

Acting as a maximalist secretary of state is a difficult undertaking in contemporary American politics. A modern president is widely perceived as the nation's "chief diplomat," a perception heightened by the summit diplomacy and the state of permanent crisis that have characterized foreign affairs in the last three decades. In addition, as the head of a government department, a secretary of state must compete with other cabinet officials for any policy preeminence and is immediately suspect to White House officials, who place compliance with the president's programs and politics on a higher plane than organizational loyalties and institutional perspectives. But Dulles was never challenged by a rival "foreign office" in the White House. Because he enjoyed a special relationship with Eisenhower and had some independent standing within the Republican party, he was recognized as the embodiment of American foreign policy. Dulles also realized the boundaries of his role; for example, he did not interfere in affairs of the Treasury Department or the Pentagon. And he never forgot that the source of his power was the president's confidence, which

48. Kinnard, *Eisenhower and Strategy Management,* 18. See also Divine, *Eisenhower and the Cold War,* 22.

is the necessary condition for the authority of any secretary of state—maximalist or otherwise.[49]

The Decline of the State Department

Despite the presidential confidence Dulles enjoyed, the State Department did not share in his prestige or influence. Not only did Dulles rarely call upon his department to assist him institutionally in advising the president, but he distanced himself from departmental administration and worked through a small personal office. Moreover, the department continued to be the subject of intense political controversy as Republican members of the Senate railed against the policy transgressions of the previous administration. The State Department has never had a political base comparable with other cabinet departments because of the absence of strong constituency support within American society (see Chapter 2). The Defense Department, on the other hand, can command the loyalty of retired military personnel and weapons contractors. But there is only a small clientele, mostly foreign policy specialists, for the State Department's programs, and diplomacy does not provide the tangible benefits for national security that a missile silo does. Also, during the Truman and Eisenhower eras, career Foreign Service officers were singled out for particularly sharp attack as the "architects of appeasement" who were responsible for the "loss of China," and the containment policy supposedly derived from the "Acheson school of treason," which was composed of Communists, "fellow travelers" and their sympathizers.

The loyalty investigations of the late 1940s and the even more virulent attacks of Sentator McCarthy in the early 1950s left the Foreign Service shaken and demoralized. Before Dulles took office, a special subcommittee of the Senate Foreign Relations Committee chaired by Millard Tydings (D-Md.) had scrutinized the personnel files of suspected State Department employees. On July 17, 1950, the subcommittee had reported that McCarthy's allegations constituted "the

49. Hoopes, *The Devil and John Foster Dulles*, 197. See also Halperin, *Bureaucratic Politics and Foreign Policy*, 121.

most nefarious campaign of half-truths and untruths in the history of this republic," and Tydings himself had expressed confidence in the public servants who ran the State Department's loyalty program.[50]

Dulles might have been the perfect secretary—"solid, solemn, God-fearing, and thoroughly Republican"—to fend off McCarthy's later inquisitions of the State Department officials, but he did not. One reason was that, when he was chairman of the board of trustees of the Carnegie Endowment for International Peace and Hiss was its president, he had spoken out in defense of Hiss. Dulles would not testify at the Hiss trial, and he believed himself to be badly compromised by that association and vulnerable to McCarthy's attacks. Dulles also had substantial foreign policy differences with McCarthy and other members of the Republican right wing over Chiang Kai-shek, NATO, and foreign aid, among other issues. Most important, Dulles was aware of Eisenhower's refusal to engage McCarthy in a direct confrontation, even when his mentor, George Marshall, was concerned. Although Fred Greenstein argues that Eisenhower's strategy was to neutralize McCarthy by denying him the dignity of direct White House replies, this "hidden-hand leadership" sometimes appeared as presidential appeasement of the junior senator from Wisconsin.[51] And Dulles was not inclined to do anything that would jeopardize his privileged association with Eisenhower, however detrimental the consequences might be for the State Department as an institution.

The security program that Dulles allowed to be installed at the State Department was no half measure. Officially, Scott McLeod was the head of the Bureau of Security and Consular Affairs, which had been created as a direct result of McCarthy's attacks; unofficially, McLeod was McCarthy's political commissar at the State Department. "Congress wants heads to roll, and I let 'em roll" was how McLeod put it. His primary responsibility was to investigate the backgrounds of the department's eleven thousand employees for any evidence of shaky loyalty, such as reputed Communist ties or sympathies, or habits that might lead to lax security, such as excessive drinking, gossip-

50. David Caute, *The Great Fear: The Anti-Communist Purge Under Truman and Eisenhower* (New York, 1978), 303–24.

51. David M. Oshinsky, *A Conspiracy So Immense: The World of Joe McCarthy* (New York, 1983), 261; Greenstein, *Hidden-Hand Presidency*, 182.

ing, or sexual impropriety. Dulles may have thought that this was the price that he needed to pay to avoid the congressional antipathy that plagued Acheson's tenure as secretary. But "the McLeod appointment was one of the worst blunders that Dulles would make as Secretary," as David M. Oshinsky has noted. "He had done it primarily to appease the McCarthyites, to get them to take the heat off his department. As one analyst noted, Dulles was willing to 'cave in on the sides in order to salvage the core—retaining executive control over the affairs of the Department. . . .' The problem, of course, was that once McLeod was appointed, Dulles found it impossible to fire or even to discipline him without offending his supporters."[52]

These rather tortured personnel policies inevitably drove off some exceptional Foreign Service officers. Paul Nitze was forced out as head of the Policy Planning Staff despite his distinguished record and his status as a registered Republican. According to Emmett John Hughes, Nitze was "blackballed" by Senate Majority Leader William Knowland and other congressional Republicans who complained of seeing the "same old tired faces" who had been testifying under the Democrats. (Nitze later returned to public service under presidents of both parties, most recently as arms control negotiator for the Reagan administration.) As one of the principal architects of containment, George Kennan knew that he would be better off out of public life, but his letter of resignation went unacknowledged by Dulles, who planned to allow Kennan to be terminated automatically upon non-assignment after three months. Hughes and Sherman Adams arranged for "a respectful and presidential letter" to be sent out in recognition of Kennan's distinguished ambassadorial service in Moscow and elsewhere.[53]

Perhaps the most disturbing case was the drawn out confirmation proceedings that took place upon Charles Bohlen's nomination to be ambassador to the Soviet Union. Bohlen was Eisenhower's personal choice for this critical diplomatic post. The president had known Bohlen when the latter had served in the Paris embassy in the years after World War II, and he evaluated him in glowing terms: "So fully

52. Oshinsky, *A Conspiracy So Immense*, 262, 264. See also Gould-Adams, *Dulles: A Reappraisal*, 58–60.
53. Hughes, *Ordeal of Power*, 119–20.

did I believe in his tough, firm but fair attitude . . . that I came to look upon him as one of the ablest Foreign Service officers I had ever met." [54]

By contrast, Senator McCarthy said that Bohlen's "entire history is one of complete, wholehearted, 100 percent cooperation with the Acheson-Hiss-Truman regime." McCarthy also pictured Bohlen as "a guy who hits only to left field" and whose "admiration of everything Russian is unrivalled outside the confines of the Communist party." Bohlen's chief crime was to have been part of the American delegation to the Yalta Conference and President Roosevelt's interpreter. Dulles wavered and considered withdrawing Bohlen's name. Eisenhower, however, dug in his heels and fought for the Bohlen confirmation, which passed the Senate, 74 to 13. Eleven of the dissenting votes came from Republicans who deliberately defied their party's first president to occupy the White House in two decades. Eisenhower provided a succinct epilogue to the affair: "Bohlen went on to serve with distinction, first in Moscow, then in Manila, and finally in Washington as a special assistant to the Secretary of State." [55]

In his administration of the State Department, Dulles operated through a small staff in the office of the secretary. Included among its number were his press aide from the 1950 senatorial race and a young Foreign Service officer, William Macomber, who became deputy under secretary for administration in the 1970s. Dulles' preference for a "private office" could be attributed to a suspicion of the department's career officers, who had, after all, risen in the service of very different political masters. It is also true that administrative matters did not interest Dulles, who had contemplated serving as a special presidential adviser on foreign affairs so as to avoid the management of a cabinet department. Thomas Dewey is said to have observed that, like most lawyers, Dulles was no executive. He certainly "carried the State Department in his hat," which only in part refers to his being the most-traveled secretary of state of his time (or any other). [56] Dulles' penchant for "personal diplomacy" may also have stemmed from a desire to avoid the demands of departmental management and

---

54. Eisenhower, *Mandate for Change*, 212.

55. *Ibid.*, 213; Parmet, *Eisenhower and the American Crusades*, 241; Hughes, *Ordeal of Power*, 93.

56. The discussion of Dulles and his administration of the State Department is based on Hoopes, *The Devil and John Foster Dulles*, 141–48.

congressional testimony, as well as diplomatic receptions and press conferences.

Under Secretary of State Bedell Smith was an extremely capable administrator, but he was never given responsibility for day-to-day departmental administration. Smith was succeeded by two more very able administrators—Herbert C. Hoover, Jr., the former president's son, and Christian Herter, who served as secretary of state after Dulles' death. The assistant secretaries of the regional bureaus in effect shifted for themselves without department-wide coordination. The under secretary for administration, Don Lourie, former president of the Quaker Oats Company, was generally regarded as ineffectual; he was also responsible for the McLeod appointment. Dulles was jealous of his time and only reluctantly met with these principal line officers. Robert Murphy, the deputy under secretary for political affairs, was trusted as an experienced diplomatic negotiator though not valued by Dulles for his political acumen. The counsellor, Douglas MacArthur II, nephew of the famous general, served as coordinator for overseas conferences and for Dulles' many trips abroad. A Harvard Law School professor, Robert Bowie, served as director of policy planning. However, owing to Dulles' style, with its emphasis on one-man operations and short-term tactics, the planning staff as a whole, which had been envisioned as the creative center of the State Department during the Acheson era, fell progressively into disuse.

A major impediment to creative policy making was the nature of Dulles' thinking. He was possessed of a powerful intellect, but one that had ideas that were for the most part fully developed and in need only of refinement. He debated tactical aspects of policies to improve his public presentation or bargaining position. He also drafted his own speeches, memoranda to the president, position papers, cables, and press releases. This gave him a strong analytical grasp of policy but also permitted him to exercise a greater degree of intellectual arrogance. Dulles effectively made himself "the sole intellectual wellspring of conception and action in foreign policy during his period in office." Townsend Hoopes concludes that no other aspect of Dulles' behavior did more "to wither the creative impulses of the Foreign Service; weaken its sense of purpose and self-esteem; and sap its morale." But Dulles seemed not to be greatly concerned with the State

Department as a corporate body. As Hoopes said: "The Secretary was one thing; the department another. But it was the Secretary who formulated, recommended, and carried out, relegating the corporate competence of the career service to a narrow advisory role, precluding it from significant initiatives, and rarely giving it his full confidence."[57] That Dulles was one of the most powerful secretaries of state in American diplomatic history is not a matter of disagreement, though many might debate the success of his policies. It is equally clear that Dulles' power was essentially personalistic and did not extend to the State Department institutionally.

For all of his formidable personal powers, in the last analysis he consigned the State Department to a very circumscribed role in foreign policy making. By failing to redefine the department's functions beyond diplomatic representation, Dulles missed the opportunity to give it a competitive edge that might have allowed it to withstand not only aggressive challenges from other bureaucratic actors, particularly the Defense Department in the 1960s, but also the effects changing conceptions of foreign affairs, particularly the notion of national security policy. Dulles did not act like Robert McNamara did at the Department of Defense; that is, he did not undertake the kinds of major policy reconceptualizations and managerial changes that were associated with DOD's emergence as a major foreign policy making agency.

Dulles was adamant about maintaining his position as the president's principal foreign policy adviser, and, as long as no one personally challenged that prerogative, he was content. Moreover, he did not wish to jeopardize that position by involvement in international economic affairs, where he would have had to challenge Secretary of the Treasury Humphrey, or in military matters, where Eisenhower was de facto secretary of defense. The farther an issue from traditional foreign policy concerns, the less likely it was that Dulles would assert himself. The result was to delimit the State Department's bureaucratic mission in an age when international politics and the international position of the United States went through radical changes.

Despite the care with which Dulles guarded his status as the administration's major diplomatic spokesman, he was no Alexander

57. *Ibid.*, 143.

Haig incessantly asserting his claims of suzerainty over foreign policy (see Chapter 8). Dulles recognized the basic fact that decisions about which department is to be the senior participant in a policy area, and what rules are to be observed, are almost exclusively presidential decisions.[58] Any president can choose to act as his own secretary of state, as FDR did, or to designate a surrogate, such as Henry Kissinger, to act on his behalf. A successful secretary of state will realize that he must accept this reality and act accordingly. Asserting one's claims to be the "vicar of foreign policy" will not make him a maximalist secretary of state if the president is indifferent to such claims or wants other agencies involved as decision-making coequals.

Nowhere did Dulles' indifference to organizational matters eventually cause greater problems for his department than in his inattention to the institutional groundwork being laid for the National Security Council decision-making system and the special role of the assistant for national security affairs, and nowhere was Eisenhower's administrative acuity better demonstrated. Dulles may be forgiven for not foreseeing the rise of a Kissinger, but even the powers of Eisenhower's national security assistants were far from inconsiderable. The so-called "NSC policy hill" was arguably the most significant administrative innovation of the Eisenhower administration in foreign policy making. At the time, however, its operating procedures were widely misunderstood and their future significance greatly underestimated.

The NSC was designed to function as a presidential advisory body: to provide the chief executive with the information and perspective necessary to make complex foreign policy decisions. President Truman's assistant in charge of the NSC staff, Sidney W. Souers, stressed that the NSC's role was not to determine policy; rather, "it prepares advice for the President as his Cabinet level committee on national security."[59] For Eisenhower, the NSC was to foreign policy what the cabinet was to domestic policy—a forum for the exchange of views among the relevant departments and a mechanism for ensuring

---

58. Halperin, *Bureaucratic Politics and Foreign Policy*, 111.
59. Sidney W. Souers, "Policy Formulation for National Security," *American Political Science Review*, XLIII (July, 1949), 536.

government-wide policy coordination. While the cabinet meetings tended to be ritualized and informational, the Thursday NSC meetings were more highly regarded and given a higher priority in the allocation of Eisenhower's time and attention.

Robert Cutler, a retired general and banker who was special assistant for national security affairs (SANSA) during much of the Eisenhower administration, said that Eisenhower believed that top-level decision-making bodies should provide general direction and guidance. "The Council dealt with strategy, not tactics," Cutler stated. For example, in each year of the administration, the NSC conducted a review of basic national security policy (BNSP) that set forth a national strategy for achieving American objectives through political, economic, and military means.[60] Eisenhower also used the NSC "for considering matters of current importance," and in the open discussion that was characteristic of NSC debate, he could debate each alternative while hammering out a policy. The NSC system that was constructed infused new order in decision making and brought departments together in cooperative action; it was "an ideal forum" for achieving consensus and coordination in foreign policy making. In sum, according to Patrick Anderson, "In Eisenhower's own mind, there is no doubt that his organization and use of the NSC contributed significantly to his ability to cope with the complexities of the Cold War, and his NSC operations must be viewed as a landmark in the history of presidential administration."[61]

Eisenhower's formalized NSC system was not without vocal critics, especially Senator Henry Jackson (D-Wash.), who found fault with it for "papering over" differences, not allowing expression of the full range of opinions, and being incapable of policy innovation.[62] On the

---

60. Robert Cutler, *No Time for Rest* (Boston, 1965), 300, 306–307. See also Kinnard, *Eisenhower and Strategy Management*, 17.

61. Keith C. Clark and Lawrence J. Legere (eds.), *The President and Management of National Security*, (New York, 1969), 176; Stanley Falk, "The National Security Council Under Truman, Eisenhower, and Kennedy," *Political Science Quarterly*, LXXIX (September, 1964), 423–24; Kinnard, *Eisenhower and Strategy Management*, 134; Patrick Anderson, *The President's Men*, (Garden City, N.Y., 1968), 179–80.

62. See U.S. Congress, Senate, Committee on Government Operations, *Hearings Before the Subcommittee on National Policy Machinery* (2 Vols.; Washington, D.C., 1961). This committee was chaired by Senator Jackson. In the view of Douglas Kinnard, "Jackson seems to have misled a decade of scholars with this rather simplistic critique of the Eisenhower NSC system, which was subsequently accepted as the conventional wisdom in the 1960s." Kinnard, *Eisenhower and Strategy Management*, 133.

other hand, the planning process prompted a large measure of inter-departmental debate and forced officials "to confront major issues of national security and to evaluate the options." Fred Greenstein maintains that the conduct of the NSC meetings "refutes the premise of Eisenhower's critics that formalized advisory procedures stultify vigorous exchanges of views among advisers."[63]

What is clear is that the NSC became institutionalized as part of the foreign policy decision-making process, and though deemphasized under Presidents Kennedy and Johnson, it emerged again, albeit transformed, in the Nixon administration. The Eisenhower NSC was institutionalized in another sense as well—the pattern by which the issues were debated: "The characteristics of the pattern are regular attendance and participation by the President at NSC meetings; regular meetings which held top priority with members of the Council; detailed agendas; and a much broader view of Council functions. In short, the NSC under Eisenhower was a full partner involved in all aspects of national security policy from policy formulation (the Planning Board) to implementation and evaluation (the OCB)."[64]

Robert Cutler liked to describe the Operations Coordinating Board (OCB) as the downward slope of a "policy hill." It was OCB's job to see that NSC decisions were translated into plans. "The image was misleading, however," Greenstein said, "in that the NSC and its extension the OCB were involved in conceptualizing policy and the procedures for implementing it, not in making concrete operating decisions." In other words, the NSC did not supplant the cabinet departments and their secretaries, but served as a mechanism for interdepartmental policy making and execution. Similarly, it was Cutler's responsibility as chairman of the Policy Planning Board (composed of assistant secretaries and under secretaries from the relevant departments) to ensure that all differences among participants were brought into the open and clearly stated. These policy splits were sometimes put in parallel columns, identified by agency, and circulated to the NSC members in advance of each meeting. Greenstein has described what happened next: "Although all participants had the documents well in

63. Kinnard, *Eisenhower and Strategy Management*, 134; Greenstein, *Hidden-Hand Presidency*, 126.
64. Michael P. McConackie, "The National Security Council: Patterns of Use of Presidents Truman and Eisenhower" (Paper presented at the annual meeting of the Southwest Political Science Association, Houston, March 16–19, 1983), 20.

advance of the NSC meetings and had discussed them with their representative on the Planning Board, the special assistant [Cutler] had the responsibility of initiating discussion by summarizing each paper. He would bring explicit attention to the splits, labeling them by agencies that had advocated various positions, and a free-flowing discussion would ensue, with each agency representative defending his side of the disagreement."[65] Eisenhower, of course, made the final decisions.

The Eisenhower-Dulles Record Reviewed

Thus, the Eisenhower presidency's most lasting contribution to foreign affairs may have been in its administrative machinery, actual and proposed. When the American public was asked as he left office what was Eisenhower's greatest single achievement, of course, the reply was more basic: "He kept the peace."[66] And not just abroad. Eisenhower came to office at a time of deep partisan divisions over foreign policy. It is doubtful that a better team than Eisenhower-Dulles could have been found to defuse the charges of treason and appeasement leveled at the Truman-Acheson policies while at the same time containing the isolationism and McCarthyism of the Republican right wing. The nomination of Senator Taft or the election of Adlai Stevenson would have certainly led to very different foreign and domestic policies.

The image of Eisenhower that emerges from a close look at his administration of foreign policy may seem at odds with other interpretations—both traditional and revisionist. Stressing the paramount role that Dulles played (*because* of the presidential confidence that he enjoyed) clearly does not denigrate Eisenhower's premier role in decision making and policy formulation. Global issues—political, military, and strategic—were Eisenhower's principal interests, and he was intimately involved in their management. In particular, the traditional view of a passive Ike, dominated by a saber-rattling Dulles,

65. Greenstein, *Hidden-Hand Presidency*, 133, 129. See also Cutler, *No Time for Rest*, 314–15.
66. Parmet, *Eisenhower and the American Crusades*, 573; Divine, *Eisenhower and the Cold War*, 154–55.

does not stand up in the face of the record. Not only was there no armed conflict involving American soldiers during his tenure in office, but numerous incidents may be recounted in which Eisenhower restrained his more bellicose advisors and decided against military intervention in international crises. Yet the image of Eisenhower's steady hand on the tiller, which has come into sharper focus with time's passage, was not universally shared in his day—especially concerning the navigation of foreign waters.

That Eisenhower consciously cultivated a stance that appeared to place him above, or make him seem indifferent to, major policy debates—Greenstein's thesis of the "hidden-hand presidency"—is an important revision. But recognizing Eisenhower's activity behind the scenes does not alter the fact that he was judged by many in the press and the foreign policy community to be weak and vacillating. That this was style, not substance, has come to be appreciated, and as a political tactic, it had its advantages. Yet, presidents have an obligation to educate public opinion and to share their strategic conceptions with the electorate. Eisenhower chose not to speak out in this fashion, at least not until the last two years of his presidency. His decision not to assert himself in certain controversies left the stage to others and cultivated the impression of presidential acquiescence or lassitude.

But these are largely matters of interpretative emphasis. Stephen Ambrose's assessment of Eisenhower the president is accurate and to the point: "What the documents show . . . is how completely Eisenhower dominated events. Eisenhower, not Charlie Wilson, made defense policy; Eisenhower, not Dulles, made foreign policy. . . . Whether the policies were right or wrong, whether they reflected ambivalence and hesitation, or revealed the way in which Eisenhower was a prisoner of the technologists and scientists, or displayed bold and aggressive action, they were Eisenhower policies. He ran the show."[67]

The relationship between Eisenhower and Dulles was, as we have stressed, a collaborative one, and if the secretary of state acted like the chief spokesman for American foreign policy, it was because the president wished him to act that way. Dulles was insightful enough to understand the basis of his power and was assiduous in cultivating

67. Ambrose, *The President*, 10.

this relationship. Furthermore, the conducting of foreign affairs seems to work best when presidents exercise leadership over it. On this score, President Eisenhower and "Foreign Secretary" Dulles shared great success. In shaping foreign policy, a hidden hand is clearly better than no hand at all.

Still, the results of the long collaboration between Dulles and Eisenhower in foreign policy making were highly ambivalent in character. Although Eisenhower made strong overtures toward improving American-Soviet relations in the last year of his administration, invoking the "spirit of Camp David," the administration's record is better characterized as the avoidance of war rather than the active promotion of peace. Incidents in Indochina, Quemoy and Matsu, Berlin, and Lebanon all brought the United States to the brink of war. It is this "brinksmanship" and Dulles' bellicose rhetoric that people remember, but peace reigned even if sabers rattled. Much of the 1950s seems to have been a holding operation. The containment policy was codified and perhaps also overextended in the regional defensive arrangements like SEATO and CENTO, with which Dulles was much concerned. Unlike NATO, in which there was a clearly agreed-upon delineation of American-Soviet interests, these pacts may not have done more than draw highly artificial and evenly rigid lines where no such agreed-upon limits had been reached. Inevitably, when the logic of these "neo-containment" policies was tested, most dramatically in Vietnam, the results were highly debatable.

Except for minor offensive operations, such as the CIA-assisted overthrow of the leftist Arbenz government in Guatemala in 1954, the Eisenhower-Dulles approach to international politics accepted the post–1948 stalemate.[68] While contributing to a stable world order, it also led to a codification of Cold War policies that was not revised until the early 1970s, with détente and the first steps toward normalization of relations with the People's Republic of China. The Eisenhower-Dulles years also witnessed good European relations, especially with West German Chancellor Konrad Adenauer, but poor, often inflammatory, relations with former colonial nations, for example, in the debacle over the Aswan Dam project. Along with reduced military spending, there was the reliance on the "massive retaliation" doctrine

68. Richard H. Immerman, "Guatemala as Cold War History," *Political Science Quarterly*, XCV (Winter, 1980–81), 629–53.

of nuclear deterrence that has come to plague contemporary efforts at arms control. There was a strong—even maximalist—secretary of state but also a department of ever-waning influence in the policy making process. (Dulles' successor, Christian Herter, was little more than a departmental caretaker while Eisenhower acted as his own secretary of state.)

What accounted for Dulles' maximalism was the personal relationship that he enjoyed with Eisenhower. Contrary to what was widely assumed by contemporaries, it was the president who made foreign policy, not the secretary of state. Eisenhower is appreciated now for the behind-the-scenes, "hidden-hand" quality of his leadership, but for many at the time these techniques seemed more like diffidence and abdication. The administration's public posture, in particular, led to widespread misunderstanding at home and abroad about the real nature of American foreign policy objectives. In balancing the historical record, it is important to distinguish the rhetoric of Dulles from the actions of Eisenhower. But the self-righteousness and bellicosity did not go unnoticed at the time, and it was not without long-term effect.

6

Decision Making by Consensus: LBJ and Rusk

Among the individuals who have served as secretary of state in the history of the American republic, Dean Rusk has the distinction of having held the position longer than any recent incumbent, and in all of the nation's history his tenure was exceeded only by the eleven-year record of Cordell Hull. Appointed to office by President John F. Kennedy in 1961, Rusk continued to serve as the president's chief foreign policy adviser until the end of the presidency of Lyndon B. Johnson early in 1969.

Under the direction of Presidents Kennedy and Johnson, Rusk was in charge of the State Department during one of the most traumatic periods of American diplomatic experience—the era of the Vietnam War. Since the Kennedy administration only lasted "a thousand days" and was not the war's heyday, the central focus of this chapter will be upon the relationship between President Johnson and his foreign policy advisers.

The diplomacy of the 1960s was dominated by the prolonged and agonizing Vietnam War. For a number of reasons, this was an important chapter in American diplomatic history, not least perhaps because this was the first major foreign military engagement that the United States "lost" since the War of 1812. That fact alone was sufficient to create pervasive internal dissensions within the United States about America's involvement in external affairs.

The initial American commitment to preserve the independence of South Vietnam from Communist hegemony can be traced back at least to the presidency of Eisenhower and possibly to that of Truman.

Long a major colonial possession of France, Indochina had emerged from World War II a divided nation: the seventeenth parallel (intended originally as a military demarcation line for the purpose of receiving the Japanese surrender) in time became the de facto boundary between North and South Vietnam and remained so until the end of the war in the early 1970s. Led by Ho Chi Minh, the Marxist regime of North Vietnam claimed jurisdiction over the entire country. Ho was widely revered as an anticolonial spokesman; his political movement, the Viet Minh, was determined to end French colonial hegemony. Meanwhile South Vietnam remained closely linked with the West, initially with France and, after the evacuation of the French in 1954, with the United States.[1]

After Kennedy entered the White House in 1961, the American commitment to the independence of South Vietnam significantly expanded. He viewed the independence of Southeast Asia from Communist control as a vital diplomatic interest of the United States, and many of his aides envisioned the Communist challenge to South Vietnam as a test case in America's ability to respond successfully to the kind of "wars of national liberation" that the Soviet Union and Communist China advocated and supported. By the late fall of 1963, the United States was spending $1.5 million daily to preserve the security of South Vietnam, and the American military commitment for that purpose had risen to nearly twenty thousand troops. Yet JFK also believed that, in the final analysis, the government and people of South Vietnam had to assume the primary responsibility for the country's security.[2]

When he entered the White House on November 22, 1963, Lyndon Johnson pledged to continue the programs and policies of his predecessor, including the obligation to preserve the independence of South Vietnam. Under the Johnson administration, the American commit-

1. For background on America's involvement in Indochina see Peter A. Poole, *Eight Presidents and Indochina* (Huntington, N.Y., 1978); and Paul M. Kattenburg, *The Vietnam Trauma in American Foreign Policy, 1945–75* (New Brunswick, N.J., 1980).

2. Authoritative treatments of the Kennedy administration's policies toward Southeast Asia include Theodore C. Sorensen, *Kennedy* (New York, 1965), 639–61; Arthur M. Schlesinger, Jr., *A Thousand Days: John F. Kennedy in the White House* (Boston, 1965), 320–43, 532–51, 981–98; and Roger Hilsman, *To Move a Nation: The Politics of Foreign Policy in the Administration of John F. Kennedy* (Garden City, N.Y., 1967) 91–159, 413–541. An informed and balanced analysis of the Vietnam conflict is Timothy J. Lomperis, *Viet Nam: The War Everyone Lost—And Won* (Baton Rouge, 1983).

ment to that goal grew rapidly, reaching a peak of 543,000 troops by 1969. By the end of the war (a cease-fire officially went into effect on January 27, 1973), America's armed forces had suffered nearly 48,000 battlefield deaths and another 11,000 deaths off the battlefield); some 155,000 Americans were wounded in the conflict. Before Johnson left office, it was estimated that the cost of the Vietnam War for the United States had risen to $500 million per week, or some $24 billion annually, in direct costs (exclusive of the cost of veterans' benefits, interest on the national debt, and other long-term liabilities).

The war had several major implications for the problem of fragmentation in American foreign policy making. It was an outstanding example of the process of incremental decision making—diplomatic behavior undertaken as the result of a series of separate and seemingly unrelated steps over time. Both the Kennedy and Johnson administrations, for instance, repeatedly disclaimed the idea that the United States should assume the principal responsibility for preserving the security of South Vietnam. Despite such assertions, the conflict in the end largely became "America's war." As a result of incremental decision making, the United States found itself increasingly burdened with an unwanted obligation.[3]

In addition, a salient characteristic of the period was the existence of a high degree of consensus among the president and his principal advisers in the decision-making process regarding Southeast Asia. One early critic of America's growing involvement in the Vietnam conflict was Under Secretary of State George Ball, who was joined in time by former Secretary of State Dean Acheson. In the main, however, the impetus for a reexamination of America's role in Southeast Asia came mainly from outside the State Department: it was supplied by the findings of the Central Intelligence Agency, as subsequently revealed in the *Pentagon Papers*, and by Clark Clifford, who became secretary of defense at the end of the Johnson administration, and by other officials of the Defense Department.[4] Secretary of State Rusk, on the other hand, became identified as one of the most indefatigable champions of the escalation of the Vietnam conflict, a tireless de-

3. Hilsman, *To Move a Nation;* Townsend Hoopes, *The Limits of Intervention: An Inside Account of How the Johnson Policy of Escalation in Vietnam Was Reversed* (New York, 1969).
4. Neil Sheehan *et al.* (eds.), *The Pentagon Papers* (New York, 1971).

fender of the Johnson administration's policies in Southeast Asia and elsewhere.

Eventually, it is true, Rusk accepted (it would be more accurate perhaps to say that he acquiesced in) the views of those who urged the president to terminate the conflict in Southeast Asia. Yet, during most of his tenure as the head of the State Department, he symbolized the kind of policy consensus that underlay the Johnson administration's diplomacy. To critics of LBJ's foreign policy record, this consensus was objectionable for several reasons. It appeared to result from the consideration of a narrow range of options in which some alternatives, such as liquidation of America's military involvement in Southeast Asia, were arbitrarily excluded. It was maintained only by silencing or refusing to listen to those voices inside and outside the government who challenged bureaucratic inertia and mindless reiteration of old cold war slogans and dogmas. For some antiwar critics, Secretary of State Rusk was also identified as an active accomplice in the more questionable activities engaged in by the Johnson White House. These included efforts from time to time, such as in the Vietnam conflict and in the intervention in the Dominican Republic, deliberately to deceive the American people and Congress concerning Washington's diplomatic moves and generally to impose what came to be called an "imperial presidency" upon the American society.

The growing divisiveness within the United States about the Vietnam War had two other far-reaching results for the American foreign policy process. One was the growth of pervasive legislative disaffection with the conduct of the war, a primary factor producing congressional assertiveness in the foreign policy field in the years that followed. (Many legislators subsequently forgot or ignored the fact that Congress had joined with the White House in supporting measures contributing to the escalation of the conflict). As part of the effort to prevent "another Vietnam," Congress was determined to assert its prerogatives in the foreign policy field, as exemplified by the passage of the War Powers Resolution (1973) and the imposition of other restrictions upon the president's diplomatic freedom of action.[5]

5. See Cecil V. Crabb, Jr., and Pat Holt, *Invitation to Struggle: Congress, the President, and Foreign Policy,* (2nd ed.; Washington, D.C., 1984); John V. Lindsay, "For a New Foreign Policy Balance," *Foreign Affairs,* L (October, 1971), 1–15; and J. William Fulbright, *The Crippled Giant: American Foreign Policy and Its Domestic Consequences* (New York, 1972), 177–204.

The second lasting result of the Vietnam conflict was the dissolution of the anti-Communist consensus that had existed in American public opinion since the early post–World War II period. This consensus had sustained the containment policy, which had been followed by successive administrations in responding to the challenge of expansive communism since the late 1940s. For some twenty years, American people had repeatedly expressed their opposition to communism and their determination to oppose its adventurist foreign policy moves. After Vietnam, there emerged what was widely described as the "post–Vietnam War syndrome," in which American public opinion toward foreign affairs appeared to be genuinely bewildered and confused, burdened with self-doubts and guilt, and inclined to turn inward toward the solution of domestic problems. In its most extreme form (and anti–Vietnam War critics, it must constantly be remembered, did not comprise a monolithic group), the feeling existed that since the United States had been defeated in its attempt to achieve its goals in Southeast Asia, it could not accomplish its objectives anywhere beyond its own borders. For many years after the war's end, pervasive anxieties about "another Vietnam" became a kind of national phobia that conditioned American attitudes toward regions like Latin America and the Middle East.[6]

But potent as the anti–Vietnam War syndrome was during the 1970s, events by the end of the decade indicated that the American people's long-standing apprehension about Communist expansionism had by no means totally disappeared. Before the Carter administration left office, millions of Americans had become deeply concerned about events like the collapse of the Iranian monarchy, the weakening of the American position in the Persian Gulf area, and Communist gains in Latin America. The election of Ronald Reagan—who had campaigned on the pledge to "make America great again"—to the presidency in 1980 was persuasive evidence that a majority of Americans believed that the United States was still a superpower and that it had unavoidable international responsibilities.[7]

6. John E. Reilly, "The American Mood: A Foreign Policy of Self-Interest," *Foreign Policy*, XXIV (Spring, 1979), 74–87; Daniel Yankelovich, "Farewell to 'President Knows Best,'" *Foreign Affairs*, (Special issue, 1978), 670–93; James Chace, "Is a Foreign Policy Consensus Possible?" *Foreign Affairs*, LVII (Fall, 1978), 1–17.
7. Ellis Sandoz and Cecil V. Crabb, Jr. (eds.), *A Tide of Discontent: The 1980 Elections and Their Meaning* (Washington, D.C., 1981), esp. Ch. 8.

The Vietnam War, of course, was not the only significant foreign policy development during the Johnson administration. As always, Soviet-American relations were perhaps the centerpiece of American diplomacy and the key to world peace. America's growing involvement in Vietnam, along with the Soviet-American confrontation in Cuba in 1962, meant that cold war tensions continued throughout the 1960s. The Soviet Union's ruthless suppression of dissent in Czechoslovakia in 1968 provided new evidence to the West that the era of peaceful coexistence, proclaimed by Soviet Premier Nikita Khrushchev, signaled no end to cold war suspicions and animosities. Yet despite such developments, President Johnson held a summit meeting with Soviet leaders at Glassboro, New Jersey, in June, 1967. An Anglo-American-Soviet agreement to ban above-ground nuclear testing was reached on July 25, 1963, and in 1968 the United States, the USSR, and fifty-nine other nations signed an accord to ban the proliferation of nuclear weapons. Although ideological suspicion between the superpowers remained intense, they did draw back from the brink of nuclear war in Cuba, and they carefully avoided converting the Vietnam conflict into a direct Soviet-American encounter.[8]

In inter-American relations, the Kennedy-Johnson-Rusk era witnessed several noteworthy developments. In 1961, in response to long-standing Latin American complaints about Washington's neglect of their problems, the Kennedy administration launched the "Alliance for Progress," a comprehensive and long-range program designed to promote Latin American modernization and development. A dominant goal of the undertaking was strengthening democracy within a region where authoritarian (often military-dominated) governments had long been the norm. President Johnson continued America's commitment to this program. Although some progress was recorded in achieving its objectives, in the main the principal goals of the Alliance for Progress, especially the enhancement of democracy south of the border, largely remained elusive.[9]

Also under the Kennedy administration, there occurred one of the

8. Lyndon B. Johnson, *The Vantage Point: Perspectives of the Presidency, 1963–1969* (New York, 1971), 462–93; Joseph L. Nogee and Robert H. Donaldson, *Soviet Foreign Policy Since World War II* (New York, 1981), 102–256; Anatol Rapoport, *The Big Two: Soviet-American Perceptions of Foreign Policy* (Indianapolis, 1971), 154–204; Adam B. Ulam, *The Rivals: America and Russia Since World War II* (New York, 1971), 299–397.

9. J. Warren Nystrom and Nathan A. Haverstock, *The Alliance for Progress* (Prince-

strangest episodes in the history of American diplomacy: the Bay of Pigs crisis on April 17, 1961, when an American-supported group of Cuban exiles attempted to overthrow the Communist-controlled government of Cuba. The undertaking was an unmitigated failure, coming just a few weeks after President Kennedy entered the White House. Predictably, the Bay of Pigs encounter added a new source of tension to Cuban-American relations. Its main consequence for the foreign policy making process, however, was to make Kennedy extremely distrustful thereafter of the advice offered him by his aides, especially his military and intelligence advisers, who had assured him that the Bay of Pigs venture would succeed.[10] Johnson, who was vice-president during the episode, may well have come to share JFK's distrust of the CIA, leading him during the ensuing Vietnam War to discount CIA-sponsored studies showing that the United States was losing the contest in Southeast Asia.

Some eighteen months later, another challenge involving Cuba— the Cuban missile crisis of 1962—confronted the Kennedy White House. In contrast to the earlier Bay of Pigs disaster, the resolution of the Cuban missile crisis was widely interpreted as an outstanding diplomatic victory for the United States. The crisis erupted as the result of a series of developments that convinced the Kennedy administration that the Soviet Union was seeking to convert Cuba into a missile base in the Caribbean area. Moscow's adventurism was a blatant challenge to the oldest principle of American foreign policy, the Monroe Doctrine of 1823, and to repeated warnings to the Kremlin by successive chief executives not to intervene in the Western Hemisphere.

By 1962, reports were widely circulating that Moscow was constructing missile sites in Cuba. Finally, after obtaining photographic confirmation of this fact, President Kennedy on October 22, 1962, addressed the American people, informing them of Moscow's activity. In effect, he presented the Kremlin with an ultimatum to remove its offensive missiles from Cuba and ordered the United States Navy to impose a "quarantine," or blockade, of Cuba to assure that no

ton, 1966); Edwin Lieuwen, *U.S. Policy in Latin America: A Short History* (New York, 1965), 83–139; Richard B. Gray (ed.), *Latin America and the United States in the 1970s* (Itasca, Ill., 1971), 75–137.

10. Sorensen, *Kennedy*, 291–310; Schlesinger, *A Thousand Days*, 233–67.

new missiles were introduced onto the island. The United States and the Soviet Union, American officials believed, had gone "eyeball-to-eyeball" over Cuba, and the USSR had blinked first. Faced with Kennedy's decisiveness, the Kremlin ordered its ships that were bringing new missiles to Cuba to change course, and a direct Soviet-American conflict was averted. Significantly, the most ominous face-to-face confrontation between the United States and the Soviet Union since World War II occurred in the Western Hemisphere.

Insofar as the American foreign policy process was concerned, the major results of the Cuban missile crisis were perhaps twofold. First, Kennedy became more persuaded than ever of the value of relying upon a select group of his advisers, such as the Executive Committee of the National Security Council (ExComm), in dealing with international crises. Second, throughout the policy-making process in the Cuban missile affair, Kennedy demanded and enforced the utmost secrecy from his advisers. For example, Secretary of State Rusk was precluded by the president's injunction from conferring with his colleagues in the State Department. Such "lessons" on how to respond to a foreign crisis successfully were not lost on Kennedy's successor, Lyndon Johnson.[11]

The fourth major development in United States–Latin American relations occurred under the Johnson administration, when the White House ordered the marines to land in the Dominican Republic in the spring of 1965. The avowed purpose of the intervention was to protect the lives of Americans and other foreigners threatened by the revolutionary upheaval and violence sweeping the country, for which President Johnson and his advisers blamed Communist elements, who were in turn encouraged and aided by Havana and Moscow. The American military contingent in the country was in time replaced by an inter-American peace-keeping force under the auspices of the Organization of American States (OAS); as the result of subsequent national elections, a new civilian government took power that was able to maintain relative stability for a number of years in the strife-torn country.

11. Robert F. Kennedy, *Thirteen Days: A Memoir of the Cuban Missile Crisis* (New York, 1969). See also Sorensen, *Kennedy*, 667–719; Schlesinger, *A Thousand Days*, 794–819; and Andres Suarez, *Cuba: Castroism and Communism*, (Cambridge, Mass., 1967), 131–86.

The Dominican intervention had several lasting consequences for American foreign policy. It resulted in widespread criticism of the United States throughout Latin America and in other countries, since it appeared to signify a return to the kind of "big stick" diplomacy practiced by President Theodore Roosevelt and other chief executives before World War II. The Dominican crisis also provided a new source of internal disaffection with the diplomacy of the Johnson administration, particularly among his fellow Democrats and other liberal groups. Critics alleged that the officials of the Johnson administration had a fixation with communism as the major cause of global and regional tensions, that they relied too heavily upon military solutions of complex political and economic problems, and that President Johnson and his advisers had deceived the American people and Congress about the nature of the problem in the Dominican Republic and the purposes of America's intervention.[12]

In relations with Western Europe during the 1960s, the United States faced several significant developments. As always since 1949, the North Atlantic alliance (NATO) was in a condition of greater or lesser disarray. Disagreements among its members concerning the geographic scope of the alliance, differing conceptions of NATO defense strategy, and efforts to achieve a higher degree of diplomatic cohesion among the members of NATO were among the continuing sources of contention in European-American relations.

For over a decade (1958–1969), American foreign policy toward Western Europe was preoccupied also with the movement known as Gaullism. The president of the Fifth French Republic, General Charles de Gaulle, was determined to assert France's independence from both the United States and the Soviet Union. Upon de Gaulle's insistence, France withdrew from the NATO organization (though it remained a formal member of the Western alliance), and Paris developed its own independent nuclear capability, the *force de frappe*. Even after de Gaulle's death, many of his ideas continued to influence French and, more broadly, European attitudes toward regional and global problems.[13]

12. John B. Martin, *Overtaken by Events: The Dominican Crisis from the Fall of Trujillo to the Civil War* (Garden City, N.Y., 1966). See also Abraham F. Lowenthal, *The Dominican Intervention* (Cambridge, Mass., 1972); and Cecil V. Crabb, Jr., *The Doctrines of American Foreign Policy: Their Meaning, Role, and Future* (Baton Rouge, 1982), 253–78.
13. Schlesinger, *A Thousand Days*, 343–79, 842–89; Johnson, *The Vantage Point*,

During the 1960s the Middle East witnessed an intensification of the long-standing Arab-Israeli conflict, which erupted into a third round of overt hostilities in the Six-Day War of June, 1967. This new wave of violence, in which Israel launched a preemptive air strike that largely eliminated the Egyptian air force on the ground, resulted in an overwhelming Israeli military victory against Egypt, Syria, and other Arab forces.

The Six-Day War removed none of the underlying sources of tension between Israel and its Arab enemies; nor did it bring Israel the security that its citizens ardently sought. After the conflict, for example, the Palestine Liberation Organization (PLO) and other Arab guerrilla groups intensified their opposition to Israel, and many Arab leaders looked forward to a "fourth round" of fighting against the Israeli enemy. (It came in 1973 in the Yom Kippur War, in which Arab forces imposed heavy casualties upon Israel, though Israeli forces were in the process of winning the contest when a cease-fire was arranged). Throughout the 1960s Washington, while continuing to provide massive economic and military support to Israel, endeavored to serve as a peacemaker in this controversy, but its efforts met with no conspicuous success.[14]

One other outstanding diplomatic development during the 1960s remains to be mentioned. For over a decade after 1949 the United States was confronted with a seemingly monolithic Sino-Soviet axis. Officials of the Kennedy and Johnson administrations were convinced, for example, that the Communist threat to Indochina derived ultimately from a global Marxist offensive in the Third World orchestrated by Moscow and Peking. But by the early 1960s, informed students of Asian affairs detected evidence of deep fissures in the wall of proclaimed Sino-Soviet solidarity. Growing ideological differences between the two Communist giants, personal jealousies and distrust among their leaders, rival territorial and historical claims and disputes, Soviet interference in Chinese internal affairs, Peking's deter-

---

305–22. Gaullism is examined in Roy C. Macridis (ed.), *De Gaulle: Implacable Ally* (New York, 1966); and Harold van B. Cleveland, *The Atlantic Idea and Its European Rivals* (New York, 1966).

14. Walter Laqueur, *The Road to War: The Origin and Aftermath of The Arab-Israeli Conflict, 1967–68* (Baltimore, 1968); Trevor N. Dupuy, *Elusive Victory: The Arab-Israeli Wars, 1947–1974* (New York, 1978), 221–387.

mination to become a nuclear power in the face of Soviet-imposed obstacles—these were among the leading causes of the emerging schism between the Soviet Union and the People's Republic of China.

By the late 1960s the cracks in the Sino-Soviet alliance had become too wide to conceal. Globally, the disintegration of international communism into various forms of "national communism" was one of the most significant tendencies affecting the nature and future of the international system. According to critics, officials of the Johnson administration did not correctly assess this profound change in Sino-Soviet relations or adjust American foreign policy to it successfully. It was left for President Nixon to exploit the "opening" when he visited China early in 1972. Several more years elapsed before the Carter administration normalized relations with China by the exchange of ambassadors in 1979.[15]

The Appointment of Dean Rusk

According to one of his closest advisers, President Kennedy devoted considerable care to the selection of his cabinet—and he "worried longest over his selection of a Secretary of State." After prolonged deliberation, he chose Dean Rusk for the position, passing over such better-known and more politically influential figures as Adlai Stevenson, Democratic presidential nominee in 1952 and 1956, and Chester Bowles, former Democratic governor of Connecticut and an influential spokesman for the liberal wing of the Democratic party. Stevenson was offered and accepted the position of American ambassador to the United Nations, while Bowles became under secretary of state and later United States ambassador to India.[16]

Rusk possessed a number of qualities that appealed to President Kennedy. One was that, as a former military officer and experienced State Department official, he was a noncontroversial figure whose appointment, it was believed, would not cause dissension among the various factions of the Democratic party. He was not a political aspi-

15. Hilsman, *To Move a Nation*, 275–361; Roderick MacFarquhar (ed.), *Sino-American Relations, 1949–1971* (New York, 1972); A. Doak Barnett and Edwin O. Reischauer (eds.), *The United States and China: The Next Decade* (New York, 1970).
16. Schlesinger, *A Thousand Days*, 138–39; Sorensen, *Kennedy*, 257.

rant or a possible political rival of the new president. The Rusk appointment was commended to JFK by former Secretary of State Dean Acheson and other experienced State Department officials. As a Democrat and an avowed admirer of Adlai Stevenson, Rusk could also be counted upon to work cooperatively with the latter in his new position as head of the American UN delegation.[17]

Rusk's highly varied experience in the armed forces, at the State Department, and at the Rockefeller Foundation equipped him for his new position. Born in 1909, Rusk became a Rhodes scholar to Great Britain and served in the army in the Pacific Theater during World War II, where he rose to the rank of colonel. He entered the State Department in 1946 and subsequently held the positions of assistant secretary of state for UN affairs and for Far Eastern affairs. He also acquired broad management experience as deputy under secretary of state, when he supervised liaison between the State and Defense departments.[18]

In his previous State Department career, Rusk had been directly involved in a number of major diplomatic undertakings. For example, he had urged his superiors not to extend recognition to the new Communist regime in China; he was convinced that Soviet influence over Mao Tse-tung's regime was massive and decisive. He also participated in the formulation of the Marshall Plan for reconstructing postwar Europe and in the creation of NATO, and he played a role in drafting the Japanese peace treaty, signed on September 8, 1951.[19]

When North Korean forces crossed the South Korean frontier in June, 1950, Rusk urged Secretary of State Acheson and President Truman to resist this Communist intrusion. During the Korean conflict, he also recommended that the president involve the United Nations in the defense of South Korea, advice that Truman followed. In time, Rusk joined Truman's other advisers in urging him to relieve General MacArthur of his command. Also during the early 1950s Rusk recommended that the Truman White House extend military aid to

17. Schlesinger, *A Thousand Days,* 140–41; Dean Acheson, *Present at the Creation: My Years in the State Department* (New York, 1969), 432; John B. Martin, *Adlai Stevenson and the World* (Garden City, N.Y., 1977), 558.

18. Hilsman, *To Move a Nation,* 572; Acheson, *Present at the Creation,* 255.

19. Hilsman, *To Move a Nation,* 129; Harry S. Truman, *Years of Trial and Hope, 1946–1952* (Garden City, N.Y., 1956), 407–408. Vol. I of Truman, *Memoirs;* Hugh Sidey, *John F. Kennedy, President* (New York, 1963), 17.

the French-controlled government of South Vietnam. Then, as president of the Rockefeller Foundation from 1952 to 1960, he acquired considerable experience with, and insight into, the kinds of health, educational, and developmental problems pervasive throughout the Third World.[20]

Rusk also possessed certain personal traits that President Kennedy believed qualified him to lead the State Department and that induced President Johnson to retain Rusk after Kennedy's death. One associate has described Rusk as a "decent and thoughtful man." Rusk's model for a presidential adviser was Secretary of State George C. Marshall, who has been described as playing "an Olympian role" as a taciturn judge "among the squabbling bureaucrats" surrounding him in the Truman administration. One of Marshall's prime administrative principles was reserving final judgment on important policy questions "until he and the president were alone." Rusk endeavored to follow this principle as secretary of state. At one critical stage of decision making during the Vietnam War, when President Johnson and his advisers were confronted with accumulating evidence that the war was being lost, one commentator reports that "Rusk said little . . . it being a familiar trait of his to remain relatively silent at meetings he did not himself conduct, preferring to reserve his position for the President's ear." Subsequently, Rusk did not attend the sessions of LBJ's advisers that were devoted to considering this evidence and its implications.[21] In some cases (the Bay of Pigs episode in 1961 was a notable example), Rusk's customary silence in group deliberations might well have been interpreted by his colleagues, and by the president, as acceptance of the decision reached.

Rusk's personal traits were deemed especially suitable for serving President Kennedy, a chief executive who was keenly interested in foreign affairs and who believed that, as a result of his service in the Senate, he had acquired insights and useful experience into this aspect of national policy. Increasingly, Kennedy became "his own secretary of state," and if he had lived, JFK might well have come to

20. Acheson, *Present at the Creation*, 402, 423; Gaddis Smith, "Dean Acheson," in Robert H. Ferrell (ed.), *The American Secretaries of State and Their Diplomacy* (New York, 1972), 226–27; David S. McLellan, *Dean Acheson: The State Department Years* (New York, 1976), 320; Schlesinger, *A Thousand Days*, 140.
21. Hoopes, *The Limits of Intervention*, 172.

emulate the earlier model provided by President Franklin D. Roosevelt (see Chapter 3).

As an experienced public servant, Rusk understood that, in the final analysis, any incumbent president is always free to function as his own secretary of state, and he continued to serve both presidents Kennedy and Johnson loyally and conscientiously. Kennedy found Rusk to be "quiet, courtly and cautious, noncommittal in his press conferences and unaggressive in his excellent relations with Congress." Kennedy viewed Rusk's advice to him as "intelligent and well informed." Rusk "chose his words coolly and carefully, avoiding unnecessary controversies with bland and lucid logic," and he was never patronizing in his relations with the chief executive. He understood clearly that the president ultimately determines the foreign policy of the United States.[22]

Presidential Styles During the 1960s

As secretary of state, Dean Rusk not only had an extraordinarily long tenure in his position, but he served two chief executives whose personal and administrative styles and procedures were in some respects quite dissimilar. On one hand, President Kennedy designated Rusk as his principal foreign policy adviser and expressed confidence in him. On the other hand, JFK more and more centered the decision-making process in the White House, relying upon *ad hoc* mechanisms, such as the Executive Committee of the National Security Council, to advise him in dealing with major foreign policy issues, like the Cuban missile crisis of 1962.[23]

After Johnson became president, the diplomatic policy-making apparatus came to be elaborate and complex. Formal advisory mecha-

22. Sorensen, *Kennedy*, 270; Schlesinger, *A Thousand Days*, 141–42; Dean Rusk, "The President and the Secretary of State," in Kenneth Thompson (ed.), *Virginia Papers on the Presidency* (Washington, D.C., 1980), 9.

23. The membership of ExComm during the Cuban missile crisis consisted of the president, Secretary of State Rusk, Secretary of Defense Robert McNamara, CIA director John McCone, Secretary of the Treasury Douglas Dillon, White House national security adviser McGeorge Bundy, and the chairman of the Joint Chiefs of Staff, General Maxwell Taylor. The viewpoints of several other advisers, such as Under Secretary of State George Ball and Soviet specialist Charles Bohlen, were solicited on various aspects of the crisis. Kennedy, *Thirteen Days*, 30.

nisms were overlaid with a number of informal processes, all designed to produce a massive flow of information and policy recommendations directed at the Oval Office. One study of LBJ's administrative approach has observed that he "frequently engaged in a wide range of personal consultations both inside and outside government through individual conversations, phone calls, or *ad hoc* meetings. There was no predictable pattern to such consultation, and even the closest members of the President's official family were unable to follow it. At the end, a decision emerged." After he left the White House, Johnson contended that throughout his tenure as chief executive, "There was no shortage of information at any time. The information I received was more complete and balanced than anyone outside the mainstream of official reporting could possibly realize."[24]

In effect, under both Presidents Kennedy and Johnson (but especially under the latter) the foreign policy decision making process existed on two levels: an intricate formal system and a highly personal and fluid informal system. Created in 1947 (see Chapter 2), the National Security Council had been established as the primary mechanism available to the president for coordinating military and diplomatic aspects of national policy. President Kennedy's choice to direct that staff agency was Dean McGeorge Bundy of Harvard University, whom he had also seriously considered as a possible secretary of state. Bundy served as NSC director under both JFK and LBJ until his resignation in 1966. His replacement was the economist W. W. Rostow, who had previously served in the State Department and was considered perhaps the most "hawkish" member of Johnson's inner circle on the Vietnam War. Owing largely to the influence of Bundy and Rostow, by the late 1960s the role of the president's national security adviser in foreign policy decision making had been significantly enhanced (see Chapter 7).

For many observers, Bundy exemplified the attitudes prevailing in Washington during the period of the New Frontier. A member of the eastern intellectual establishment, he was a highly intelligent, incisive, and dedicated staff assistant who appeared to be totally convinced that officials in Washington both understood international problems correctly and could devise effective solutions for them.

24. Keith C. Clark and Laurence J. Legere (eds.), *The President and the Management of National Security* (New York, 1969), 83; Johnson, *The Vantage Point*, 64.

Both JFK and LBJ exhibited great confidence in Bundy, valued his insights and devotion, and relied heavily upon him to clarify and present policy alternatives for presidential consideration. Bundy was widely viewed as a capable and pragmatic "problem solver" who had a facility for cutting through red tape and facilitating the making of diplomatic decisions. Along with President Kennedy, Bundy was skeptical that the vast and inertia-ridden State Department was capable of providing the required diplomatic leadership; at a minimum, the department needed continual prodding and monitoring by the White House staff to make it responsive to the president's wishes. Rostow's service as director of the NSC staff was characterized mainly by his innovative ideas and proposals, by his strong antipathy toward communism, and by his unswerving conviction that American goals in Southeast Asia were being achieved.

Dependent as Presidents Kennedy and Johnson were upon their White House staff, however, neither was inclined to rely upon the formal NSC mechanism per se for advice. Johnson particularly preferred to consult trusted individuals and small groups of advisors. When he convened the NSC, it was primarily to inform its members of impending decisions and allow them some limited opportunity to participate in them. For Johnson the presence of Bundy and Rostow on the White House staff also served another purpose: they were the administration's resident intellectuals, whose presence, it was hoped, would impart legitimacy to its policies at home and abroad. However, along with Secretary of State Rusk, these White House aides came to be widely viewed as prominent examples of the "yes-men" who comprised LBJ's inner circle and whose primary function was to protect him from dissident opinion on the war and other diplomatic undertakings.[25]

In making crucial foreign policy decisions, both Kennedy and Johnson relied heavily upon *ad hoc* and informal mechanisms. Kennedy's creation of the Executive Committee of the National Security Council has already been noted. Under Johnson, a major administrative innovation was the creation of the Senior Interdepartmental Group (SIG).

25. Lincoln P. Bloomfield, *The Foreign Policy Process: A Modern Primer* (Englewood Cliffs, N.J., 1982) 46–52; Alexander L. George, *Presidential Decisionmaking in Foreign Policy: The Effective Use of Information and Advice* (Boulder, 1980), 157–59; I. M. Destler, *Presidents, Bureaucrats, and Foreign Policy: The Politics of Organizational Reform* (Princeton, N.J., 1972), 97–118.

Chaired by the under (later renamed the deputy) secretary of state, SIG included representatives from the Defense Department, the Treasury Department, the CIA, and other governmental agencies. At a lower level, several interdepartmental regional groups were also created. Headed by an assistant secretary of state, each group was expected to study international problems affecting particular areas. Theoretically, in both SIG and the regional groups, the primacy of the State Department in the foreign policy process was preserved. Yet, the precise purpose of organizational innovations like SIG and the regional groups was never altogether clear, and their actual contribution to foreign policy decision making during the Johnson era is even more questionable. One well-informed commentator, for example, is convinced that these mechanisms were in reality a "kind of window-dressing" designed perhaps to create an atmosphere of support and legitimacy for policies to which LBJ was already committed and to give the public an impression of "change, movement, and novelty" in American foreign relations when, in reality, no fundamental changes in policy were contemplated or undertaken.[26]

By contrast, Johnson's "Tuesday lunch group" was a novel and highly influential advisory mechanism that evolved out of luncheon meetings between the president and selected cabinet members. In time, the group's regular participants included Johnson, Rusk, McNamara, the director of the CIA, the president's national security adviser, the presidential press secretary, and, when their advice was needed, the Joint Chiefs of Staff. This mechanism reflected Johnson's preference for discussions with small groups of advisers in whom he had confidence, rather than large and complex structures like the National Security Council. The membership of the Tuesday lunch group was "flexible enough to include whomever the President wanted and felt he needed for the work at hand." According to Rusk's account, discussion among members of the Tuesday lunch group was candid and sometimes spirited. Yet even within the Tuesday lunch framework, the president leaned most heavily upon two members—Rusk and McNamara—for advice.

The president's preference for this device created a number of problems for his official family. The agenda of the Tuesday lunch group, for

26. James A. Nathan and James K. Oliver, *Foreign Policy Making and the American Political System* (Boston, 1983), 49–52, Bloomfield, *The Foreign Policy Process*, 50–51.

example, was often inadequately prepared and sometimes unknown in advance. The spontaneous introduction of new topics during the discussions meant that agencies whose responsibilities and interests were directly affected were not represented in the deliberations. No written records of the Tuesday lunch discussions were kept; in effect, each official present had to recall what was discussed, what was decided, and his agency's responsibility was for policy implementation. Given Johnson's insistence upon secrecy, other members of the State Department were not infrequently in the dark about the latest policy developments and about actions required of them.[27]

For major policy questions, after full discussion had occurred within the Tuesday lunch group and a de facto decision had been reached on the course of action, President Johnson would normally present the issue to the National Security Council for further deliberation. This step permitted other agencies, such as the Treasury Department, to express their viewpoints on foreign policy questions affecting their interests. Yet, according to an official who served under both Presidents Kennedy and Johnson, the actual purpose of the NSC meeting was twofold: to inform those officials present of the president's decision and to give the members of NSC "at least the illusion of participation" in it.[28]

Supplementing this informal advisory system was Johnson's tendency to rely upon a wide circle of close friends and personal advisers whose viewpoints he valued. At one stage in the Vietnam conflict, for example, LBJ solicited the advice of a group of former public servants called "the Wise Men", including former Secretary of State Acheson, former Under Secretary of State George Ball, former White House aide McGeorge Bundy, and General Omar Bradley. Johnson also sought the advice of the prominent Washington attorney, Clark Clifford (who in 1968 would succeed McNamara as secretary of defense), and in company with every president since World War II, he utilized elder statesman Averell Harriman for counsel and diplomatic missions.[29]

27. Clark and Legere, *The President and the Management of National Security*, 88–89; Bloomfield, *The Foreign Policy Process*, 50–51; Rusk, "The President and the Secretary of State," 18.

28. George W. Ball, *Diplomacy for a Crowded World: An American Foreign Policy* (Boston, 1976), 199.

29. Johnson, *The Vantage Point*, 409; Hoopes, *The Limits of Intervention*, 124, 150–55.

Thus, President Johnson's style of foreign policy decision making was a highly flexible and personal one. Even his closest advisers were hard pressed to discover exactly how and when LBJ made a final decision. Throughout the process, however, in company with President Kennedy and other chief executives before him, LBJ insisted upon the principle that final decisions in the foreign policy field were made by the president. "I make the decisions here," he observed in 1965. In contrast to his predecessor, however, Johnson entered the White House with little or no background or experience in foreign affairs. His prior legislative service had focused mainly upon domestic problems. Indeed, some observers are convinced that he exhibited a genuine aversion to international politics, believing, as isolationists did before World War II, that the foreign policy realm was a hostile and dangerous environment for the American democracy, inevitably leading to trouble. Until the Vietnam War became the dominant policy question of his administration, LBJ devoted his attention mainly to internal issues. One commentator states in fact that President Johnson regarded foreign policy as a kind of "black art," requiring special skills which he did not possess.[30]

After Kennedy's assassination, Johnson decided to retain Dean Rusk as secretary of state. LBJ numbered Rusk among his advisers who served him "with fidelity, brilliance, and distinction." He came to regard Rusk as "a loyal, honorable, hard-working, imaginative man of conviction." Contrary to the popular depiction of Rusk, LBJ recalled, he shared "the President's load of responsibility and abuse," and was no yes-man, who merely told the president what the latter wanted to hear. Rusk could be quite determined when he was telling his superior in the White House not to "do something that I felt needed to be done," LBJ said. In 1969 Johnson awarded Rusk the Medal of Freedom in recognition of his meritorious service to the nation.[31]

Like his predecessor, Johnson also distrusted the State Department, though perhaps less strongly. His attitude exhibited a long-standing "populist" skepticism toward the diplomatic elite, whose members

---

30. Morton Berkowitz, P. G. Bock, and Vincent F. Fuccillo, *The Politics of American Foreign Policy: The Social Context of Decisions* (Englewood Cliffs, N.J., 1977), 188; Destler, *Presidents, Bureaucrats, and Foreign Policy,* 105.
31. Johnson, *The Vantage Point,* 20, 567.

traditionally were drawn from Ivy League institutions and represented high social circles. Johnson was less outspoken than Kennedy in lamenting the lack of creativity on the part of the State Department bureaucracy, but he was known to share many of JFK's doubts about the department. As a rule, LBJ did not seek advice directly from lower-level State Department experts and specialists on particular foreign policy issues. His general attitude was conveyed by an assertion he made during the Dominican crisis in 1965: "I talk to Dean Rusk, not to some fifth desk man" in the State Department. "If Dean Rusk doesn't know more than the fifth desk man, he shouldn't be Secretary of State."[32]

Lacking background in the foreign policy field, Johnson was inclined to lean heavily upon his advisers, who were drawn from outside, no less than inside, the government. His approach to major national policy issues tended to be highly informal and flexible. His tendency was to "stalk" a problem—to consider it fully from several perspectives—before reaching a decision. In this stage he consulted with a wide range of official and unofficial advisers. Perhaps more than any chief executive since Franklin D. Roosevelt, LBJ involved himself personally in the minutiae of policy questions—to the extent, for example, of specifying the exact targets to be bombed by the air force in Viet Nam. Once the president had reached a decision, he expected unquestioning loyalty from his subordinates in carrying it out.[33]

A recurrent criticism of the decision-making process of the Johnson administration was that it was rigged, or inherently structured to yield predetermined results in foreign policy. This criticism has taken two forms. One version of it holds that, perhaps without deliberate intent or design, the process produced "groupthink," or a kind of mindless conformity among LBJ's advisers, leading them time and again to arrive at a consensus on the Vietnam War and other diplomatic issues. This interpretation emphasizes the idea that President Johnson possessed an overweening ego and had a psychological com-

32. Berkowitz, Bock, and Fuccillo, *The Politics of American Foreign Policy*, 188.
33. Destler, *Presidents, Bureaucrats, and Foreign Policy*, 104–106; Eric F. Goldman, *The Tragedy of Lyndon Johnson* (New York, 1968), 452–53; Rowland Evans and Robert Novak, *Lyndon B. Johnson and the Exercise of Power* (New York, 1966), 375.

pulsion to be liked, leading him to surround himself with aides who became little more than sycophants. From this system of decision making, therefore, the diplomatic options LBJ considered were extremely limited and did not include fundamental reorientations of external policy, which might, presumably, have prevented the Vietnam fiasco.[34]

At least two questions can be raised, however, about this analysis of the Johnson administration's decision-making process. One is whether any other model of executive decision making, such as that followed by President Roosevelt or President Truman, would have necessarily yielded a different result. Diplomatic miscalculations, of course, are sometimes made in any system of policy making. The second question is why, if this explanation is correct, a quite different system of decision making, such as that followed in Congress during most of the Vietnam War, also produced overwhelming support for the Johnson-Rusk diplomacy toward Vietnam and on other major external policy issues during the 1960s.

A different interpretation of the diplomatic errors made during the Johnson-Rusk period is to account for them on the basis of *intentional* efforts by the president and his advisers to deceive the American people, Congress, and the world about their true goals in Southeast Asia, Latin America, and other regions. This is the explanation preferred by a wide circle of revisionist historians and commentators on the Vietnam War and the Dominican intervention. The underlying problem with this approach is that there are almost as many explanations of the underlying or "real" causes of American interventionism abroad as there are commentators who believe the Johnson administration deliberately fostered it. These explanations include the influences of the "military-industrial complex" on the foreign policy process; the dominant role played by a small policy elite, sometimes called "the national security managers" or "crisis managers"; the ingrained anti-Communist impulses of President Johnson, Secretary of State Rusk and other high-ranking officials; America's desire to domi-

34. Irving L. Janis, *Groupthink: Psychological Studies of Policy Decisions and Fiascoes* (Boston, 1982); Goldman, *The Tragedy of Lyndon Johnson*, 451–55, 473–75; Doris Kearns, *Lyndon Johnson and the American Dream* (New York, 1976), 2–3, 274–75; Charles Yost, *The Conduct and Misconduct of Foreign Affairs: Reflections on U.S. Foreign Policy Since World War II* (New York, 1972), 140–41.

nate other countries economically and to exploit their raw materials; bureaucratic inertia and an unwillingness to adapt American foreign policy to new conditions overseas; a congenital bias against revolution in the Kennedy and Johnson administrations.[35]

Until quite late in LBJ's administration (the turning point probably came early in 1968, when Secretary of Defense Clifford began to express doubts about the war), a high degree of consensus was unquestionably a hallmark of the decision-making process of the Johnson White House.[36] As a rule, discussions among LBJ's advisers were concerned primarily with how to achieve Kennedy's and Johnson's announced goals in Southeast Asia rather than with whether America had a vital interest in the region or whether its goals were attainable at a cost acceptable to Congress and the American people.

Evidence can be cited also to support the contention that in time President Johnson became psychologically resistant to dissenting viewpoints, which he seems to have interpreted as evidence of disloyalty to his administration, and refused to consider them. In terms of his personality traits, the reserved and unobtrusive Rusk was not temperamentally suited for the role of forceful policy critic; nor is there any reason to doubt that during most of the period he headed the State Department he believed in the wisdom of America's diplomatic course in Southeast Asia.

An alternative explanation of the policy consensus that existed during most of the Johnson-Rusk period—one for which there is as much evidence as other interpretations of American diplomacy during the 1960s—is that it emerged and was perpetuated primarily by two factors. One was ignorance on the part of Johnson and his advisers—and of the American people—about conditions and societies abroad in general, and particularly about Southeast Asia. Before the 1960s,

---

35. For representative revisionist studies, see Robert J. Lifton (ed.), *America and the Asian Revolutions* (Chicago, 1970); Richard J. Walton, *Cold War and Counter-Revolution: The Foreign Policy of John F. Kennedy* (Baltimore, 1973); Claude Julien, *America's Empire* (New York, 1973); Richard Barnet, *Roots of War: The Men and Institutions Behind U.S. Foreign Policy* (Baltimore, 1973); John C. Donovan, *The Cold Warriors: A Policy Making Elite* (Lexington, Mass., 1974); Gabriel Kolko, *The Roots of American Foreign Policy* (Chicago, 1971); William A. Williams, *The Tragedy of American Diplomacy* (2nd ed.; New York, 1972); and Melvin Gurtov, *The United States Against the Third World* (New York, 1974).

36. Hoopes, *The Limits of Intervention*, 167–81.

Southeast Asia had been a region remote from American interests; the United States possessed few specialists on the region, some of whom, it must be emphasized, supported the Johnson administration's policies in Southeast Asia.

The second reason why consensus marked the decision-making process of the Johnson administration toward the Vietnam War (and toward other crises, such as the intervention in the Dominican Republic) was a conviction by President Johnson and his closest advisers that a commitment to defend the independence of South Vietnam had already been made by his predecessors. LBJ believed that he was obliged to fulfill that obligation after he entered the White House. The strategy of containment was not devised by the Johnson-Rusk foreign policy team. It had guided American foreign policy toward the Communist challenge since the early post–World War II period (see Chapter 4). The idea that containment might not apply to Southeast Asia—the notion that containment doctrine ought to be applied selectively—was not a principle that was widely accepted by the American people and their leaders in the early 1960s. Moreover, the Johnson White House received little useful guidance from critics of the Vietnam War concerning how the scope of the containment policy ought to be narrowed or concerning criteria that ought to govern its application globally.

The consensus reflected among Johnson and his advisers extended beyond the executive branch of the American government. During most of the 1960s, fundamental agreement also existed within Congress in support of the administration's external policies. Time and again, the House and Senate were afforded opportunities to express their opposition to the Vietnam War, such as when Congress annually considered the defense budget. Down to the late 1960s, little evidence existed that legislators seriously dissented from the course of action proposed by the White House. Not until President Nixon had indicated that American troops were being withdrawn from Southeast Asia did Congress officially terminate the war in Southeast Asia.[37]

37. Richard Nixon, *The Memoirs of Richard Nixon* (2 vols.; New York, 1978), II, 433–36.

Rusk as Manager of the State Department

Critics of American foreign policy during the 1960s have shown no hesitation in judging Dean Rusk a failure as the director of the State Department. More than any other official in Washington except President Johnson himself, Rusk became a symbol of the Vietnam War and a favorite target of antiwar sentiment. For reasons that are still not altogether clear, his even more "hawkish" colleague during most of this period—Secretary of Defense McNamara—largely escaped the onus for the Vietnam fiasco.

As secretary of state, Rusk had two convictions that directly affected the ability of the United States to influence the course of global events favorably. One was his idea that the normal condition of the international system is upheaval and chaos and, not infrequently, violence. In Rusk's view, the external environment was, as a rule, hostile to the achievement of American diplomatic goals. The other idea was that though the United States was a superpower, its ability to influence developments abroad in a manner congenial to its interests was extremely limited. After his retirement Rusk said that the words inscribed at the entrance to Dante's Inferno—ABANDON HOPE ALL YE WHO ENTER HERE—were a proper inscription for the main entrance to the State Department.[38]

From the time he joined the State Department, Rusk had been known as a "cold warrior" who feared the consequences of Communist expansionism for the security of the United States, its allies, and other independent nations. He had participated in the formulation of the containment strategy, urged President Truman to defend South Korea, and urged both JFK and LBJ to prevent the communization of Southeast Asia. As Rusk assessed it, communism was not the answer to the problem of national development throughout the Third World. Rather, "it was the most effective and brutal means known to history for exploiting the working class." The emerging Sino-Soviet dispute, in his view, provided no real comfort for Americans, since it was fundamentally a quarrel over the best means for fomenting world revolution and defeating the United States. To his mind, the main

38. Rusk, "The President and the Secretary of State," 9.

problem of American foreign policy remained the containment of expansive communism.[39]

In a number of respects, Rusk could properly be called a traditionalist secretary of state. He venerated the diplomatic process and the customary procedures of the State Department. He believed that a paramount goal of diplomacy was to get international issues "off the front page," and he himself became the epitome of the kind of quiet diplomacy he preferred. He took Presidents Kennedy and Johnson literally when they repeatedly asserted that, under White House direction, the State Department was in charge of American foreign policy and that the secretary of state served as the president's chief diplomatic adviser. On numerous occasions, Rusk praised the American diplomatic corps, expressing the view that it was one of the best in the world. He observed that in the 1960s, more than in any previous era of American history, diplomatic officials were called upon to respond to unending crises overseas; they had to maintain relations with some 110 independent nations and sometimes represent the United States abroad at the risk of their lives.[40]

Rusk believed that under the American constitutional system the president ultimately made the nation's foreign policy. In doing so, of course, the chief executive leaned heavily upon the secretary of state and other advisers. Rusk also understood and accepted the fact, however, that "the President is free to seek and get advice from anyone in the wide world, from his chauffeur if he wants to, from senators, congressmen, people in the media," or any other source. Yet the chief executive "must always be available to and hear the views of the Secretary of State." Consistent with this principle, Rusk was totally opposed to the idea, which emerged during the Nixon administration and after, that members of the White House staff should in any way impede the secretary of state's access to the Oval Office or "get between" him and the president. He was not enthusiastic about special

39. "Secretary Rusk Interviewed on 'Today' Show," *Department of State Bulletin*, XLIV (February 27, 1961), 305; "Seventh Meeting at the Council of Ministers," *ibid.*, XLIV (April 17, 1961), 548; "American Republics Unite to Halt Spread of Communism in Western Hemisphere," *ibid.*, XLVI (February 19, 1962), 272–73; Dean Rusk, "America's Goal—A Community of Free Nations," *ibid.*, XLVI (March 19, 1962), 449–51; Rusk, "Winning Worldwide Victory for Freedom," *ibid.*, XLVII (September 3, 1962), 343.

40. Dean Rusk, "The Realities of Foreign Policy," *ibid.*, XLVI (March 26, 1962), 487–88; "The Making of Foreign Policy," *ibid.*, L (February 3, 1964), 164–76.

assistants to the president who performed diplomatic functions while maintaining little liaison or consultation with the State Department.[41]

Rusk recognized the increasingly difficult problem of coordinating the activities of the executive branch successfully in the foreign policy field. At the same time he had little confidence in elaborate administrative mechanisms or structures for doing so. The coordination of foreign policy activities by executive agencies, he once stated, must not become "a device to spread hidden vetoes around the city of Washington." To his mind, successful policy coordination could only be achieved "by the assignment of central responsibilities to identifiable individuals and departments" rather than to anonymous bureaucracies and committees. In practice this meant that the secretary of state or other high-ranking officials of the State Department should assume the main responsibility for unifying executive activities in foreign affairs.[42]

As secretary of state, Rusk's administration of his department was guided by several principles. He held daily staff meetings with his closest State Department advisers, and he met less frequently with other officials under his jurisdiction. Much of his time was spent in this activity; sometimes there were as many as thirty meetings within a working day. Rusk encouraged junior officers within the department to meet with him from time to time, in part because he believed it bolstered their morale to do so. With his advisers, he was a good listener, usually reserving his own judgment (and often leaving them mystified concerning his own position).[43]

Secretary of State Rusk was admittedly not enthusiastic about reorganization as a method for improving the State Department's efficiency or performance. For example, he largely left the implementation of the Herter committee's reforms (see Chapter 2) to his subordinates, and changes ultimately made seldom produced the results the committee's advocates expected. To his mind, the crucial factor determining the department's performance was the relationship existing between the secretary of state and the chief executive.[44]

41. Rusk, "The President and the Secretary of State," 10–11.
42. Dean Rusk, "Charter Day Address," *Department of State Bulletin*, XLIV (April 10, 1961), 515–19; "Secretary Rusk Interviewed on 'At the Source' Program," *ibid.*, XLV (July 24, 1961), 149.
43. Rusk, "The President and The Secretary of State," 14–15, 26–27.
44. *Ibid.*, 33–34.

Rusk was, of course, familiar with the long-established precedent that a chief executive not only appoints his own secretary of state (with the confirmation of the Senate) but frequently selects other high-ranking State Department officials as well. As often as not, these appointments are made by the president for personal, domestic political, and other extraneous reasons having little to do with the individual's qualifications for a diplomatic assignment. A prominent example during the 1960s was President Kennedy's designation of Adlai Stevenson to head the American delegation to the United Nations. In this role, Stevenson did not hesitate to communicate his viewpoints directly to the White House, and the UN delegation's liaison with the State Department was sometimes less than ideal.[45] Similarly, in an episode known as the Thanksgiving Day Massacre, Kennedy ordered a wholesale reassignment of high-level State Department officials, a decision in which Secretary Rusk played a relatively minor role.

Under Rusk's administration, long-range diplomatic planning within the State Department received a relatively low priority. (As emphasized in Chapter 4, the planning function had begun to decline by the early 1950s.) During the 1960s, the line between planning and direct operational responsibilities within the department continued to be eroded, if it did not altogether disappear.[46]

On the basis of his own experience and observations within the State Department, even Rusk shared some of the misgivings expressed by President Kennedy and others about its performance. For example, he publicly criticized the existence and apparently endless growth of excessive bureaucratic "layering" within the department, which created the necessity for an almost infinite number of clearances by one administrative unit after another before communications could be sent from the department to overseas missions. But he was skeptical about the notion that bureaucrats in the State Department and other governmental agencies were engaged in a relentless pursuit of power or that they devoted their efforts primarily to decision making. In reality, Rusk was convinced, that was not the case at all. To his mind,

45. Martin, *Adlai Stevenson and the World*, 579–865; Arnold Beichman, *The "Other" State Department: The United States Mission to the United Nations—Its Role in the Making of Foreign Policy* (New York, 1968), 143–64.
46. Hilsman, *To Move a Nation*, 50–55; Schlesinger, *A Thousand Days*, 406–17; Destler, *Presidents, Bureaucrats, and Foreign Policy*, 226–28; Bloomfield, *The Foreign Policy Process*, 174.

the natural tendency of State Department officialdom was to avoid making decisions; rather than pursuing power, the bureaucratic inclination was "to avoid responsibility" whenever possible. As one of his former subordinates expressed it, Rusk believed that "part of the organizational shuffling (or reorganization) in Washington . . . is a scramble to get off target zero." Implicitly, he agreed with Kennedy's assessment that it was a continuing challenge to get the State Department to produce creative and effective proposals responsive to the challenges confronting the United States overseas.[47]

Although Rusk was accessible to his aides, conferred with them, and listened courteously to their ideas, he rarely insisted that State Department expertise on areas such as Latin America and Southeast Asia be considered by the president, the Tuesday lunch group, or other advisory councils before final diplomatic decisions were made. At the same time, he did not overtly block attempts by his subordinates to develop their own channels of communication to the White House. Concepts like counterinsurgency and "nation-building"—key ideas upon which American strategy in Southeast Asia was based—had been accepted by the Kennedy White House, for example, largely at the instigation of State Department officials like W. W. Rostow and Roger Hilsman. Several years later, Under Secretary of State George Ball became one of the first members of the Johnson foreign policy team to raise fundamental questions about America's participation in the Vietnam War.[48]

The belief within the State Department and other governmental agencies that decision making toward Vietnam was narrowly confined to LBJ's inner circle of intimate advisers—and the feeling that other high-ranking officials were largely excluded from the process—unquestionably contributed to a problem that continually irritated the president but that he appeared powerless to stop: leaks of information to the press and Congress by officials who disagreed funda-

47. "Secretary Rusk Interviewed on 'Today' Show," 305–306; Dean Rusk, "A Fresh Look at the Formulation of Foreign Policy," *Department of State Bulletin*, XLIV (March 20, 1961), 395–99; "United States Foreign Policy in a Period of Change," *ibid.*, XLIV (March 27, 1961), 439–40; "The Making of Foreign Policy," *ibid.*, L (February 3, 1964), 164–76; Destler, *Presidents, Bureaucrats, and Foreign Policy*, 69; Hilsman, *The Politics of Policy Making in Defense and Foreign Policy* 152.

48. Hilsman, *To Move a Nation*, 52–53; W. W. Rostow, "Guerrilla Warfare in the Underdeveloped Areas," *Department of State Bulletin*, XLV (August 7, 1961), 233–38; Janis, *Groupthink*, 266–67; Hoopes, *The Limits of Intervention*, 28–29.

mentally with the administration's diplomatic moves. Such disclosures were perhaps the inevitable response of bureaucrats who felt that their viewpoints were not being adequately considered in the decision-making process.

In 1966 a White House staff report found that under Rusk's management, the State Department was "not an organization in the usual sense," but "a constellation of small power centers—some moving, some standing, some competing, some hiding, some growing . . . but more breaking apart into smaller fragments." The report noted that in recent years the department had tended to become protective and defensive in an effort to retain primacy within a relatively limited sphere of foreign relations, while implicitly conceding predominance in some fields, such as military policy, to other federal agencies. Yet, in the process the department's historic function of providing leadership across the entire spectrum of diplomatic issues had declined dramatically, with no other department now equipped to play this role. Under these conditions, it was perhaps inevitable (see Chapter 7) that a "rival State Department" should emerge in the White House.[49]

During the 1960s the principal rival to the State Department's position in the foreign policy process came from the Department of Defense, headed from 1961 until 1968 by perhaps the most dynamic and forceful secretary of defense since World War II, Robert McNamara. Like Rusk, McNamara was a holdover from the Kennedy administration. His tenure at the Pentagon was distinguished by numerous innovations, his introduction of new management techniques, and—an accomplishment that particularly appealed to President Johnson— his forceful assertion of the principle of civilian control over the military establishment. McNamara and his team of "Whiz Kids," as they were called, appeared to epitomize the kind of vigorous departmental leadership and imaginative administration that Presidents Kennedy and Johnson desired (but often did not get) in other departments.[50]

Secretaries Rusk and McNamara were opposite personality types and exhibited vastly different administrative styles. While the former was modest, unobtrusive, and reflective, the highly intelligent Mc-

49. Destler, *Presidents, Bureaucrats, and Foreign Policy*, 158–60; Ball, *Diplomacy for a Crowded World*, 200–201.

50. William W. Kaufman, *The McNamara Strategy* (New York, 1964); C. W. Borklund, *The Department of Defense* (New York, 1969), 3–163.

Namara was self-confident, assertive, and a formidable opponent in debate on issues affecting the Pentagon's responsibilities. Almost inevitably, McNamara was well prepared and had marshaled his facts and statistics impressively; his proposals normally also reflected a high degree of unity within the Defense Department. By contrast, uncertainty often existed about what Secretary Rusk really thought and about whether his viewpoint reflected the thinking of his colleagues within the State Department. Accordingly, during the Johnson administration, especially on decision making related to the Vietnam War, relations between the two departments were widely depicted as resulting from McNamara's "imposition" of his position upon a passive and compliant Rusk and perhaps even upon President Johnson himself.

This image, however, distorts reality and omits several salient factors accounting for a high degree of rapport between the State and Defense departments during the 1960s. One of these was the fact that, though it was never officially declared by Congress, the United States was at war in Southeast Asia, and traditionally during such periods military considerations are paramount in national policy. Rusk had spent twenty-five years in the armed forces, including years on active duty. Moreover, he was convinced that since the end of World War II the main business of the United States diplomatically was to meet the Communist challenge abroad, a threat he identified as stemming primarily from aggressive impulses by the Soviet Union, Communist China, North Vietnam, Cuba, and other Communist nations. Time and again, Rusk called attention to the intrinsic relationship existing between military power and diplomacy. In 1963, for example, he declared, "Today the military men and diplomats work together in the closest cooperation to protect the safety and vital interests of the American people." He therefore advocated "powerful military defenses," which he deemed essential for the United States. Rusk did not believe that there was undue military influence in national decision making; nor was he worried about the risk of military usurpation of civilian authority. In his view a potent military component was a vital adjunct to American diplomacy.[51]

51. Dean Rusk, "The Underlying Crisis: Coercion vs. Choice," *Department of State Bulletin*, XLV (July 31, 1961), 175–79; Rusk, "The Current Danger" *ibid.*, XL (September 25, 1961), 507–10; Rusk, "The Realities of Foreign Policy," *ibid.*, XLVI (March 26, 1962),

During most of the 1960s an effective working partnership, therefore, existed between the State and Defense departments, though many officials in Washington judged it an unequal partnership largely dominated by Secretary McNamara and his Pentagon advisers.[52] As much as any other single factor perhaps, McNamara's computer-generated analyses showing that the United States was winning the war in Southeast Asia—or could do so soon if the level of American military involvement were raised—lay at the center of the Johnson administration's miscalculations. As time passed, the evidence indicated that these statistical projections were seriously flawed. Yet, in most cases Rusk's own public statements indicated that he accepted them. More than once, for example, he asserted that the American military effort in Southeast Asia had "turned the corner" and was in the process of achieving victory.[53] If he showed little disposition to contest the Pentagon's optimistic analyses of the course of the war, it should be noted that other experienced State Department officials, such as George Ball and former Secretary of State Acheson, did in time raise fundamental questions about them. Analysts within the Central Intelligence Agency also doubted the reliability of Defense Department studies predicting ultimate American victory in Southeast Asia.[54]

From the perspective of administrative theory, the cooperative relationship between Secretaries Rusk and McNamara during the 1960s could also be accounted for by the former's approach to bureaucratic challenges to the State Department's customary jurisdiction. Heading a department that since World War II had witnessed steady encroachments upon its domain by other executive agencies, Rusk was inclined to be protective and to deal with rivals like the Defense Department on the basis of "tacit non-aggression treaties." His principle was that the State Department "steers clear of military tactics so the military will keep out of diplomacy." Yet, even more than in earlier conflicts like World War II, in Southeast Asia this approach encoun-

487–88; Rusk, "Winning Worldwide Victory for Freedom," *ibid.*, XLVII (September 3, 1962), 344–45; Rusk, "Unfinished Business," *ibid.*, XLIX (September 30, 1963), 490–96.

52. Hilsman, *To Move a Nation*, 58–60.

53. Dean Rusk, "The Road Ahead," *Department of State Bulletin*, XLVIII (March 4, 1963), 311–12; "Secretary Rusk's News Conference of March 8," *ibid.*, XLVIII (March 25, 1963), 435–36; Rusk, "The Stake in Viet-Nam," *ibid.*, XLVIII (May 13, 1963), 727–35.

54. Sheehan *et al.* (eds.), *The Pentagon Papers*.

tered the increasingly difficult problem of differentiating clearly between political and military policy questions. (Indeed, the kind of counterinsurgency strategy employed by the United States in Vietnam assumed that political and military problems were indissolubly related.)[55] The problem of relations between the State and Defense departments during the Johnson administration underscored a reality that became increasingly evident in American foreign relations after the Vietnam conflict. The United States is poorly prepared to fight limited wars successfully. Few Americans, including even the highest officials of the government, understand or are willing to accept the principle of subordinating military strategy to the achievement of limited political objectives.

Executive-legislative relations during the 1960s were marked by paradoxes and anomalies. As a former member of the House and Senate, Lyndon Johnson had entered the White House attuned to legislative attitudes, desires, and procedures on national policy questions. As chief executive, his legislative record was outstanding, perhaps the most noteworthy achievement of his administration. He was convinced that his predecessor, President Truman, had made a serious mistake in 1950 when he did not formally involve Congress in waging the Korean War, with the result that the Korean encounter became widely known as "Mr. Truman's war." LBJ was determined not to repeat that error. On numerous occasions, therefore, President Johnson, Secretary of State Rusk, and other high-ranking officials of the administration briefed legislators on the Vietnam War and other major foreign policy developments, answered their questions, and endeavored to supply information requested by congressional committees interested in external issues. The president in fact once informed his principal advisers that he "never wanted to receive any recommendation for actions [in Southeast Asia] we might have to take unless it was accompanied by a proposal for assuring the backing of Congress."[56]

Rusk was no less mindful of Congress' vital role in the foreign policy process, and he was committed to the principle of bipartisanship in foreign relations. He had impressed President Kennedy favorably

55. Destler, *Presidents, Bureaucrats, and Foreign Policy,* 160–61.
56. Johnson, *The Vantage Point,* 115–16; Goldman, *The Tragedy of Lyndon Johnson,* 449–50.

by his patient and intensive efforts to win support on Capitol Hill for the president's foreign policy program. According to one Kennedy aide, Rusk "proved the most effective Secretary of State [on Capitol Hill] since Cordell Hull."[57] On several occasions Rusk underscored the bipartisan continuity of American foreign policy since World War II, emphasized the importance of executive-legislative collaboration in behalf of diplomatic programs and policies, and called for the establishment of an effective partnership between the president and Congress in dealing with major foreign policy questions.[58]

Yet, a significant irony of the Vietnam War period was that, despite the Johnson administration's recognition of the increasingly influential role of Congress in the foreign policy process, executive-legislative relations deteriorated to the lowest level reached since World War II. The defection of influential Democrats on Capitol Hill, some of whom in time became leaders of the antiwar movement, provided graphic evidence of this phenomenon. A prominent example was Senator J. William Fulbright (D-Ark.), who became an outspoken critic of Johnson-Rusk diplomacy.

The erosion of bipartisanship was graphically illustrated by the administration's experiences with the Tonkin Gulf Resolution, passed by overwhelming majorities in both houses of Congress in the summer of 1964. The resolution had been proposed by the White House after reports were received of two successive attacks (on August 2 and 4) upon American naval vessels by North Vietnam in the Gulf of Tonkin. After the second incident, President Johnson and his advisers were certain that Hanoi's aggressiveness was intentional and that North Vietnam was testing America's resolve in the Vietnam War. He believed that this test must be met decisively. Accordingly, he asked Congress to pass a resolution expressing America's determination to resist Communist aggression in Southeast Asia. The provisions of the resolution stated that Congress approved "all necessary measures to repel any armed attack" against American forces in Southeast Asia and to "prevent further aggression" in the region. The resolution asserted that America was prepared, "as the President determines, to

57. Schlesinger, *A Thousand Days*, 433.
58. "Secretary Rusk Interviewed on 'Today' Show," 306; "Secretary Rusk Holds Press and Radio News Briefing at Los Angeles," *ibid.*, XLVIII (March 11, 1963), 363; Dean Rusk, "Some Current Issues in U.S. Foreign Policy," *ibid.*, XLVIII (May 6, 1963), 682–83.

take all necessary steps including the use of armed force" to preserve the security of the region. Secretary of State Rusk and other State Department officials played a key role in formulating the resolution and gaining legislative support for it.[59]

Few developments during the war, however, ultimately proved as controversial as the Tonkin Gulf Resolution. Critics of the Johnson-Rusk diplomacy in time regarded it as a typical exercise in LBJ's duplicity and his attempt to manipulate Congress into supporting his foreign policy ventures. Meanwhile, time and again the Johnson White House cited the resolution as an important source of its authority for military escalation in Southeast Asia and as irrefutable evidence that the nation's policy there was supported by legislative, no less than by executive, policy makers.[60]

By the end of the Johnson-Rusk era, little semblance of bipartisanship remained in American foreign policy. Democrats were in open revolt against the administration's policies in Southeast Asia, Rusk's credibility on Capitol Hill had declined sharply, and the steady erosion of his political base convinced President Johnson not to seek reelection in 1968.

The failure of the Tonkin Gulf Resolution and other measures to create and maintain bipartisan cooperation between the executive and legislative branches during the 1960s calls attention to a fundamental problem in the American foreign policy process. Perhaps the outstanding feature of the Vietnam conflict vis-à-vis other military contests fought by the United States since the War of 1812 is that the nation *lost* the war in Southeast Asia. The model of successful bipartisan cooperation in foreign affairs was the period of World War II and the early postwar era (see Chapters 3 and 4). Except for "the loss of China" to communism, during that period the United States experienced no overt and dramatic diplomatic defeats, and it had a number of notable successes to its credit, such as the successful containment of communism in Greece, the reconstruction of Western Eu-

59. The resolution was embodied in House Joint Resolution 1145; after it was signed by the president on August 7, 1964, it became Public Law 88-408. The resolution was approved by the House of Representatives by a vote of 414-0 and by the Senate, 88-2. A detailed discussion of the meaning and consequences of the resolution can be found in Crabb, *The Doctrines of American Foreign Policy*, 191–234. See also Johnson, *The Vantage Point*, 114, 117–18.

60. Johnson, *The Vantage Point*, 117–19; Fulbright, *The Crippled Giant*, 177–204; J. William Fulbright, *The Arrogance of Power* (New York, 1966), 44–67, 106–39.

rope, and the defense of Western Europe from Soviet expansionism. The outcome of the Vietnam War alone could easily account for the collapse of bipartisan unity in foreign relations.

While he was secretary of state, Rusk on one occasion called for "vigorous discussion" throughout American society on foreign policy questions. In his view, at least every two or four years, during national elections, there should be a "great debate" on external, as well as internal, policy issues. Such a debate would in the end strengthen the kind of bipartisan foundation that had supported the nation's foreign policy since the period of the Truman administration.[61] In conformity with the democratic principle of accountability, it was perhaps both desirable and inevitable that such a great debate would occur over the Vietnam War as an indispensable step in the reorientation of American diplomacy after that traumatic encounter.

A related dimension of the secretary of state's responsibilities involves the increasingly influential role of public opinion in the American foreign policy process. Rusk was fully attuned to this aspect of his duties, and it is another irony of the Vietnam conflict that in time he became perhaps the most unpopular head of the State Department since World War II. To Rusk, public understanding and support were essential for American diplomatic success. He expressed great confidence in the good judgment of the American people, in their underlying common sense in comprehending the realities confronting the United States abroad, and in their ability to demonstrate "the nerve and the will" required to defend the diplomatic vital interests of the non-Communist world. He believed that if Moscow and other foreign capitals became confused about the determination of the American people to support the policies of their government, the prospects for instability and conflict abroad would be greatly increased. Rusk also believed, in contrast to the views of his superior in the White House, that, with rare exceptions like the Cuban missile crisis, foreign policy decisions in the United States could not and should not be enveloped in secrecy.[62]

61. "Secretary Rusk Holds Press and Radio News Briefing at Los Angeles," 363.

62. "Secretary Rusk's News Conference of February 6," *Department of State Bulletin*, XLIV (February 27, 1961), 296–97; Dean Rusk, "A Fresh Look at the Formulation of Foreign Policy," *ibid.*, XLIV (March 20, 1961), 398; Rusk, "Building an International Community of Science and Scholarship," *ibid.*, XLIV (May 1, 1961), 625; Rusk, "The Realities of Foreign Policy," *ibid.*, XLVI (March 26, 1962), 489; Rusk, "Security and Freedom: A Free World Responsibility," *ibid.*, XLVIII (March 18, 1963), 383.

Until the closing months of the Johnson administration, Johnson and Rusk were convinced that their policies were supported by the mainstream of American public opinion. The evidence indicates that this assessment was in general correct. During the 1960s most Americans wanted to avoid both the extremes of all-out war and capitulation to communism in Southeast Asia, which is another way of saying they shared the White House goal of keeping the Vietnam War limited. Throughout most of the war, the majority of the American public was neither overwhelmingly "hawkish" nor "dovish." The people were prepared to accord wide latitude to the chief executive to pursue his diplomatic goals within these broad parameters. Admittedly, the ordinary American had only a rudimentary and poorly thought out understanding of what "winning" a limited war against communism in Southeast Asia really meant in terms of the costs or consequences involved. And as always, during the 1960s the average American's understanding of foreign affairs was primitive, fragmentary, marked by ambivalences and contradictions, and reflective of a large measure of indifference toward many problems and conditions overseas.[63]

After an awareness of the magnitude of the rising American military and economic commitment to the defense of South Vietnam characterized public attitudes—and after the American people sensed the costs and consequences of continuing this commitment—public support for the Johnson administration's policies in Southeast Asia eroded. To a degree which has not yet been determined and is difficult to document, the government of North Vietnam and its supporters, of course, encouraged the withdrawal of the public mandate for the Johnson administration's policies in Southeast Asia. A comparable approach by Hanoi had earlier undermined the French government's position in Southeast Asia. At any rate, President Johnson's dramatic announcement on March 31, 1968, that he would not seek reelection amounted to an admission that his foreign policies were no longer acceptable to the American people.[64]

63. Our analysis of public opinion during the Johnson-Rusk era relies heavily upon the evidence presented in Seymour M. Lipset, "The President, the Polls, and Vietnam," in Lifton (ed.), *America and the Asian Revolutions*, 101–16; John E. Mueller, *War, Presidents and Public Opinion* (New York, 1973), esp. 23–65. See also the poll data presented in Crabb, *The Doctrines of American Foreign Policy*, 193–277.

64. See the discussions of the impact of public opinion upon the Johnson administration's diplomacy in Southeast Asia in Lipset, "The President, the Polls, and Vietnam," 101–17; Nelson W. Polsby "Hawks, Doves, and the Press," in Lifton (ed.), *America*

The more extreme and sometimes violent manifestations of public opposition to the Vietnam War (and to a lesser degree to the Dominican intervention)—such as sit-ins, clamorous public demonstrations, and disruptive protests—played a relatively minor role in changing the course of American foreign policy during the Johnson-Rusk period. Indeed, some students of American public opinion are convinced that extreme forms of protest may have *prolonged* the war in Vietnam. The protests engendered a kind of siege mentality among the president and his advisers, and they convinced LBJ as a matter of principle not to yield to what he viewed as the uninformed demands of extreme antiwar critics. They also generated sympathetic public support from ordinary citizens for the beleaguered White House. More than once, President Johnson, Secretary of State Rusk, and other officials asserted that they would not permit Ameican foreign policy to be "made in the streets" by extremist groups.

Yet despite such disclaimers, the numerous and graphic antiwar demonstrations unquestionably did in time affect the conduct and viewpoints of Johnson, Rusk, and other key members of the administration. In part from their concern about the physical safety of the president and his chief advisers, officials of the Johnson administration reduced their public appearances and their attempts to defend the nation's diplomatic conduct abroad. This, of course, severely curtailed the level of public discourse about the war. Hanoi and other Communist capitals were supplied with daily evidence of domestic American opposition to prevailing policy, while the decrease in appearances by administration spokesmen created an impression that the Johnson White House had been intimidated by its outspoken critics. Finding their policies under severe attack and their ethics and moral principles impugned by some outspoken critics, officials of the Johnson administration became highly protective and more inclined than ever to clothe their diplomatic deliberations in secrecy. This tendency incensed legislators and members of the news media and encouraged political commentators to get their information from leaks, such as the *Pentagon Papers.*

---

and the Asian Revolutions, 61–79; Richard A. Brody, "Vietnam and American Elections," in *ibid.*, 79–101; and Henry Kissinger, *White House Years* (Boston, 1979), 254–55, 292–93.

The dominant "lesson of Vietnam" as it relates to the role of public opinion in American foreign relations, however, perhaps lay in calling attention to the indispensable role of legitimacy as the foundation of any democratic nation's foreign policy. Critics and supporters of the Johnson-Rusk approach to the Vietnam War alike would agree that in time it lost the necessary legitimacy, and this was a crucial development leading to the Vietnam failure. The Johnson-Rusk foreign policy team plainly did not discover a solution to this conundrum.

The Johnson-Rusk Relationship in Perspective

Although it is still subject to the kind of reexamination that has been carried out on the diplomacy of the Eisenhower-Dulles period, the prevailing judgment is that despite his long tenure in office Dean Rusk would not be numbered among the outstanding secretaries of state in American history. Rusk led the State Department during one of the most internally divisive eras of the nation's experience, and President Johnson steadily lost credibility with the electorate primarily because of his foreign policy record. In the eyes of some, Johnson, along with his successor, Richard Nixon, exemplified the kind of perversion of the executive office implied by the term *imperial presidency*. The Johnson-Rusk diplomacy provided a powerful stimulus for the kind of congressional assertiveness in foreign relations that occurred during the 1970s. Inevitably perhaps, the blame for the defeat in Vietnam—along with lesser setbacks, such as the deterioration in United States–Latin American relations and the eruption of a new round of violence in the Arab-Israeli dispute—was attributed to President Johnson and his principal foreign policy adviser, Dean Rusk.

Among students of the 1960s, considerable attention has been devoted to the foreign policy consensus that has been singled out as a crucial element in accounting for America's involvement in Vietnam. Rusk came to be widely regarded as epitomizing the kind of "groupthink" that was responsible for the nation's diplomatic misadventures under the Johnson administration. Theoretically, of course, there is nothing wrong with a high degree of unity among executive officials concerning the nation's foreign policy goals. The later experiences of the Nixon, Carter, and Reagan administrations provide convincing evidence that chronic disagreement and conflict within the executive branch can be just as serious an impediment to the realization of American diplomatic goals. And a high level of consensus among executive officials also existed during the Truman administration, when some of the most noteworthy diplomatic accomplishments in the post–World War II era were achieved (see Chapter 4). As a recurring problem in the management of American foreign relations, therefore, the challenge is to achieve consensus within the national government in behalf of foreign policies that are creative and effective.

Rusk's predicament as an influential member of the Johnson administration exemplified the dilemma of the average American in adapting his world view to an unfamiliar, rapidly changing international environment. Inevitably perhaps, his tendency is to cling to policies with which he is familiar and that have been successful in the past. Rusk finally, with evident reluctance and an overt lack of enthusiasm, modified his position on the Vietnam War. In that respect he was joined by millions of his fellow citizens. Yet, in the process he produced no new and successful strategy for achieving American objectives in Southeast Asia or, more broadly, in the kind of unstable and revolutionary situations confronting the United States throughout the Third World. Faced with these challenges, Rusk was unable to evolve a response that met two crucial criteria—one that would both be capable of achieving American objectives overseas and also command and maintain a broad consensus of support at home.

If that may legitimately be construed as a momentous failure by the secretary of state, it was one in which the president, other high-ranking executive officials, members of the House and Senate, anti–Vietnam war critics, and the American people all shared. In the years that followed, this defect continued to pose a formidable obstacle to an effective role by the United States in the international system.

7

The Emergence of a Rival State Department: Nixon and Kissinger

International politics, like its domestic counterpart, sometimes presents dramatic reversals of fortunes and policies, reversals that can be replete with ironies. The strange career of Richard Nixon as politician and president exemplifies this observation. In collaboration with his national security adviser (and de facto secretary of state), Henry Kissinger, Nixon promulgated far-reaching revisions in post–World War II foreign policy. Whatever the judgments that history may make about the Nixon presidency on moral and constitutional grounds, there can be little question of the momentous impact that his tenure had for the conduct of American foreign affairs. Nixon's impact was felt in several ways—in the theoretical framework in which his foreign policy initiatives were cast (the so-called "Nixon Doctrine"); in the specific content of the policies themselves (for example, in détente and the normalization of Sino-American relations); and in the process by which these policies were formulated, especially regarding the role of Kissinger and his White House staff. In foreign affairs Nixon realized the "New American Revolution" that eluded him in domestic politics. His administration also came close to avoiding the intra–executive branch conflict that has plagued postwar foreign policy making, though this was accomplished by effectively displacing the secretary of state from any meaningful role and substituting the national security adviser in his place.

The Nixon foreign policy record is an ironic one. For one thing, a conservative American president, who had made anticommunism a major tenet of his political rhetoric for two decades, embraced the Soviet head of state and negotiated the first and only substantial arms control agreements to date. A president with a long record of asserting American claims to world hegemony negotiated with the Soviet Union on the basis of assumptions that effectively recognized the diplomatic coresponsibility of the Soviet Union and the United States in maintaining order for the international system. In both cases the import of the Nixon foreign policy was to recognize the co-equality of the United States and USSR in the world order. In the fifty years that the United States and the Soviet Union have had diplomatic relations (the United States recognized the Bolshevik government in 1933), the two nations have oscillated between confrontation and cooperation, though the former has clearly dominated. With the possible exception of the brief period of guarded friendship during and just after World War II, the "era of negotiation" that Nixon heralded in 1969, and realized most dramatically in the Strategic Arms Limitation Talks (SALT I) of May, 1972, saw the greatest cooperation between the two superpowers ever.

While it would certainly be denied by its formulators, the Nixon-Kissinger foreign policy initiatives constituted a major defensive reassessment of America's world position. Indeed, it bears a similarity to the controversial Yalta agreements of 1945, which conceded a Soviet sphere of influence in Eastern Europe as an unalterable *fait accompli* of World War II. Any such analogy would particularly disturb Nixon, who made denunciations of the "Yalta sellout" a staple of his early political rhetoric. In effect, the Nixon Doctrine recognized the undeniable fact that by the late 1960s the Soviet Union had achieved parity with the United States in overall nuclear weaponry and thus had gained the right to assert its international political interests. In the Nixon-Kissinger assessment of the world order, the United States could maintain its paramount position only by recognizing that its power, while preeminent, was not omnipotent. What was needed (and what Nixon claimed to offer) was a redefinition and redeployment of American power.

The Nixon Doctrine

The Nixon Doctrine, unlike the Truman Doctrine (see Chapter 4), was not a specific formulation. Rather, it was a set of policy guidelines that offered a flexible course of action in foreign policy making (some would say so flexible as to be vague or "slippery," a characterization not unfamiliar to Nixon in other contexts). A key element of the Nixon Doctrine was the idea that retrenchment was necessary in the foreign commitments of the United States to allow American power to be used more effectively and efficiently. As President Nixon put it, "I began with the proposition that we would keep all our existing treaty commitments, but that we would not make any more commitments unless they were required by our own vital interests." [1] With this realpolitik, Nixon and Kissinger placed the issue of American power at the forefront of foreign policy considerations. Given the American experience with a long, divisive war in Vietnam that ended in defeat, the need for a reassessment of the nation's military capabilities and international priorities was painfully evident.

From this perspective the restoration of American power required, first, a liquidation of the Vietnam conflict in a way that would avert a dangerous polarization of American society and still preserve the reputation of the United States as a country that sustained its commitments; second, a realistic reordering of the nation's priority interests so as to avoid squandering its resources in the service of idealistic goals peripheral to the central balance of military and geopolitical power; third, the development of a concept of international order that—while consistent with the priority interests of the United States—would provide a standard of legitimacy to which most nations could attach themselves; and, finally, purposeful and dramatic action on global issues so that this country's leaders, once again, would be looked to as the main pace setters in the international arena. [2]

According to the Nixon Doctrine, given the "balance of terror" implied in the nuclear parity between the two superpowers, the United States needed to be most concerned with the conventional

1. See President Nixon's "Second Annual Report to Congress on United States Foreign Policy," in *Public Papers of the Presidents of the United States: Richard Nixon, 1971* (Washington, D.C., 1971), 219–345; Richard Nixon, *The Memoirs of Richard Nixon* (New York, 1978), 395.
2. Seyom Brown, *The Crises of Power: An Interpretation of United States Foreign Policy During the Kissinger Years* (New York, 1979), 2–3.

warfare likely to be associated with "wars of liberation," which might be backed by the Soviet Union, and other localized conflicts. As a response to this problem, the Nixon Doctrine stated that the United States would honor its treaty commitments but that it should not be expected to assume the primary burden of the manpower necessary for another nation's defense. Economic and military assistance would be furnished as appropriate, and the United States would provide a "shield" if "a nuclear power threatens the freedom of a nation allied with us or of a nation whose survival we consider vital to our security and the security of the region as a whole." However, while the United States would continue to support its allies, the Nixon Doctrine sought to clarify that this nation could not, and would not, "conceive *all* the plans, design *all* the programs, execute *all* the decisions, and undertake *all* the defense of the free nations of the world."[3]

Even before President Nixon addressed these words to Congress, Henry Kissinger, who was then an adviser to Nelson Rockefeller, a rival of Nixon's for the 1968 Republican presidential nomination, argued similarly that the United States was no longer able to effect global management: "We can continue to contribute to defense and positive programs, but we must seek to encourage and not stifle a sense of local responsibility. Our contribution should not be the sole or principal effort, but it should make the difference between success and failure." A key tenet of the Nixon Doctrine was the requirement that an endangered ally supply the manpower and, most important, demonstrate the will to provide for its own security; the United States would supply logistical and material support. "The willingness of the country concerned to make its assigned contribution would be a precondition for the provision of American aid."[4]

When Richard Nixon proclaimed that America's interests must shape its commitments, rather than the other way around, he was reflecting a basic dogma of international relations that has been termed realpolitik. As a principle for governing foreign affairs, realpolitik posits the primacy of power (and the balance of power) and national

3. Richard Nixon, *U.S. Foreign Policy for the 1970s: A New Strategy for Peace* (Washington, D.C., 1970), 5–6.
4. Henry A. Kissinger, "Central Issues in American Foreign Policy," in Kermit Gordon (ed.), *Agenda for the Nation* (Washington, D.C., 1968), 612; Cecil V. Crabb, Jr., *The Doctrines of American Foreign Policy* (Baton Rouge, 1982), 285.

interest.[5] As nations seek to maximize their position in the world, the practitioner of realpolitik believes that a central goal of American foreign policy should be to foster an international environment that is conducive to its own security and well-being. Implicit in many realpolitik conceptions of a stable international order is a recognition of the interests that other nations have in the outcomes of world political events. George Kennan, for example, has argued that a stable political system could have emerged after World War II if there had been a clear recognition of the various spheres of influence enjoyed by the various Allied nations in Europe, particularly the interest that the Soviet Union had in maintaining its sphere of influence in Eastern Europe. Similarly, Anatol Rapoport has argued that successful détente between the United States and the Soviet Union must be predicated on a de facto acceptance of the interest that each has in maintaining its respective international interests and influence.[6]

The Nixon Doctrine saw the maintenance of détente as a necessary precondition for the president's "structure of peace." Realization of détente as a general goal entailed negotiation of specific arms-control agreements and an overall reduction in competitive tensions. This, in turn, required acceptance by both the United States and the USSR of a basic parity in weaponry and a recognition of each other's security interests. The realism involved in such a policy was never popular with either end of the American political spectrum. For many conservatives it smacked of appeasement, while for many liberals it seemed Machiavellian or, given Kissinger's background, Bismarckian. For both camps the Nixon-Kissinger approach fell short of more far-reaching goals such as military superiority or a just world order. Yet, the Nixon Doctrine was "liberal" in its desire to reduce the level of suspicion and propensity for hostilities between the two superpowers. On the other hand, it was "conservative" in its goal of efficient use of American power to maximize the nation's international political interests.

In essence, the Nixon Doctrine represented an effort to come to

5. For a full discussion of realpolitik, see Cecil V. Crabb, Jr., *Policy-Makers and Critics: Conflicting Theories of American Foreign Policy* (New York, 1976), 165–214.

6. George F. Kennan, *Memoirs, 1925–1950* (New York, 1969), 262, 266; Anatol Rapoport, *The Big Two: Soviet-American Perceptions of Foreign Policy* (New York, 1971), 86.

terms with the realities of a world after Vietnam. From this viewpoint, the United States could no longer seek to maintain a "territorial empire"—one in which American manpower would be directly responsible for perimeter defense and internal security. Maintaining a territorial empire required the United States to act as the "policeman of the free world" and inevitably involved the commitment of American forces to situations that might be decidedly local, and even more decidedly peripheral, to the nation's central security concerns. What Nixon and Kissinger proposed, in effect, was a "hegemonic empire"— one in which there are demarcations among differing spheres of control and in which allied or client states are responsible for local defense and internal security. Thus, as an alternative model of strategic thinking, the Nixon Doctrine represented an effort to reassess the conduct of American international relations in the light of the Vietnam experience.[7] It should be understood as seeking "to enable the United States to do essentially as much in the world as before, but with an economy of means, a fairer distribution of burdens, and a more rational allocation of tasks among allies."[8]

Détente as Foreign Policy

The most immediate and irksome foreign policy problem that faced Nixon was achieving an honorable resolution to the war in Vietnam. Four years after he assumed office, this goal was realized with the official termination of hostilities on January 27, 1973. Accomplishing the disengagement of the United States from this "endless war" proved to be a longer and politically more volatile undertaking than was the process by which the military commitments were originally made. Nixon and Kissinger devised a two-pronged approach for the realization of this objective. First was the phased withdrawal of American combat troops from involvement in the ground war. Meanwhile, the

7. The models of territorial and hegemonic empires are developed by Edward N. Luttwak, *The Grand Strategy of the Roman Empire* (Baltimore, 1976), 13–50. Luttwak is a distinguished writer on nuclear strategy, not an ancient historian. Consequently, his analyses of Roman military concepts may be fairly judged to have applications for contemporary defense concerns.

8. Earl C. Ravenal, "Nixon's Challenge to Carter," *Foreign Policy*, XXIX (Winter, 1977), 37.

continuation of the American air war would serve to prod the North Vietnamese government to negotiate an end to the hostilities on the basis of diplomacy rather than force. The corollary to the "de-Americanization" of the war was its "Vietnamization"—the modernization and professionalization of the South Vietnamese army to allow it to take over full combat responsibility. American troops would gradually be withdrawn from Vietnam; as this process went forward, the United States would "train, equip, and inspire the South Vietnamese to fill the gaps."[9]

This two-pronged strategy for ending America's war in Vietnam also had a double-edged danger. First, the administration's critics at home would be quick to protest if the withdrawal of American troops stalled or if the scope of the war broadened. Protests are exactly what occurred when South Vietnamese and American forces invaded (it was officially an "incursion into") Cambodia in 1970 to wipe out North Vietnamese sanctuaries and supply columns. President Nixon argued that such an operation was necessary to forestall a North Vietnamese invasion and to provide the South Vietnamese government with the time necessary to maintain its own defenses.[10] Domestic critics, including prominent politicians both within and outside the Nixon administration, felt differently and regarded the Cambodian operation as regionalizing a local conflict—creating an "Indochinese War"—and reneging on the promise of peace. Major universities around the United States were closed down in the wake of antiwar protests and large-scale demonstrations were staged in Washington and other American cities such as those that had traumatized domestic politics during the previous Johnson administration. The tragic shootings at Kent State University may have represented a symbolic end to the tactic of mass confrontation, but the spontaneity and the size of the protests clearly signaled that the American people wished surcease from the interminable struggle.[11]

The second difficulty in Nixon's Vietnam strategy involved the North Vietnamese. Much of the success of Vietnamization was predicated on the willingness of the Hanoi government to allow its adversaries

9. Nixon, *Memoirs*, 392.
10. Richard M. Nixon, *The Real War* (New York, 1981), 105–36.
11. Nixon, on the other hand, had unrelenting contempt for the personal and political values of the antiwar demonstrators. Nixon, *Memoirs*, 398–404.

in Saigon the breathing space to rearm and redeploy as the American troop presence diminished. When the North Vietnamese launched a surprise attack with conventional weapons that included tanks and artillery, the northern provinces of South Vietnam fell, and only massive American air strikes prevented worse losses. The United States also partially "re-Americanized" the war by mining the harbor of Haiphong to interdict supplies and reintroducing large-scale bombing of North Vietnam. This dramatic reescalation of the war occurred just as President Nixon was to visit Moscow to negotiate détente with Soviet leader Leonid Brezhnev. Significantly, the Soviet Union did not call off the scheduled summit; presumably the future of the détente was more important than the fate of its client state. In this diplomatic isolation North Vietnam agreed to a cessation of hostilities that entailed substantial concessions on both sides. All American troops were to be withdrawn from Vietnam in two months, prisoners of war would be exchanged, and commissions representing all political persuasions would make recommendations for restructuring the South Vietnamese government. Most significant, the North Vietnamese agreed to recognize the political sovereignty of the American-backed regime, which allowed the Nixon administration to retreat with the appearance of honor. What the North Vietnamese conceded in January, 1973, however, they took back in the spring of 1975 when the red flag was raised over Saigon.

The "loss of Vietnam" is often cited as proof that the United States lacks not only omnipotence but merely determination to honor its commitments. On the other hand, this defeat freed the United States to refocus its attention on the crucial matter of the strategic balance between itself and the USSR. As John Spanier said, "At the center of détente with the Soviet Union stood the Strategic Arms Limitation Talks (SALT)."[12] While the United States was distracted in Indochina, the Soviet Union had moved from a position of nuclear inferiority in 1962 to one of parity and, according to some estimates, of superiority, at least in certain categories of weapons. By the beginning of the Nixon presidency significant elements within the foreign policy community had come to believe that the quantitative and qualitative development of the Soviet nuclear arsenal had undermined the "bal-

12. John Spanier, *American Foreign Policy Since World War II* (9th ed., New York, 1983), 191. See also Coral Bell, *The Diplomacy of Détente* (New York, 1977).

ance of terror" upon which the system of mutual deterrence was predicated. In particular, the Nixon administration had concluded that the Soviets had developed a first-strike capacity that would allow it to destroy American land-based missiles without fear of retaliatory annihilation. If the two superpowers could work out a mutually acceptable arms agreement, it would sanctify the strategic parity and diplomatic equivalence between the two nations. That was the reasoning behind détente. "SALT, in brief, became a symbol of détente," Spanier noted. "With it, détente seemed to be blossoming; without it détente seemed to be fading. A SALT agreement or failure to arrive at an agreement became the barometer of détente." Negotiations directed at achieving a Soviet-American arms control agreement began in late 1969 and culminated on May 26, 1972, when Nixon and Brezhnev signed the SALT accords. These efforts led to an agreement upon a quantitative limitation of nuclear arms—a treaty that limited the number of delivery vehicles, such as missiles and bombers, that each country could possess. (In contrast to the SALT II agreement of the late 1970s, which was never ratified, SALT I did not restrict the overall nuclear firepower allowable to each nation.) In essence, SALT sought to preserve the prevailing nuclear symmetry by freezing the number of missile launchers of each country. It also prohibited both countries from converting short-range missiles into long-range ones and from taking other steps that would alter the military equilibrium that had been established.[13]

When SALT was signed in 1972, the United States possessed 1,054 land-based intercontinental-ballistic missiles (ICBMs) and the Soviet Union 1,618. SALT did not apply to mobile ICBMs, and it allowed the development of the "mobile experimental" (MX) missile system. Neither did it apply to the nuclear weapons of the NATO countries, a source of much adverse Soviet comment whenever there is any question about their greater number of missiles. It might also be remembered that the "medium range" missiles now being deployed in Europe have a range that includes Moscow, though they are not a violation of SALT.

As an arms-control measure that dealt only with the quantitative aspects of nuclear weapons, SALT did not limit the firepower, de-

13. Spanier, *American Foreign Policy*, 193.

structiveness, accuracy, or other characteristics of existing weapons systems. The United States and the Soviet Union could, and did, introduce qualitative improvements without violating the SALT accords. What may be more important, however, is that SALT represented the first time in which the two superpowers had agreed to place limits on each side's number of missiles. If nothing else, SALT established a precedent for superpower cooperation in limiting their nuclear arsenals.[14]

To speak of détente as if it were only a Soviet-American matter is a decided though common mistake. Along with Vietnamization and SALT, the "normalization" of relations with the People's Republic of China was the other element in the Nixon Doctrine's defensive reassessment. In fact, it can be argued "that détente with China was a prerequisite to détente with the Soviet Union."[15] From a realpolitik perspective, this presented an opportunity for the United States to take advantage of a falling out between its adversaries to achieve a rapprochement with China.[16] Britain traditionally had allied itself with the second-greatest continental land power (whether Prussia or France) against the greatest (the other of the aforementioned pair); this strategy had been the touchstone of its foreign policy. The possibility of a Sino-American alliance presented a similar opportunity for creating a new balance of power within the international system. The power balance in such a system would be a limited de facto entente, in which China, along with NATO, would counter the Soviet Union's conventional military power as the United States (with its NATO ancillary) countered its nuclear power.

To engage in even so implicit a defensive alliance represented a historic diplomatic *volte-face*, an almost unprecedented turnabout in the foreign policies of the two nations, especially of the United States and

14. For detailed analyses of SALT see Richard Burt, "The Scope and Limit of SALT," *Foreign Affairs,* LVI (July, 1978), 751–71; Aaron L. Friedberg, "What SALT Can and Cannot Do," *Foreign Policy,* XXXIII (Winter, 1978–79), 92–101; Paul Nitze, "Nuclear Strategy: Détente and American Survival," in James P. Schlesinger (ed.), *Defending America: Toward a New Role in the Post-Détente World* (New York, 1977), 97–109.

15. Spanier, *American Foreign Policy,* 187–88.

16. The realpolitik approach "argued that the Soviets were more likely to be conciliatory if they feared we would otherwise seek a rapprochement with Peking." Henry Kissinger, *White House Years* (Boston, 1979), 182. Kissinger observes that on China, "not surprisingly, I was on the side of the Realpolitikers." *Ibid.* For his overall views on China, see *ibid.* 163–95, 684–788, 1049–97. See also Nixon, *Memoirs,* 544–80, 878–83; and Nixon, *The Real War,* 137–62.

its president. It could be judged hardly less than "a major event in American foreign policy when a President declared that we have a strategic interest in the survival of a Communist country, long an enemy and with which we had no contact." Nixon's visit to China in 1972 and his public embrace of Mao Tse-tung and Chou En-lai symbolized nothing less than a revolution in Sino-American relations. "And it was on this level of shared geopolitical interest transcending philosophies and history that the former Red-baiter and the crusaders for world revolutions found each other," Kissinger recalled.[17]

The "China card" that the United States played in normalizing relations with the People's Republic was meant to trump the Soviet Union's long suit in conventional military forces. All trumps, however, have to be played carefully and selectively. The Chinese-American defensive relationship as constructed by Nixon and Kissinger was one in which the two nations would reinforce each other without explicitly coordinating their diplomatic and military tactics. But it was this very flexibility that was the China card's principal value. As the United States was careful to remind the USSR, the Sino-Soviet rapprochement had not resulted in a defensive alliance between the two countries; nor was the United States, as the architect of détente, interested in intensifying conflict between the Soviet Union and other nations. American (and Soviet) officials were aware, nonetheless, of the strategic and military advantages of a close relationship with China. These advantages were influential in changing the course of Soviet-American, as well Sino-American, relations.[18]

The "New Nixon" as President

For all the dramatic foreign policy initiatives associated with the Nixon Doctrine, it is ironic that President Nixon's personal and political legacy should be in such great disrepute. Nixon's tattered reputation is largely a domestic phenomenon. Abroad, Nixon, in and out of office, has enjoyed an easy familiarity with Soviet and Chinese politi-

17. Kissinger, *White House Years*, 182, 1089.
18. Actual diplomatic recognition did not come until January 1, 1979. During the 1970s the two nations drew closer together through scientific and cultural exchanges, expanding trade relations, and diplomatic conversations.

cal leaders and received high marks for strong leadership from most members of the European foreign policy community. Both Brezhnev and Chou En-lai were said to have hoped for his reelection in 1972 as necessary for the future of détente and the normalization of Sino-American relations. Yet, in a recent rating of presidents by American historians, published in the *Journal of American History*, Nixon ranked in the bottom three, with Grant and Coolidge, as an unqualified failure.[19] How do we explain this radical difference in the personal stature of a leader among his own countrymen compared with his reputation in other nations?

No public figure is immune to the analytical couch of "psychobiography." Nevertheless, it would be hard to think of a president who has been the subject of more inquiries into his psychological makeup than has Nixon.[20] From his earliest days in politics, questions about Nixon's judgment, honesty, sense of fair play, and emotional stability have persistently been raised. During the almost thirty years that he was an active political figure (and afterward as well), Nixon has been capable of arousing an extraordinary degree of hatred from among some fellow politicians, members of the press, and the public at large. Sizable numbers of the electorate chose to identify themselves as "Nixon-haters." He ended his famous valedictory press conference in 1962 with the taunt "You won't have Nixon to kick around anymore." And, of course, to avoid certain impeachment, he became the only president to resign from office.[21]

The Nixon who entered that Oval Office in 1969 was associated with a very different set of foreign policy views than those constituting the Nixon Doctrine. As president, he seemed to have undergone one of those metamorphoses that would lead periodically to talk of a "new Nixon." After twenty-five years of a political career whose foundation was anticommunism, Nixon initiated détente. After two

19. This survey was conducted by Robert K. Murray of Pennsylvania State University and was reported in *U.S. News and World Report*, November 21, 1983, p. 54.

20. James David Barber, *The Presidential Character* (2nd ed.; Englewood Cliffs, N.J., 1971), 347–442; and Bruce C. Mazlish, *In Search of Nixon: A Psychohistorical Inquiry* (New York, 1972).

21. On Nixon's early political career see Fawn M. Brodie, *Richard Nixon: The Shaping of His Character* (New York, 1981), 362–76; Earl Mazo and Stephen Hess, *Nixon: A Political Portrait* (New York, 1968); and Garry Wills, *Nixon Agonistes: The Crisis of the Self-Made Man* (New York, 1970). For Nixon's own description of the ups and downs of his prepresidential political career, see his *Six Crises* (New York, 1962).

decades of excoriating "Red China," he now spoke of "the People's Republic" and went off to pay homage to Chairman Mao. Policies with which he had been long identified—indeed that he had culti- vated and exploited for political advantage—were quickly jettisoned. Discarding his persona as crusading cold warrior, Nixon became the great architect of accommodation with the Soviet Union, offering an American version of "peaceful coexistence" while proposing a new international balance of power.

Ultimately, any discussion of Nixon, even one concerned solely with the administration of foreign affairs, must come to terms with his personal tragedy. To an extent that was unparalleled in American political history, public policy making became intertwined with as- sessments of the president's psychological makeup. In her study of Nixon's character, historian Fawn Brodie summarized the impetus for his political career: "The sense of being unloved led to that of being essentially unlovable, to self-loathing. As a defense against this, the fantasy life took over. Nixon became intent on being a president, first of the Whittier High student body . . . finally vice president and president of the United States. Obtaining ever-greater glory and ever- increasing power became the most powerful motivating force in his life."[22]

Even so different a historian as Arthur Schlesinger concluded that the domestic and international crises that led to a diametric expan- sion of presidential power in the postwar period found in Nixon "a President whose inner mix of vulnerability and ambition impelled him to push the historical logic to its extremity. . . . The structural forces tending to transfer power to the Presidency were now reinforced by compulsive internal drives—a sense of life as a battlefield, a belief that the nation was swarming with personal enemies, a flinching from face-to-face argument, an addiction to seclusion, a preoccupa- tion with response to crises, an insistence on a controlled environ- ment for decision. For a man so constituted, the imperial Presidency was the perfect shield and refuge."[23]

The downfall of Richard Nixon personally and the destruction of his "imperial presidency" are inextricably linked with the term *Watergate*. Yet, what Nixon defenders liked to dismiss as a "third-rate

22. Brodie, *Richard Nixon*, 503. See also Nixon, *Memoirs*, 4, 7.
23. Arthur M. Schlesinger, Jr., *The Imperial Presidency* (New York, 1974), 216.

burglary" may have been just that when compared with the Nixon administration's record of constitutional abuses. This is not the place to analyze the threats to constitutional regularity perpetrated during the Nixon presidency.[24] British commentator Godfrey Hodgson asserted that even a cursory list suggests how expanded a view Nixon took of presidential prerogative: nonenforcement of statutes, vastly expanded use of the pocket veto, unprecedented claims in the name of executive privilege, national security, and the impoundment of appropriated funds. "In short," Hodgson said, "Nixon from time to time claimed powers and immunities for his office that, if successfully asserted, would have the effect of radically upsetting the constitutional system of checks and balances and of replacing the constitutional President with a new style of chief executive whose virtually absolute power was justified by the supposed requirements of 'national security' and qualified only by the need to win a 'mandate' from the voters every four years."[25]

The prospect of what Hodgson describes as a "plebiscitary presidency" had been first and most frequently predicted in the area of foreign affairs. Even at the height of their diplomatic successes, Nixon and Kissinger were often faulted for the secretive and extraconstitutional processes by which their policies were fashioned.[26] The foreign policies of the Nixon administration were never so tainted by the Watergate affair as to leave them discredited. Indeed, in the last days of Nixon's tenure, these foreign policy achievements were the embattled president's principal claim to exculpation. What must remain one of the most fascinating paradoxes of Nixon's political career is that the foreign policy objectives associated with the Nixon Doctrine essentially involved a retrenchment of American global power. As vice-president and presidential candidate, Nixon had taken an aggressive and expansive position about the role of the United States in

24. See, for example, Jonathan Schell, *The Time of Illusion* (New York, 1976); Louis Fisher, *The Constitution Between Friends* (New York, 1978); Richard Nathan, *The Administrative Presidency* (New York, 1983).

25. Godfrey Hodgson, *All Things to All Men: The False Promise of the Modern American Presidency* (New York, 1980), 43.

26. For example, see William Shawcross, *Sideshow: Kissinger, Nixon, and the Destruction of Cambodia* (New York, 1979); and Seymour M. Hersh, *The Price of Power: Kissinger in the Nixon White House* (New York, 1983).

world affairs. As president, however, he executed what was a major contraction in American diplomatic influence, even though it was justified as a strategic redeployment.

The Presidential Assistant as "Foreign Minister"

From the very outset of his administration and despite much talk about a commitment to cabinet government, President Nixon was determined that foreign policy would be directed from the White House. His dislike for bureaucracy in general, and the foreign policy bureaucracy in particular, was one of his most deeply held convictions—a distrust that was also shared by Kissinger.[27] Moreover, Nixon demonstrated a need for tightly controlled decision-making procedures and disliked the face-to-face confrontations that are often required in the formulation and execution of any policy. As he said in his *Memoirs*, "Therefore I regarded my choice of a National Security Adviser as crucial." Nixon describes his choice of Kissinger as "uncharacteristically impulsive," especially given the unique importance that the assistant for national security affairs would enjoy in the conduct of American foreign policy. To a degree that was not equaled by his predecessors, Kissinger constructed an administrative apparatus in the White House that not only coordinated departmental proposals but was capable of generating foreign policy options independent of the departments of State and Defense. He was a very extraordinary presidential adviser, effectively the head of a White House foreign ministry, for the life of the Nixon administration and beyond. As Nixon himself observed, "The combination was unlikely— the grocer's son from Whittier and the refugee from Hitler's Germany, the politician and the academic."[28]

It may be that the virulence of university politics (the characterization is attributed to former Princeton University president Woodrow Wilson) provides a good training ground for the bureaucratic battlefield of the White House. Kissinger was hardly the first college pro-

27. On the organization of foreign policy decision making in the Nixon White House, see Kissinger, *White House Years*, 38–48.
28. Nixon, *Memoirs*, 340, 341.

fessor to hold high public office or to serve as a White House aide; both the Franklin Roosevelt and Kennedy-Johnson administrations made extensive use of professorial talent. In the early Nixon White House, assistant for urban affairs Daniel Patrick Moynihan was, like Kissinger, a Harvard professor, and both had doctoral degrees in political science. (Moynihan, now a Democratic senator from New York, was later ambassador to the United Nations.) Kissinger's immediate predecessors as national security adviser, McGeorge Bundy and Walt Rostow, were also professors. (Rostow was a distinguished economist, and Bundy had been dean of arts and sciences at Harvard.) Nonetheless, it is fair to observe that no one prior to Kissinger had assumed this position with such a well-defined theory of international relations, and no one in the post–World War II period has commanded the foreign policy making process so effectively for so long.

What also distinguished Kissinger from his predecessors was not only the unusual way he exercised this power (from the White House rather than the State Department) but his unusual background, which was reflected in his accent. Of German-Jewish birth, Kissinger fled Hitler's regime with his family and settled in New York City, where he attended high school and went to college for a year. It was during his wartime army service, however, that he discovered his real interest—international politics—under the tutelage of Fritz Kramer, a similarly unusual fellow soldier sixteen years his senior, a political exile from Germany with the rank of private, who was well-versed in European philosophy. After being discharged from the army as a sergeant, Kissinger attended Harvard College on the GI Bill and graduated summa cum laude. His 377-page senior thesis was modestly entitled "The Meaning of History: Reflections on Spengler, Toynbee, and Kant."

In his Harvard doctoral dissertation, Kissinger articulated a full-scale interpretation of international relations under the rubric of an analysis of European diplomatic history in the generation after Napoleon's fall. Published in 1957, *The World Restored: Castlereagh, Metternich, and the Restoration of Peace, 1812–1822* was an atypical academic exercise in that it was a combination of *tour d'horizon* and personal reflection—both unusual forms of academic expression, at least for a Ph.D. student in political science. Kissinger's adviser for both his undergraduate and graduate theses was William Y. Elliott, a flamboyant and controversial member of Harvard's government department with ties to the Departments of State and Defense.[29]

What is more remarkable is that as a student, Kissinger had formulated certain basic notions, such as the distinction between "legitimate" and "revolutionary" states, that were to inform not only his later writings but, most important, his policies as national security adviser and secretary of state. Kissinger may or may not have "turned scholarship into projective biography," but it has been often observed that a distinctive characteristic of his writing has been to derive generalized conclusions from the analysis of historical cases.[30] "Through these generalizations Kissinger developed, articulated, and outlined his operational code and provided a guide to his future behavior," Harvey Starr has claimed.[31] John Stoessinger put the argument for continuity in Kissinger's thinking more simply: "His diplomacy as Secretary of State is deeply rooted in the insights of the young doctoral student at Harvard. . . . It is, in fact, a virtual transplant from the world of thought into the world of power."[32]

Kissinger has certain principles that he believes are the scaffolding on which any system of international relations must be constructed, whether it be the Congress of Vienna system that prevailed from 1815 to 1914 or the Nixon Doctrine. The fundamental requirement of any foreign policy is to guarantee international stability. Kissinger's great admiration for Metternich was rooted in a recognition of the founda-

29. Bruce Mazlish, *Kissinger: The European Mind in American Policy* (New York, 1976), 17–82; David Landau, *Kissinger: The Uses of Power* (New York, 1972), 14–72; Stephen R. Graubard, *Kissinger: Portrait of a Mind* (New York, 1974), 1–12.

30. Harvey Starr, "The Kissinger Years," *International Studies Quarterly*, XXIV (December, 1980), 488; Mazlish, *Kissinger: The European Mind*, 151.

31. Starr, "Kissinger Years," 474. The term *operational code* denotes an approach to the study of international relations that seeks to understand a policy maker's belief system through a content analysis of his writings. Once an individual's beliefs have been "coded," the code is used to explain his policy decisions. See Alexander L. George, "The Causal Nexus Between Cognitive Beliefs and Decision-Making Behavior: The 'Operational Code' Belief System," in Lawrence S. Falkowski (ed.), *Psychological Models in International Politics* (Boulder, 1979).

32. John G. Stoessinger, *Henry Kissinger: The Anguish of Power* (New York, 1976), 7. Stoessinger was a graduate student at Harvard with Kissinger in the early 1950s. Kissinger's thinking about international relations cannot be fully treated in the present work. There is a convenient summary in Graubard, *Kissinger: Portrait of a Mind*, 13–53. For a critical view see George Liska, *Beyond Kissinger: Ways of Conservative Statecraft* (Baltimore, 1975). For Kissinger's thinking about Soviet-American relations and thermonuclear war, see his *Nuclear Weapons and Foreign Policy* (New York, 1975), and Graubard, *Kissinger: Portrait of a Mind*, 54–111.

tion that the Austrian foreign minister laid for a century of peace. Metternich devised a "congress" system that was to provide for consultation among the European powers to ensure that local conflicts would not escalate into general war. This system was cumbersome, its political principles were questionable, and it was hardly free of violence (for example, the Crimean War of 1856). On the other hand, there were no wars on the scale of those of the Napoleonic era until World War I destroyed not only this Concert of Europe, but European world hegemony as well. More important, Metternich and Kissinger recognized that the guarantee of a stable world order is not in the particular structural mechanism established, but in a shared belief in the legitimacy of the world order. It was Metternich's fundamental insight about Napoleon (as it was Churchill's about Hitler) that the French emperor's ambitions could not be realized within the state system that had prevailed since the Treaty of Westphalia in 1648. Napoleon represented a revolutionary force and would have to go if Austria, Prussia, and Britain (the nation most difficult to convince) were to be secure in their borders.

Kissinger's fundamental insight was that the USSR and People's Republic of China had ceased to be revolutionary powers and had come to accept the basic distribution of international power in the post–World War II age. Indeed, he argued that the Sino-Soviet ideological split and the Soviet-American nuclear parity gave everyone concerned a stake in the survival of the current international order— flaws and all. The great challenge confronting a statesman was to accommodate these legitimate, if competing and conflicting, interests, without recourse to general war. This basic requirement was made particularly important when such a war would involve an all-out thermonuclear exchange. For Kissinger, this meant that it was necessary for foreign policies to maintain the balance of power—not as a static system but as a dynamic process that could respond and adapt to developments within the status quo.[33] An ongoing equilibrium had to be maintained among the various nations (especially between the superpowers) that sought to further their interests vis-à-vis other national contenders.

33. The ongoing Soviet-American competition in the Third World, for example, could hardly be reconciled with a static conception of the balance of power. In many Third World nations, open border conflicts between the two superpowers or their surrogates sometimes threaten broader international stability, for example in Afghanistan

There is nothing strikingly original in this theoretical conception of international relations, but the very lack of originality points up the durability of the concepts involved. Most significant, Kissinger as statesman incorporated these theoretical concepts into a doctrine to govern American foreign policy that was manifested in détente, SALT, and the normalization of Sino-American relations. Positing laws of history or even historical analogies is the riskiest of intellectual activities. On the other hand, the laws that Kissinger discerned were, in effect, procedural rules that governed how nations should behave, not what they might want. Kissinger's debt to Metternich (and Castlereagh) can be briefly summarized: 1) Then, as now, a stable world order was the necessary precondition for a peaceful world. 2) Then, as now, stability rested upon a shared belief in the inherent legitimacy of the world order. 3) Then, as now, the ever-changing political goals of nations had to be accommodated within a model of dynamic equilibrium through periodic reformulations of the balance of power. For Kissinger these principles of international order represented the basis for Soviet-American diplomatic cooperation.

Kissinger enjoyed some public recognition for his *Nuclear Weapons and Foreign Policy* (commissioned by the prestigious Council on Foreign Relations in 1957), as a sometime White House consultant during the 1960s, and as Nelson Rockefeller's foreign policy adviser before and during his unsuccessful campaign for the 1968 Republican presidential nomination. Kissinger's selection as Nixon's national security adviser was unusual because they had little prior acquaintanceship. Moreover, Kissinger was clearly associated with an archrival and in the past had offered somewhat uncomplimentary evaluations about Nixon.[34] On the other hand, Kissinger's initial appointment did provide some assurances to the eastern wing of the Republican party. It was not until after the Cambodian invasion of 1970 that Nixon and Kissinger became personally close. In the face of resignations on his

---

and Angola. Kissinger, for his part, did not demonstrate a great interest in these matters except to remind the Soviet Union that any sponsorship of "wars of national liberation" inimicable to American security interests would undermine détente. For his views on the principle of "linkage" as a key element in détente, see *White House Years*, 129–30.

34. But after an interview with President-elect Nixon concerning a possible job in the new administration, Kissinger "was struck by his perceptiveness and knowledge so at variance with my previous image of him." Kissinger, *White House Years*, 12.

own staff and concerted opposition from his past academic colleagues, Kissinger provided unflagging support. It was this loyalty, "when Nixon was being portrayed by his critics as having taken leave of his senses, that established the real bond between them."[35]

Kissinger became the most successful of the "foreign policy intellectuals" who have come to power in the postwar era. This new class of actors in the foreign policy making process is a loose collection of individuals associated with major university research centers, such as the School of Advanced International Studies at Johns Hopkins University, certain "think tanks" specializing in the study of national security issues, such as the California-based RAND Corporation; well-established philanthropic organizations, such as the Rockefeller Foundation; and prestigious public-interest groups such as the Council on Foreign Relations in New York City. Connections between the "foreign policy intellectuals" and the "foreign policy making establishment" are quite strong. Kissinger was also a distinguished member of this latter group: professor at Harvard with close ties to the Council on Foreign Relations, frequent contributor to *Foreign Affairs*, consultant to the State Department and various arms-control panels, foreign policy adviser to the Rockefeller family. He was also Europe-oriented and an internationalist. Despite his claim that he is not a member of such an establishment because of his foreign background, insofar as the group exists at all, Kissinger is a member. Given Nixon's famous antipathy toward the "Eastern establishment," Kissinger's association with him is the more ironic.[36]

What distinguished Kissinger from other intellectuals in government, such as McGeorge Bundy and Zbigniew Brzezinski, was his unparalleled success. He surpassed earlier White House foreign policy advisers like Woodrow Wilson's Colonel House and Franklin Roosevelt's Harry Hopkins. Indeed, Kissinger was clearly one of the most influential presidential assistants in the administrative history of the presidency. His influence was restricted to foreign affairs, but no White House aide has ever enjoyed greater command of such a key element of American public policy. In domestic affairs only Sherman Adams in the Eisenhower administration, Harry Hopkins as head of

35. Marvin Kalb and Bernard Kalb, *Kissinger* (Boston, 1974), 168.
36. On Nixon's distrust of the "Eastern establishment," see Kissinger, *White House Years*, 257, 299, 944.

the Works Progress Administration, and H. R. Haldeman before he fell victim to Watergate could be said to rival Kissinger in political importance. And, even so powerful a White House chief of staff as Haldeman did not encroach on Kissinger's foreign policy turf.[37]

A contemporary account of the Nixon administration certified Kissinger's importance and added, "What no one saw at first, though, was that he would quickly become the President's closest confidant, his principal negotiator, his troubleshooter, his First Minister, over-shadowing members of the Cabinet—would become . . . no less than the second most powerful man in the world."[38] Kissinger enjoyed the status he did largely because he served Nixon's interests and ambitions. In a sense, of course, this is the case with most successful administrative officials. But Nixon and Kissinger complemented each other intellectually, politically, and psychologically. Nixon may have had no idea that Kissinger would have such a flair for bureaucratic politics and journalistic favor. Kissinger, for his part, probably did not begin his tenure with a grand design for dominating foreign policy making. However, the presidential paralysis brought on by Watergate presented him with an unprecedented opportunity to conduct the nation's foreign affairs and guarantee international stability. He did not hesitate to rise to the occasion.

While Kissinger's preeminence in foreign policy making was unquestionable, it would be a major error to jump to any conclusions that the presidential assistant superseded the president. Even more than a cabinet secretary, who may enjoy the protection of a powerful interest group, a White House aide must be careful to faithfully mirror the interests of his sole protector. For all of his independent stature, Kissinger was no different; he himself commented about how one reversal could undo an assistant's power, however many successes there may have been in the past. White House aides must cater carefully to the president's whims; an assistant's power is like that of the courtier—absolutely dependent on the ruler's favor.[39] This presidential confidence is the essential glue for any enduring policy-making

37. Generally, Haldeman was concerned with procedural questions of White House administration and with the management of the president's time and personal needs. For Kissinger's relations with Haldeman, see Kissinger, *Years of Upheaval* (Boston, 1982), 95–97.

38. Henry Brandon, *The Retreat of American Power* (New York, 1973), 24.

39. George Reedy, *The Twilight of the Presidency* (New York, 1970).

relationship, whatever the administrative arrangement or policy area. To use the historical comparisons with which discussions of Kissinger are so replete, Kissinger was no Cardinal Richelieu to King Louis XIII or Chancellor Bismarck to Kaiser Wilhelm I. What came to be termed the Nixon-Kissinger approach to foreign policy making was still fundamentally Nixonian.

It cannot be emphasized too strongly that Kissinger's influence was so great because his views were in alignment with Nixon's. It happened that they saw eye to eye on the objectives of American foreign policy. When Nixon said that "the only time in the history of the world that we have had extended periods of peace is when there is a balance of power," he was not echoing Kissinger's *The World Restored;* rather, both men shared a conception of world order at least as old as Metternich. Both also found congenial a notion of realpolitik in American foreign policy that would allow the national interest to be furthered even when this entailed alliances made on the basis of geopolitics rather than ideology or principle. Kissinger was able to give the president's policy instincts intellectual content. Kissinger could supply the ideas, while Nixon provided the political authority, except toward the end, when Watergate left him more to reign than to rule.[40]

If Nixon was the princely patron, Kissinger was the court architect. Kissinger also supplied the bureaucratic support that would translate these presidential instincts into foreign policies. For example, he had secret meetings with Chinese leaders to map out the specific details of bilateral agreement that allowed Nixon and Mao Tse-tung to negotiate the broad principles of mutual understanding. The president and the presidential assistant would meet several times a day, and Kissinger became the only post-1968 associate to enter Nixon's inner circle. Since Nixon had an intense dread of meeting new people or of seeming ill-prepared at meetings, Kissinger had meticulous briefing papers prepared, which Nixon would then commit to mem-

40. *Time,* January 3, 1972; Brandon, *Retreat of American Power,* 39; Bell, *Diplomacy of Détente,* 48. See also Mazlish, *Kissinger: The European Mind,* 233–62. Kissinger was careful to keep a low profile with the press during his first two years as national security adviser so as to avoid provoking presidential jealousies or those of other staff members. However, the constant publicity that followed disclosure of Kissinger's trip to China did strain relations with Nixon and his close associates, who resented any insinuation that the central role was played by Kissinger. See Kissinger, *White House Years,* 1410, 1455, and *Years of Upheaval,* 770–71.

ory.[41] Kissinger also briefed the press (which Nixon distrusted), chaired interdepartmental committees, served as the administration's foreign policy spokesman, and conducted the detailed and prolonged personal negotiations required to achieve diplomatic agreements. However, anyone confused about who was in control of the foreign policy making process should ponder Kissinger's remarks: "Presidents, of course, are responsible for shaping the overall strategy. They must make the key decisions; for this they are accountable and for it they deserve full credit no matter how much help they receive along the way. When they attempt the tactical implementation of their own strategy they court disaster. Nixon never made that mistake."[42]

Nixon did make many other mistakes, however, especially those that are associated with Watergate. As this affair grew from a case of campaign chicanery to a constitutional crisis, there were inevitable concerns among American allies and others about how long the United States could go on with the presidency paralyzed. As the momentum for impeachment grew with the revelations of increasingly more compromising conversations recorded on the White House tapes, Kissinger moved more and more to the forefront with assurances about the stability and continuity of American foreign policy. In other words, he was implying that the international community need not worry about Nixon's ability to conduct foreign affairs, because Kissinger was in control. In the last days of the Nixon presidency, Kissinger and Haldeman's successor as White House chief of staff, General Alexander Haig, who had been Kissinger's deputy for two years, played extraordinary roles in the Watergate melodrama, as they eased the distraught and discredited president into voluntary resignation while maintaining a semblance of governmental normality. It is difficult to conceive of a more unlikely occurrence in American political history: two presidential assistants, one a foreign-born college professor and the other a professional soldier, both of whom had risen to prominence because of President Nixon's patronage, assuming, for all intents and purposes, primary responsibility

41. Landau, *Kissinger: The Uses of Power*, 140; Kissinger, *White House Years*, 78. For some of Kissinger's observations about Nixon's personality (including his much discussed *l'horreur de face à face*) and work habits, see *White House Years*, 45, 480–82, 917, 1475–76, and *Years of Upheaval*, 103, 1181–84.

42. Kissinger, *White House Years*, 142.

for the affairs of state. As Kissinger recalled: "Haig dealt with the domestic issues; I was responsible for foreign policy. I made no major recommendations to Nixon without discussing them with Haig; he kept me generally informed of key developments on the domestic side, and especially Watergate, that might affect foreign policy. Together with others we sought to hold the ship of state steady even while its captain was gradually being pushed from the bridge."[43] It is another of the ironies that pervade the Nixon presidency that the White House staff system that had been intended as the means for Nixon to master the bureaucracy became at the end a bureaucratic substitute for a paralyzed president.

A Rival State Department

It is not unusual for a president to act as his own secretary of state, such as Franklin Roosevelt and John Kennedy did. Nor was it unknown before the Nixon administration for presidents to engage foreign policy advisers from outside the State Department—Colonel House and Harry Hopkins, for example. Even extraordinary foreign policy making groups, such as the Tuesday lunch group of the Johnson administration, were not unknown. Presidents have always been free to seek advice from whomever they wished and to make decisions in whatever manner they see fit. Yet, while the State Department may have gradually been losing its traditional primacy since Franklin Roosevelt's administration, none of its institutional rivals, such as the Defense Department and the CIA, had ever been able to assert its own unchallenged preeminence. Under the Nixon administration, however, as the decline of the State Department reached its nadir, a rival institution achieved such preeminence.

The National Security Council staff, under the direction of Henry Kissinger, emerged as not simply a claimant for presidential attention in foreign policy making but as the principal vehicle for the ar-

43. Kissinger, *Years of Upheaval,* 110, 1196, 1204–1206. Kissinger provides a chilling description, though one intended to be laudatory, of how much power had accrued to Haig as White House chief of staff: "He furnished psychological ballast to a desperate President. He did so without catering to Nixon's every prejudice; he insured that Nixon's preferences and orders would be screened by a governmental structure capable of advising the President in a mature way about the national interest." *Ibid.,* 109.

ticulation and implementation of the administration's objectives. Kissinger's influence upon the diplomacy of the Nixon administration can hardly be exaggerated. For one thing, the national security adviser spent more time in consultation with the almost reclusive president than did any cabinet officials. Physical propinquity does create special relationships—in bureaucratic politics and international relations as elsewhere. But there is little evidence that a domineering assistant forced his views on a complacent president. As Kissinger observed, "the influence of a Presidential Assistant derives almost exclusively from the confidence of the President." Nixon was familiar with Kissinger's thinking about foreign policy and found that it coincided with his own thinking.[44]

Nixon and Kissinger shared a strongly negative assessment of government bureaucracies in general and of the foreign policy making bureaucracy in particular. Nixon as vice-president and Kissinger as a White House consultant had each acquired decidedly unfavorable impressions of the State Department. Both men had come to view it as too parochial, that is, too prone to see a foreign policy problem from the other country's point of view. They thought it was too bogged down in bureaucratic inertia: its administrative structure created a need for time-consuming clearances from its various semiautonomous fiefdoms. They also believed the State Department lacked creativity, that the policy proposals that emerged from it were overly vague and lacking sharp analytical focus. To Kissinger, "Nixon had always distrusted the State Department, which he considered both fuzzy-minded and a nest of holdover liberal Democrats." In any event, Nixon was determined to run foreign policy from the White House, and he had a willing accomplice in Kissinger. "As time went by, the President, or I on his behalf," Kissinger recalled, "came to deal increasingly with key foreign leaders through channels that directly linked the White House Situation Room to the field without going through the State Department—the so-called backchannels. This process started on the day after Inauguration."[45]

At first glance the appointment of William Pierce Rogers as secretary of state would seem to augur good times for the State De-

44. Kissinger, *White House Years*, 47; Nixon, *Memoirs*, 340–42.

45. Kissinger, *White House Years*, 27, 29, 589, 1127; Kissinger, *Years of Upheaval*, 439, 442, 418.

partment. The personal relationship between the secretary and the president, of course, is more important than any administrative arrangement for determining the State Department's formal standing in foreign policy making. Rogers had been deputy attorney general and later attorney general in the Eisenhower administration, and he was a respected member of the "eastern establishment." He was a highly regarded member of the New York bar at the time of his appointment and a friend of Nixon's from vice-presidential days. He had no practical experience in international affairs and little knowledge of the institutional interests and political forces that shape foreign policy. Rogers was a respectable nominee but an inadequate secretary. From almost the very first it was clear to Washington insiders that Rogers would face a strong rival for President Nixon's attention in National Security Adviser Kissinger. With rare exceptions, Rogers was simply unable to succeed in such efforts; in fact, Nixon observes that the secretary was most concerned that he be kept "informed of what was going on" in foreign affairs. For example, the State Department did not learn of Nixon's plans to visit Rumania until an hour before the official announcement—even though this was the first visit of an American president to a Communist nation.[46] The arrangements had been made through one of Kissinger's "backchannels." Under Rogers the State Department largely functioned as the draftsman of the Nixon-Kissinger blueprint.

In fairness to Secretary Rogers, he cannot be made to accept personal blame for his department's influence having declined to its lowest point since the last years of Hull's tenure (see Chapter 3). As Kissinger observes, "Rogers was in fact far abler than he was pictured; he had a shrewd analytical mind and outstanding common sense." But these capabilities did him little good, since Nixon and Kissinger had already constructed a full-blown design for American foreign policy. As Seymour Hersh said, "In reality, Kissinger won his bureaucratic wars not because Rogers did not try, but because Nixon wanted it that way."[47] Even Rogers' past collegial association with Nixon did not help him when the president avoided open-ended exchanges with colleagues in favor of detailed memoranda to subordi-

46. Nixon, *Memoirs*, 433; Rowland Evans, Jr., and Robert D. Novak, *Nixon in the White House* (New York, 1971), 97.
47. Kissinger, *White House Years*, 31; Hersh, *Price of Power*, 32.

nates. Most damaging for Rogers and his department, Nixon and Kissinger began office determined to manage foreign affairs unchallenged from the White House. With Rogers as secretary, the State Department remained weak and ineffectual, leaving the White House dominant.

Whether Nixon had deliberately chosen a weak secretary of state may be debatable, but regardless of intent, the result was clear, as Kissinger wrote in his memoirs: "Once Nixon had appointed a strong personality, expert in foreign policy, as national security advisor, competition with the Secretary of State became inevitable. . . . The two positions are inherently competitive if both incumbents seek to play a major role." Given the situation, what followed was not surprising: "Whether Nixon planned it that way or simply permitted it to happen—probably a combination of both—the relationship between Rogers and me soured beyond recovery. We had begun with the customary protestations that we would not repeat the frictions of the previous administrations. We soon found ourselves at loggerheads. I was too arrogantly convinced of my superior knowledge, Rogers was too insistent on his bureaucratic prerogative, for the acts of grace that would have permitted both of us to escape the treadmill on which we found ourselves, and, more important, to serve the nation better."[48]

Kissinger concluded that the situation was unworkable, and in 1973 he became the first—and because of legislation passed in 1974, probably the last—national security assistant to also serve as secretary of state. In the post–World War II struggle for control of the foreign policy making process, the White House had emerged triumphant over the venerable Department of State. Even the Defense Department, which had been so influential in foreign policy making during the 1960s, was relatively quiescent during the Kissinger years.[49] The president's personal adviser on foreign affairs was now also in control of the major institution responsible for its implementation.

What enabled Kissinger to maintain, expand, and consolidate the president's confidence in him was the institutional support provided

48. Kissinger, *White House Years*, 30; Kissinger, *Years of Upheaval*, 419.
49. Geoffrey Piller, "DOD's Office of International Security Affairs: The Brief Ascendancy of an Advisory System," *Political Science Quarterly*, XCVIII (Spring, 1983), esp. 70–74. The Defense Department made something of a comeback in foreign policy making under Caspar Weinberger's aggressive leadership in the Reagan administration.

by the staff of the National Security Council. As assistant to the president for national security affairs, Kissinger used his position as the NSC's executive director to develop an administrative apparatus that could provide the technical support necessary for the successful execution of policy. Whereas presidents before Nixon might have sought to challenge the State Department's authority, the Kissinger NSC sought to supplant the department as a policy-making body. The elaborate staff that Kissinger headed was designed to achieve that end.[50] The backchannels had become the main channel for the flow of foreign policy making.

Quantitatively, the NSC staff that Kissinger directed was expanded to some 150 analysts during the Nixon administration, as contrasted with an average of 10 during the Truman administration. Qualitatively, the caliber of the NSC personnel was judged to be first-rate.[51] Kissinger had a reputation as a stern taskmaster, and professional staff turnover was high during his tenure as staff director. Yet, the quality of the analyses produced was so good and so consonant with the thinking of Nixon that NSC's influence on policy making became almost immediately pervasive. Structurally, the displacement of the State Department was facilitated by the reorganization of the NSC staff into regional and functional units that competed with the bureaus of the traditional departments. Administratively, Kissinger (not a State Department official) chaired several important interdepartmental committees, such as the Washington Special Action Group, which was designed to deal with international crises, and the Senior Policy Group, a top-level deliberative body for reviewing policy studies. Politically, the White House Situation Room replaced the "Seventh Floor" of the State Department as the locus of American foreign policy making.

From the earliest days of the Nixon administration, because of a mutuality of interests with the president, Kissinger acquired "a near

---

50. On Kissinger's staff, see John P. Leacacos, "Kissinger's Apparatus," *Foreign Policy*, V (Winter, 1971–72), 3–28.

51. Among its prominent members were Helmut Sonnenfeldt, chief of Soviet research for the State Department; Morton Halperin, deputy assistant secretary of defense for international security affairs; and Lawrence Lynn, deputy assistant secretary of defense for systems analysis. Interestingly, many key NSC staffers under Kissinger had served in previous Democratic administrations; many also served in high State Department positions in succeeding administrations. For a very critical view of Kissinger's relations with his NSC staff, see Hersh, *Price of Power*, 98–104.

monopoly on the time, attention, and respect of the President of the United States on all matters of foreign policy." The NSC system that was authorized in National Security Memorandum 2 shortly after the inauguration in January, 1969, installed Kissinger at the center of the foreign policy making process. Kissinger would be "firmly atop the bureaucratic structure with decisive control over both the formulation and conduct of policy, and thus *de facto* powers greater than the *de jure* constitutional authority of the Secretaries of State and Defense. Exploited and extended to become a vehicle for Kissinger's extraordinary talents, that position of power created a new pattern of government in Washington for foreign relations."[52] Kissinger placed the origins of the new policy-making procedures in Nixon's long-standing determination "to conduct foreign policy from the White House, his distrust of the existing bureaucracy, coupled with the congruence of his philosophy and mine and the relative inexperience of the new Secretary of State."[53]

In the face of such formidable obstacles, Rogers' tenure as secretary of state was bound to be uncomfortable. It is somewhat remarkable that he continued in office throughout the whole course of the first Nixon administration. In his repeated confrontations over foreign policy making with Kissinger, Rogers could only assert the theoretical primacy of his hierarchical position. Kissinger was unwilling to grant any bureaucratic deference to the secretary of state, and he also realized that the personal relationship between a president and his NSC adviser—or any official seeking influence in the making of foreign policy—was all-important.[54] In Kissinger's accurate assessment, Rogers lacked the "intangible ingredient" of a close personal relationship with Nixon.[55]

52. Roger Morris, *Uncertain Greatness: Henry Kissinger and American Foreign Policy* (New York, 1977), 145, 47. State Department official Lawrence S. Eagleburger, soon to be one of Kissinger's chief deputies, reacted to the new system with the remark "What ever happened to the Secretary of State?" *Ibid.*, 83.

53. Kissinger, *White House Years*, 47.

54. *Ibid.*, 30–31. Kissinger observed that the last strong secretary of state had been John Foster Dulles, and "Dulles's influence had derived from the President's confidence in him and not from the State Department machinery." *Ibid.*, 43. See Chapter 5.

55. *Ibid.*, 31. In discussing the various rebuffs that Rogers faced in trying to assert his views as secretary, Kissinger confesses: "The procedures so painful to Rogers were clearly instigated by Nixon; it is equally evident that I nurtured them. Neither Rogers nor I mustered the grace to transcend an impasse that we should have recognized was not in the national interest." *Ibid.*, 589.

Rogers was finally replaced by Kissinger in August, 1973, when, as the Watergate scandal was gaining momentum, it was felt necessary to reassure the public at home and abroad of the stability of American foreign policy. The new secretary of state, however, also kept his position as national security adviser until he was succeeded by Brent Scowcroft in November, 1975. Kissinger got on famously with Scowcroft, who had served as his deputy in the White House. Moreover, as a professional soldier, Scowcroft also possessed the "passion for anonymity" that is supposed to characterize all presidential assistants and that was conspicuously absent in the case of Kissinger. Since Nixon's successor, Gerald R. Ford, was a novice in foreign affairs, Kissinger came increasingly to represent an element of "continuity, legitimacy and success" in the governmental process.[56]

Despite his professed pique at being removed from his position as presidential assistant, Kissinger acknowledged that the administrative dualism involved had in fact proved irksome. He reiterated that the relationship between the secretary of state and the president is what gives the State Department its role in foreign policy making— not the chairing of interdepartmental committees. It is certainly true that administrative arrangements do not of themselves make for success in bureaucratic politics. But it is equally true that occupying a position that claims to stand above the fray of departmental interests and to offer the president "disinterested advice" is an enormously important power base. In any event, Kissinger as secretary of state, was not challenged by a national security adviser with an expansive notion of his personal and institutional prerogatives in foreign policy making.

After he left the government, Kissinger provided a delineation of the roles and responsibilities associated with the two positions.

A determined Secretary of State cannot fail to have his view heard whoever chairs the committees. The security adviser's contact with media and foreign diplomats should be reduced to a minimum; the articulation and conduct of foreign policy should be left in the main to the President and the Secretary of State (and of course their designees). The preparation of options, which is in the main what interdepartmental machinery does, should be the province of a security adviser chosen for fairness, conceptual grasp, bureaucratic savvy, and a willingness to labor anonymously. (General Andrew

56. Kissinger, *Years of Upheaval*, 418–23; Bell, *Diplomacy of Détente*, 39.

Goodpaster under Eisenhower and General Brent Scowcroft under Ford are two outstanding examples.) The influence of the Department of State would flow from the personal confidence between the President and the Secretary and the quality of the analytical work produced by the Department.[57]

One cannot help but wonder how Secretary of State Rogers would have fared if National Security Adviser Kissinger had followed his own advice during the first Nixon administration.

The Nixon-Kissinger Record Reviewed

The demise of his reputation as a great architect of foreign affairs must have been the most bitter disappointment for Nixon to accept. After his departure from the White House, there were to be few references to the Nixon Doctrine as a touchstone of American foreign policy. But in the years that have passed since the Watergate scandal toppled his presidency, the principles of the Nixon-Kissinger approach to international relations continue to influence significant contemporary debates about the proper role of the United States in world affairs. Ironically, the most sustained opposition to these principles has come from conservative critics who have argued that détente was based on a fundamental misconception—that the Soviet Union would become a responsible international actor if its insecurity were diminished by military parity with the United States. Liberal critics have never been comfortable with the primacy that the Nixon-Kissinger foreign policy attached to geopolitical or realpolitik considerations and its indifference to such goals as seeking economic justice and promoting human rights. Critics with no ideological concerns have questioned what common elements in SALT, the normalization of Sino-American relations, improved regional stability, and the multiplication of economic ties can be used to produce a diplomatic blueprint that will spare the United States future diplomatic misadventures, such as "another Vietnam."

Like many policies that are loudly heralded as new, the Nixon-Kissinger strategy was in fact based on the evocation of some of the oldest concepts of diplomacy. Indeed, much of the importance of the

57. Kissinger, *Years of Upheaval*, 437.

Nixon administration's foreign policy was in its reassertion of certain basic diplomatic axioms that, however, had been anything but axiomatic in the thinking of many American policy makers. One of these precepts is that a nation's foreign policy commitments should approximate its capabilities. In particular, this reassessment of American capabilities helped the United States adapt to the Soviet Union's achievement of an irreversible equality in strategic nuclear weapons. More broadly, the Nixon-Kissinger foreign policy reflected a realization that the United States could no longer serve as the world's policeman. Imperfect though it was, this policy recognized that a great power is not an omnipotent power: "The Nixon Doctrine was a needed corrective to the almost limitless diplomatic ambitions of the United States from the end of World War II until the Vietnam War."[58]

Another fundamental aim of the diplomacy that underlies the Nixon Doctrine was a desire to give the Soviet Union a stake in preserving the stability of the international system. In effect, the USSR was being offered full international legitimacy "in a consultative, coequal superpower relationship with the United States." In exchange, the Soviet Union would forgo any revolutionary aspirations and agree to a policy of international moderation and restraint in exploiting any power vacuums that might affect American interests. As Seyom Brown observed: "U.S.–Soviet arms control efforts, particularly the Strategic Arms Limitations Talks (SALT), were linked by Nixon and Kissinger to this grand strategy. SALT became the most visible and dramatic symbol—and test—of the Soviet's willingness to moderate their power competition with the United States and be bound by mutually acceptable rules."[59] In effect, Nixon and Kissinger were asking the Soviet Union to enter into a cooperative arrangement to guarantee international equilibrium—a new world concert.

Although associated with some well-established principles of international relations, the Nixon-Kissinger foreign policy ignored, and eventually ran afoul of, some fundamental rules associated with domestic politics in the United States. The particulars of official wrongdoing and political subversion that were associated with the Watergate scandal led to a general public repudiation of the Nixon

58. Crabb, *Doctrines of American Foreign Policy*, 320–21.
59. Brown, *Crises of Power*, 143.

administration and its policies—foreign as well as domestic.[60] The re-action of political leaders to Watergate was often greater in intensity than that of the public at large. Watergate triggered a new militancy on the part of Congress to reassert its traditional constitutional pre-rogatives in public policy making. Congressional frustration over the "imperial presidency" was perhaps greatest in foreign affairs, where the executive branch had achieved nearly absolute power. The War Powers Resolution of 1973, which dealt with presidential foreign poli-cies involving military hostilities, was Congress' most dramatic as-sertion of its rights (see Chapter 1). Although the importance of the resolution may be more symbolic than actual, it served notice on Nixon and future presidents that Congress would demand to be in-cluded in the policy-making process as a political partner, even if a junior one.

Similarly, Congress protested against the nonaccountability of the president for foreign policy initiatives formulated and executed by presidential assistants under the protection of executive privilege. Nor was the NSC staff to be allowed to engage in secret diplomacy that left the State Department and Congress in ignorance of even the basic objectives being negotiated, even if such diplomacy involved détente or other policies of major significance. In particular, there were to be "no more Kissingers" at the White House beyond the reach of congressional oversight, let alone one occupying positions at the White House and State Department simultaneously (see Chapter 8). Defenders of a strong presidency rightly pointed out the necessity of allowing the chief executive the discretion necessary to act quickly and decisively in the conduct of foreign affairs; the Supreme Court, most legislative leaders, and the general public have consistently affirmed this necessity.

Kissinger (and Nixon) may have been too enamored of the nine-teenth-century Concert of Europe to realize that such a system could not be reconstructed in the twentieth century, at least not without significant structural modifications. Unlike a balance of power sys-tem, which requires a relative equality among at least a few nations

60. Kissinger, *Years of Upheaval*, 122–27, 300–301, 414–16; Chalmers McRoberts, "Foreign Policy Under a Paralyzed Presidency," *Foreign Affairs*, LII (July, 1971), 675–89; McGeorge Bundy, "Vietnam, Watergate, and Presidential Powers," *Foreign Affairs*, LVIII (Winter, 1979–80), 397–407.

(five is often suggested) that will automatically readjust as changing fortunes dictate, a concert system can exist in a world of modified bipolarity. For the concert to work, however, certain conditions must prevail. These include support for the continuity of the principles underlying the system, a shared sense of values among the policy makers, a mechanism for making the necessary adjustments in power relations, acceptance of the moral and political equality of the system's members, and an international politics that was at least relatively insulated from short-run political shifts. Above all, all members of a concert must have a stake in the survival of the system and hence in making the diplomatic efforts necessary to ensure its well-being.[61]

There is clearly a case to be made that the Nixon-Kissinger foreign policy sought to create a concert system such as was established in the aftermath of the Napoleonic wars—an international order that would allow a rational and controlled management of power relations. The thrust of the Nixon Doctrine was to repudiate the major policies of the cold war—verbal confrontation and military containment—in favor of an approach that accepted the legitimacy of the Communist political systems. Nixon's visit to Peking clearly signaled the end of the old policies. American acceptance of Soviet strategic nuclear parity, implicitly agreed to in the 1960s and formalized in the first SALT treaty, was another development that suggested a "Concert emergent." And "linkage" was to be the *modus operandi* for interaction among the superpowers. For the Nixon-Kissinger concert, as with the Concert of Europe, international questions were seen as closely interrelated, and peace was predicated upon the acceptance of mutual responsibility for the maintenance of the international order over short-run political gains. Linkage was the essential element of Nixon-Kissinger policies toward China and especially the Soviet Union (see Chapter 8).[62] It cannot be certain that Peking and Moscow have had a parallel commitment to a revived concert, and part of Kissinger's insistence on the principle of linkage was to emphasize that the continued success of détente could not be guaranteed in the

61. James A. Nathan, "Commitments in Search of a Roost: The Foreign Policy of the Nixon Administration," *Virginia Quarterly Review*, L (Summer, 1974), 338–39.
62. Stephen A. Garrett, "Nixonian Foreign Policy: A New Balance of Power—or a Revived Concert," *Polity*, VIII (Spring, 1976), 408, 398, 411.

event of any Soviet or Chinese machinations in the Third World, such as sponsoring "wars of national liberation." Nevertheless, the Nixon Doctrine represented a pragmatic attempt to create a new international order based on a mutual awareness that, in the nuclear age as in the Napoleonic, order is fundamentally preferable to disorder.

Apart from its doctrinal significance, the Nixon-Kissinger era will have continuing import for the changes that were introduced in the foreign policy making process. For the first time in American history, the secretary of state was effectively excluded from diplomatic decision making, with the national security adviser serving as de facto secretary. From the beginning, Kissinger recognized the potential importance of this White House office, and he acted decisively to expand his power. Although he had the advantage of a strong background in foreign affairs, he also realized that his position on the White House staff gave him the incomparable advantage of physical proximity to the president. Most important, Kissinger realized that national security is a peculiarly presidential responsibility and that presidents are likely to find White House aides more reliable than cabinet secretaries. Statutory provisions will prevent another Kissinger from serving as both de facto and de jure secretary of state. But the success of Kissinger's "rival State Department" serves as a possible model for presidents and their national security advisers who seek to dominate foreign policy making from the White House.

8

A Vicar of Foreign Policy: Reagan, Haig, and the White House

Our final case study is something of a departure from the earlier ones. In the earliest case studies, the key foreign policy makers were the president and the secretary of state and, secondarily, the secretary of defense, the secretary of the treasury, and the director of the CIA, with the national security assistant in a staff position. However, beginning with McGeorge Bundy in the Johnson administration and culminating in Henry Kissinger under Presidents Nixon and Ford, a trend developed that in time led the assistant to the president for national security affairs to become the equal of the secretary of state and in some cases even his superior in the foreign policy process. Moreover, the staff of the National Security Council, with the presidential assistant as director, came to be institutionalized as a policy-making body. It came to have some continuity from one administration to the next, to be large enough for area and subject specialization and a formal hierarchy, and to enjoy such importance in decision making that it could initiate policies on its own as well as evaluating and coordinating those of cabinet departments—including the Department of State (see Chapter 9 for more details).

By the 1980s, unlike in the periods dealt with in our previous case studies, the national security assistant could assert his primacy over any cabinet secretary because he could comprehend the full scope of American international relations and the policy options involved, whereas cabinet members represented specialized bureaucratic interests. In addition, the White House staff in the 1980s had come to involve itself directly and actively in the foreign policy making process.¹ Previously, the political and domestic assistants to the president had largely eschewed involvement in diplomacy, which had been the preserve of a separate foreign policy advisory system that included, of course, the assistant for national security affairs. The fates of both Cyrus Vance and Alexander Haig, however, suggest that in any struggle between the State Department and the White House for control of foreign policy, it was necessary for the secretary of state to reach an accommodation with the presidential staff. No secretary of state could maintain his power by simply asserting his preeminence in foreign policy making.

The efforts of the secretary of state to claim a privileged position as *the* presidential adviser on foreign policy were ultimately unsuccessful. Perhaps the most significant failure was that of Alexander Haig, who attempted to make himself the "vicar" of foreign policy—the president's chief deputy or surrogate in the foreign policy field. To understand Haig's repeated claims to this status properly, it is necessary as background to comprehend the relationship of Secretary of State Cyrus Vance and National Security Adviser Zbigniew Brzezinski in the Carter administration. While not claiming the designation of vicar, Vance believed himself to be the rightful spokesman for American foreign policy. Events revealed that his efforts were to be as unsuccessful as those of Haig. Vance ran afoul of an ambitious presidential assistant in the person of Brzezinski, and Haig entertained a conception of his office that did not correspond to the realities of national security policy making. Both, however, should have realized that their persistent problems testified to the impossibility of their claims. Competition between the nation's chief diplomat and the president's chief White House adviser for international affairs has become endemic to the process of foreign policy making. What is presently unclear is whether such policy-making fragmentation will permanently characterize American foreign relations.

1. As used here, the term *White House staff* refers to the political associates of the president responsible for his personal and political fortunes. They are usually policy generalists who come from the campaign or who have past political ties with the president. The *NSC staff*, while serving at the president's pleasure, also serve as an institutional arm of the presidency and are sometimes retained despite a change in administrations or parties. As subject-matter specialists, they are more often recruited from government, the armed services, foundations, and universities.

Détente Recast: The Carter Administration's Foreign Policy

The 1970s and 1980s has been an era in which the specifics of détente as the doctrinal basis of American foreign policy have been evaluated and debated. Some aspects of Soviet-American relations have engendered sharp debate in the United States, questions such as the level of military preparedness necessary for a credible defense posture and the degree of long-range Soviet fidelity to the requirements of restraint and responsibility necessary for continued détente.[2] By the late 1970s, a number of incidents in different parts of the world, particularly the Soviet invasion of Afghanistan in 1979, had given rise to great concerns, across a wide swath of the domestic and international political spectrum, that American power vis-à-vis the Soviet Union had seriously deteriorated. The belief was voiced that the credibility of the United States as a superpower was in jeopardy, and the future of détente was called into question. As Richard Tucker put it, "The invasion of Afghanistan, coming as it did on top of the Iranian crises, had obviously dealt the *coup de grâce* to the Carter administration's foreign policy."[3]

This sequence of events within a few months led to a dramatic shift in American foreign policy, as signified by President Carter's speech to a joint session of Congress on January 23, 1980. The "Carter Doctrine" proposed a number of diplomatic and defensive measures designed to signal the Soviet Union that the United States was prepared to resist any further Soviet expansionism. The countermeasures associated with the Carter Doctrine were certainly a reversal of that president's previous emphasis on cooperation with, and goodwill toward, the Soviet Union.[4]

The expressed failure of the early Carter policies also made the rhetoric of Ronald Reagan more believable. That Carter largely abandoned détente after the Soviet invasion of Afghanistan made Reagan's subsequent diplomatic revisionism more plausible. Carter re-

2. See, for example, Robert W. Tucker, "America in Decline: The Foreign Policy of Maturity," *Foreign Affairs*, LVIII (Special Issue, 1980), 449–84.
3. *Ibid.*, 480.
4. Zbigniew Brzezinski, *Power and Principle: Memoirs of the National Security Adviser, 1977–1981* (New York, 1983), 53–57; Cyrus Vance, *Hard Choices: Four Critical Years in Managing America's Foreign Policy* (New York, 1983) 27–28.

luctantly, and Reagan enthusiastically, abandoned the "Vietnam reticence" that had been said to account for American hesitancy abroad during much of the 1970s; he forcefully reaffirmed strong international security interests and increased the pace of weapons development.

Carter's main concern in foreign policy making was to establish an administrative process that would avoid the extreme centralization of power that occurred in the Nixon administration when Kissinger, as the assistant for national security affairs, virtually displaced the secretary of state and ultimately held both positions simultaneously. To avoid the rise of "another Kissinger," Carter wanted the secretary of state, Vance, to be his principal adviser for foreign policy and the State Department to provide the necessary staff work. The assistant for national security affairs, Brzezinski, and the NSC staff were to play a less active and less assertive role in the foreign policy making process. In particular, policy coordination among the principal actors— the secretaries of state and defense, the presidential assistant, the CIA director, and the vice-president—was to be achieved through collegiality rather than by means of a national security adviser serving as an omnipotent chief of staff for foreign policy.[5] However, like many earlier administrations that have begun with a commitment to cabinet government and collegial decision making, the politics of foreign policy making produced other, and sometimes unintended, administrative arrangements.

Despite his very limited background in foreign affairs, which of course is not unusual for a president, Carter saw himself "as a policy initiator and manager who would make his own decisions from the range of views provided by his senior advisers."[6] His desire to have the option of acting as his own secretary of state would in itself limit any secretary of state's freedom to act as a presidential surrogate for foreign policy. Moreover, in the White House, Brzezinski proved to be aggressive in gaining the president's confidence and access to his presence. With the career of Kissinger as precedent,

5. Alexander George, *Presidential Decisionmaking in Foreign Policy: The Effective Use of Information and Advice* (Boulder, 1980), 159, 160.
6. I. M. Destler, "National Security II: The Rise of the Assistant," in Hugh Heclo and Lester M. Salamon (eds.), *The Illusion of Presidential Government* (Boulder, 1981), 272; Hamilton Jordan, *Crisis: The Last Year of the Carter Presidency* (New York, 1983), 46–47.

any assistant for national security affairs would have reason to entertain visions of administrative grandeur. Brzezinski was also no ordinary presidential assistant. As a professor of political science at Columbia University and a member (along with both Carter and Vance) of the Trilateral Commission that studied international political and economic problems during the 1970s, he had strong views about American foreign policy, especially toward the Soviet Union, that he was accustomed to arguing for with great force. To expect Brzezinski to take a backseat in foreign policy making, especially when sitting next to the driver in the White House, was to ask him to become a different person.

Ultimately, the very qualities that made Brzezinski valuable to Carter became the source of antagonism between the secretary of state and the national security adviser. As Brzezinski came to define and defend the administration's foreign policy objectives with increasing force and frequency, Vance repeatedly objected to these intrusions on the prerogatives of the State Department and its secretary. As time passed, Brzezinski acted more and more as Carter's foreign policy spokesman, and by the middle of 1978 Brzezinski had transformed his role of private presidential adviser to one of vigorous public advocate for important foreign decisions, especially those concerning the Soviet Union and, later, Iran. "By 1978," as I. M. Destler noted, "a serious Brzezinski-Vance split was publicly visible."[7]

President Carter, apparently at the secretary of state's request, restrained his national security adviser from speaking out on foreign policy issues in ways that pointed out differences between the White House and State Department.[8] Such attempted restraint, however, did not last long; indeed, it could not be expected to be effective given the circumstances. The reality was that Brzezinski spoke out as forcefully as he did because the president encouraged his activities. Brzezinski was not only an eager and indefatigable defender of the president's

7. George, *Presidential Decisionmaking in Foreign Policy*, 200; Destler, "National Security II," 273; Raymond A. Moore, "The Carter Presidency and Foreign Policy," in M. Glenn Abernathy *et al.*, *The Carter Years: The President and Policy Making* (New York, 1984), 63.

8. The best single source on Brzezinski's performance as special assistant for national security affairs during the first six months of the Carter administration is the profile "A Reporter at Large: Brzezinski," by Elizabeth Drew, *New Yorker*, May 1, 1978, pp. 90–130.

policies, but, in contrast to Vance, he willingly served as a lightning rod for criticism that would otherwise have been directed at Carter. An assistant like this can prove an invaluable asset for any president.

The competition between Vance and Brzezinski continued unabated and unresolved until April, 1980, when the secretary of state resigned because of his disagreement with Carter and Brzezinski over the mission that was proposed and initiated (and subsequently aborted) to rescue the American hostages in Iran.[9] By that time, however, the Carter administration's foreign policy had become widely characterized as severely fragmented, badly designed, and poorly managed.[10] Just before Vance's resignation, an interesting exchange took place between him and Senator Edward Zorinsky (D-Neb.) at a hearing of the Committee on Foreign Relations.

SENATOR ZORINSKY: As you know, Mr. Secretary, I have sponsored legislation to require Senate confirmation of the President's Assistant for National Security Affairs. Next month, this committee is planning to hold hearings on this matter.

With all due respect, isn't it true that we really have at least two Secretaries of State, you and Dr. Brzezinski? Why should one be subject to Senate confirmation and not the other when, in fact, both play a significant role in the foreign policy of this country?

SECRETARY VANCE: The answer is no, there is only one Secretary of State. I am the Secretary of State. The Security Adviser has a very important role to play as an adviser to the President of the United States. This has long been the case, not only with this President but with other Presidents, and it is appropriate that this should be the case.

The only persons who speak for the United States, and the President has made this clear, in terms of foreign policy are the President of the United States and the Secretary of State.[11]

As we know, however, there has often been more than one secretary of state at a time, as was most certainly the case in the Carter administration.

---

9. Vance, *Hard Choices*, 410–12. See also Gary Sick, *All Fall Down: America's Tragic Encounter with Iran* (New York, 1985).

10. See, for example, Stanley Hoffman, "The Hell of Good Intentions," *Foreign Policy*, XXIX (Winter, 1977–78), 3–26; and Thomas L. Hughes, "Carter: The Management of Contradictions," *Foreign Policy* XXXI (Summer, 1978), 34–55.

11. U.S. Congress, Senate, Committee on Foreign Relations, *The National Security Adviser: Role and Accountability* (Washington, D.C., 1980), 173.

NSC Versus the State Department

In a commentary about the continuing rivalry between Vance's successor as secretary of state, former Senator Edmund S. Muskie, and Brzezinski for control of American foreign policy, former State Department official Leslie Gelb argued that behind the competition for personal power was a more fundamental competition. At a deeper level, these struggles derived from the conflict and differing perspectives of two institutions: the White House, in the form of the national security adviser along with the National Security Council staff, and the secretary of state, who represented the views of his department. The saga is really a modern replay of the historical conflict between palace guard and king's ministers or between any personal staff and the line officers in any organizational structure. From this perspective, Brzezinski's assertiveness was simply indicative of a process that had begun with McGeorge Bundy in the 1960s and was most dramatically exemplified by Henry Kissinger—the emergence of the White House assistant "as a major, visible foreign policy figure in his own right."[12]

Brzezinski made clear in his memoirs that he regarded himself as equal to the secretaries of state and defense, with these three officials comprising a policy-making triad in foreign affairs. If he was not to become a Kissinger dominating the policy-making process in the White House, neither was Vance to be a John Foster Dulles monopolizing the president's attention for the State Department. Brzezinski also realized that, as the president's assistant, the national security adviser was the guardian of the "presidential perspective" in decision making. This required a viewpoint that transcended the interests of the various foreign policy bureaucracies—the diplomatic bureaucracy, the military and intelligence bureaucracies, and the bureaucracies that deal with the international economy. Accordingly, Brzezinski used his National Security Council staff to help shape those decisions, by sifting through the policy proposals that come for presidential action, to find those that would further Carter's avowed goals. According to Brzezinski, "Coordination is predominance: and the key to asserting effective coordination was the right of direct ac-

12. Leslie H. Gelb, "The Struggle over Foreign Policy," *New York Times Magazine*, July 20, 1980, pp. 26–27ff; Destler, "National Security II," 274.

cess to the President, in writing, by telephone, or simply by walking into his office."[13]

What Vance forgot—and Brzezinski had the perspicacity to notice—was that there is no perfect process for foreign policy making, only one that is acceptable to and serves the needs and interests of an incumbent president. And, as Kissinger has observed, Brzezinski was aware that "every president since Kennedy seems to have trusted his White House aides more than his Cabinet."[14]

In such a circumstance, it is unlikely that a president will enforce the prohibition on political activity or the limitation of policy-making scope that has been periodically proposed by advocates of a preeminent position for the secretary of state. Presidents have chosen to work through a strong secretary of state, as Eisenhower did with Dulles, or to rely exclusively on the assistant for national security affairs, as Nixon did with Kissinger. Carter preferred a middle course, in which the secretary of state and the national security adviser competed for control of foreign policy making. There is nothing necessarily wrong with such a policy-making model: a certain amount of rivalry, even friction, among institutional actors can contribute to more effective policy. Bureaucratic conflict is also probably inevitable and might be constructively formalized. Yet, it is no less true that a president needs to avoid an institutionalized conflict between the State Department and the NSC staff that produces nothing more than fragmented policy proposals and leaves the decision-making process in disarray. When President Carter could not, or would not, settle the differences between Vance and Brzezinski, this was precisely the result.[15] By relying on his national security adviser to retain control over foreign policy issues, Carter fatally undermined Vance's authority as secretary of state. The irony is that where Carter entered office pledged to replace the Kissinger model of foreign policy making, the actual result was a concentration of power nearly as great as that in the Nixon administration.

In seeking to avoid the extreme centralization of decision-making power that characterized the Kissinger era, the policies of the Carter

13. Brzezinski, *Power and Principle*, 63. For a description of the NSC staff in the Carter administration, see *ibid.*, 74–78; and Moore, "The Carter Presidency and Foreign Policy," 61–63.

14. Henry Kissinger, *White House Years* (Boston, 1979), 47.

15. Gelb, "Struggle over Foreign Policy," 39–40.

administration had an equal and opposite effect. By allowing the competition between his two top foreign policy advisers to escalate into open rivalry, Jimmy Carter produced a degree of disunity and divisiveness that seriously undermined the credibility of American foreign policy. Ronald Reagan and his advisers were determined to correct this state of affairs and to have a strong secretary of state. Part of Alexander Haig's tenacity as the "vicar" of American foreign policy came from his belief that this was his proper role.

Détente Revised: The Reagan Administration's Foreign Policy

Ronald Reagan, both as candidate and president, had been sharply critical of détente as the basis of Soviet-American relations. Clearly repudiating the basic premises of the Nixon-Kissinger foreign policy, the 1980 Republican party platform called for a strategy of "peace through strength" that would involve the achievement of overall military and technological superiority over the Soviet Union, the rejection of any arms-control agreements "which lock the United States into a position of military inferiority," and creation of the level of forces necessary "to prevail in conflict in the event deterrence fails."[16] These were clearly "fighting words," and though party platforms are often rhetorically overblown, these ideas represented a rejection of such basic assumptions as military parity, renewed SALT agreements, and the military doctrine of "mutually assured destruction."

In Reagan's view, America's position in international affairs had been badly compromised during the Carter administration. Indeed, he viewed his decisive electoral victory as a mandate on foreign policy to reverse the decline of American power and to reestablish the United States as a nation that could not be pushed around. The principal means by which the reassertion of American power was to be accomplished was by direct diplomatic confrontation with the Soviet Union where American interests were involved and a decisive buildup of military forces—conventional and nuclear. President Reagan and his principal foreign policy advisers, especially his first secretary of state, Alexander Haig, were quick to assert the presence of a Soviet-

16. *Congressional Quarterly Weekly Report*, XXXVIII (July 19, 1980), 2005–2008.

inspired conspiracy behind many international disruptions, such as political terrorism and "wars of national liberation." They also spoke of the Soviet Union in sharply critical, even provocative, language. In his January 29, 1981, news conference, for example, Reagan said of the leaders of the Soviet Union that "the only morality they recognize is what will further their cause, meaning they reserve unto themselves the right to commit any crime, to lie, to cheat, in order to obtain that. . . . I think when you do business with them, even at a détente, you keep that in mind." [17]

The basic premise of the Reagan administration's foreign policy has been the assumption that the Soviet Union is pursuing imperialist objectives with its vastly expanded military capacity. [18] The Afghanistan invasion was only the most dramatic example. More typical of Soviet imperialism, according to the Reagan-Haig formulation, was reliance upon its client states to undermine American interests, such as Syria has supposedly done in the Middle East, and to foment rebellion in states aligned with America, such as Cuba has supposedly done in El Salvador. This Soviet aggressiveness required a firm American response wherever it was manifested in the world, especially after the fall of Vietnam and the Iranian hostage crisis. The American military occupation of Grenada can probably be best understood as a symbolic "show of will"—a clear sign that the United States was ready and able to use military force to protect its security interests. The internal political situation on a small Caribbean island probably did not constitute any danger to American security, but the successful invasion indicated the importance that the Reagan administration attached to Central American affairs. [19]

El Salvador, and its relationship with neighboring Nicaragua, was the first and most persistent foreign policy problem for the administration. Shortly after taking office, Secretary of State Haig denounced the leftist rebels in El Salvador and asserted that the Sandinista government of Nicaragua was supplying the rebel forces with arms pro-

17. Seyom Brown, *The Faces of Power: Constancy and Change in United States Foreign Policy from Truman to Reagan* (New York, 1983), 571.
18. Haig testified before the Senate Foreign Relations Committee that in recent years the Soviet military had been transformed from a continental to a global power capable of supporting an imperial foreign policy. New York *Times*, January 10, 1981.
19. See the official white paper—"Special Report on Communist Involvement in the Insurrection of El Salvador," *Department of State Bulletin*, LXXXI (March, 1981), 1–11.

vided by Cuba and the Soviet Union.[20] The Reagan administration dramatically stepped up military assistance to El Salvador and committed American military advisers to train the El Salvadoran (and Honduran) military forces. Nicaragua was also subjected to intense diplomatic pressure to cease any support for the rebel movement in El Salvador, and the Central Intelligence Agency provided very open "covert support" for anti-Sandinista guerrilla forces.

Central America was the hot seat of the Reagan administration's foreign policy, but it was not the only geographic region in which American interests were judged to be at stake. The Middle East in general and Lebanon in particular came to involve a significant military and diplomatic commitment. In the words of one commentator, "The revival of the policy of global, all-continents, coercive containment of the USSR and its proxies, and of negotiation from strength, presumed credible capabilities for brandishing military power— anywhere and at any level—from paramilitary through strategic confrontations."[21]

The Reagan administration, therefore, engaged in a major overhaul of the nation's defense posture and arms-control strategy. This involved three broad programmatic developments. First, overall Defense Department spending was projected for a five-year buildup of $1.6 trillion—a real average increase of 7 percent a year. Second, several new offensive and defensive weapons were introduced: the B-1 bomber, the Trident II missile for submarines, the MX missile, and, most recently, the "Star Wars" defense scheme. The MX was very controversial, as it had been for President Carter, but President Reagan decided to proceed with its deployment. Although it was deployed only in stationary sites that had been "hardened" (the government did not invest in the vastly more expensive mobile versions), this concession did little to mollify its critics. For some, the MX seemed the worse of both worlds: a provocative new weapon meant to compen-

---

20. For contrasting views about what should be the basis of American foreign policy in Central America, see *The Report of the President's National Bipartisan Commission on Central America* (New York, 1984) and Martin Oisken (ed.), *Trouble in Our Backyard: Central America and the United States in the Eighties* (New York, 1984). The National Bipartisan Commission was chaired by Henry Kissinger. For a critical perspective that views these regional security problems as outside the scope of Soviet-American conflict, see Robert S. Leiken (ed.), *Central America: Anatomy of Conflict* (New York, 1984).

21. Brown, *Faces of Power*, 590.

sate for the vulnerability of American ICBMs to a Soviet preemptive strike but one that was itself highly vulnerable.

Third, the Reagan administration was committed to closing the "window of vulnerability" that some arms-control analysts said threatened the credibility of an American response to a Soviet first strike. Since the deterrence doctrine of "mutually assured destruction" required a credible counterforce capacity (that is, one in which enough missiles would survive an attack to annihilate the other side), it was necessary to maintain parity, which some viewed as an overall balance, whereas others saw it as equality within each category of weapons. The MX was one response that sought to prevent any destabilization in the strategic situation by matching the numerical superiority of Soviet warheads with a more powerful and accurate missile, one that would not be destroyed before being launched. Similarly, the deployment of intermediate-range Pershing missiles in Europe was meant to counter the Soviet Union's SS-20s, as well to have the potential for "theater use" in a conventional European war.

The strategic thinking underlying the Reagan administration's policy making was far removed from that of the Nixon administration, which had emphasized reductions in nuclear weaponry and a general relaxation of tensions between the superpowers. The Reagan White House's continual questioning of Soviet intentions and expressions of skepticism about whether sufficient verification existed in the arms-control process led some to speculate whether the administration had rejected the concept of strategic parity between the United States and the USSR upon which détente was based. Yet for all the rhetorical denunciations of Soviet international adventurism and possible violations of the SALT agreements, deterrence and détente were not completely excluded from American strategic thinking and diplomatic policy. Under Reagan, ideology gave way to pragmatism in the implementation of specific policies. The Reagan administration, in practice, has been much softer in dealing with the Soviet Union than its rhetoric would have suggested. For example, the economic boycott that was imposed by President Carter to protest the Afghanistan invasion has been lifted, protests concerning human rights violations by the Soviet government have been mild, and the Reagan White House's response to the Korean Air Lines incident was tempered. Similarly, under Reagan the Polish government was provided with urgently needed loans to prevent a default to its international creditors, and relations with the People's Republic of China have been normalized. Détente has been revised and recast, but it has not been rejected or replaced.

Haig Versus the White House

Few secretaries of state have come to the office as well versed in White House politics as Alexander Haig. As former deputy assistant to the president for national security affairs under Henry Kissinger, he served in the White House when it was the locus of American foreign policy making. During his service on the NSC staff, Haig, who had won the Distinguished Service Cross as a battalion commander in Vietnam, rose from colonel to major general in the United States Army. After the resignation of H. R. Haldeman as Nixon's White House chief of staff, Haig served in this position through the Watergate crisis. His role in the final days of the Nixon administration was one of the most remarkable ever played by a presidential assistant. He essentially orchestrated President Nixon's resignation while seeing that the basic functions of government operated despite a constitutional crisis.[22] President Gerald Ford appointed Haig, who was now a four-star general, to be supreme commander of NATO, a position in which, despite concern because of his involvement in the Watergate scandals, he enjoyed great success with the European military and diplomatic community.

Haig's almost meteoric ascent was accompanied by criticism that he was a "political general." He had jumped over thousands of other officers in his rapid rise from colonel to major general and was the only four-star general never to have been a divisional commander. Critics also claimed that Haig owed his political preeminence to an unseemly facility for bureaucratic intrigue and to his uncritical service to Kissinger. Still others have been sharply critical of Haig for his role in the "Saturday Night Massacre," during which Haig told the acting attorney general to fire the Watergate special prosecutor with the warning "Your Commander in Chief is giving you an order."[23]

22. Henry Kissinger, *Years of Upheaval* (Boston, 1980), 109–10.
23. William Safire, in New York *Times*, November 24, 1980; Bob Woodward and Carl

There were also allegations that Haig was involved with illegal wiretapping of government officials, including his own colleagues on the NSC staff, when he served as Kissinger's deputy. One commentator put the strongest anti-Haig case in these terms: "General Haig is the exemplar of the careerist: a man who will do anything for his master—anything likely, that is, to advance his own career. He evidently has no feeling for American constitutionalism, for restraint in the exercise of power."[24]

Despite the questions raised about Haig's connections with the Nixon administration, especially the Watergate scandal, his designation as secretary of state was considered a major commitment by the Reagan administration to a new direction in foreign policy making. In particular, Haig was judged to have received a mandate to take command of the White House in order to prevent a repetition of the vacillation and uncertainty that had characterized American foreign policy in the Carter administration because of the feud between Vance and Brzezinski. What surprised most observers, including the Reagan White House staff, was how quickly, insistently, and dramatically Haig asserted his prerogatives—not only as secretary of state but as the principal national security policy maker and premier cabinet secretary. According to one senior official, "He acts more like an assistant President than a coequal Cabinet member."[25]

For all the problems of "turf and temperament" that later developed between the State Department and the White House, Alexander Haig and Ronald Reagan shared the same world view, especially about the need to counter the growing power of the Soviet Union. Both were sharply critical of the Carter administration for pursuing an overly conciliatory policy toward Moscow. Despite his own participation in formulating the Nixon-Kissinger foreign policy, in 1980 Haig declared that the "twin pillars" of that policy, détente and deterrence, had failed.[26] At the core of Haig's foreign policy was a commitment to resisting Soviet expansionism beyond Eastern Europe. Ac-

---

Bernstein, *The Final Days* (New York, 1976), 61. Haig, for his part, voiced surprise that his role in the Nixon White House should be an issue in his nomination for secretary of state. Alexander M. Haig, Jr., *Caveat: Realism, Reagan, and Foreign Policy* (New York, 1984), 40.

24. Anthony Lewis, in New York *Times*, December 4, 1980.

25. New York *Times*, February 8, 1981.

26. *Ibid.*, December 18, 1980. See also Haig, *Caveat*, 46, 105, 129, 232.

cording to what has been called the "Haig Doctrine," increased security assistance would be provided to Third World countries to increase their internal stability and ability to resist externally sponsored aggression.[27]

Yet, despite such hard-line positions Haig was a moderating influence in foreign policy making. He was strongly opposed, for example, to ideas identified with right-wing Reagan supporters such as Senators Jesse Helms (R-N.C.) and John Tower (R-Tex.), along with certain members of the National Security Council staff. The secretary of state was particularly upset by suggestions of Richard Pipes, a Harvard professor and Eastern European analyst for the NSC, that seemed to countenance the use of a preemptive nuclear strike by the United States, as well as by the derogatory comments of Richard Allen, the assistant for national security affairs, concerning the pacifist sentiments of many Europeans involved in the campaign against the deployment of the Euromissiles.[28] In general, Haig was highly regarded by Europeans for his firmness of manner and knowledge of international issues.

At home, however, Haig became increasingly embroiled in syntactical and procedural quarrels. In his speaking, Haig became associated with the use of awkward and disjointed circumlocutions in which a simple declaration would have been fine. Asked once if anything was new in Poland, he once replied, "No, not in an instantaneous sense." It reminded Watergate phraseology such as "at this point in time" to mean "now." Haig also consistently referred to subcabinet officials at the State Department as "his nominees," though these are, of course, presidential appointments. The use of the possessive case would have been less consequential had the qualifications of these appointees been different. As it was, many of these officials, like the under secretary for political affairs (Lawrence Eagleburger) and certain regional assistant secretaries (like Richard Burt for European affairs and John Holdridge for Far Eastern affairs), had also been members of the Kissinger NSC staff, and conservative Republican senators opposed their confirmation on the grounds that such appointments were a betrayal of the Reagan foreign policy principles.

27. *Newsweek*, April 6, 1981, p. 32. Haig, *Caveat.* 129.
28. *Newsweek*, April 6, 1981, p. 37.

The degree to which the evaluation of a policy's substance is affected by style and personality is certainly debatable. Regardless, Haig's personal manner became the source of much controversy from the early days of the Reagan administration. White House aides, in particular, were reported to have concluded that tensions between themselves and the secretary had been exacerbated by Haig's "volatile" and "unusual" temperament.[29] The most dramatic example of Haig's unpredictable behavior occurred on March 30, 1981, when President Reagan was wounded in an attempted assassination. In the resulting confusion and in the absence of Vice-President George Bush, Haig arrived at the White House and announced before the assembled press corps, "I'm in charge here." That such an announcement was obviously wrong (the constitutional order of succession goes through the vice-president to the speaker of the House of Representatives and the president *pro tempore* of the Senate) was bad enough.[30] What was worse was his televised appearance: he seemed shaken, exhausted, and anything but in control. It may be that Haig's reputation never recovered from that event. While his intention must have been to assure the nation and the world that the machinery of government was operating efficiently, it appeared to be pushy and presumptive. For the White House Staff this incident was typical of his petty obsession with matters relating to his privileges as secretary of state. Haig's legendary bureaucratic skills and unequaled background in foreign affairs had led both political insiders and the general public to expect him to be the most powerful figure in the Reagan administration. But as Roger Morris said, "in barely two months, he is reported angry, brooding, near resignation over a series of poisonous bureaucratic struggles with the White House, whose power in such matters he knows so well, or should."[31]

Haig's difficulties with the White House reached major proportions in the contretemps over who was to head the crisis management team established by President Reagan—the secretary of state or the vice-president. Both Kissinger and Brzezinski had used their posi-

29. New York *Times*, July 2, 1981.
30. Haig must have been acting on the assumption that the Twentieth Amendment, which did provide for presidential succession by the secretary of state after the vice-president, was valid. But it had been superseded by the Twenty-fifth Amendment in 1967.
31. Roger Morris, *Haig: The General's Progress* (New York, 1982), 399.

288 PRESIDENTS AND FOREIGN POLICY MAKING

tions as crisis managers to make the Situation Room of the White House a focal point for policy making. Brzezinski, for example, had used crisis management to formulate Persian Gulf policy independently of the Departments of State and Defense. Haig was determined to prevent the growth of a competing foreign policy center in the White House such as had bedeviled his immediate predecessors; he wanted a return to the Dulles-Eisenhower model, according to which the secretary of state acted as crisis manager. This struggle over who would head the crisis management team was also one over who would eventually control policy making. Haig stressed that he had the president's mandate to be the "chief formulator and spokesman for foreign policy," in Reagan's phrase. To designate crisis management responsibilities to another official, therefore, would be to diminish his authority.[32] After a highly publicized series of rumors (including that Haig had threatened resignation and had leveled accusations against Chief of Staff James A. Baker, Jr., and Counselor Edwin Meese III), the White House announced that the vice-president would head the crisis management team that, as part of the national security system, would coordinate federal resources in response to an emergency situation.[33] Haig did not resign, though he publicly blamed the senior White House staff for mishandling the matter. President Reagan reaffirmed Haig's position as his "primary adviser on foreign affairs," while blaming reporters for the controversy over the secretary's remarks.[34]

Haig was reported to be a "wounded lion" in the aftermath of the crisis management incident and to be particularly resentful of the role of the White House staff in orchestrating the affair.[35] The secretary had reason to believe that he had been "had" by the White House staff, but he behaved in a way that demonstrated a fatal misunderstanding of the realities of decision-making power in the Reagan administration. First, by publicly criticizing Baker and Meese, Haig transformed a rivalry into a public feud, formalizing a breach between the White House and the State Department over foreign policy making. Second,

32. New York *Times*, March 29, 1981.
33. For the text of the White House statement, see New York *Times*, March 25, 1981.
34. *Ibid.*, March 26, 1982.
35. *Ibid.*, March 28, 1981. Haig has stated that a high White House aide, possibly James Baker, said that the secretary would have to be gotten rid of quickly, "and we are going to make it happen." Haig, *Caveat*, 302, and see also 148.

his actions confirmed the growing belief of the Reagan staff that the secretary was not a "team player" in an administration that strongly emphasized such behavior. Third and most important, the White House became convinced that Haig was preempting the president's role as the nation's chief diplomat; one presidential assistant was quoted as saying, "Haig thinks he's President."[36] Since he was a past party to this kind of palace intrigue under the Nixon administration, it is a wonder that Haig should have underestimated the influence wielded by the senior White House staff, whatever may have been President Reagan's expressed commitment to cabinet government.

Fourth, Haig made a serious strategic error by overreacting to the designation of Vice-President Bush to chair the crisis management team. As a former CIA director and ambassador to China, Bush had a background in foreign affairs second in the Reagan administration only to Haig's; moreover, as vice-president, Bush could assert authority in the president's name that could transcend the perspective of a particular department. Haig was undoubtedly correct in his assessment that the White House staff was determined to "clip his wings" by limiting his complete authority over foreign policy, but he might have noted that it was the vice-president who was in the chair, not the assistant for national security affairs, as had been the case with Kissinger and Brzezinski.

Fifth, Haig was too quick to point up John Foster Dulles as the appropriate model for the conduct of foreign affairs. What Haig seemed not to understand was that Dulles' preeminence was principally the result of his intimate relationship with President Eisenhower rather than simply his position as secretary of state (see Chapter 5). Haig forgot that fundamental tenet of successful relations between the president and secretary of state in foreign policy making—that it is the president who makes policy and that he is free to consult whomever he wishes and to establish whatever structural processes he deems appropriate.

Sixth, Haig should have realized that, though White House aides like Baker and Meese had no particular expertise or interest in foreign affairs, they had an inordinate interest in the president's political well-being. Reagan himself had no interest in the daily manage-

36. New York *Times*, March 26, 1981.

ment of foreign affairs and was strongly committed to Haig as a necessary antidote to the divisiveness and incoherence of the Carter administration's foreign policy making. The White House staff, however, did not wish to allow Haig to preempt complete responsibility for national security to the exclusion of Secretary of Defense Caspar Weinberger or even CIA director William Casey. Haid should have realized that his Dulles analogy neglected the momentous changes that had served to broaden the scope of foreign policy beyond the State Department's institutional interests. Moreover, he "tried to broaden the State Department's reach at a time when the growing interrelationship between diplomacy and domestic politics on such issues as energy, auto imports, and immigration made the White House reluctant to delegate this huge domain to diplomats alone."[37] Without a strong national security adviser, the White House staff was understandably fearful that a president who lacked a background in diplomatic and defense issues (unlike Eisenhower, who had been knowledgeable about both) would become the creature of departmental interests. As the keepers of Reagan's political future, Baker and Meese would inevitably have to counter Haig's demands to dominate the process of foreign policy making, or else they would seem to have surrendered control to him. Their situation was different from that of White House Chief of Staff Sherman Adams, who could rely on President Eisenhower to handle foreign affairs while Adams himself concentrated on the domestic policies, where the president was weaker. But with Alexander Haig as vicar, Ronald Reagan might be seen as only a titular bishop of the diocese of foreign affairs.

Haig might have achieved a de facto primacy in foreign affairs. But in a memorandum on Inauguration Day he insisted upon a de jure grant of presidential authority that was more sweeping than had been accorded to his predecessors.[38] Although Haig did not get all that he proposed in his original memorandum, he was granted much broader authority over foreign policy making than his recent predecessors. For example, the secretary of state was designated as chair-

37. Hedrick Smith, in *Ibid.*, March 29, 1981.
38. Destler, "National Security II," 282. See also New York *Times*, January 27, 1981. Haig apparently did not push this twenty-page memorandum on Reagan while the president was still in formal dress after viewing the parade. Instead, he submitted it to Meese to bring to Reagan's attention. Despite Haig's reminders, Meese waited three months before doing so.

man of a variety of interdepartmental working groups, though not those involving defense or international economic policy. Since all these committees had in the recent past been chaired by the assistant for national security affairs, this agreement was a major victory for Haig even if it was not the complete triumph that was envisioned in his Inauguration Day memorandum. There was a pyrrhic quality to Haig's organizational victory, however, because it put the White House staff and the cabinet secretaries on alert that he was attempting a power play at their expense. A White House aide was quoted as observing that for Haig "everything beyond the water's edge was foreign policy." The inevitable reactions were "battles over turf," as the secretary of defense asserted his primacy in areas such as the development of the neutron bomb and the MX missile system and the secretaries of commerce and the treasury claimed leadership in questions involving foreign trade and international economic policy. The three-month delay before action was taken on Haig's original memorandum suggests that Meese deliberately stalled its implementation in order to allow a groundswell of opposition from within the administration to develop.[39] This should have been a signal to the secretary of state that his plans for consolidation of his power over the foreign policy making process would not occur without substantial opposition.

While Haig was seeking to aggrandize his personal and institutional power, the assistant for national security affairs was doing a "disappearing act," in accordance with the president's publicized intention to make the secretary of state his principal foreign policy adviser. Like Brzezinski under Carter, Richard Allen came to this White House position from an advisory position in the Reagan campaign in which he had enjoyed considerable public exposure. Unlike Brzezinski or Kissinger, however, he was not a member of the foreign policy establishment; nor did he have a reputation as a scholar or conceptualizer of foreign affairs. Allen consistently endorsed a low-profile, facilitator conception of his job as presidential assistant, and he asserted that his intention was not to make policy "but only to help coordinate the work of the various agencies in foreign policy."[40]

39. New York *Times*, February 27, 1981, March 26, 1981.
40. Destler, "National Security II," 281; New York *Times*, January 27, 1981.

In a sharp break with a twenty-year tradition, the role of the national security adviser and his staff was deliberately scaled down, and the NSC was placed under the direct control of Presidential Counselor Edwin Meese. One would have to return to the Eisenhower national security system to find Allen's administrative counterpart. Indeed, Allen likened himself to Eisenhower's aide Gordon Gray, who was one of those presidential assistants with a "passion for anonymity" as NSC staff secretary. Whereas previous national security advisers had had direct access to the president, Allen operated through Meese, though he continued to provide the daily presidential briefing on the world situation and to prepare memoranda on "talking points" for the president's conversations with foreign leaders. The NSC staff, however, was downgraded from a policy-making and control group to a conduit for departmental policy proposals. More significant, Allen and his staff did not involve themselves either in day-to-day operations of foreign policy or in independently formulating policy initiatives. As Allen put it, "The policy formulation function of the national security adviser would be offloaded to the Secretary of State." Theoretically, the national security adviser in the Reagan administration would focus on interagency coordination and "long-range thinking."[41] Appointees to the NSC staff positions were largely of a strongly conservative viewpoint and, with certain exceptions (such as the controversial Harvard professors Samuel Huntington and Richard Pipes), lacked the academic or bureaucratic visibility and experience that had been typical of earlier NSC staffs. In the administrative hierarchy, Allen would rank as a deputy secretary, in contrast to the cabinet-level status of his immediate predecessors and of his supervisor, Meese. A visible symbol of this difference in Allen's status was that his office was in the basement of the West Wing of the White House while Meese was down the hall from the Oval Office in a corner suite that Brzezinski had occupied.

Open warfare broke out between Haig and the White House staff less than three months into the new administration. The incident involving the crisis management team came after a mounting series of complaints from Haig that the White House was out to undermine his authority, demands that NSC staffers clear their speeches

41. New York *Times*, March 4, 1981, November 19, 1980.

with him, accusations by both sides of inadequate or tardy briefing papers, claims and counterclaims of improper policy statements, leaks by the State Department, and actions by White House underlings meant to settle their bosses' scores with the other side. At one point, Haig charged that someone in the White House, as yet unidentifiable (but not Allen), was waging a "guerrilla campaign" against him. (It was widely rumored to be the chief of staff, Baker.) And some White House senior staff members, recognizing Allen's reduced role but wary of Haig's monopolistic goals, moved into the foreign policy area themselves.[42]

Allen was eased out as national security adviser in January, 1982, ostensibly for not reporting a thousand-dollar honorarium he had received from a Japanese magazine but really for his poor management of the NSC staff.[43] His successor was Deputy Secretary of State William P. Clark, who chose Robert McFarlane to serve as his deputy. It was alleged that Judge Clark, an old political friend of Reagan's who had been appointed to the California Supreme Court when Reagan was governor, had been sent to Haig's department so he could look out for the president's interests there. Clark's lack of experience in foreign affairs and repeated stumbling over the capitals of other nations during his confirmation hearings raised embarrassing questions about his qualifications for the department's second position. But he received high marks for his on-the-job learning and proved an invaluable emissary between Haig and the increasingly hostile senior presidential staff. In his move to the White House, Clark upgraded the status of the position of national security adviser, since he reported directly to the president rather than through Meese. As a longtime friend of Reagan's, he enjoyed an ease of access denied to Allen (and to Haig). There was talk that the White House triumvirate (Baker, Meese, and Deputy Chief of Staff Michael Deaver) was becoming a quadrumvirate with the addition of Clark to the senior staff.

Clark and Haig had enjoyed a good working relationship at the State Department, but any hopes for improved relations between the secretary of state and the White House were quickly dashed. For one thing, Clark was closer to Reagan's own hard-line views about the So-

42. *Ibid.*, March 24, 1981; Washington *Post*, November 6, 1981.
43. Richard Hallman, "Reagan as Commander-in-Chief," *New York Times Magazine*, January 15, 1984, p. 57.

viet Union than was Haig. There were also recurring tensions about protocol and privileges with Haig reported to have "bruised feelings" about slights to him in official ceremonies. By June, 1982, he and Clark were reported to have confronted each other in what aides described as "shouting matches" on several issues.[44] When Haig finally resigned on June 26, 1982, citing unhappiness with the administration's foreign policy and his role as its director, his act was greeted as a forgone conclusion and, for the White House staff, one long overdue. While Reagan had come to respect Haig's intellect, he had also come to find his temperament intolerable.[45] Clark's attitude was crucial: he had come to the White House as an admirer of Haig, but quickly became disillusioned with the secretary's unwillingness to recognize that foreign policy making was a presidential prerogative, not Haig's.

The new secretary of state, George P. Shultz, a former treasury secretary in the Nixon administration, stood in sharp contrast to Haig. Where the general was mercurial, aggressive, and a political loner, the former economics professor was evenhanded, conciliatory, and a team player. Whereas Haig (at least publicly) had a confrontational posture in diplomatic matters, Shultz deliberately opted for quieter, behind-the-scenes diplomacy to win his point. Most important, at least from the White House's perspective, Shultz was said to hold the view that as secretary of state he had no foreign policy of his own, only that of the president. It was quickly noted that "Shultz goes to extraordinary lengths to emphasize that Reagan is responsible for making foreign policy."[46] Shultz's preference for conciliation and compromise did cause speculation that he would lack the determination necessary for strong policy making. On the other hand, the incessant bureaucratic feuding of Haig's tenure had "projected a picture of a chaotic U.S. foreign policy and in the end sapped Haig's influence with the President."[47]

44. New York *Times*, June 22, 1982. Leslie Gelb also reported, "Unlike Mr. Haig who seeks the limelight, 'Judge' Clark is always careful to insure that it is his boss, the President, who gets the credit for making foreign policy." Haig has said that Clark told him in June, 1982, "You better understand that from now on it's going to be the President's foreign policy." Haig, *Caveat*, 307.
45. New York *Times*, June 27, 1981.
46. *U.S. News and World Report*, November 8, 1982, p. 27.
47. *Ibid.*, 26; New York *Times*, July 18, 1982. See also I. M. Destler, "'Faith Without Works?' The Enigma of Reagan Foreign Policymaking" (Paper presented at the Woodrow Wilson School of Public and International Affairs, Princeton University, November 19–20, 1982).

Noticeably absent with Shultz at the State Department was the internecine warfare between the secretary of state and the national security adviser. There was no Clark-Shultz feud.[48] Both Shultz and Clark were personally loyal to Reagan and shared his desire that he should be seen as clearly in charge of foreign policy. Clark, in particular, enjoyed an ease of access to the president, and shared with him a nearly identical feeling about the role of the United States in world affairs, particularly vis-à-vis the Soviet Union. Clark bore no similarity to past national security advisers, such as Kissinger and Brzezinski, who liked to conceptualize about foreign policy on a grand scale; even Richard Allen had had a reputation as a coordinator of somewhat grandiose foreign policy formulations. Other than during his year as deputy secretary of state, Clark was almost devoid of an interest in foreign affairs. Nevertheless, he had the president's ear and, even with a scanty knowledge, he was able to interest Reagan in the issues.[49]

Despite Clark's proximity (personal and political), Shultz continued to retain Reagan's confidence. Although no personal confidant, Shultz was regarded as able and loyal and as possibly the administration's most competent official. Differences did occur between the State Department and the White House—over American military activities in Central America, for example. Despite his team-player standing, Shultz has also had major differences with Defense Secretary Caspar Weinberger. In general, Shultz counseled a more moderate foreign policy while Clark and Weinberger favored a harder line. Conflicts, however, never became conflagrations, as they often did with Haig and the White House. When Clark left to become secretary of the interior, it was because of a personal preference to work on issues with which he was more familiar rather than foreign policy where he was, by self-admission, out of his depth.

It is widely agreed that Shultz is "conservative, methodical and calm" and that as an administrator he is "an incrementalist, a problem solver and a mediator". Yet, these very qualities also earned Shultz criticism: his calm was seen as passivity, his team playing as timidity. While his views are virtually identical to Haig's, he did not

48. *U.S. News and World Report*, September 19, 1983, p. 30.
49. Steven Weisman, "The Influence of William Clark," *New York Times Magazine*, August 14, 1983, pp. 17–20ff.

have wide experience in foreign affairs. But as Leslie Gelb has said: "Unlike Mr. Haig, he does not push those positions that are contrary to what he thinks are Presidential inclinations. Unlike Mr. Haig, he subordinates himself at every opportunity to Mr. Reagan." Of course, this was one of Shultz's major goals: to end the rancor that had existed when Haig was secretary of state. Shultz is fond of saying that "It is Mr. Reagan's policy." But many critics maintained that, with a president who has not developed a cohesive global strategy and a secretary of state who is not inclined to develop one himself, American foreign policy remained incapable of decisive actions.[50]

The Vicar General

Haig's biggest problem as secretary of state was the perception of the president's men that his desire to take command of foreign policy was really an attempt to upstage Reagan and usurp his policy-making prerogatives. For his part, Haig chafed at having to work through the senior White House staff (the Baker-Meese-Deaver triumvirate, or "three-headed monster," as Haig called it) that guarded President Reagan, much as Haig had guarded President Nixon. While Haig would have been expected to understand the parochial and protective mentality of White House staff, he complained persistently about their "intruding on foreign policy, stabbing nominations for political reasons and leaking 'disinformation' about him to the press."[51] General Haig should have realized that engaging in a full-scale bureaucratic war could only serve to damage his credibility as a member in good standing of the administration.

Whatever the personal problems, which were considerable, Haig's behavior as secretary of state cannot be understood apart from his determination to become the vicar of foreign policy. In Haig's conception this was not simply a matter of expanding turf; it was a matter of "coherence—a single integrated foreign policy that reaches across

50. The quotations in the preceding paragraph are from Leslie Gelb in New York *Times*, August 1, 1983. For a description of Shultz's tenure, which has some parallels to that of Dean Rusk, see the commentary by Bernard Gwertzman, New York *Times*, May 23, 1984.

51. "Haig vs. the White House," *Newsweek*, April 6, 1981, p. 29.

traditional jurisdictional lines into questions of economics, energy, and defense as well."[52] The coherence that Haig was proposing, however, would have required a Department of National Security Affairs, and such a departmental archdiocese would also require a vicar general, not just a vicar. Before the realization of any such administrative resolution, General Haig could be assured of intense opposition from other prelates in the cabinet and the White House with an interest in foreign policy.

As Reagan himself joked, Haig was inclined to confuse being vicar with being pope. A vicar is the bishop's chief assistant in the administration of diocesan affairs. His ecclesiastical authority emanates from the bishop, and what power the vicar wields depends on his personal relationship with the bishop. Haig seemed to forget that Reagan did not abdicate his presidential responsibility for the conduct of foreign affairs when he designated the secretary of state as his "chief spokesman and adviser," and the White House staff was there to provide constant reminders of who was still president.[53] In fact, Reagan had granted Haig a broader swath of foreign policy making authority than any secretary of state had enjoyed since Dulles. Like Eisenhower's secretary of state, however, Haig should have been more solicitous of the president and more conscious of how his assistants would react to exorbitant claims to foreign policy making power. Prerogatives are not power, and power is not indivisible. Haig might have had the reality of policy-making power even without the formalities; by insisting on an unattainable status, he lost the president's confidence, which was his real power as vicar from the start.

The administration of foreign policy in the Carter and Reagan administrations highlighted the difficulty of the problem of determining the primacy of the secretary of state as against the national security adviser. Brzezinski has argued that a "secretarial" model of foreign policy making, in which responsibility for direction and coordination is vested in the secretary of state, is clearly inferior to a "presidential" model, in which these tasks are performed by the as-

52. *Ibid.*
53. At a State Department dinner given in honor of Secretary of State Shultz, Dean Rusk observed, "Dean Acheson once remarked that in the relations between a President and a Secretary of State, it was always of the greatest importance that each of them understand at all times which one is President." "State Department According to Rusk," New York *Times*, February 11, 1984.

sistant to the president for national security affairs. To Brzezinski, three reasons necessitate a presidential model: First, in an age of dramatic global crises "the nerve center for national security is bound to be increasingly the White House"; second, foreign policy requires the integration of diplomacy, defense, intelligence, and international economics, whereas the State Department is concerned largely with diplomatic issues alone; and third, coordination is more effectively realized if attempted from the White House, which is better able to rise above narrow bureaucratic concerns than a cabinet department.[54] In sum, pretense that the secretary of state can serve as the chief architect of foreign policy should be given up; only a White House official close to the president can pull all the competing bureaucratic interests together.

Brzezinski's proposal has aspects of special pleading about it, since it can be seen as a justification for his own actions in the messy battle over control of foreign policy making during the Carter administration. Various models of the relationship among the president, secretary of state, and national security adviser will be analyzed in Chapter 9, along with several proposals for reforming the foreign policy making process. It be observed here, however, that no proposal for restructuring the policy-making process can be effective unless it suits the president's decision-making preferences. A strong secretary of state can be in full command when he is diplomatically knowledgeable and also enjoys the full confidence of the president, as with Dulles and Eisenhower; in such a situation it is less likely that the national security assistant will attempt to maximize his power potential. In other situations, the national security assistant will seek to expand his power at the expense of the secretary of state and with the concurrence of the president, such as happened with Bundy versus Rusk under Johnson. Alternatively, there will be a constant battle to control the president in situations where the chief executive does not, or cannot, choose an appropriate model, which is what occurred under Carter and Reagan.[55] There is simply no substitute for a presi-

54. Brzezinski, *Power and Principle*, 533–35. To legitimate the assistant's central role in coordination, Brzezinski thinks that the office should be subject to Senate confirmation. *Ibid.*, 536.
55. Margaret Wyszomirski, "The De-Institutionalization of Presidential Staff Agencies," *Public Administration Review*, XLII (September, 1982), 453; Stanley Hoffman, "In Search of a Foreign Policy," *New York Review of Books*, September 29, 1983, p. 51.

dent sufficiently knowledgeable and sure of himself to set policy and to determine how he wants to structure the policy-making process.

Haig's ambition to be the vicar of American foreign policy failed because he lacked the institutional resources to counter opposition from the senior White House staff, the personal characteristics that would have enabled him to function in situations of administrative ambiguity, and, most important, the presidential support that would have enabled him to consolidate control over the policy-making process. Alexander Haig's failure, however, was more basically Ronald Reagan's, because it is a presidential obligation to create and control a decision-making system. By not delegating to someone responsibility for the day-to-day conduct of the nation's global strategy and by allowing a debilitating bureaucratic war to wage unabated, Reagan became liable to the criticism that his foreign policy, like Carter's, was uncoordinated and directionless. "The problem posed by the lack of machinery to coordinate foreign policy effectively is compounded by the persistent failure to spell out a coherent international strategy," as *U.S. News and World Report* put it. The debacle in Lebanon, arguably the worst foreign policy disaster for the United States since Iran, pointed up the disarray in the decision-making process. Administration officials delivered confusing and often contradictory statements raising questions about who was in charge and what American objectives really were. Most important, it also dramatized the consequences for foreign policy of a disengaged president and badly coordinated advisers. "There is a total absence of decisionmaking at the top," complained one bewildered Defense Department official. "I've never seen anything like this. It's scary."[56]

A New Equilibrium in Foreign Policy Making

The Reagan administration could justifiably lay claim to a series of significant foreign policy successes.[57] Besides an overall greater asser-

56. *U.S. News and World Report*, May 11, 1981, p. 29; "The Price of Failure," *Newsweek*, February 27, 1984, p. 15.
57. See Robert W. Tucker, "Toward a New Detente," *New York Times Magazine*, December 9, 1984, pp. 70–71ff. For a sharply contrasting evaluation, see William D. Anderson and Sterling J. Kernek, "How Realistic is Reagan's Diplomacy?" *Political Science Quarterly*, C (Fall, 1985), 389–409.

tiveness in the defense of American global interests, Reagan's supporters could point to a renewed parity in Soviet-American strategic weaponry, the successful invasion of Grenada, the relative stability of the Duarte government in El Salvador, good relations with the Western European defense community, further normalization of relations with China as signified by the president's trip there, and a Middle Eastern situation that might easily have been much more. Unquestionably, however, the unseemly displays that characterized Haig's disputes with the White House damaged the administration's credibility in foreign policy making. The impression lingered of a rudderless ship of state with an indifferent captain and officers on the bridge unable to share authority or steer a straight course.

The perception of a presidency on "automatic pilot" in the conduct of foreign affairs made the Reagan administration very sensitive about any situation that seemed to suggest the absence of firm presidential control. Yet, Haig's departure did not guarantee instant harmony among the Reagan's foreign policy makers. A well-publicized feud simmered between Caspar Weinberger and George Shultz, the secretary of state's style raised questions about his ability to assert control over foreign policymaking, and the role of the national security advisor needed to be defined. The emergence of Robert McFarlane as an honest broker among the competing factions within the administration was particularly important for restoring some order to the foreign policy making process.

Disputes between the secretary of state and the secretary of defense were hardly unique to Shultz and Weinberger. For example, Secretary of State Henry Kissinger and Secretary of Defense James R. Schlesinger were frequently at odds over relations with the Soviet Union during the Ford administration. Nor, as bureaucratic wars go, were the Shultz-Weinberger battles particularly bloody.[58] Indeed, much of the fighting took place by proxy, especially the struggle over arms-control strategy waged between the Assistant Secretary of State for European Affairs Richard Burt and Assistant Secretary of Defense for International Security Affairs Richard N. Perle.[59] In the end Shultz

58. Philip Taubman, "The Shultz-Weinberger Feud," *New York Times Magazine,* April 14, 1985, p. 81.

59. "The war of the two Richards" figures prominently in Strobe Talbott, *Deadly Gambits: The Reagan Administration and the Stalemate in Nuclear Arms Control* (New York, 1984).

prevailed, as shown by the appointment of Paul Nitze as the secretary of state's advisor for arms-control talks and the administration's decision not to renounce the unratified SALT II agreements. These developments, which were viewed as breaking a policy impasse within the administration, were judged a defeat for Defense Secretary Weinberger and his congressional allies. Although he rode out strong pressures to resign (for his intransigence on defense spending and MX missile development, as well as on arms control), Weinberger remained in place, largely because of his long personal association with the president rather than for any political indispensability.[60]

It may be that Shultz's low-key, reserved style served him well in the sharply fought bureaucratic battles of the Reagan administration. Newspaper headlines of stories about the secretary of state's tenure are highly suggestive: WATCHING GRASS GROW, PAINT DRY AND SHULTZ WAIT; SHULTZ SCORES A BACKSTAGE VICTORY; NO HEADLINES, NO FANFARE: THIS IS SHULTZ; RETICENCE AND FOREIGN POLICY.[61] However, after Haig's combativeness and Weinberger's intractability on major international issues, Shultz's style must have seemed immensely reassuring to the senior White House staff as well as to President Reagan. What were supposed to have been liabilities—Shultz's distaste for publicity and public combativeness, his calmness (which to his critics was diffidence), and a loyalty to the president bordering on self-abnegation—proved ingredients for a successful stay at the State Department. In particular, Shultz was willing to act simply as a "senior aide"—not even a *primus inter pares*, let alone a vicar—in the foreign policy making process. He cultivated a good reputation for behind-the-scenes diplomacy, not only avoiding headlines but having all foreign policy announcements issued from the White House Press Office rather than the State Department. After the mercurial, headline-grabbing Haig and with the uncompromising and argumentative Weinberger still around, Shultz must have seemed increasingly attractive to Reagan and White House Chief of Staff Donald Regan.

Finally, it needs to be emphasized that Shultz emerged as the administration's principal foreign policy official not only because of his administrative tenacity and personal self-effacement but because of an important political alliance with the White House. As Robert

60. New York *Times*, December 6, 1984, December 10, 1984, June 11, 1985.
61. *Ibid.*, May 23, 1984, December 9, 1984, May 17, 1985, October 8, 1985.

McFarlane, the assistant for national security affairs, grew more self-assured (following widespread stories that he had been seen as a non-threatening, compromise choice) and gained President Reagan's confidence (and, not inconsequentially, Mrs. Reagan's as well), he was able to use his influence to solve many Shultz-Weinberger impasses. Moreover, as a former staff member on the Senate Armed Services Committee, Kissinger's former NSC deputy, and Haig's counselor at the State Department, McFarlane had greater experience in foreign affairs than either Shultz or Weinberger, especially on arms control and the Middle East. At first, the national security adviser was content to mediate the conflict between Shultz and Weinberger; as this proved unsuccessful, he began tilting increasingly toward the more flexible Shultz.[62] This Shultz-McFarlane axis allowed the secretary of state to emerge as the administration's premier foreign policy maker, while ensuring that the prerequisite for that preeminence was White House support.

It may have been inevitable that there would be a shift toward the State Department, given the insistent involvement by Weinberger and the Defense Department in political matters long acknowledged to be in the domain of diplomacy. Moreover, Shultz's success was largely proportionate to Weinberger's aggressiveness; as the secretary of defense became more insistent, the secretary of state appeared more reasonable. On the other hand, there were also strong personal factors in play. Both Shultz and McFarlane were cautious consensus seekers in an administration that prized team playing above all other virtues. As managers, both Shultz and McFarlane gravitated toward pragmatic solutions that could be expected to enjoy broad support; this immediately contrasted with the increasingly, and often inexplicably, doctrinaire Weinberger. Shultz also had his predecessor as an example of how not to further one's claims to speak for American foreign policy: do not claim a complete prerogative; do not assert extreme positions; do not squabble in public; do not contradict the White House; and do not seek to upstage the president. Haig—and to a lesser degree Weinberger—violated all of these precepts. Shultz operated in a manner that appeared to incorporate such precepts as personal attributes.

62. *U.S. News and World Report,* June 24, 1985, July 1, 1985, July 8, 1985; Leslie H. Gelb, "Taking Charge," *New York Times Magazine,* May 26, 1985, pp. 20–21ff.

In surrendering any pretensions to a vicarage over American foreign policy, George Shultz has defined a role for the secretary of state as part of a foreign policy team in which he and the national security advisor can maintain an approximate coequality. To designate Shultz the "minimalist" secretary of state may not be fair, but it is a diminished office and a State Department with a more subservient role than has been the case throughout most of American history. Shultz reigns by conceding to the Defense Department an equal status in arms-control and strategic policy making and by granting the national security advisor a veto over policy and ultimate authority for monitoring compliance with presidential policies. In fairness it must be said that Shultz may have salvaged the best deal possible under the circumstances, and he clearly won a hard-fought victory over Weinberger in arms negotiations. In an administration disposed to collective decision making and with a president who delegates broad authority to the departments for policy making, some sort of collegial arrangement for the management of foreign affairs, with the White House acting as umpire, was the most likely outcome. The possible fatal flaw in this system is that, if foreign policy is not simply to be the lowest common denominator of bureaucratic interests, there must be a president knowledgeable about world affairs, confident in his grasp of international politics, and possessed of a clear sense of diplomatic goals, to provide the necessary leadership. Unfortunately, such presidents seem to be rare. Indeed, in the period since World War II, perhaps only Richard Nixon, for all of his faults, approximated this admittedly idealized conception of a "diplomat in chief."

9

Conclusion

Forty years after the end of World War II, the problem that provides the central focus of this study—conflict, fragmentation, and incoherence within the executive branch on diplomatic issues—appears to be a permanent feature of the American foreign policy process. The diplomatic records of the Carter and Reagan administrations (see Chapter 8) leave little doubt that this conclusion is justified.

The effectiveness of the Carter administration's diplomacy, for example, was significantly impaired by the recurrent lack of coherence among the president and his chief foreign policy advisers in dealing with such varied issues as détente with the Soviet Union, the presence of Soviet combat troops in Cuba, the Iranian hostage crisis, and the Soviet invasion of Afghanistan. To no inconsiderable degree, the "indecisiveness" exhibited by President Carter in responding to these and other external challenges could be attributed to fundamental disagreements and conflicts among his principal aides on particular foreign policy questions. Secretary of State Cyrus Vance's resignation in April, 1980, was prompted, for example, when Carter decided over Vance's objections to undertake the ill-fated military mission to rescue the American hostages in Iran. Along with nearly every secretary of state who has served since World War II, Vance relinquished his office with feelings of disappointment and frustration growing out of the obstacles he encountered in endeavoring to restore the primacy of the State Department in the foreign policy process.[1]

1. Jimmy Carter, *Keeping Faith: Memoirs of a President* (New York, 1982), 510–20.

The experience of the Reagan administration in the foreign policy field was not fundamentally different. In its approach to foreign affairs, the Reagan White House began inauspiciously, with the widely publicized and divisive activities of Secretary of State Alexander Haig. Haig's conception of his role as vicar of American foreign policy ultimately led to his resignation, giving him one of the briefest tenures in office of any secretary of state in American history, eighteen months. His successor, George Shultz, administered the State Department more quietly and with more finesse; unlike Haig, he was usually careful to acknowledge that in the last analysis President Reagan determined the foreign policy of the United States. Shultz was also less politically ambitious and personally abrasive than his predecessor.

Yet, under Reagan, deep and recurrent divisions continued to exist within the executive branch on major foreign policy questions, and in a number of instances they posed serious impediments to American diplomatic success. The failure of the Reagan administration's diplomacy in Lebanon, for example, was a leading case in point. The coherence of governmental policy on the Lebanese question in fact was jeopardized by two primary causes of disunity. One of these was fundamental disagreement between the executive and legislative branches over the goals and methods of American diplomacy in the Middle East. As in the past, the lack of collaboration between the White House and Congress in dealing with foreign policy issues continued to pose serious problems for the United States in foreign affairs.[2]

The other ongoing source of governmental disunity in external affairs is intraexecutive conflict. This problem can, and not infrequently does, exacerbate misunderstandings and tensions between the president and Congress in the foreign policy field. Within the Reagan administration, several specific causes or manifestations of this problem could be identified. One recurrent disagreement was between the White House staff and the State Department, a conflict that did not end after Haig's replacement by Shultz. Another was policy differences between the secretary of state and the secretary of defense over the desirability, goals, and duration of American military inter-

2. See Cecil V. Crabb, Jr., and Pat Holt, *Invitation to Struggle: Congress, the President, and Foreign Policy* (2nd ed.; Washington, D.C., 1984); and John Spanier and Joseph Nogee, *Congress, the Presidency, and American Foreign Policy* (New York, 1981).

vention in Lebanon. After the intervention was carried out, differing views were expressed from time to time by executive officials over the mission of American forces in Lebanon. Still another source of intra-executive disunity was a series of statements by President Reagan and several of his high-level advisers concerning American goals in Lebanon and the precise role of the armed forces in achieving them. Basic differences also existed within the State Department regarding the underlying causes of political strife in Lebanon and America's most effective response to them.

Not untypically, after American forces were withdrawn from Lebanon in mid-February, 1984, much of the blame for the "failure" of Washington's diplomacy in the Middle East was placed upon Secretary of State Shultz and the State Department. In the weeks that followed, as other secretaries of state had often done before him, Shultz served as a lightning rod for congressional and public discontent over the Reagan administration's diplomatic activities in the Middle East. By early 1984, therefore, it was not altogether surprising that reports of Shultz's impending resignation were widespread in the news media. As was also typical, during this period the president took pains to express confidence in, and high regard for, his secretary of state.[3]

One lasting consequence of the Lebanese misadventure was to raise recurrent questions among informed observers concerning who if anyone was actually in charge of the American foreign policy process. In contrast to the experience of the Carter administration, the diplomatic setback in Lebanon did not appear to affect Reagan's personal popularity with the American people. The Great Communicator seemed impervious to the kinds of charges of diplomatic mismanagement that had destroyed Carter politically. Yet, as one commentary observed, the Lebanese case illustrated the hazardous consequences "of a foreign policy run by a disengaged president and a team of badly coordinated and overly turf-conscious advisers." The abortive Lebanese venture, this study concluded, indicated convincingly that "there is a total absence of decision making at the top."[4]

From the evidence provided by the experiences of the Reagan,

3. New York *Times*, February 3, 1984, February 9, 1984, March 3, 1984; William B. Quandt, in *ibid.*, October 27, 1983; Nicholas Von Hoffman, in Baton Rouge *Morning Advocate*, February 29, 1984.
4. *Newsweek*, February 27, 1984, pp. 15–23.

Carter, and other administrations since World War II, several conclusions about the problem of intraexecutive conflict in foreign affairs are warranted. First, the problem—which, as Chapter 3 emphasized, came to the forefront of attention during World War II—is obviously endemic in the American foreign policy process. It shows no sign of disappearing, and its existence appears to be independent of whether the White House is occupied by a Democratic or a Republican president.

Second, various proposals and remedial steps designed to eliminate or substantially mitigate the problem have thus far clearly failed to do so. These include the president's serving as his own secretary of state; designation of the secretary of state as the president's chief foreign policy adviser and spokesman; establishment of the National Security Council in 1947 and the evolution of the office of national security adviser; innumerable major and minor reorganizations of the State Department since World War II; reliance upon interdepartmental committees and various informal *ad hoc* coordinating mechanisms; and several other devices and improvisations that have sought to impart greater unity to executive branch activities in the foreign policy field. By some criteria, the problem of conflict and fragmentation within the executive branch in dealing with foreign policy questions may be more critical today than it was during the Truman and Eisenhower administrations.

Third, a number of these remedial measures—and the outstanding example perhaps is the creation and expansion of the National Security Council—have, in the popular phrase, become part of the problem. As exemplified by the career of Henry Kissinger in the Nixon and Ford administrations, the emergence of the president's national security adviser as a forceful—in Kissinger's case, a dominant—actor in the foreign policy process has introduced a new source of contention, rivalry, and jealousy among officials involved in diplomatic decision making.

Fourth, the existence of the problem of perennial and deeply ingrained disunity among executive officials concerned with foreign affairs has significant and far-reaching consequences for the role of the United States in international relations. In his classic study *Democracy in America* (1835), Alexis de Tocqueville expressed doubt that the American democratic system was inherently capable of managing foreign affairs successfully vis-à-vis autocratic, authoritarian, and (he would add today) totalitarian governments.[5] Since World War II, Tocqueville's skepticism has been reiterated by innumerable commentators on American foreign relations, especially those who are concerned about the disadvantages that a democracy faces in dealing with nondemocratic systems. In his analysis of twentieth-century American diplomacy, for example, George F. Kennan expressed doubts about the nation's ability to conduct foreign relations effectively.[6] Walter Lippmann was another influential commentator who had many comparable misgivings about the American society's ability to implement the containment policy successfully for an indefinite period of time in the future.[7] After the failure of the Reagan administration's diplomacy in Lebanon, many observers at home and abroad questioned America's staying power in behalf of a diplomatic goal that was not, and perhaps inherently could not be, achieved quickly.[8]

Before World War II—and even in the doubts expressed by more recent commentators such as Kennan and Lippmann—skepticism about American democracy's ability to conduct foreign affairs was directed primarily at two specific problems: the always difficult challenge of maintaining cooperative executive-legislative relations in the foreign policy field and the question of whether American public opinion was capable of understanding and supporting the government's diplomatic activities. These commentators were seldom concerned about conflict among the members of the president's own foreign policy team in responding to crises and challenges overseas.

In one respect, however, the existence of persistent intraexecutive disunity in foreign affairs may be an even more critical problem than the lack of harmonious executive-legislative relations or public ignorance and apathy. Formulating a unified and cohesive foreign policy position within the executive branch is an essential prerequisite for

5. Alexis de Tocqueville, *Democracy in America*, ed. Henry S. Commager (New York, 1948), 138.
6. See the implicit and explicit criticisms of the American foreign policy process in George F. Kennan, *American Diplomacy, 1900–1950* (New York, 1952).
7. Two of Walter Lippmann's numerous publications raise serious questions about America's ability to conduct foreign affairs successfully. See *The Public Philosophy* (Boston, 1955); and his critique of the containment policy in *The Cold War* (New York, 1957).
8. See the Arab reactions to the withdrawal of American armed forces from Lebanon in *Newsweek*, February 27, 1984, pp. 15–23.

constructive relations between the president and Congress on diplomatic questions; it is also a vital necessity in constructing a foundation of public acceptance and legitimacy for external policy. As Senator Vandenberg expressed it in the early postwar period, a cohesive and successful foreign policy is likely to emerge only if the United States has "one secretary of state at a time."

The Sources of Intraexecutive Disunity

The evidence presented in the preceding chapters calls attention to a number of fundamental sources of continuing disunity within the executive branch in dealing with foreign policy issues. While no effort is made here to list these causes in order of importance or priority, they can be briefly summarized.

The decline of the State Department. As observed in Chapter 2, the decline of the State Department from its once premier position in the foreign policy hierarchy is a process that began well before World War II. Indeed, some of its causes, such as long-standing American skepticism toward diplomacy and officials engaged in it, can be traced back to the colonial period.

For a number of reasons, World War II and its aftermath accelerated this decline. One potent reason, of course, was President Franklin D. Roosevelt's domination of the foreign policy process, as explained in Chapter 3. The State Department's lack of preparation for the postwar era—together with its reluctance to exert leadership in responding to postwar problems—further diminished its standing in the eyes of the president, Congress, and informed citizens. The McCarthy era in the late 1940s and early 1950s, during which the careers of a number of State Department officers were ruined and the reputations of countless officials and other public figures badly tarnished, severely impaired the department's morale and public image.

Beginning with the Korean War in 1950 and extending through the failure of the Reagan administration's diplomacy in Lebanon in 1984, the State Department has been widely blamed for a series of diplomatic reverses and fiascoes. During the 1960s, for example, next to President Lyndon B. Johnson himself, Secretary of State Dean Rusk became the primary target of anti–Vietnam War critics. To many minds, Rusk appeared to epitomize what was wrong with the Department of State. As explained more fully in Chapter 6, Rusk was a State Department traditionalist who believed that his department should be in charge of American foreign policy under the president's direction. But Rusk appeared to have neither the incentive nor the talents required to defend that principle against a growing circle of bureaucratic intruders. He also led a department in which highly diverse ideas often existed concerning America's proper course of action in Southeast Asia and other locales. For these and other reasons, during the Vietnam War he seldom gave the impression of being at the forefront of the policy-making process or of challenging prevailing orthodoxies.

After the Vietnam War, the decline of the State Department continued. As national security adviser under Presidents Nixon and Ford, Henry Kissinger, whose disdain for the State Department was legendary, emerged as the de facto secretary of state and in time combined both offices in his own person. During the 1970s, the public mood of diplomatic caution and retrenchment acted as a brake against diplomatic activism by the president and his foreign policy aides. The decade of the 1970s was also an era of strong legislative assertiveness and militancy in foreign affairs. In the light of the Vietnam fiasco, many legislators believed that Congress should be entrusted with a larger (some believed, a dominant) role in the foreign policy process. Congress, it was thought, could be counted upon to avoid "another Vietnam" and lesser diplomatic reverses. Under the Reagan administration, the widely publicized tribulations of Secretary of State Alexander Haig, culminating in his forced resignation, did not improve the public image of the State Department. Under Secretary of State Shultz, the difficulties encountered in achieving American diplomatic objectives in Western Europe, Latin America, the Middle East, and other settings likewise did little to enhance the department's image or to inspire confidence about its performance as a key actor in the diplomatic decision-making process.

Accused by left-wing critics of exhibiting a congenital opposition to communism and to radical political change abroad and by right-wing critics for failing to devise a "winning" diplomatic strategy for the United States, the State Department continues to lack a stable and influential domestic constituency that will champion its cause.

Indeed, its constituency base is probably narrower today than it was at the end of World War II.

Changes in the international system. The State Department's decline as the agency incontestably in charge of American foreign policy is related to another phenomenon—fundamental changes in the international system since World War II.

When the United Nations was created in 1945 and established the following year, 51 nations served as founding members of the organization (most of the former Axis powers were initially excluded from membership). By the 1980s, the United States maintained diplomatic relations with approximately 160 independent nations.

The international system has not only changed in size; it has become infinitely more complex and diverse than was true in 1945. Among the Big Five that largely created the UN and formulated the peace that ended World War II—the Soviet Union, the United Kingdom, France, China, and the United States—there were four Western nations (and China was in effect only an honorary member of this select group). With the process of decolonization and the emergence of the Third World, mankind's attention has now become focused upon a wide range of novel and difficult problems for which Western ideas and experience often seem irrelevant or poorly adapted.

The State Department and other executive agencies in the United States, therefore, have been compelled to give attention to a growing number of states belonging to the contemporary international system. At the same time, they have been required to reorder American diplomatic priorities to take account of the dominant interests and concerns of this still-expanding international system. As most of the Third World members of the system see it, achieving their goals will require renewed American interest in, and new levels of American assistance to, these countries in the years ahead.

The new international agenda. One of the most crucial factors engendering disunited efforts within the executive branch regarding foreign policy issues is the changing nature of the international agenda in the postwar period. By the "agenda" is meant those issues that are at the forefront of global and regional concern and that require responses in the form of policies and programs by the members of the international system.

Today, "foreign affairs" embrace a multitude of activities and programs by governments that were often unknown or relatively un-important in the pre–World War II era. In addition to the customary political and economic issues with which governments have long been concerned, foreign affairs now include cultural, propaganda, informational, and related activities, as illustrated by the Voice of America radio broadcasts and faculty- and student-exchange programs; foreign military, economic, and technical assistance programs; efforts to stabilize the price levels of global commodities and to regulate the value of major currencies; "alliance maintenance" or membership in regional defense pacts and efforts to strengthen the alliance's cohesion and defense capabilities; ties among many of the world's labor unions and movements; relations with multinational corporations, whose activities cut across national frontiers; efforts to solve global and regional environmental problems often involving collaboration among several agencies of the American and other governments; and space programs that frequently have major international political and military implications. Almost every year, some new item is added to the ever-growing international agenda.

These developments have had a three-fold impact on the American foreign policy process. First, as never before, the new international agenda has drawn established executive departments and agencies into the process of foreign policy decision making. As the State Department has often viewed the matter, the circle of foreign policy "kibitzers" has been too greatly enlarged. In some cases—as in the Agriculture Department's key role in the Food-for-Peace Program—these agencies exercise a potent influence upon the foreign policy process in the United States.

Second, the contemporary international agenda has resulted in the creation of a host of new executive agencies, many of which have significant international responsibilities. Postwar administrative units such as the CIA and other agencies that comprise the complex "intelligence community," the Arms Control and Disarmament Agency, the United States Information Agency (USIA), the Department of Health and Human Services, the Department of Transportation, the Department of Energy, the Drug Enforcement Agency—these are only some of the administrative units created since World War II whose responsibilities have significant international dimensions.

Third, the new international agenda has in turn largely eroded the traditional distinction between foreign and domestic affairs. Today, these two realms are no longer separate and distinguishable. As the Johnson administration discovered during the Vietnam War, for example, a massive overseas commitment by the United States has momentous domestic consequences. America's involvement in the war largely prevented LBJ from achieving the Great Society program to which his administration was committed; it generated new inflationary pressures for the American economy; and it had several crucial consequences for the American political system—not excluding Johnson's own political repudiation and demise. The boycott on petroleum shipments imposed by the oil-producing states of the Middle East in 1973 had comparable domestic implications for the American society.[9]

The "domesticization" of the American foreign policy process, therefore, is another postwar tendency eroding the traditional role of the State Department in foreign relations. It has induced growing fragmentation in the executive branch's efforts to formulate and administer a unified foreign policy for the United States.

The impossible demands of the American presidency. Another tendency contributing to intraexecutive disunity and fragmentation in foreign affairs has attracted renewed concern by political scientists and other informed students of American government in recent years. This is the nature and responsibilities of the presidential office in the United States. In the contemporary period—and no reason exists for believing that significant improvement will occur in the years ahead—the presidential office is widely viewed as an "impossible" position, exceeding the capabilities of any single individual to perform adequately. The mounting burdens of the presidency have produced a situation today that is almost guaranteed to result in public disillusionment and dissatisfaction with the performance of the incumbent.[10]

9. The domestic impact of the Vietnam War, including the extent to which it gravely impaired President Johnson's commitment to creating the Great Society, is a major theme of David Halberstam, *The Best and the Brightest* (New York, 1983).

10. For more detailed analysis see Theodore C. Sorensen, *A Different Kind of Presidency* (New York, 1984); Robert S. Hirschfield (ed.), *The Powers of the Presidency: Concepts and Controversy* (2nd ed.; Chicago, 1973); Thomas E. Cronin (ed.), *Rethinking the Presidency* (Boston, 1982); Thomas E. Cronin and Rexford G. Tugwell (eds.), *The Presidency Reappraised* (2nd ed.; New York, 1977).

This tendency obviously has direct and significant implications for the problem of intraexecutive disunity in foreign policy. One effect of it, for example, is that few chief executives now have the time or the stamina required to become well informed about even a small number of the nearly 160 nations belonging to the international system. As Chapter 3 emphasized, President Franklin D. Roosevelt was determined to serve as his own secretary of state, but this was a time when the international system consisted of approximately one-third as many members as it does today. Presidents Kennedy and Johnson were the most recent chief executives who were prone to follow FDR's example. Kennedy of course did not complete a full presidential term. The results in Johnson's case do not provide reassurance that a president's serving as his own secretary of state is an approach that promotes the diplomatic and security interests of the United States. The Vietnam War was a conspicuous diplomatic failure for America, and this outcome had many negative consequences for LBJ's domestic programs. Johnson's own knowledge of foreign affairs was severely limited, and he never succeeded in creating an advisory system that supplied him with accurate and objective information about the course of the Vietnam War and certain other major developments in foreign relations. His foreign policy was therefore judged a failure by the American people.

Any incumbent American president must delegate a large share of his responsibilities in both domestic and foreign affairs to his advisers and subordinates while reserving for himself the power to serve as the "ultimate decider" in both policy realms. The question then becomes: What forms or patterns of such delegation and policy coordination will produce wise, effective, and unified policy decisions by the executive branch? We shall return to that fundamental and difficult question.

Congressional assertiveness in foreign relations. Especially since the Vietnam War, another phenomenon—congressional assertiveness in the foreign policy field—has contributed to intraexecutive differences in foreign affairs. In the light of the Vietnam debacle, Congress has forcefully asserted its prerogatives in external affairs. Many members of the House and Senate are determined to prevent another "imperial president" from leading the nation astray diplomatically and in the process deceiving or manipulating Congress to achieve his goals. In the view of many legislators today, a transcendent lesson of the Vietnam conflict was that congressional insights and judgments about complex foreign policy questions must be carefully considered by executive officials before important diplomatic decisions are arrived at and announced publicly. In some cases Congress appears determined to make or decide the foreign policy of the United States.

Diplomatic assertiveness by Congress since the Vietnam War has provided new opportunities and avenues for executive agencies to take their case to Capitol Hill and to develop close links with a growing list of congressional committees active in the foreign policy field. For many years, certain executive agencies have had close and continuing ties with committees of the House and Senate, such as the Defense Department has had with the House and Senate Armed Services committees. Such connections have grown in the recent period, as nearly every major committee of Congress has assumed responsibilities in the sphere of foreign relations. If their positions and bureaucratic interests are not sympathetically considered by the State Department or the White House, executive agencies may now "appeal" their cases to the legislative branch, where they are likely to find one or more committees receptive to their viewpoints.

In their mood of diplomatic activism, many legislators welcome evidence of divisiveness within the executive branch on foreign policy questions. Such fragmentation provides members of the House and Senate with ready-made opportunities to gain allies for their particular foreign policy orientations. The existence of such divisions also inevitably weakens the position of the president in dealing with Congress on diplomatic questions.

The "institutionalization" of executive conflict. Finally, in explaining the recurrence of intraexecutive branch conflict in foreign affairs, full account must be taken of the degree to which the forces generating such conflict have tended to become "institutionalized" and perhaps self-perpetuating since World War II. Fundamental policy and sharp personal disagreements by executive officials involved in foreign policy decision making have been given momentum in some measure by the growth of the executive bureaucracy in the postwar period; by the crucial importance of foreign policy, not only for the American people but for the world and the destiny of the planet; and by the natural inclination of high-level bureaucrats to advance their personal ambitions, to expand their power and influence of their agencies, and to engage in bureaucratic in-fighting to protect their turf.

These tendencies have been most graphically illustrated by the establishment and evolution of the National Security Council, whose director serves as the president's national security adviser. As explained in Chapters 3–6, the role of the National Security Council in the Ameican foreign policy process was relatively limited from the Truman to the Johnson administrations. In recent years, the two best-known directors of the NSC, Henry Kissinger under the Nixon and Ford administrations and Zbigniew Brzezinski under the Carter administration, have aggressively advanced their influence and that of the NSC staff.

During Kissinger's tenure as national security adviser, the NSC in fact became a "rival State Department," and his influence upon the foreign policy process greatly eclipsed that of Secretary of State William Rogers, who had been chosen by President Nixon because he would be a weak head of the State Department. Kissinger possessed the qualities required to compete successfully against the State Department and to win worldwide recognition as the Nixon administration's leading foreign policy spokesman. He had impeccable academic credentials and was extremely well informed on the history and theory of modern diplomacy. He was highly articulate and persuasive in presenting his ideas. He had a strong ego and much ambition, and he was skillful in bureaucratic intrigue and manipulation. Perhaps most important, he enjoyed the confidence of President Nixon and had almost unlimited access to the Oval Office. His physical proximity to the presidential office conferred advantages upon him that rivals were unable to match. Under these conditions, Kissinger and the National Security Council had little difficulty displacing the State Department as the most influential executive agency involved in foreign policy decision making in the early 1970s. Brzezinski, when serving as national security adviser under Carter, tried unsuccessfully to emulate Kissinger. On the other hand, Brzezinski was still in office at the end of the Carter presidency, after Vance, a far more experienced and formidable adversary than Rogers, had resigned in protest.

Recent diplomatic events provide ample evidence of the opportunities that exist within the executive branch for the emergence of a "rival State Department." Given the right combination of personalities, administrative structure, and opportunities, other agencies can (and do) contest the centrality of the State Department's historic role of diplomatic leadership. It should be noted that the NSC's challenge to the State Department was undertaken from an administrative base created since World War II. Theoretically, the National Security Council and its staff were established to serve as a high-level coordinating mechanism, whereby diplomatic and military components of external policy were to be successfully blended into a unified "national security policy" for the United States. In theory, the chief executive should perform this function if he has the ability and inclination. When the president is unwilling or unable to coordinate national policy, however, then a new source of intraexecutive disunity is injected into the foreign policy process.

Patterns of American Foreign Policy Making

Throughout this study we have made and reiterated the point that the postwar American foreign policy process has become increasingly characterized by an absence of unity and cohesion. The president is the ultimate foreign policy decision maker, and he comes to his decisions nearly always after consultation with one or more advisers. From one administration to another, the nature of these policy-making interactions varies widely, especially the relative influence and effectiveness of the primary actors themselves. The character of intraexecutive branch relations in the various administrations studied in Chapters 3–8 may be conveniently summarized in a typology and graphically represented by schematic diagrams like the one below. The diagram of each type, or pattern, of foreign policy making will indicate the relative influence of the three principal actors in the executive branch who are involved in the process: the president (P), the secretary of state (S), and the White House assistant for national security affairs (N).

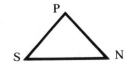

Attached to the symbol for each actor will be a rating that represents our judgment of the individual's overall influence in the foreign policy process at the end of his term of office. Detailed item-by-item ratings assigned to the key actors for each administration are included in the Appendix. The ratings assigned for each type depicted in the diagrams in the chapter are *overall scores* representing a summation of the appropriate criteria for each major actor. The ratings and their symbols are:

− −	very weak
−	weak
O	average
+	strong
+ +	very strong
N.A.	not applicable

These ratings are not intended as evaluations of the diplomatic success or effectiveness of the particular administration concerned. They are intended only to convey graphically the relative influence of each actor in the decision-making process, from dominance to ineffectualness. It should also be noted that, as with all summary representations, a certain oversimplification is involved, particularly in the reduction of the principal actors to only three. In previous chapters, it has been noted on several occasions that a major difficulty in arriving at and maintaining a coherent foreign policy is the multiplicity of actors involved—for example, the CIA director and the UN ambassador; often the secretaries of commerce and the treasury and even agriculture; and increasingly since World War II, the secretary of defense. We would argue that, with rare exceptions, the official roles in the foreign policy making process of all but the latter official are either peripheral or ancillary. Moreover, only two secretaries of defense have sustained a long involvement with American foreign policy making, and both situations have been peculiar. Robert McNamara was a key figure in the conduct of the Vietnam War, and Caspar Weinberger has been a keen advocate in the Reagan administration for advanced strategic weapons such as the MX and "Star Wars" systems. Both were concerned with national defense—the ability to project force—rather than the broader issues of foreign policy.

In the postwar era secretaries of defense have often argued and contended for a broader role for the Pentagon in foreign policy making. There is no question that for cases in which military operations or weapons systems are involved, the Defense Department will inevitably play a major decision-making role. This was certainly the case with McNamara and, to some extent, with Weinberger, too. But diplomacy, at least as traditionally conceived, has not normally been a province of the secretary of defense, and his involvement will be considered here only as it affects the roles of the principal actors.

On the other hand, it is now beyond question that the president's assistant for national security will play a leading role in American foreign policy making. One of the inescapable conclusions about the past few decades has been the gradual, inexorable, and seemingly irreversible rise of this presidential assistant to the status of an influential actor in foreign affairs. Lacking the institutional prerogatives of a cabinet chief, but not burdened by institutional interests, the White House national security adviser has frequently emerged as the secretary of state's most aggressive competitor for influence. Since 1947 successive national security assistants have found that their proximity and access to the president is an asset equal to the historical prestige of the secretary of state and the traditional expectations about his diplomatic duties. The success of either actor depends largely on his relationship with the president and the president's conception of his own foreign policy making role.

Employing a typology to explain the problem of executive disunity in the formulation and administration of foreign affairs obviously has certain defects and shortcomings. A typology can in no sense account for all influential sources of intraexecutive policy incoherence, such as those created by personality idiosyncrasies or the impact of crucial developments abroad (the impact of the Soviet invasion of Afghanistan, for example, on President Carter's attitudes toward Moscow). In addition, the formulation of specific criteria by which to evaluate the influence of major foreign policy actors entails subjective and arbitrary judgments with which some well-informed students of postwar American diplomacy might well disagree. Moreover, it is acknowledged freely that any typology does not adequately differentiate between two quite dissimilar situations—peacetime and wartime—

which can fundamentally affect the relationship existing among the key actors.

A typology inevitably oversimplifies reality. In practice, as each of the case studies showed, the foreign policy process involves many major and minor actors. Sometimes an official not represented here, such as Secretary of Defense McNamara, may have considerable influence in foreign policy decision making. A significant role may also be played by informal advisers, who have been relied upon at some point by nearly every chief executive since World War II. Examples are Clark Clifford and Averell Harriman. As former Secretary of State Dean Rusk has observed, a president is free even "to consult his chauffeur" in arriving at foreign policy decisions if he desires.

This leads to another caveat. For each of the primary actors involved in the foreign policy process—the president, the secretary of state, and the national security adviser—seven criteria have been formulated and employed to arrive at a reasonable approximation of their influence in diplomatic decision making during the administrations examined in the case studies (see Table 3). For the purposes of calculation and comparability, the criteria are identical for comparable actors throughout the postwar period. But there are two problems presented by this approach. One is that the typology makes no attempt to determine or take account of the relative importance of each criterion. Experience since World War II, for example, has demonstrated convincingly, however, that the determination of the president to inject himself actively and directly into the foreign policy field can—and probably will—be the most decisive fact in determining the pattern of executive relationships related to foreign affairs during his administration. Compared with the impact of this factor, many of the other criteria on the list may be of relatively minor importance.

The other admonition is highlighted by recalling former Secretary of State Dean Acheson's observation that, in the final analysis, the wellsprings of American foreign policy are "unknown and unknowable." The implication of Acheson's judgment is that the question of precisely how and why an incumbent president decides to adopt a specific policy in foreign affairs may often be unanswerable—even by the president himself. Why, and exactly when, for example, did Presi-

Table 3   Criteria Used to Evaluate the
Influence of the Major Diplomatic Actors

The President
   Active involvement in foreign policy decision making
   Support given to the secretary of state; prevention of policy incoherence
   Background in foreign affairs
   Negotiating skill
   Ability to influence public opinion
   Ability to influence Congress
   Prestige abroad

The Secretary of State
   Support received from the president
   Background in foreign affairs
   Political assets
   Administration of the State Department
   Ability to influence public opinion
   Rapport and influence with Congress
   Skills for bureaucratic in-fighting

The National Security Adviser
   Relations with the president
   Desire to play an active policy-making role
   Ability to articulate foreign policy and influence public opinion
   Background in foreign affairs
   Belief that the State Department is weak, that a policy vacuum exists
   Skills for bureaucratic in-fighting and desire to enlarge the NSC's role
   Management of NSC

dent Truman decide to adopt a firm policy toward the Soviet Union? Why did President Johnson make his apparently unshakable decision to achieve victory in Vietnam, and why did he hold to it for so long, even in the face of accumulating evidence that achieving the goal was impossible?

The general answer applicable to these and many other questions is that, with the assistance of their formal and informal advisers, presidents arrive at their foreign policy decisions over time as a result of the interplay of a number of influences and factors motivating them, not excluding domestic political calculations, their own unique administrative styles, and such irrational and emotional forces as their own ego involvement in particular diplomatic alternatives. It is probably impossible for any typology of diplomatic decision making that is applied uniformly to several post–World War II administrations to reflect these realities adequately.

But even with these limitations, using a typology contributes to a more informed understanding of the recurring problem of intraexecutive disunity and incoherence in the sphere of American foreign relations. A formal construct like a typology calls attention to the fact, for example, that on the basis of some forty years' experience since World War II, certain definable patterns of relationships among the major executive actors in the foreign policy process may be discerned. It is not unreasonable to expect that these patterns or this particular combination of relationships may reemerge in the future. Moreover, insofar as students of the American system believe that one pattern is preferable to others, the first step in endeavoring to eliminate or mitigate the problem of executive incoherence in American foreign relations is to identify clearly the diverse relationships among foreign policy actors that have appeared since World War II and to call attention to the principal consequences and implications of each pattern identifed. Our typology is offered in an effort to achieve that goal.

In the series of types portrayed in Figures 1–6, it will be noted that the usual policy-making relationship is triangular—involving presidents, secretaries of state, and national security advisers. Exceptions to this pattern exist in certain situations involving the national security adviser. In the Roosevelt administration, the position did not exist. In some cases, such as that of Sidney Souers under President Truman, the national security adviser has been almost anonymous; in other situations, several individuals have held the position—Robert Cutler, Gordon Gray, and Dillon Anderson in the Eisenhower administration, for example. In the case of the Reagan administration, it can be argued that the position of national security adviser has been both multiple and anonymous. In each of these exceptional cases, the name of the national security adviser was not included in the model.

Figure 1   The Patriarchial Pattern: Roosevelt-Hull

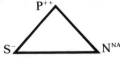

Salient characteristics of the type:

- international crises that greatly enhance executive leadership; a need for secrecy in wartime decision making
- a popular president who involves himself actively and decisively in military and diplomatic decision making
- presidential reliance upon a wide range of formal and informal advisers, with minimal liaison among them; little formal coordination of executive activities; rapid growth of the federal bureaucracy
- a secretary of state who plays a largely symbolic role in foreign relations, articulating the president's viewpoints, embodying the nation's moral principles, and cultivating relations with Congress
- a State Department whose role in the foreign policy process deteriorates and is increasingly challenged by other agencies that acquire growing responsibilities in foreign affairs
- momentous international decisions affecting the nation's future are made primarily by the president, with or without consulting his advisers; American diplomatic efforts exhibit a "dilettantish" and uninformed quality; extreme diplomatic activism may impair the president's health; but his vice-president has little preparation or training in foreign affairs

In this pattern the president serves as "his own secretary of state." President Roosevelt almost totally dominated the decision-making process in his administration. By the late 1930s, nearly every key foreign policy decision bore his personal imprint, reflected his policy preferences, and was influenced by his ideological inclinations and prejudices. Under the American constitutional system, it is of course always possible for "another FDR" to emerge, especially during wartime. Theoretically, any president is free to serve as his own secretary of state, and since World War II some, such as President Kennedy, have clearly emulated FDR's example. A president should do so, however, only in full awareness of what were perhaps certain inevitable consequences of FDR's approach: inadequate American preparation for crucial international negotiations with foreign governments, several ill-considered diplomatic agreements and understandings, serious neglect of the State Department with an ensuing decline in its influence, and a heavy physical and psychological toll exacted on the president himself.

Figure 2   The Classical Pattern: Truman-Acheson

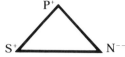

Salient characteristics of the type:

- major diplomatic challenges cause growing public concern about future international stability
- a president who is inadequately prepared for diplomatic leadership but who, after consultation with his advisers, is determined to make final decisions in foreign affairs
- a well-qualified and forceful secretary of state, who is determined to maintain State Department primacy in foreign relations; he keeps the president fully and frequently informed about diplomatic developments; the president in turn supports and defends his secretary of state
- the secretary of state manages his department capably and consults with highly qualified State Department subordinates; he defends the department from bureaucratic rivals and attacks from political opponents
- the president's national security adviser plays a nominal and relatively insignificant role in decision making
- several crucial policies and programs adopted and successfully implemented in foreign affairs; there is an unusually high degree of bipartisan collaboration in the diplomatic field and a low level of executive dissonance and policy incoherence in foreign relations

This pattern recognizes the constitutional authority of the president as ultimate decision maker while clearly vesting responsibility for the conduct of foreign relations in the secretary of state and the State Department. Time and again, President Truman expressed his desire that Secretary of State Acheson manage foreign relations, and when necessary the chief executive invoked the power of his office to enforce this maxim against challengers. An extremely high degree of confidence and rapport existed between Truman and Acheson. In turn, the secretary of state relied upon a corps of experienced and talented subordinates to provide creative ideas and policy proposals that were uniquely responsive to external challenges confronting the United States in the early postwar era. This pattern is associated with perhaps the most diplomatically creative period of post–World War II American foreign relations. It has not been witnessed since the Truman administration—and may never be witnessed again.

Figure 3   The Personalistic Pattern: Eisenhower-Dulles

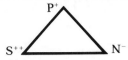

Salient characteristics of the type:

- a president who possesses great popularity and prestige, who has military expertise and experience in public affairs, though not much in foreign affairs; he delegates responsibility for managing foreign affairs to the secretary of state while making ultimate policy decisions himself
- the secretary of state is personally admired and respected by the president and has high level of knowledge and background in foreign affairs; he has close ties with members of the president's political party; he preserves a close rapport and communicates frequently with the president on foreign policy issues
- the secretary of state appears to be minimally interested in the State Department's institutional role in policy making; the Foreign Service plays only a tangential decision-making role; morale within the State Department declines sharply
- the national security adviser serves mainly as a policy facilitator and expediter, maintaining a low profile in the foreign policy process
- few innovative diplomatic undertakings or expansion of American commitments abroad; American policy has a high "moralistic" content; established policies are largely continued

This pattern can be found in the successful relationship between President Eisenhower and Secretary of State Dulles. Because Eisenhower chose not to involve himself directly in day-to-day foreign policy making, Dulles' preeminent position was both desired and defined by the chief executive. But there was never any question about who was in command of American foreign relations. Dulles never forgot that it was Eisenhower's foreign policy. He carefully courted the president's confidence, followed his directions, and kept him fully informed about the specifics of policy formulation and execution. Dulles' personal power was great, but it was due to his standing with Eisenhower and did not carry over to the State Department. Dulles was relatively indifferent to the concerns and morale of the Foreign Service and uninterested in matters of departmental administration. His administration of the State Department was as personalistic as was his domination of foreign affairs. Dulles was the model of a dominant secretary of state, whereas Acheson stood for a dominant State Department. Dulles' tenure marked the beginning of a dramatic decline in the State Department's institutional influence and professional prestige.

Figure 4   The Consensual Pattern: Johnson-Rusk-Bundy/Rostow

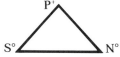

Salient characteristics of the type:

- a president who enters office without a strong personal mandate and perhaps overshadowed by a popular predecessor; he has little background or interest in foreign affairs and is heavily dependent upon his advisers and values unity among them
- an escalating, costly, and traumatic limited-war situation in a region poorly understood by official and public opinion in America
- a secretary of state with extensive diplomatic and military experience, whose main rival is a capable and forceful secretary of defense, and who has little skill and inclination for bureaucratic in-fighting
- the secretary of state relies upon and consults his State Department subordinates, but does little to maintain the overall primacy of his department in bureaucratic rivalries and the decision-making process
- the president's national security advisers emerge as informed and influential aides; they are protective of the president and seek to shield him from uncongenial and dissident ideas
- the pattern of intraexecutive relations promotes "groupthink" and enforced unanimity among key participants; there is a growing level of congressional and public disaffection with course of the war; the administration's diplomacy eventually loses legitimacy and is repudiated by public opinion and Congress

This pattern is associated with the Johnson administration's policies during the Vietnam War. President Johnson inherited a diplomatic commitment that he felt it was his duty to honor. As America's presence in Southeast Asia escalated, so did the military component of external policy: as in World War II, military considerations were accorded high priority while the war was in progress, and these were forcefully asserted by a persuasive and aggressive secretary of defense. Yet the Pentagon's analyses of developments in Southeast Asia proved increasingly faulty. An inordinate desire for unity among the president's advisers meant that in practice dissenting viewpoints were discouraged, if not suppressed. "Groupthink" became the basis of decision making. Dissent took the form of policy "defections" by key officials and leaks to the press. In time, the administration's diplomatic course in Southeast Asia lost public acceptance and the American presence in Southeast Asia was liquidated.

Figure 5 The Palace Guard Pattern: Nixon-Rogers-Kissinger

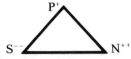

Salient characteristics of the type:

- a president who endeavors to end an unpopular war and to avoid commitments likely to lead to new diplomatic failures
- the president is reasonably well informed about and interested in foreign affairs and determined to play a crucial role in reformulation of American foreign policy
- the president is distrustful of the State Department and desires to center diplomatic decision making in the White House
- the secretary of state has no discernible background or qualifications in foreign affairs; he is chosen because he will be a weak head of the State Department
- the national security adviser is a highly knowledgeable, ambitious, and articulate aide who holds strong views about American policy; he has little confidence in State Department and uses his proximity to the president and his talents to become *de facto* secretary of state, with the president's explicit and implicit support
- there are several substantive achievements in foreign affairs; the national security adviser emerges as dominant actor in the policy process, but criticism of his role mounts in Congress; the president's position and prestige are fatally impaired by a domestic political crisis

In considering foreign affairs his strong suit, Richard Nixon was not a typical president. He was determined to exercise control over the formulation and execution of foreign policy from the White House. Moreover, his psychological needs and political methods dictated a policy-making process dominated by a few trusted advisers—a White House "Palace Guard." With his "rival State Department" in the West Wing of the White House, National Security Adviser Henry Kissinger personally initiated and managed the momentous shift in American foreign policy represented by détente and the normalization of relations with China. Kissinger's succession as secretary of state was simply a *de jure* recognition of a *de facto* reality established early in the Nixon administration. He was not only the most active and influential national security assistant to date, but he transformed the office from a staff position with limited advisory powers to one with major operational responsibilities. On the other hand, the atmosphere was so conspiratorial as to give rise to great fears about constitutional accountability. The Palace Guard, of which Kissinger was a key commander, led to criticism that Nixon's was an "imperial presidency," criticisms that eventually compromised the administration's foreign policy.

Figure 6 The Anarchical Pattern: Reagan-Haig

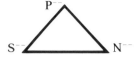

Salient characteristics of the type:
- the president enters office after pledging to reverse America's declining diplomatic and military fortunes abroad
- the president has poor preparation in, and understanding of, foreign affairs and is heavily dependent upon his advisers, permitting high degree of policy dissonance among them
- the secretary of state is moderately well informed in foreign affairs and is determined to preside over American foreign policy making under the president's direction; he is often politically maladroit and antagonizes other presidential advisers
- the national security adviser has little or no background in the foreign policy field; yet he often has strong ideological viewpoints and seeks to protect the president from assertive advisers and unwelcome ideas
- some substantive achievements occur, but in general, there is a series of foreign policy setbacks and failures; the administration of foreign relations gives the impression of uncertainty among executive officials and continuing policy incoherence

"Anarchical" is a highly negative assessment of an administration's foreign policy. However, the open warfare between Secretary of State Alexander Haig and the Reagan White House seriously endangered the administration's international and domestic credibility. Especially since the president expressed little interest in foreign affairs, the decision-making structure could not have been much worse; it led to a recurring pattern of dissonance and disunity within the executive branch. With the secretary of state trying to act like a foreign policy "vicar," the White House staff quickly saw a threat to the president's political prestige. Without a strong national security adviser as an enemy, the secretary of state was emboldened to try to assert complete control over foreign policy. The White House staff was determined that Reagan should be pope and exercise his authority over the meddlesome Haig. After eighteen months, Haig finally resigned. While claiming to emulate Dulles as secretary of state, he seems not to have understood the personalistic nature of Dulles' success. In addition, foreign policy making may have grown too complex for supervision by a cabinet secretary, and so politicized as to call for a personal presidential assistant rather than an accountable departmental secretary.

The Future of Foreign Policy Making

All of the types presented are admittedly approximations of a more complex foreign policy making reality. Constructing even the simplest typology also doubtless reveals the presence of personal preferences held by the authors concerning foreign policy making. Especially given the highly negative assessment that was offered of the Reagan administration, it should be stressed that such assessments are of the *process* of foreign policy making, not the substantive content of the policy.[11] For example, the Carter administration has a strong claim to designation as "quasi-anarchistic," with its pattern of indecisiveness, intraexecutive branch disunity, and resultant lack of credibility. Bad policy making is not the product of any particular foreign policy approach. In both the Carter and Reagan administrations, however, presidents were unable or unwilling to impose a preferred alternative, and presidential direction is a crucial element in sound foreign policy making.

Given the fragmentation, competitiveness, and lack of cohesiveness demonstrated in the case studies, proposals for structural reform of the foreign policy making process have recurred with considerable regularity in the post–World War II period. As I. M. Destler has said, "Few problems have been probed as often since World War II as that of organizing our government for coherent and purposive foreign policy." In 1972 he cited thirteen major studies or proposals that have sought, often with some form of official sponsorship, to restructure the government to facilitate a more effective system for the formulation and administration of foreign affairs.[12] Although reorganization

11. The record of the Reagan administration in foreign policy, of course, has not been without success. It might also be noted that the term *anarchical* is used to characterize the foreign policy record of Reagan and Haig. The relations of Reagan, Shultz, and the White House staff proved to be decidedly more collegial. See Chapter 8.

12. I. M. Destler, *Presidents, Bureaucrats, and Foreign Policy: The Politics of Organizational Reform* (Princeton, 1972), 16. Among the major postwar reorganization proposals are the Hoover commission report of 1949; *The Administration of Foreign Affairs and Overseas Operations,* published by the Brookings Institution in 1951; a second Brookings report in 1960, *The Formulation and Administration of United States Foreign Policy;* the Rockefeller proposal submitted to the Jackson Subcommittee on National Policy Machinery in 1960; the Herter committee report of 1962; and the 1968 report of the American Foreign Service Association, *Toward a Modern Diplomacy.* For a complete list of these studies see Destler, *Presidents, Bureaucrats, and Foreign Policy,* 323–24.

proposals were most common in the first two decades of the Cold War era, recent years have seen little slackening in the frequency of solutions to the "foreign affairs organizational problem."

Most proposed reforms involve the designation of some extraordinary cabinet-level official to be responsible for the coordination of foreign affairs. For example, Herbert Hoover in 1955 suggested the creation of a vice-president for foreign affairs, which would, of course, require a constitutional amendment. In 1960 Nelson Rockefeller submitted a proposal to Senator Henry Jackson's Subcommittee on National Policy Machinery, which was involved in an extensive review of the foreign policy making process, for the creation of a "First Secretary of Government." This First Secretary, who would receive his authority from the president and act in his behalf, would serve as "Executive Chairman" of the NSC and would supervise its staff, as well as represent the United States internationally. The goal of this proposal was to create a new position for an official who could supervise foreign policy without any departmental associations. A related proposal in 1960 came from the Brookings Institution, which called for a new "Secretary of Foreign Affairs"—essentially a strengthened secretary of state who would preside over a "consolidated department" that would include the foreign aid and international information agencies.[13]

All of the proposals for reorganizing the foreign policy process seek to realize a greater degree of organizational coherence than is currently the case, particularly by strengthening presidential authority in the struggle of bureaucratic interests. As Destler posits it, the question should not be whether someone should serve as the president's agent of coordination but *who* should do so—the secretary of state or the national security assistant. The answer must be closely related to the president's administrative style and personal preferences: "For no president will stick to a general organizational design if it doesn't work for him in daily procedure." Of the reforms mentioned above, all suffered a common fate: polite reception and political inaction because of the scope of the constitutional and administrative changes involved.[14]

13. Destler, *Presidents, Bureaucrats, and Foreign Policy*, 26.
14. *Ibid.*, 259. In any discussion of proposed federal government policy, Lyndon Johnson is said to have admonished his advisers to limit the number of constitutional amendments requested to one per proposal. His irony was appropriate.

The most realistic proposals for reforming the foreign policy process have involved defining the scope and authority of a chief presidential adviser. Traditionally, such administrative reform has centered around the restoration of the power that the secretary of state
and the State Department enjoyed in its last golden era under Dean
Acheson and General George Marshall. A "neoclassical pattern" of
foreign policy making would involve the realization of several personal and institutional arrangements. The secretary of state and the
president would need to have so close a working relationship that
the Secretary approaches (though no one can probably attain it) the
status of a presidential alter ego for foreign affairs. Additionally, the
secretary of state would have to serve as the chief manager of foreign
policy, including its day-to-day operations, while transcending the
parochial concerns of the Department of State. Of course, such secretarial primacy would inevitably involve a dimunition in the influence
of the national security adviser and his staff. Theodore Sorenson, former counsel to President Kennedy, believes that such a diminution is
both desirable and possible: "Friction between the Secretary of State
and the President's National Security Adviser, which for fifteen years
or more has recurringly given this country a split-screen image around
the world, is not inevitable if the President will make clear that the
Secretary is the government's chief diplomatic spokesman and that
the Adviser is to confine his advice to the President."[15]

For the secretary of state to be strong, the national security adviser's role would have to be modeled on that of Brent Scowcroft during the Ford-Kissinger years or Gordon Gray under Eisenhower and
Dulles. In such an "ANSA-free world," the assistant for national security affairs (ANSA) would be "anonymous, efficient, and supportive of
the president" but not threatening to the secretary of state's privileged
position. A national security adviser who acts as simply a "custodian"
(sorting out departmental options for the president) or, alternatively,
serves as a "facilitator" (guiding the flow of departmental options)
presupposes a president who is highly confident of his own understanding of international relations and his mastery of the foreign policy process.[16]

15. *Ibid.*; Sorensen, *A Different Kind of Presidency*, 94–95.
16. Lincoln Bloomfield, *The Foreign Policy Process* (Englewood Cliffs, N.J., 1983), 57;
Alexander L. George, *Presidential Decisionmaking in Foreign Policy: The Effective Use of
Information and Advice* (Boulder, 1980), 195–200.

Such a neoclassical pattern of foreign policy making is represented in the following diagram:

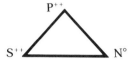

There are major problems with this hypothesized pattern. It is highly idealistic in its expectations about proper role behavior by the principals, particularly in the assumption that the national security adviser will be content with so modest a mandate. This typology may also be highly unrealistic in the assessment of the foreign policy making skills of American decision makers, including the president. Expert knowledge of foreign affairs is neither a prerequisite nor even particularly an asset in contemporary American politics. Moreover, when presidents have come to concern themselves with foreign affairs, increasingly in recent years they have turned to the White House staff for policy recommendations and political advice.[17]

Critics of the neoclassical pattern are quick to point out that it is highly outmoded, particularly since the tenure of Henry Kissinger as national security assistant. The NSC advisory system has become institutionalized as part of the policy-making process, and the assistant will always be looking for the opportunity (amply provided by presidential propinquity) to influence foreign policy—a propensity aided by the facilities afforded by the West Wing's Situation Room and the NSC staff's professional skills. Moreover, various commentators, Zbigniew Brzezinski for example, have argued that the secretary of state is too encumbered with the State Department's bureaucratic rigidity, resistance to change, and diplomatic world view to make an effective presidential spokesman for foreign affairs. In addition, foreign policy directed by the State Department would almost certainly have a long-term, "diplomatic" character, as distinct from other orientations that might favor military actions, ideological goals, or quick-fix "political" solutions. Unfortunately, what makes for better international relations is not necessarily good domestic politics. Ad-

17. For example, see the view expressed by Richard Nixon as president-elect to his future national security adviser, in Henry Kissinger, *White House Years* (Boston, 1979), 15.

mittedly, the centralization of policy making in the White House probably encourages greater compatibility between foreign and domestic elements of national policy than would be the case in the proposed neoclassical pattern.

The strongest arguments for White House–centered foreign policy making concern the nature of bureaucratic and presidential politics. For the neoclassical pattern to work, the State Department would have to be given responsibility for the coordination and implementation of foreign policy as well as for its formulation and articulation. Such a bureacratic arrangement would necessarily subordinate the Defense Department and CIA to their coequal, the State Department. Moreover, these departments would certainly argue that such an administrative arrangement violated the formal hierarchy and that the State Department lacked the expertise to evaluate strategic doctrines and intelligence operations. It would also be argued strenuously that the imperatives of national security policy making transcend the boundaries and competence of any one department, even the one traditionally responsible for external affairs.[18]

A different approach—creation of a "Department of National Security Affairs"—would constitute a mortal threat to *all* the executive departments, would threaten to impose the excessive layering typical of "mega-departments," and would raise the possibility of overt bureaucratic warfare such as characterized the Defense Department for over a decade after its formation in 1947.

In contrast, a "White House pattern" would recognize that "on foreign policy matters the president needs someone close to him who shares his 'presidential perspective' and who can rise above narrower bureaucratic concerns."[19] Theoretically, that official is the assistant to the president for national security affairs. The following diagram represents the White House pattern for foreign policy making.

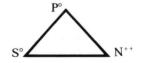

18. Zbigniew Brzezinski, *Power and Principle: Memoirs of the National Security Adviser, 1977–1981* (New York, 1983) 534–35.
19. *Ibid.*, 535.

This pattern can be recommended immediately for its realism. There is no assumption in it that the president will be especially knowledgeable about foreign affairs or directly involved in its day-to-day administration. Recent history suggests that it would be wise not to expect future presidents to perform overly well in these matters.

This scheme does not propose an overly assertive role for the secretary of state, despite the strong traditional arguments favoring his preeminence. As recently as 1974, George Kennan argued that, subject only to presidential direction, the secretary of state "should have authority to direct not only the activities of the Department of State, but all activities conducted by other departments of the government, including economic, social, military, informational, intelligence-gathering, etc., which have a significant impact on the nation's external relations."[20] With all due respect to the noted diplomatic historian and distinguished former ambassador, there is little evidence in America's postwar foreign policy record that would suggest the feasibility of such a solution. Certainly, the case studies presented in Chapters 3–8 lend little support to Kennan's proposed solution.

There have, of course, been distinguished and forceful postwar secretaries of state—Acheson, Dulles, and Kissinger. In the main they have measured up to the criteria that have been judged necessary for the secretary to function as the president's chief foreign policy adviser, namely "not only intellectual breadth, relevant experience, and political sense, but initiative and energy."[21] However, in all three of these cases the source of their power derived essentially from their personal relationship with the president. And with the exception of Acheson, who presided over a beleaguered department, these secretaries virtually ignored the State Department as an institution.

The presidency has come to dominate foreign affairs, and in recent years when presidents have sought a strong arm to assist them, they have increasingly looked to their assistants for national security affairs. Henry Kissinger, then, represents the model for one who would successfully manage foreign policy making—but in his capacity as

20. Testimony of George Kennan before the Commission on the Organization of the Government for the Conduct of Foreign Policy, September 24, 1974, quoted in Graham Allison and Peter Szanton, *Remaking Foreign Policy: The Organizational Connection* (New York, 1976), 121.
21. *Ibid.*, 132.

national security adviser, not as secretary of state. This seems to be an incontrovertible feature of American foreign affairs policy making for four reasons: 1) the national security adviser shares the president's unique perspective, and his personal fate is closely tied to the president's political fortunes; 2) centralization of policy making in the White House permits a closer integration of foreign and domestic policy and puts the president's chief adviser for foreign affairs in a close working relationship with the president's domestic advisers; 3) as the focus of foreign policy has broadened to encompass so many diverse activities, it has been revealed that the State Department simply lacks the expertise to challenge the other departments and the power to enforce its primacy;[22] and 4) there is no way that a department secretary can match the advantage provided by the national security assistant's physical presence in the White House itself. By setting up a foreign policy shop in the basement of the West Wing, Kissinger successfully eclipsed his bureaucratic rivals and institutionalized the policy-making role of the national security adviser.

In effect, the White House pattern concedes that, regrettable as it may be, there is little likelihood of a return to the classical form of strong secretarial leadership. Too much has happened to the detriment of the State Department for this historic pattern to be revived. The White House pattern recognizes that interdepartmental coordination and comprehensive policy making are, in the last analysis, presidential responsibilities. The White House—in the form of the national security adviser and his staff—has come to be best situated to assist the president with these tasks. It is also recognized, however, that a cloistered palace guard, insulated from congressional inquiry and public accountability, must be avoided.

Certain political and administrative arrangements could be introduced to keep the White House from becoming a foreign policy making cloister. One innovation would be a statutory requirement that the position of assistant for national security affairs be subject to senatorial confirmation. When this was first suggested in the aftermath of Kissinger's tenure in the White House and the Watergate scandal, confirmation was viewed as a device to limit presidential authority. However, former National Security Assistant Brzezinski argues to the

22. Brzezinski, *Power and Principle*, 534–35.

contrary that confirmation would "legitimate the Assistant's central role in coordination and thus also in shaping national security policy." To Brzezinski, the position should be similar to that of the director of the Office of Management and Budget (OMB), who since 1973 has been subject to senatorial confirmation and who enjoys cabinet status as the president's principal controller of departmental spending. Brzezinski proposes that the presidential assistant be redesignated the "Director of National Security Affairs" in order to underscore the parity between the two positions: "If the President wishes to make the White House the center of decisionmaking, the source of policy initiation, and an effective instrument for coordination of the extremely complex governmental machinery in the area of national security, then a step along these lines would greatly enhance clarity and the legitimacy of White House preponderance."[23]

Another step that would strengthen the White House pattern is an expanded and revitalized State Department. The secretary of state is no longer typically the chief coordinator of American external relations. On the other hand, the State Department "is the principal repository of knowledge about foreign societies; and a main source through political and economic reporting of new information about events abroad."[24]

This description suggests a clear, and highly significant, role for the State Department in foreign policy making. It is a role that also could be augmented by expanding its administrative jurisdiction over certain agencies that have developed virtual autonomy from the secretary of state: the Agency for International Development, which has responsibility for foreign economic and technical assistance programs; the United States Information Agency, which operates official propaganda operations such as the Voice of America, as well as educational and cultural exchange programs; and the Arms Control and Disarmament Agency, which is responsible for negotiations concerning a reduction in nuclear and conventional weapons. It goes without saying that maintaining and improving the professional qualifications and status of the Foreign Service (perhaps through establishment of a National Academy of Foreign Affairs) would further

23. *Ibid.*, 536, 537.
24. Allison and Szanton, *Remaking Foreign Policy*, 124–25.

enhance the State Department's effectiveness and improve American foreign policy.

A politically aware secretary of state and a well-regarded State Department have a vital role to play in charting the course for the United States in international relations. If there is to be proper balance in the National Security Council's deliberations, it is essential that the political, social, cultural, historical and all other dimensions of a foreign policy be considered along with the strategic, military, economic, and ideological components. Indeed, the NSC might be restructured to facilitate a more active role in foreign policy making. Not since the Eisenhower administration has the NSC itself (as distinct from its staff) been used for foreign policy making, though the ExComm of the Kennedy administration and the Tuesday Lunch Group of the Johnson years were de facto "NSC subcommittees." Yet, an executive committee at the highest levels of political and military authority could provide the forum in which a coherent foreign policy might be formulated, overseen, and evaluated. The assistant for national security affairs would have a pivotal role as the NSC's executive secretary—directing its staff, routing the flow of departmental policy proposals and memoranda, coordinating interdepartmental groups, and structuring alternatives for presidential review and decision.[25] The number and variety of departments and the level of representation, however, suggest the need for a presiding official who transcends both existing organizational loyalties and parochial interests.

Since the president may be occupied with other matters or wish to avoid involving himself in preliminary policy debates and bureaucratic battles, he might well delegate this task to the vice-president. The president may, in fact, wish to delegate a broad vice-presidential responsibility for supervising foreign affairs. In particular, the vice-president, whose existing duties are nebulous and who is far from overburdened, could chair major NSC committees—for example, the

25. I. M. Destler argues that the title and functions of executive secretary of the NSC should substitute for the broader responsibilities currently borne by the assistant to the president for national security affairs. According to Destler, this administrative rearrangement would enhance the secretary of state's proper position as the president's foremost foreign policy counselor. See Destler, "A Job That Doesn't Work," *Foreign Policy*, XXXVIII (Spring, 1980), 86–88; and I. M. Destler, Leslie H. Gelb, and Anthony Lake, *Our Own Worst Enemy: The Unmaking of American Foreign Policy* (New York, 1985).

SALT verification panel and the Senior Review Group. As the official assigned responsibility for crisis management in both the Carter and Reagan administrations, the vice-president has already established a claim to be the presidential surrogate for foreign affairs. A new "Vice-President for Foreign Affairs" has been prominent among proposed reforms of the policy-making process. Our proposal, however, does not require a constitutional amendment but simply an administrative order. As chairman of the National Security Council, the president need only delegate to the vice-president, as deputy chairman, such responsibilities as he believes desirable. De facto, the vice-president would enjoy the power associated with the de jure title, and White House responsibility for foreign affairs would be strengthened.[26]

"Accidental presidencies" have occurred with enough frequency in recent decades to recommend a major and continuing role for the vice-president in diplomatic decision making, regardless of the particular pattern that a president may utilize to conduct foreign affairs. It should be reemphasized that, as the chief diplomat, the president is always free to choose whatever administrative arrangement best suits his political and personal needs. What is essential, however, is that he *choose*. Failure by a president to make clear his preferences for administering foreign affairs leads to the anarchy or near anarchy characteristic of the first eighteen months of the Reagan administration.

In formulating foreign policy there is no substitute for a president actively involved in the process and knowledgeable about its substance. As Brzezinski has put it: "Given the nature of our political system, any effort to generate a meaningful sense of direction will have to originate with the President. He alone can mobilize the national will and also educate the country to the dilemmas—and imperatives—of the new world situation."[27] Essentially, the president may choose to work through a strong secretary of state, which would require his direct involvement in day-to-day administration, or through

26. On vice-presidents as "assistant presidents," see Thomas E. Cronin, "Rethinking the Vice-Presidency," in Cronin, *Rethinking the Presidency*, 330–33. Given his standing as presidential timber, any vice-president who would serve as an assistant president for foreign affairs, as we have proposed, would have to possess something of a "passion for anonymity" in serving as the president's surrogate, which is rare among politicians. Is it too much to ask of a presidential aspirant? And for a vice-president for foreign affairs to function effectively, he would need to be careful never to forget that he is responsible for executing the president's policy, not his own.

27. Brzezinski, *Power and Principle*, 533.

a strong White House staff, especially a powerful national security assistant representing his interests in foreign policy making. Whatever mechanism is chosen, it must be capable of ensuring that a presidential perspective is imposed on the array of foreign policy activities scattered across the American national government.

Regardless of whether a president chooses to manage foreign affairs through a strong secretary of state or a strong national security adviser, an enhanced vice-presidential role seems highly desirable. As the constitutionally sanctioned "second-in-command" of American government, the vice-president is ideally situated, politically and administratively, to aid the president in the conduct of foreign policy. Politically, the vice-president is, at least formally, the president's electoral colleague and the only other nationally elected official. Administratively, the vice-president is an ideal presidential deputy because he represents no institutional interest, and he lacks an independent power base. By establishing the vice-president as his de facto deputy for foreign affairs, the president places a "transdepartmental" official in a key policy-making position, with an official status transcending cabinet secretaries and presidential assistants. Moreover, a president could accomplish this objective simply by formalizing and broadening the vice-president's current responsibilities for crisis management in National Security Memorandum 1, by which successive presidents have allocated responsibilities for managing national security.

This administrative change would seem to remedy a number of problems. It would certainly enhance the stature of the vice-presidential office, which has suffered a political eclipse until recent years. Early in the history of the Republic, the vice-presidency served as a stepping-stone to the presidency. More recently, however, FDR's first vice-president, John Nance Garner, described the office as "not worth a bucket of warm spit," or words to that effect. Recent incumbents have been more visible political figures and some, like George Bush and Richard Nixon, have shown some facility in foreign affairs. The wonder is that more has not been done to upgrade the authority and responsibility of the vice-presidency. The president could use the assistance that this official would be uniquely qualified to provide. Moreover, the incidents of vice-presidential succession have occurred with alarming frequency in the last few decades, and the possible consequences of such succession in the nuclear age are increasingly perilous. The proposal suggested here would help reduce the danger and instability involved by providing for an orderly transition in the conduct of foreign policy.

No proposed reform in the foreign policy making process, including the one suggested here, is a panacea for the problems of incoherence and fragmentation. We have noted that the sources of much of the dissonance and dissension in foreign policy making are complex and long-standing. Scholars doubtless are especially susceptible to the rationalist fallacy—the assumption that, because there should be a solution, one is available. A certain measure of policy-making confusion is inherent in the conduct of American foreign affairs and will persist despite such proposed reforms as injecting the vice-president actively in the foreign policy process. As vice-presidents discover when they sit in the Oval Office themselves, no previous job or training can really prepare them for the perspective and power of the president of the United States in public policy making in general and foreign policy making in particular. Only the specialized on-the-job training of being chief executive prepares the incumbent for the awesome power associated with diplomatic policy making in the nuclear age.

Appendix
Patterns of American Foreign Policy Making: Itemized Ratings

The Ratings and Their Symbols

− −	very weak
−	weak
0	average
+	strong
+ +	very strong
N.A.	not applicable

Type 1 The Patriarchial Pattern: Roosevelt-Hull

THE PRESIDENT	Negative	0	Positive
Active involvement in foreign policy decision making			+ +
Support given to the secretary of state; prevention of policy incoherence	− −		
Background in foreign affairs		0	
Negotiating skill			+
Ability to influence public opinion			+ +
Ability to influence Congress			+ +
Prestige abroad			+ +
OVERALL			+ +
THE SECRETARY OF STATE			
Support received from the president	−		
Background in foreign affairs		0	
Political assets			+
Administration of the State Department	−		
Ability to influence public opinion			+
Rapport and influence with Congress			+
Skills for bureaucratic in-fighting	− −		
OVERALL	−		
THE NATIONAL SECURITY ADVISER*			
Relations with the president		NA	
Desire to play an active policy-making role		NA	
Ability to articulate foreign policy and influence public opinion		NA	
Background in foreign affairs		NA	
Belief that the State Department is weak, that a policy vacuum exists		NA	
Skills for bureaucratic in-fighting and desire to enlarge the NSC's role		NA	
Management of NSC		NA	
OVERALL		NA	

*This position was not created until the National Security Act of 1947.

Type 2   The Classical Pattern: Truman-Acheson

THE PRESIDENT	Negative	0	Positive
Active involvement in foreign policy decision making			+
Support given to the secretary of state; prevention of policy incoherence			+ +
Background in foreign affairs	− −		
Negotiating skill	−		
Ability to influence public opinion		0	
Ability to influence Congress			+
Prestige abroad		0	
OVERALL			+
THE SECRETARY OF STATE			
Support received from the president			+ +
Background in foreign affairs			+
Political assets	−		
Administration of the State Department			+
Ability to influence public opinion	−		
Rapport and influence with Congress	− −		
Skills for bureaucratic in-fighting			+
OVERALL			+
THE NATIONAL SECURITY ADVISER			
Relations with the president		0	
Desire to play an active policy-making role	− −		
Ability to articulate foreign policy and influence public opinion	− −		
Background in foreign affairs	−		
Belief that the State Department is weak, that a policy vacuum exists	− −		
Skills for bureaucratic in-fighting and desire to enlarge the NSC's role	− −		
Management of NSC		0	
OVERALL	− −		

Type 3 The Personalistic Pattern: Eisenhower-Dulles

THE PRESIDENT	Negative	0	Positive
Active involvement in foreign policy decision making	−		
Support given to the secretary of state; prevention of policy incoherence			+
Background in foreign affairs		0	
Negotiating skill		0	
Ability to influence public opinion			+ +
Ability to influence Congress	−		
Prestige abroad		0	
OVERALL			+
THE SECRETARY OF STATE			
Support received from the president			+ +
Background in foreign affairs			+ +
Political assets			+
Administration of the State Department	− −		
Ability to influence public opinion	−		
Rapport and influence with Congress	−		
Skills for bureaucratic in-fighting			+ +
OVERALL			+ +
THE NATIONAL SECURITY ADVISER*			
Relations with the president			+ +
Desire to play an active policy-making role		0	
Ability to articulate foreign policy and influence public opinion	−		
Background in foreign affairs		0	
Belief that the State Department is weak, that a policy vacuum exists	− −		
Skills for bureaucratic in-fighting and desire to enlarge the NSC's role	−		
Management of NSC			+
OVERALL	−		

*This is a composite rating of the performance of Robert Cutler, Dillon Anderson, and Gordon Gray.

Type 4   The Consensual Pattern: Johnson-Rusk-Bundy/Rostow

THE PRESIDENT	Negative	0	Positive
Active involvement in foreign policy decision making			+
Support given to the secretary of state; prevention of policy incoherence			++
Background in foreign affairs	−		
Negotiating skill		0	
Ability to influence public opinion	−		
Ability to influence Congress			+
Prestige abroad	−		
OVERALL			+
THE SECRETARY OF STATE			
Support received from the president			++
Background in foreign affairs			+
Political assets	−		
Administration of the State Department			+
Ability to influence public opinion	−		
Rapport and influence with Congress	−		
Skills for bureaucratic in-fighting	−		
OVERALL		0	
THE NATIONAL SECURITY ADVISER*			
Relations with the president			+
Desire to play an active policy-making role		0	
Ability to articulate foreign policy and influence public opinion	−		
Background in foreign affairs		0	
Belief that the State Department is weak, that a policy vacuum exists		0	
Skills for bureaucratic in-fighting and desire to enlarge the NSC's role		0	
Management of NSC		0	
OVERALL		0	

*This is a composite rating of the performance of McGeorge Bundy and Walt Rostow.

Type 5 The Palace Guard Pattern: Nixon-Rogers-Kissinger

THE PRESIDENT	Negative	0	Positive
Active involvement in foreign policy decision making			+
Support given to the secretary of state; prevention of policy incoherence	− −		
Background in foreign affairs			+ +
Negotiating skill			+
Ability to influence public opinion	−		
Ability to influence Congress	−		
Prestige abroad			+
OVERALL			+
THE SECRETARY OF STATE			
Support received from the president	− −		
Background in foreign affairs	− −		
Political assets	−		
Administration of the State Department		0	
Ability to influence public opinion	− −		
Rapport and influence with Congress	−		
Skills for bureaucratic in-fighting	− −		
OVERALL	− −		
THE NATIONAL SECURITY ADVISER			
Relations with the president			+ +
Desire to play an active policy-making role			+ +
Ability to articulate foreign policy and influence public opinion			+
Background in foreign affairs			+
Belief that the State Department is weak, that a policy vacuum exists			+ +
Skills for bureaucratic in-fighting and desire to enlarge the NSC's role			+ +
Management of NSC		0	
OVERALL			+ +

Type 6   The Anarchical Pattern: Reagan-Haig

THE PRESIDENT	Negative	0	Positive
Active involvement in foreign policy decision making	– –		
Support given to the secretary of state; prevention of policy incoherence	– –		
Background in foreign affairs	– –		
Negotiating skill		0	
Ability to influence public opinion			+ +
Ability to influence Congress			+
Prestige abroad	–		
OVERALL	– –		
THE SECRETARY OF STATE			
Support received from the president	– –		
Background in foreign affairs			+
Political assets	–		
Administration of the State Department			+
Ability to influence public opinion	– –		
Rapport and influence with Congress	– –		
Skills for bureaucratic in-fighting		0	
OVERALL	– –		
THE NATIONAL SECURITY ADVISER*			
Relations with the president		0	
Desire to play an active policy-making role		0	
Ability to articulate foreign policy and influence public opinion	– –		
Background in foreign affairs	– –		
Belief that the State Department is weak, that a policy vacuum exists		0	
Skills for bureaucratic in-fighting and desire to enlarge the NSC's role		0	
Management of NSC	– –		
OVERALL	– –		

*This is a composite of the performance of Reagan's various national security advisers.

Index

of national security advisers
National Security Agency, 67
National Security Council: contribution
to intraexecutive conflict, 4; and intelligence information, 66; ExComm, 76,
205, 211, 211n, 213, 337; role of, 78–
81, 272, 273n, 307; creation of, 138;
during Truman administration, 139,
264; during Eisenhower administration, 168–69, 191–94; Policy Planning
Board, 168; during Kennedy administration, 205, 211–13, 211n; during
Johnson administration, 212, 213, 215;
during Nixon administration, 260–61,
264–65, 264n; during Carter administration, 278–80; during Reagan administration, 292; as rival State Department, 316–17, 327; restructure of,
330, 337, 337n
NATO, 124, 125, 163, 196, 206, 209, 246,
284
Neustadt, Richard, 36, 165n, 181
Neutrality. See Isolationism
Nicaragua, 281
Nitze, Paul, 187, 301
Nixon, Richard: as commander in chief,
32–33; veto of War Powers Act, 33;
move to impeach, 40, 259; influence of
Rooseveltian model, 84; as senator,
159; as vice-president, 180, 250, 339;
visit to China, 208; as imperial president, 235, 303; and American public
opinion, 248; psychological makeup,
248–50; resignation of, 248, 259, 284;
foreign leaders' opinions of, 249–50;
working relationship with Kissinger,
257–60; view of State Department,
261; ratings of, 327, 346
Nixon administration: rival State Department, 7–8, 260–67; Watergate crisis, 35, 40, 43, 249–50, 257–60, 266,
268–69, 284–85, 335; dominance of
national security adviser, 40, 79–81,
307, 316; and Office of Management
and Budget, 71; approach to international affairs, 237–38, 267–71; approach to Soviet Union, 238, 240–49,
254; realpolitik approach, 240–41,
246, 246n, 258, 267; constitutional
abuses, 250; assessment of, 267–71;
and executive privilege, 269
Nixon Doctrine, 237–42, 250, 270, 271
North Atlantic Treaty, 124, 149, 151
North Atlantic Treaty Organization. See
NATO

North Vietnam. See Vietnam War
Nuclear weapons, 5, 117, 123, 160, 161,
171, 197, 203, 207–208, 239–40, 244–
46, 254, 268, 270, 286. See also Atomic
bombs; SALT; Weapons
Nye committee, 89

OAS. See Organization of American
States
O'Connor, Roderic L., 184
Office of International Security Affairs.
See Defense Department
Office of Management and Budget, 71–
72, 336
Office of Strategic Services. See State
Department
Office of War Information, 73
Oil reserves. See Middle East
OMB. See Office of Management and
Budget
Organization of American States, 114,
125, 205
Oshinsky, David M., 187
OSS. See State Department
Owen, Ruth Bryan, 109

Parmet, Herbert, 170
Pentagon Papers, 200, 234
People's Republic of China. See China,
People's Republic of
Perle, Richard N., 300
Persian Gulf, 64, 72, 202, 288
Persons, Jerry, 169
Philippines, 126
Phillips, William, 95
Pious, Richard M., 20, 36–37
Pipes, Richard, 286, 292
Poland, 283–84, 286
Polk, James K., 21, 38–39
Presidents: constitutional powers, 11–
12, 19–26; struggle with Congress in
foreign policy making, 12; as head of
state, 13–15; leadership requirements,
13–19; as chief executive, 15–16; as
chief diplomat, 16, 184–85; as commander in chief, 17, 21–22; as world
executive, 18–19; role in treaty making, 22–24; executive agreements, 23–
24, 27–28, 89, 98–99; appointment
process, 24–25; recognition of governments, 25–26; extraconstitutional prerogatives, 26–37; war-making powers,
29–35; executive privilege, 35, 43, 43n,
269; prerogative government, 36–37;
leadership requirements, 37–40; rat-